Urbanization in
Contemporary Latin America

Urbanization in Contemporary Latin America

Critical Approaches to the Analysis of Urban Issues

Edited by

Alan Gilbert
in association with
Jorge E. Hardoy and **Ronaldo Ramírez**

JOHN WILEY & SONS

Chichester · New York · Brisbane · Toronto · Singapore

Library of Congress Cataloging in Publication Data:

Main entry under title:
Urbanization in contemporary Latin America
    Includes index
    1. Urban policy — Latin America — Addresses, essays,
lectures.   2. Social classes — Latin America — Addresses,
essays, lectures.   3. Social conflict —
Addresses, essays, lectures.   4. Housing policy — Latin
America — Addresses, essays, lectures.
I. Gilbert, Alan, 1944-II. Hardoy, Jorge Enrique-
III. Ramirez, Ronaldo.
HT127.5.U718   307.7′6′098   81–21876

ISBN 0 471 10183 4   AACR2

British Library Cataloguing in Publication Data:

Urbanization in contemporary Latin America: critical
    approaches to the analysis of urban issues.
    1. Cities and towns — Planning — Latin America
    2. Latin America — Social policy
    I. Gilbert, Alan   II. Hardoy, Jorge E.
    III. Ramírez, Ronaldo
    980′.038   HT169.L/

ISBN 0 471 10183 4

Phototypeset by Dobbie Typesetting Service, Plymouth, Devon, England
and printed in the United States of America

In memory of
LUIS UNIKEL

Contents

vii

List of Figures

Contributors

JORGE BALAN, born 1940, Argentina. Studied sociology at the University of Buenos Aires and at the University of Texas, Austin, Ph.D. 1968; Assistant professor, New York University 1968–71. Visiting Professor at the University of Minas Gerais, 1971–73. Senior Researcher at the Instituto Torcuato di Tella, 1974–76 and at CEDES, 1978 to date, both in Buenos Aires. Guggenheim Fellow during 1977. Co-author of *Men in a Developing Society: Geographic and Social Mobility in Monterrey, Mexico* and many articles on migration and urbanization in Mexico, Brazil and Argentina.

RICHARD BATLEY, born 1942, London. Studied at the University of Birmingham B.Soc.Sc. (Sociology), 1965; University of Durham, M.A., 1971; University of Sussex, D.Phil., 1981; Research Assistant, University of Sussex (Institute of Development Studies), 1974–78; Lecturer in Development Administration, Institute of Local Government Studies, University of Birmingham, 1978 to date. Research on educational policy formation and urban planning in Britain; commissioned by the British Government to evaluate the urban aid programme 1971–74. Research on housing and urban renewal policy in Brazil, 1974–78, and in Colombia and Mexico, 1980. Consultant to the ILO on the installation of basic urban services in squatter settlements in Peru and Venezuela, 1977–78, and to the Overseas Development Administration on the development of intermediate towns in Kenya, 1980–81. Co-author of *Going Comprehensive* and *The Politics of Positive Discrimination* and of various articles on urban policy implementation in Britain, Brazil, Peru and Venezuela.

RAY BROMLEY, born 1947, Shropshire. Studied at the University of Cambridge, B.A. (Geography), 1969; M.A. 1973; Ph.D. (Geography), 1975. Tutor in Geography, University College of Swansea, 1971–73; Lecturer in Social Administration, University College Swansea, 1973–76; Lecturer in

Development Studies, University College of Swansea, 1976–81; Visiting Professor, Graduate Planning Program and Local Revenue Administration Project, Syracuse University, 1981–84. United Nations Consultant on Regional and Social Planning on various occasions between 1975 and 1981, working in Ecuador, Brazil and Chile, and Consultant on Rural-Urban Market Linkages to the Regional Development Corporation of Potosí, Bolivia, in 1980. Author of *Development and Planning in Ecuador*, editor of *The Urban Informal Sector: Critical Perspectives*, coeditor of *Casual Work and Poverty in Third World Cities*, and author of various articles on market-place trade, regional development policy, employment policy and development planning.

MICHAEL EDWARDS, born 1957, Liverpool. Studied at the University of Oxford, B.A. (Geography), 1978; University College London, Ph.D. (Geography), 1982. Fieldwork in Bogotá and Bucaramanga in Colombia on renting among low-income groups, 1978–80. This is his first published work.

ALAN GILBERT, born 1944, London. Studied at the University of Birmingham, B.Soc.Sc. (Geography), 1965; London School of Economics, Ph.D. (Geography), 1970. Research Fellow, Institute of Latin American Studies, London, 1969–70; Lecturer at University College and the Institute of Latin American Studies, London, since 1970. Consultant on port expansion to the Peruvian Government, 1968–69, to the United Nations on the Bogotá Urban Development Study, 1972–73, and on population redistribution policy, 1978 and 1979, to the Venezuelan Government on satellite cities, 1975, and to the Korean Government on regional development, 1981. Co-director with Peter Ward of *Public Intervention, Housing and Land Use in Latin American Cities*, a comparative research project financed by the British Government. Author of *Latin American Development: a Geographical Perspective* and with Josef Gugler of *Cities, Poverty and Development: Urbanization in the Third World*; editor of *Development Planning and Spatial Structure*, and various articles on regional planning, industrial location, urban development and health provision in Latin America.

JORGE ENRIQUE HARDOY, born 1926, Buenos Aires, Argentina. Studied at the University of Buenos Aires (Architecture) and Harvard University, MCP (City and Regional Planning), Ph.D. (Urban Studies). Professor of Architecture and Urban Planning, University del Litoral, Rosario, Argentina, 1956–65; Director of the Centre of Urban Studies, Instituto Di Tella, Buenos Aires, 1966–69. Visiting Professor, Yale University, 1970–71. Since 1971, Head of Research, Centre of Urban and Regional Studies, Buenos Aires, Guggenheim Fellow, 1961 and 1967. Senior Research Fellow, International Development

Research Centre of Canada, 1976. Author of *Pre-Columbian Cities*; *Urban Planning in Pre-Columbian America*; *Seis ensayos sobre la urbanización contemporanea en América Latina*; *Urban Reform in Revolutionary Cuba*.

CAROLINE MOSER, born 1944, Berkshire, England. Studied at the University of Durham, B.A. (Anthropology), 1967; University of Manchester, Postgraduate diploma (Anthropology), 1969; University of Sussex, D.Phil. (Social Anthropology), 1975. Extensive field research in Colombia, Bolivia and Ecuador. Lecturer at the Development Planning Unit, University College London since 1978. Member of the DPU mission to Calcutta, 1980. Author of various articles on the 'informal sector' and urban poverty, on urban market sellers in Colombia and the survival strategies of low-income women in Ecuador.

PEDRO NIKKEN, born 1945, Caracas, Venezuela. Studied law at the Catholic University of Caracas (1968) and Paris II (D.E.S. Droit Privé 1973). Dean of the Faculty of Law and Political Science at the Central University of Venezuela 1978–81). Author of several articles in civil law.

ROGELIO PEREZ PERDOMO, born 1941, Bocono, Venezuela. Studied law at the Central University of Venezuela (1964, Dr. Der. 1975), Paris (1966) and Harvard, Ll.M. (1972). Professor at the Central University of Venezuela. Visiting fellow at the Institute of Development Studies, University of Sussex (1977). Author of several books and articles on philosophy and sociology of law.

RONALDO RAMIREZ, born 1934, Santiago, Chile. Dip. Arch. University of Chile, 1962; Dip. Urban Studies, UCL London, 1970. Doctoral work, University of Essex and London School of Economics. Professor at the University of Chile, 1964–73; visiting professor, University of California, Berkeley, 1973. Lecturer at the Development Planning Unit, University College London, 1974 to date. Author of various articles and papers on Latin American development and on Chilean urbanization.

JOHN F. C. TURNER, born 1927, London. Studied architecture at the Architectural Association in London, diploma 1954. Worked in Peru between 1958 and 1965 promoting and designing community self-help housing programmes for a variety of government housing agencies. Research Associate at the Joint Centre for Urban Studies at MIT and Harvard, 1965–67; Lecturer at the Massachusetts Institute of Technology (SPURS Programme), 1967–73; Director of nationwide study and evaluation of self-help housing in the United States for the U.S. Department of Housing and Urban Development, 1968–70; Consultant to several national and international agencies; Lecturer at the

Architectural Association, 1974–75; Lecturer at the Development Planning Unit of University College, 1976– date. Author of Freedom to Build (with Robert Fichter) and Housing by People as well as numerous articles and papers stressing the need for user control of housing resources.

LUIS UNIKEL, 1932–1981, Mexico City. Degree in Civil Engineering, National University of Mexico (UNAM), 1956; Masters in Urban Planning, Massachusetts Institute of Technology, 1958. Analyst in the Planning Directorate of the Presidential Secretariat, 1960–65; Member of the Hydraulic Commission of the Valley of Mexico, 1960–65; Professor at El Colegio de México, 1965–81; Director of the Centro de Estudios Económicos y Demográficos, El Colegio de México, 1977–81. Author of *El desarrollo urbano de México and Dinámica de la población de México* and numerous articles on urban development, regional change and industrial location in Mexico. Received the National Economic Prize of the Banco Nacional de México both in 1970 and in 1974. President of the Interamerican Planning Society, 1980–81.

PETER WARD, born 1951, Ismailia, Egypt. Studied at the University of Hull, B.A. (Geography) 1972; University of Liverpool, Ph.D. (Geography) 1976; Lecturer at University College London since 1975. Seconded by the Ministry of Overseas Development to Mexico 1978–79 to work as adviser on low-income housing policy with the Ministry of Human Settlements and Public Works (SAHOP). Author of various papers on low-income housing and editor of *Self-help Housing: a Critique.*

Preface

Since 1977, a series of seminars has been run in London on urbanization in Latin America. The seminars have been organized jointly by the Development Planning Unit at University College, the Institute of Latin American Studies, the Architectural Association's Graduate School and the International Institute for the Environment and Development. The series has attracted large audiences and some interesting and provocative papers. This volume includes a number of the best papers and is intended to stimulate interest and discussion among a wider audience. We hope that this wider readership will comprise all social scientists, architects, planners and indeed practitioners of all kinds.

We should like to acknowledge the financial help which the Development Planning Unit and the Institute of Latin American Studies provided to the seminar. We also thank Christine Daniels for preparing the maps.

Sadly, one contributor will never read the volume. Early in 1981 Luis Unikel died at the very young age of 48 years. Luis was widely admired and liked, he is much missed, and his death is a major loss to urban and planning studies in Mexico and Latin America generally. The least we can do as editors is to dedicate this volume to his memory.

Urbanization in Contemporary Latin America
Edited by A. Gilbert with J. E. Hardoy and R. Ramírez
© 1982 John Wiley & Sons Ltd.

1

Introduction

ALAN GILBERT

This book is concerned with urban problems and with the way we view those problems. It is less prescriptive than analytic: it explores a variety of approaches to understanding urban issues in Latin America and, by implication, those in other regions. The justification for such a volume is that the past decade has seen a major intellectual shift in the social sciences. The paradigm for research has shifted from a broadly positivistic and normative stance towards a more structuralist, political-economic approach to academic enquiry. In the fields of urban and development studies, the way that the academic community views the problems and causes of urban and developmental change has changed almost beyond recognition. This 'revolution' has important implications for the 'real world'. Questions which had answers under the previous paradigm have been reopened to scrutiny. The wisdom underlying conventional planning policies is now being queried. The whole nature of society is being questioned and this is having major repercussions in the fields of politics and planning. The outcome of this shift is as yet uncertain. It is not easy to predict whether it will sweep through the social sciences, embracing all disciplines and the study of all geographical areas or whether it will be a partial shift akin to that of the quantitative revolution in sociology, economics or geography. But, clearly, some evaluation of that potential contribution is now essential. The new intellectual paradigm is not going to go away and the old paradigm no longer looks so convincing. It is possible that, like all vanguards, the new paradigm is too brash, enthusiastic and confident and will eventually become more muted to be absorbed into conventional wisdom. Eventually, no doubt its teachings will be severely criticized and relegated to the 'dustbin' of the 'old paradigm'. But, for the time being, the new paradigm contains most of the life and energy of current academic enquiry and poses awkward and necessary questions for policy makers. The new approach has several distinguishing characteristics.

First, it tends to emphasize the importance of social classes and the conflicts between those classes as an explanation of concrete situations. Whereas the previous paradigm tended to assume that societies were potentially harmonious and that economic and social development would benefit all groups in society, the new paradigm stresses that the benefits from development are an outcome of class conflict. The benefits one group in society gains, tend to be won at the expense of another. At times, the new perspective suggests that economic growth is positively harmful because the form of that growth is such that it harms the poor.

Secondly, the new approach is more historically orientated. It emphasizes that current problems have historical roots and that many are associated with the expansion of colonialism and capitalism. Poverty is rarely a static phenomenon, one that is merely a continuation from the past; it has been created by the contacts between one civilization and another. To view Latin American peasants as if they have always lived as they do today, when there have been dramatic changes affecting their economic and social environment and when it is clear that many of those peasants have forebears who were members of great civilizations, is patently absurd. The new paradigm stresses the effects of capitalist expansion on the regions of what can broadly be called the Third World. This expansion has linked large areas of the world into an integrated economic and social structure. Poverty and other manifestations of development in areas such as Latin America can only be understood in the light of capitalist expansion.

Thirdly, the new paradigm emphasizes that capitalist expansion has penetrated different parts of the world differentially and brought benefits only to some. Many poorer areas are best described as going through a process of dependent or peripheral capitalism. The terms of their development are conditioned by changes and phenomena occurring in the developed world, peripheral capitalist economies lack autonomy to determine their own development path. In order to survive in the world economy, peripheral economies adapt in a variety of ways. Some such as Hong Kong, Korea and Taiwan prosper, while others become poorer; there is no inevitability about the outcome. Eventually, some economies are wholly penetrated by the capitalist mode of production, while in others precapitalist and semicapitalist forms of production and exchange survive and adapt to the dominant capitalist system. Sometimes, they survive and expand because their survival is more conducive to the continued prosperity of the dominant capitalist mode. Thus the new paradigm emphasizes the relationships between different kinds or modes of production and tends to emphasize the negative aspects of change.

Fourthly, the structural perspective of the new paradigm contrasts markedly with the emphasis upon the individual which characterized the liberal, positivist paradigm. Individuals are members of classes, groups and structures. They respond in rational and individual ways to the developments that affect them, but the opportunities and constraints to their action are determined more often than not by their class position. Social mobility there may be, but opportunities in dependent capitalist social formations are limited for members of the peasantry or the working class. Thus, current work on migration stresses not the nature of individual moves but the broad causes and consequences of those moves. It is interested in the expansion of capitalist relations into the rural areas, in the development of agribusiness and in the expulsion of labour from the countryside, rather than in the directions, or reasons why, certain individuals move.

Finally, because it views development as an outcome of historical forces and class conflict, it looks at the State and the role that it plays within the social formation of which it forms part. The State is viewed not as the benign, fair-minded stimulant of equitable development, as it was so often portrayed under 'modernization' theory, but as an integral element in class conflict. While some view the State, and specific States, as the mere instrument of the dominant social class, others see it as performing a balancing role in maintaining the socioeconomic system. However it is viewed it is a much more political and calculating entity than the governments that inhabited the previous paradigm.

We would argue that no single paradigm can satisfactorily resolve issues as complex as economic, social and political change. By its very nature, intellectual enquiry must constantly modify the questions it poses. For this reason it is important to explore all new lines of thought and to relate them to more established ways of thinking. Perhaps the integration of new and old is possible, perhaps the new approach is incompatible with the old, perhaps the new approach is superior, perhaps with hindsight little improvement. Such questions can be resolved only after careful analysis and after time has allowed deeper reflection.

The present volume is intended to contribute to the consideration of such issues. Some of the papers criticize and evaluate ideas emerging from the new paradigm, others examine the implications of the new concepts for our understanding of urban issues. Although they span the ideological, intellectual and disciplinary continuums, all are critical of the state of knowledge. Included in the volume are papers directed to specifically Marxist questions, others which are more positivist in approach, and some which are more eclectic, seeking a consensus between old and new approaches. The editors regard the diversity of approaches as a major virtue. The range of contributions offers a forum for the airing of frequently conflicting views about the nature of urban problems and solutions. For example, can housing problems be overcome by changing the attitudes of architects, builders, and planners or only by a restructuring of society? Is rampant land speculation a consequence of weak urban planning or an integral contradiction of capitalism within the urban arena? Should help be given directly to the 'informal' sector or will such assistance merely accentuate inequalities among the poor and lead to more rapid penetration by large-scale capitalist enterprise? Questions such as these are critical to our understanding of Latin American reality and to the possible resolution of social inequality and poverty. Indeed, this was the original intention of the seminar series from which this volume has emerged. The invitations to the seminar participants instructed them as follows: 'We hope that each paper will review the existing literature and isolate the key research issues for the future. More specifically, we hope that the different papers will focus on one or more of the following issues. First, what does ''dependency theory'' contribute to the study of urbanization? Is this school of thought sufficiently flexible to embrace the varied experiences of the different Latin American countries? Second, what are the principal problems afflicting urban areas in the region and to what extent do these problems differ from city to city? Finally, what roles can governments be expected to play in a capitalist system? To what extent does government action hamper the spontaneous efforts of the poor and what kinds of policy best ameliorate the main problems of poor groups?' With hindsight, we might modify those questions slightly, for example, the word dependency might well be replaced by the term 'political economy', but the intentions remain sound and important.

Unfortunately, but not unexpectedly, the volume puts forward no comprehensive answer to these questions nor recommends a single approach to their analysis. Although the authors are universally concerned by the lack of progress on redistributing income, resources and power within Latin American societies, beyond the generalizations that the poor are neglected, that power is concentrated in few hands, and that many of the problems are integral to the nature of dependent capitalist development, there is a wide range of interpretations. Indeed, it is the diversity of contemporary developments within Latin American urban society that is so intriguing a conclusion of so many of these contributions. The social repercussions of similarly unequal distributions of power vary dramatically from one city to another, let alone from one country to the next. The way the poor obtain land or services, the trends in their wage levels, the ways in which they are encouraged or discouraged to engage in politics, vary widely. If the papers point to ways in which we can understand that diversity through meaningful generalization, they are sufficiently intellectually rigorous to accept the limits and dangers of generalization. In short, one conclusion to the volume is whatever the virtues of the new intellectual paradigm, there are no simple answers.

But another trend is clear. Although the papers in this volume are drawn from a wide range of disciplines, anthropology, architecture, geography, law, planning and sociology are all represented, the papers are addressing increasingly similar issues. Under the old paradigm the disciplinary barriers remained erect, even fossilized, despite constant manifestations of the need for interdisciplinary and multidisciplinary studies. The new political-economy approach has the major virtue of forcing different disciplines to ask similar questions and to share methodologies. The current papers clearly differ in approach and retain much of their disciplinary flavour, but the trend is clear, arbitrary intellectual walls are coming down.

In the first paper, Jorge Hardoy makes a broad statement about the path of urbanization in Latin America over the last two thousand years. Although this is a volume on contemporary urbanization, it is clear that a historical backcloth is an essential prelude to such a study. His aim is to demonstrate the basic similarity in the way in which Latin American cities have always been designed and built. Classifying Latin American urbanization into three broad epochs, pre-Columbian, colonial, and postindependent, he argues that although each period contained major examples of formal planning, the most characteristic form of urban development was self-help or unplanned housing. Formal planning, in fact, has always been reserved for the buildings and urban areas dedicated to religious, administrative, ceremonial or élite functions. Teotihuacán or Cuzco were no more typical of poor people's housing than Brasília or the planned part of Ciudad Guayana are of how poor Brazilians and Venezuelans live today. Formal design in pre-Columbian America was no more relevant to the housing of the poor than it is in the twentieth century: the poor have always built their own housing within the constraints laid down by the rules of the powerful. 'Contemporary Latin American cities, like their predecessors, have been constructed by many builders, mostly anonymous, forced to find their own solutions in the face of government neglect and sometimes repression' (p.31). That view echoes much of what follows in the book irrespective of the intellectual and ideological approach of the writer.

Jorge Balán contributes a detailed empirical paper which challenges the way we think about urban change under peripheral capitalism. In the process of explaining how two Argentinian regions developed very different forms of economy and society during the nineteenth century, he both illustrates and contradicts many of the arguments about Latin American urban and regional development made by so-called 'dependency school' writers (Palma, 1978). Some members of this school have argued that Latin America's poverty, social structure, and dependent trading and financial position were outcomes of their subordinate position in the world economy. Exploited as they were first as colonies of Spain and Portugal and later as neocolonies of Britain and the United States, their economies were transformed according to the needs of the metropolitan powers. The impression given was that the development, or rather underdevelopment, of these areas was dictated by the needs of the developed countries. Latin American nations were inserted into the all embracing world economy and had little or no control over their destiny. As an antidote to the ahistorical, positivistic ideas of many development planners, who implicitly assumed that poverty was the fault of Latin Americans themselves, this was a useful contribution. But, as Dos Santos (1970), Cardoso and Faletto (1969) and others soon demonstrated, this was far too simple a view. Balán shows how the urban systems of two different regions located within the same kind of dependent economy and society and both peripheral to the main centres of national decision-making evolved in distinctive ways. The fact that neither managed to develop autonomously nor continued to grow vigorously to the present day is to be explained by their peripheral position within the Argentine space-economy. Neither managed to develop manufacturing industry beyond a rudimentary level because their economies were subjugated to the interests of political and economic groups in Buenos Aires. As Balán says 'there was no way that the provinces could confront the essential interests of the agricultural export sector'. This is not the same as saying, in the way made famous by Frank (1967), that they were merely examples of peripheries linked into the periphery-metropolis chain. Had peripheral development been as automatic as Frank suggested, local economies would have been further impoverished, would have manifest similar levels of poverty and would have had similar social characteristics. In fact, Mendoza and Tucumán emerged in distinctive ways despite their common peripheral status. The economy of Mendoza was more dynamic than that of Tucumán, it was organized more equitably, and its rural areas were more closely linked to the region's main city. The differing social and economic patterns emerging in each area demonstrate the 'conditioning', as opposed to the 'determining', role that the international context played in regional development. The main virtue of Balán's paper is that he demonstrates both the variation in regional response and provides a method of explaining how such variations can be studied. It is an excellent analysis and explanation of how flexibility can exist within essentially rigid constraints: a point also developed by Roberts (1978, 1975) in the case of Peru.

In the third chapter, Ray Bromley examines the street employment that is so characteristic of Latin American and Third World cities. He criticizes the idea that these occupations are 'marginal' to the wider urban economy and shows that the workers are closely linked to 'formal' sector activities for their very existence; working capital, materials, tools, transport, markets and protection are all provided in varying degrees by the formal sector. Indeed, Bromley shows that few street workers are truly independent, most are closely tied to suppliers, employers, contractors and money lenders. Nor is the stereotyped picture of the poverty of these workers entirely true. While the majority are poor, some street workers do very well. Street occupations are highly diversified, except that they nearly all have low social status and require long hours of work. While such workers are generally regarded as parasitic, most contribute to the urban economy by reducing distribution costs, by helping recycle waste products and generally lowering urban living costs for all social groups.

Unfortunately, this usefulness is not realized by the urban authorities who tend to harass the street workers. Under the pretext of regulating their activities, municipal government tends to limit the areas where they can work and to require their formal licensing. Bromley concludes that these policies are unfair to street workers and that such restrictions are inappropriate both to general urban needs and to the specific needs of the poor. Since so many of the street workers are very poor, their activities represent a survival strategy. By harassing them, the authorities not only make their lives more difficult but also damage respectable urban institutions and groups which use the services of these workers. Bromley recommends 'a more positive series of policies towards . . . street occupations' although it is uncertain whether governments in Latin America are prepared to accept such advice. His recommendations implicitly raise the whole question of whether government policies arise through error and misunderstanding, or whether they are the result of some deliberate action to favour other groups. After all, harassment of street traders may favour regular shops and supermarket chains whose sales may suffer from the 'unfair' competition. Harassment may also favour the police who may extract illicit payments from those they neglect to arrest. Who is to say whether harassment is the accidental outcome of a misguided policy or whether it is a deliberate act? One's interpretation is likely to depend on the picture one holds of the nature of the State. Only if the State is seen to be benign rather than malignant, or if it is seen to maintain stability in a basically fair, rather than unfair, social system is the interpretation likely to be favourable.

The nature of the State in Colombia and Mexico constitutes the main focus of the paper by Alan Gilbert and Peter Ward. Presenting some preliminary findings from their comparative study of low-income settlement, politics and public intervention, they demonstrate that the issues of land, housing and servicing in Latin America, or indeed anywhere else, cannot be understood outside an understanding of the role and nature of the State. The differences and similarities between low-income settlement formation and consolidation in Latin American cities should be analysed in terms of what individual governments do and do not do. The shape and form of low-income settlement is critically affected by the way the State controls land prices, allocates land, and organizes zoning, servicing and infrastructural provision. They examine different conceptualizations of the State, particularly those drawn from recent Marxist work. They are uncertain whether any general theory is especially useful in explaining the behaviour of individual States, but make clear that many Latin American States condone 'illegal' activities as a way to maintain social stability and rapid economic growth. For this reason, State policy generally permits low-income settlement, however illegal it may be under their own laws and regulations, because it is essential to the continued functioning of the city. Beyond this covert tolerance, Latin American governments do little to help the poor. Their overt policies tend to favour commercial, industrial and high-income groups. It is only when the poor make a sustained demand for better treatment, say by voting against the current administration, that their cause is given higher priority in resource allocation. Very rarely, as least in Bogotá and Mexico City, have governments gone out of their way to directly help low-income populations. Of course, the poor may benefit indirectly from measures intended to help other groups, they may gain from investment in, say, infrastructure, which because it creates spare capacity can be used to provide services for low-income groups, but the generalization remains sound.

The data do not suggest, however, that the poor in either city have suffered greater material deprivation as a result of recent State policies. The State has increased its involvement with low-income groups and although this has sometimes involved higher payments for services and taxes for the poor, many settlements have been serviced. Nevertheless, the poor continue to suffer from the wider consequences of governmental neglect and repression. The authors are certain that fundamental policy changes are required to improve the position of the poor, and are uncertain of the possibility of such changes in the two societies involved. Radical change may be the only route, but it is important to recognize nevertheless that the more cataclysmic interpretations of urban reality in Latin America are not true of Bogotá and Mexico City; in both cities, the poor continue to gain some benefits from economic growth and urban development. The problem is that those benefits could be increased markedly by the introduction of more equitable measures such as tax reform and controls on land and building-material speculation. Such changes would improve the environment which now limits even their self-help attempts to improve their housing situation.

Michael Edwards explores an area which has been greatly neglected by studies of housing in Latin American cities, the tenant population. In some cities more than half the population lives in some form of rental accommodation and yet we know little about their living conditions, about their aspirations, their social and political characteristics, or about their relationship with the wider urban society. This neglect has come about largely because of the fascination with irregular, shanty housing and because of the implicit belief that most renters are occupying rental accommodation temporarily: they will move into owner occupation as soon as they have become established in the labour market and/or have a family. Yet, while it is true that most owners in shanty towns were once tenants, few writers or planners have questioned whether the majority of current tenants have this move open to them. Certainly, the all too frequent conjunction of declining real wages for low-income earners, and rising prices of land and building materials suggests that ownership may be increasingly difficult to achieve. It is possible, therefore, that the tenant population now contains a substratum of very poor people comprising the old, the underemployed and the infirm. This is one of the hypotheses that Edwards has tested in his recent doctoral dissertation.

In fact, his evidence suggests that few of the rental population can be easily distinguished from low-income owner-occupiers; a conclusion that is replicated in Gilbert and Ward's work in Bogotá and Mexico City. Among the tenants are many who could afford to buy homes in the irregular settlements but who choose to spend or invest their incomes in other ways. Of course, there are tenants who are very poor, who occupy single rooms and who have little chance of moving out of rental accommodation. Some of these tenants are indeed old and infirm, but the majority comprise young families. The nature of Edwards' methodology, an analysis of the housing situation at one point in time, makes it impossible to test whether home ownership is actually becoming more difficult but the rising proportion of people renting homes in Bucaramanga suggests that it is. If this interpretation is correct, then people who would have become home owners a few years back can no longer purchase accommodation. However, this is not the same as suggesting that it is the down and outs who rent low-income housing.

What is clear is that renting, and the role that it plays in the housing system, must be viewed structurally. The proportion of families renting accommodation is a function of the ease of access to home ownership. As such, Edwards argues that diagnosis should emphasize the constraints on the supply of housing rather than the nature of demand for accommodation. The Turneresque (1967, 1968) approach which saw renting as an early stage, and home ownership as a later stage, in the work/family/migration cycle is inappropriate. That first stage is not based on a preference for rental accommodation but on lack of choice; people rent when their family is young or when they are recently arrived in the city not because they prefer it but because they cannot afford to buy property. To understand the rental/ownership balance therefore, analysis should consider the supply constraints rather than the characteristics, desires and aspirations of the population requiring accommodation. If, as in Bucaramanga, land invasions are discouraged and there are decreasingly few opportunities to buy land even in illegal subdivisions, the corollary is that large numbers of people must rent.

But, if most tenants wish to become owners, renting is not as exploitative as it is so often portrayed; it is merely a consequence of the structural situation. Most landlords are also poor and share their houses with tenants in order to supplement their incomes. There are few large-scale landlords and still fewer tenement empires. Most renters live in consolidated shanty areas not in the old decaying parts of the city centre. If renting redistributes income towards the better off, renting to the poor by the less poor does not result in a redistribution of income to the rich. Nor can the well-established political apathy of the tenants be blamed mainly on the rental situation. Edwards deduces that such apathy is more to do with the youth, low incomes and short residential experience of the tenants than with the rental situation *per se*. The fact that in Colombia MOST low-income groups are politically apathetic, is one of the outcomes of the political organization of that country.

Edwards suggests that renting should certainly be viewed positively; it is true that most people prefer to own, but the rental population does not demonstrate signs of a 'culture of poverty'. In addition, they need the homes which rental accommodation provides. Insofar as renting is retrogressive in its income effects, it is merely an outcome of the pattern of exploitation and inequality inherent in the socioeconomic system. As such, governments should seek to encourage renting if they are unable, or unprepared, to bring about more fundamental changes. If they do not, housing conditions will deteriorate. Unfortunately, past experience suggests that direct government policies are either ineffective, as rent controls have been for low-income people in Bucaramanga, or they discourage the creation of rental opportunities. The only way to handle the rental situation is by improving the supply of housing, either to make renting the normal tenure situation or by making ownership more accessible. But, this requires something of a structural transformation in society, it requires higher incomes for the poor, cheaper land and building materials, and better organized servicing policies.

Caroline Moser makes an interesting attempt to test some of the main ideas about petty commodity production of housing and its position within dependent capitalism. She is concerned with the nature of the links between small-scale self-built housing construction and the capitalist economy; specifically with the degree to which the two can be separated analytically. She also seeks to examine the apparent conflict in the Marxist literature relating to the conservation or destruction of the petty commodity sector. On the one hand, it is argued that capitalist expansion continually seeks out opportunities for further capital accumulation through the penetration of non-capitalist and partially capitalist economies; intervention which incorporates manpower into fully capitalist wage employment and increases corporate control over the means of production (Pradilla, 1976; Burgess, 1978). On the other hand, Marxist interpretations increasingly argue that the main role of the petty commodity sector in dependent capitalist economies is to subsidize the capitalist sector and thereby to allow it to survive in a highly competitive world economy. Thus evidence from Brazil suggests that rather than destroying this sector, high rates of capital accumulation have seen its expansion (Kowarick, 1975). The capitalist sector subcontracts to petty commodity producers to reduce the costs of directly employing labour in unionized factories (Roberts, 1978). In the housing field, the capitalist sector benefits from petty commodity production because it reduces the cost of reproducing labour. Specifically, demands by labour for higher wages are limited by their low costs of accommodation. The validity of these differing interpretations requires empirical verification.

Moser's analysis demonstrates beyond doubt that the self-help housing economy is integrally linked to the capitalist system of exchange and also figures in the system of production. Land is purchased at the market price, many building materials are bought commercially, paid labour is frequently used, commercial water carriers supply the settlement, and infrastructure is financed by the State and provided by large-scale capitalist enterprises. Her methodology does not allow her to demonstrate whether the petty commodity sector is expanding or being destroyed, but her paper clearly shows that there is a continuum within the *barrio* ranging from precapitalist to fully capitalist enterprise. Land is acquired by families occupying swampland and building houses for their own use while other families buy houses in the settlement at the market price. In the construction of housing, both free family labour and wage labour can be observed. Capitalist penetration has clearly occurred in the *barrio*, there is constant interaction between the petty commodity and the capitalist economies, but whether penetration is increasing or decreasing, whether the commodity sector is being conserved or destroyed is not easy to resolve.

What is very clear, as it is in numerous of the other contributions to this volume, is that the factors that determine the conditions under which the poor attempt to resolve their housing situation lie beyond their control. The fact that they are forced to occupy this swampland is determined by the nature of land ownership in the city of Guayaquil. Whether they are permitted, or encouraged, to invade land depends on the political situation both in the city and nationally. How drainage and the filling in of land is managed depends upon its profitability to large-scale producers and their influence with the urban authorities. Whether the poor are allowed to communicate their complaints to the authorities through community organizations depends whether there is a military or civilian government and upon the nature of those regimes. Undoubtedly, whether or not conservation or destruction is the principal trend, there are major limitations on self-help development. Poor people may build their own homes, but the ease or difficulty of that process is determined outside their immediate environment. Élites make decisions without reference to poor people, but those decisions have critical reper-cussions on the poor.

It is certain that those decisions are seldom intended to benefit the poor, although it is not clear that they are always harmed. Indeed, increasingly the unpredictability of relationships between capitalist and petty commodity and precapitalist modes of production seems to be dominating the current research literature (Roberts, 1978). This unpredictability clearly makes generalization difficult and is nicely illustrated by Moser's analysis of the process of land acquisition. The continuum she describes makes it difficult even to classify land acquisition adequately. Her *barrio* in Guayaquil does not demonstrate the classic, Lima-type invasion where large groups with political support occupy

large areas of land. Nor, is it the typical illegal subdivision of land characteristic of Bogotá or Mexico City. Rather it is a flexible and largely unpredictable
response to structural conditions, decided beyond the limits of the *barrio*,
often outside Guayaquil and sometimes outside Ecuador altogether. Needless
to say, these structural conditions are limited in the opportunities they offer,
and in the benefits they bring, to the urban poor.

John Turner's paper both summarizes and extends the arguments developed
in his book *Housing for People*. Although his paper does not deal with Latin
America housing *per se*, his arguments are clearly relevant to the vast
difficulties facing both urban and rural areas in the region and have been
included in this book for that reason. The broad outline of his argument is
familiar. Many people are now forced into the position of being consumers of
housing in the sense that they have little or no control over what is produced
for them. The final product is often inappropriate to their needs and the
process of production and management often produces apathy or vandalism
towards their housing environment. The costs of production are high, which
excludes large numbers of people from the potential benefits of housing
development, and which concentrates many resources into limited numbers of
housing units. Turner is essentially attacking the corporate sector and the way
that it monopolizes resources, design and production, excluding the users from
participation in the design and production of their own housing.

He believes that the main source of current housing problems lies in the
control that the 'market' and the 'State' sectors have over the 'third' or
'community' sector. The last sector is that which cares for one's dependents
and neighbours. The problem is that the 'market' and 'State' sectors dominate
housing production in both capitalist and communist countries. Turner's
argument is very similar to that of Galbraith (1975) who believes that capitalist
countries are divided into a large-scale corporate and a small-scale 'market'
sector with the former constantly improving its position *vis-à-vis* the latter.
Galbraith sees all corporations and bureaucracies as working hand in glove
because of their common institutional interests and Turner implicitly accepts
such a distinction, declaring that the distinction between private and public
sectors is no longer meaningful. Turner and Galbraith, and indeed Friedmann
and Weaver (1979) in their support for greater local or 'territorial' control in
place of 'corporate' or 'functional' control over decision-making, are all
arguing that greater popular participation is necessary to control the worst
excesses of the 'corporate' sector and indeed to restructure society. Turner's
argument is different only insofar as he includes corporate socialist regimes
within his criticism.

The difficulty, of course, with all these analyses lies in how to bring about
the transformation in decision-making. Turner recommends that people assert
their rights through direct action, that governments increase local and personal
access to resources, that people in positions of influence alter their conventions

and rules and move towards a greater balance between the 'market', 'State' and 'community' sectors. Perhaps, it is unfair criticism but few revolutions have occurred that way. Decision-makers do not make decisions in a vacuum, they make decisions with respect to budgets, existing power groups and interest groups. There are important constraints on their freedom of choice. Greater knowledge may well persuade more people of the wisdom of Turner's case, but the bureaucratic, financial and institutional constraints on most of us are such that flexibility of action is limited. Greater knowledge, if incompatible with the existing socioeconomic system, is unlikely to foster change: it is more likely to generate a whole generation of schizophrenic professionals. It is only when large numbers of communities start to practice Turner's advice that there is any hope: but can such mass mobilization come through the spread of knowledge? Some readers will agree some will not.

Turner also seeks in this paper to counter two general criticisms of his previous work. First, he makes clear that he is not recommending some kind of self-help process, not idealizing the efforts of *barriada* dwellers in Lima. In fact, he specifically condemns self-sufficiency or autarchy in housing construction in contrast to self-management. The organizing units for the design and production of housing should be community groups at the local or municipal level. As such, his programme cannot simply be placed alongside existing forms of production, as some critics suggest, it is more radical and requires the substitution of corporate by community control over a wide range of decisions. He is recommending that different levels and scales of organization perform different functions in the housing process. The corporate sector, providing it does not restrict the autonomy of the community sector, has a major role to play in the mobilization of resources for housing. Large-scale, intermediate and small-scale organizations are all required in a balanced society.

Secondly, he makes clear that the issue of access to resources is critical in his reformulation of society. This is important insofar as one of the main criticisms of his previous work (for example, Burgess, 1978) is that any widespread adoption of self-help, site-and-service and squatter upgrading schemes is likely to exacerbate the situation of the poor because of greater intervention by the capitalist sector. As such, it will accentuate the maldistribution of resources which is the key to the housing problem. Turner is, in fact, recommending something much more ambitious than such programmes and that recommendation requires that the State guarantees access to the resources needed to build housing, such as land and building materials. He cannot be criticized for not realizing the importance of resources. Further criticism must focus on his understanding of the nature of the State. In short, are we justified in trusting Latin American governments to make available resources to be used in community directed housing projects?

Rogelio Pérez Perdomo and Pedro Nikken address a much neglected aspect of low-income settlements in Latin America; how the inhabitants of such settlements are treated under the law. Unlike government or higher-income conventional housing areas which are comprehensively treated by the law, most low-income areas are technically illegal and are virtually untouched by the formal legal system. Decisions are made by the political parties which have filled the vacuum in these areas, organizing invasions, arranging servicing and arbitrating between conflicting groups. Any disputes are resolved individually by the political authorities. On the whole, this system works in the sense that systematic repression has been avoided in Venezuela and there is no real sign of political violence in the *barrios*. Obviously, the poor receive poor land, poor services and are largely excluded from the formal legal system. The only official legal intervention in the *barrios* is in the form of two municipal agencies which advise litigants in their disputes, in one case bringing the contestants together to talk about their problem. These official bodies rarely follow the letter of the law but generally make use of commonsense to resolve immediate problems. What has evolved, therefore, is an informal but official system of regulations applied by the bottom layers of the State's power pyramid. The higher levels of the State bureaucracy are not interested in applying formal legal regulations and procedures to these areas. This study poses a series of difficult questions from a policy perspective. Insofar as the Venezuelan legal system is highly bureaucratic, slow and expensive, the low-income settlers are perhaps advantaged by their neglect. Formal inclusion of their settlements and their disputes might prevent the rapid use of commonsense to resolve *barrio* disputes that is current practice. On the other hand, the fact that two low-level municipal offices are the major sources of official assistance, means that most decisions affecting the poor are highly politicized. Of course, the degree to which political parties rather than the law *per se* manipulate the situation, is part of Venezuelan reality. Whether the insertion of *barrios* into the formal legal system would change anything is a moot point. Once again, this raises the question greater government intervention in the housing, employment and situations of the poor would actually help the latter. The answer depends fundamentally on whether trust can justifiably be placed in the governmental system.

Insofar as it can, then governments should extend the law and official intervention more comprehensively to low-income settlements and thereby help overcome the insecurity and illegality of their populations. Insofar as it cannot, then low-income settlements are better left to their own devices, or at least to the pragmatic, party political, and somewhat anarchic situation that now exists. In the Venezuelan case, Pérez and Nikken clearly believe this situation has been a perfectly natural outcome of the nature of State participation in the society at large. It is therefore fanciful to anticipate any other response. Whether one believes that the same conclusion applies in other Latin American countries depends on individual beliefs and values.

Richard Batley considers a theme that has dominated recent studies of urban development in Western Europe but which has been relatively neglected in Latin America, the social and distributional effects of urban renewal (Castells, 1979; Saunders, 1979). Specifically, he examines the process of urban expulsion associated with the building of a mass-transit railway system through the centre of São Paulo. His main interest is in the procedures adopted by the Metrô Company to expropriate land and to compensate landowners in one part of the inner city. The intellectual origins of his analysis lie in the British urban planning literature. One of the themes running through his chapter is the debate about the explanatory value of the concept known as 'urban managerialism' (Pahl, 1975; Harloe, 1977). According to this concept, managers and bureaucrats determine rules which differentiate between clients of the bureaucracy. It has been suggested that most rules tend to favour middle-class and higher-income groups and prejudice low-income groups and racial and other minorities. The rules take the form they do, because bureaucrats are unaware of the effects of their decisions, are implicitly biased in favour of the groups they assist, or are more concerned with bureaucratic convenience than say equity. In the case of the Metrô Company, it is clear that the bureaucratic rules established were discriminatory: they favoured large companies and they harmed low-income groups, especially tenants. The reasons behind these rules might be due to subjectivity or other influences motivating the administrators who established the guidelines. In fact, Batley argues that the rules emerged in the form they did mainly because it was the best way to help the bureaucracy pursue its goal of building the railway. Since the company was subject to major financial and political constraints, the priority was to get the job done as quickly as possible. As a result, the procedure to negotiate the compulsory purchase of land was characterized by its emphasis on speed, the lack of advice on their rights given to the local population, and the offer of an apparently unnegotiable and technically determined sum of compensation. According to this interpretation, urban managerialism provides a less useful approach to understanding the nature of the rules than does an understanding of the structural constraints on the operation of the company. Like so many students of British planning, Batley found that the company chose the particular procedures not because of the biases of bureaucrats than because there were no real alternatives. The important issue, therefore, is not how bureaucrats decide upon procedures but upon structural limitations such as rates of return, political commitments and pressures on the company.

In the case of the São Paulo metro, large companies and those inhabitants who could afford to take their case to court gained higher compensation than small-scale owner occupiers. At Batley notes, the latter were 'isolated, under pressure and uninformed'. They were often placed in a predicament because their compensation was insufficient to buy adequate accommodation elsewhere. Tenants faired still worse because they received no compensation and were often informed very late of their imminent eviction.

In this context it is perhaps surprising that there was no protest from the local population against the procedures. After all this was a thriving community and most of the population had lived there for a number of years. Batley gives various reasons why there was little protest, most important of which was the speed and bureaucratic efficiency of the Metrô Company which made most inhabitants feel there was little to be done. This clearly had some effect but it would also seem likely that the political environment of Brazil in 1976 was a contributory factor. After all, community mobilization and political protest is not likely to flourish under a highly repressive authoritarian regime. In addition, protests over similar issues have emerged in other places when local populations have been under threat from urban renewal projects. In Bogotá, attempts to build an urban motorway through certain low-income settlements in the early seventies met with considerable resistance (Gilbert, 1978; Janssen, 1978; Revéiz et al., 1977). But such resistance did not emerge spontaneously from the settlements, it was encouraged and stimulated by opposition political groups, both within and outside government. In São Paulo, such outside support was precluded by the nature of Brazilian authoritarianism. In short, I suspect that mobilization or its absence, like bureaucratic rules, are the result of the environment in which people and institutions operate.

Batley is only interested in analysing the social effects within the area subject to urban renewal. Such an analysis is likely to conclude that poorer groups suffered as a result of the process of renewal. It is important to stress that such an analysis excludes the possible benefits that other low-income groups may receive from railway construction; a point clearly recognized by the author. Dependent on the route, many poor groups may find their access to work greatly improved, and may even find the value of their property rising. Of course, this does not vindicate unfair and differential processes of land expropriation and compensation. But, it is too simple to blame blind or uncaring bureaucrats for the procedures. Many of the inequalities, the way corporate groups benefit and individuals lose out, are built into the procedures which in turn are a direct result of the direct constraints acting upon the bureaucracy. Somehow the rules need to be changed, but to do so the nature of the economic and political model needs altering first; the recurrent question again appears.

Finally, Luis Unikel deals with an issue that has long been of major interest to Latin American planners, the problem of spatial concentration and the need to decentralize economic activity and population away from the rapidly expanding major cities. Commenting on the Mexican experience, he argues that regional policy has been ineffective in reversing the long-established trend towards spatial concentration in Mexico City. Before 1970, policy was ineffective because although government rhetoric espoused the cause of decentralization, government spending continued to favour those areas where economic growth was fastest. Such a policy may have been inevitable, but it was certainly not helped by the failure of the Mexican government to seriously evaluate its policies and programmes. Unikel argues that the only group within Mexico that has consistently monitored government policies has been the academic community; criticism that has eventually been heeded by government decision-makers. It is nice to hear praise for academic endeavour and recognition of its effectiveness even if it comes from another academic!

Despite his scepticism about the effectiveness of previous regional policies Unikel obviously believed that the Echeverría government (1970–76) had shown a strong commitment to regional development and laid the foundations for some measure of decentralization and redistribution of income. This commitment may have been the result of a growing realization of the scale of the problems emerging in as huge a metropolis as Mexico City, or it may have been the result of the growing power of state politicians; whatever the cause major legislative changes such as the Law for Human Settlements were the result. Nevertheless, Luis Unikel still detects a lack of coherence in regional and national policy. He suggests that this was an outcome of the multiplicity of interests represented in the Mexican State. Given the power of political and interest group representatives of Mexico City, for example, how can the Mexican State neglect the metropolis in order to favour other areas. Even if some of the obvious problems facing Mexico City could be temporarily neglected, could a genuinely redistributional regional programme be implemented that would help the poor of rural Mexico? Would not the nature of power in Mexico mean that it would be the most powerful and prosperous states that would benefit most from a regional development programme?

Unikel's partial answer is that nothing at all can be achieved unless planning becomes more coherent, rational and pragmatic. He makes a plea that any regional, and by implication any other, plan should be implementable rather than theoretically elegant, should define specific goals which can be monitored and evaluated, and that these goals should form part of a coherent national economic and social strategy. Clearly, if planning is to assist in the achievement of a more equitable society, such changes are essential. But, as the author clearly recognizes in his conclusion, the real answer lies beyond planning. It lies in the implementation of major structural reforms.

Alas, this is the pessimistic answer of so many of the chapters in this book although one, perhaps, that is inevitable given the current approach of social scientists. Holism and a political economy paradigm are likely to demonstrate the interrelations between social, economic and political phenomena and to recommend change on numerous fronts. But it is also the outcome of the realization that change in Latin America is not going to come from liberal minded governments introducing technical modifications in their procedures. Most governments in Latin America are not representatives of 'society as a whole' and are especially disinterested in issues such as the redistribution of power and resources; both the new paradigm and all of the authors in this book recognize that fact. Let us hope that Luis Unikel was right in his belief that governments read academic evaluations. If they do, and they read this book, then some lessons at least are very clear.

REFERENCES

Burgess, R. (1978). 'Petty commodity housing or dweller control? A critique of John Turner's views on housing policy', *World Development* 6, 1105-34.

Cardoso, F. H. and Faletto, E. (1969). *Dependencia y Desarrollo en América Latina.* Siglo XXI.

Castells, M. (1979). *City, Class and Power.* Macmillan.

Collier, D. (1976). *Squatters and Oligarchs: Authoritarian Rule and Policy Change in Peru.* Johns Hopkins Press.

Dietz, H. (1977). 'Land invasion and consolidation: a study of working poor/ governmental relations in Lima, Peru', *Urban Anthropology* 6, 371-85.

Dos Santos, T. (1970). 'The structure of dependence', *American Economic Review* 60, 231-6.

Frank, A. G. (1967). *Capitalism and Underdevelopment in Latin America: Historical Studies of Chile and Brazil.* Monthly Review Press.

Friedmann, J. and Weaver, C. (1979). *Territory and Function: the Evolution of Regional Planning.* Edward Arnold.

Galbraith, J. K. (1975). *Economics and the Public Purpose.* Penguin. Original 1973.

Gilbert, A. G. (1978). 'Bogotá: politics, planning and the crisis of lost opportunities'. In Cornelius, W. A. and Kemper, R. V. (eds.), *Metropolitan Latin America, Latin American Urban Research* 6, 87-126.

Harloe, M. (1977). *Captive Cities.* John Wiley.

Janssen, R. (1978). 'Class practices of dwellers in *barrios* populares: the struggle for the right to the city', *International Journal of Urban and Regional Research* 2, 147-59.

Kowarick, L. (1975). *Capitalismo e Marginalidade na America Latina.* Paz e Terra.

Pahl, R. E. (1975). *Whose City?* Penguin Books.

Palma, G. (1978). 'Dependency: a formal theory of underdevelopment or a methodology for the analysis of concrete situations of underdevelopment?', *World Development* 6, 881-924.

Pradilla, E. (1976). 'Notas acerca del "problema de la vivienda" ', *Ideología y Sociedad* 16, 70-107.

Revéiz, E. *et al.* (1977). *Poder e información.* Universidad de los Andes, Bogotá.

Roberts, B. (1978). *Cities of Peasants: the Political Economy of Urbanization in the Third World.* Edward Arnold/Sage.

Roberts, B. R. (1975). 'Centre and periphery in the development process: the case of Peru'. In Cornelius, W. A. and Trueblood, F. M. (eds.), *Urbanization and Inequality, Latin American Urban Research* 5, 77-106.

Saunders, P. (1979). *Urban Politics: A Sociological Interpretation.* Hutchinson.

Turner, J. F. C. (1967). 'Barriers and channels for housing development in modernizing countries', *Journal of the American Institute of Planners* 32, 167-81.

Turner, J. F. C. (1968). 'Housing priorities, settlement patterns and urban development in modernizing countries', *Journal of the American Institute of Planners* 34, 354-63.

Urbanization in Contemporary Latin America
Edited by A. Gilbert with J. E. Hardoy and R. Ramírez
© 1982 John Wiley & Sons Ltd.

2

The building of Latin American cities

JORGE E. HARDOY

This short essay covers two thousand years of Latin American urban history. The aim is to introduce the reader to the ways in which different societies sought to plan and build their cities. Throughout this period most cities were constructed by individuals, supplemented by the results of occasional collective efforts. Self-help was as characteristic of the past as of the present Latin American city. In both, the self-built shelter of the majority surrounded the small city core built for pre-Columbian, colonial or national élites. The core always exhibited street plans, land uses and building standards very different from the rest of the city; the difference between ruler and ruled was established long ago.

PRE-COLUMBIAN URBAN DEVELOPMENT

The flourishing of regional states during the first millenium B.C. marked the beginning of urban development in several parts of present-day Latin America (Lanning, 1967; Lumbreras, 1969; Sanders and Price, 1968; Krickeberg, 1961). Possibly during the late formative period (600–0 B.C.), the cultures living in the Central Valley of Mexico, in Hidalgo, in Oaxaca, in Puebla-Tlaxcala and in other regions of present-day Mexico developed an advanced hydraulic technology as an answer to the demands of a growing population increasingly concentrated in larger villages (Palerm, 1973). In Peru's coastal valleys, major irrigation works were built during the early horizon period (900–200 B.C.), based on many centuries of communal works of growing complexity (Kosok, 1965). As food supplies and population increased, closer commercial links between the different ecological areas developed, encouraging an increase in local production for export to other regions.

Increased control of the rural environment meant that the original agricultural communities lost their independence. Consolidation of social organization, the centralization of economic decisions, the specialized

19

organization of labour and the regulation of trade represented a step towards a
new sociopolitical system and the beginnings of a state bureaucracy. Thus, in
Mesoamerica and the Andean region, much of the rural population and most
of what we might call urban artisans, were engaged in producing a surplus for
a ruling élite. Sometime during this long formative period, the ruling
theocracies began to organize economic institutions which helped trade and
production, thus encouraging the formation of towns.

Urban centres did not evolve simply as a consequence of population growth
supported by higher agricultural production and more intensive commercial
relationships. It was not a linear process taking place simultaneously in all
centres. Almost certainly, new political organizations emerged during the
middle and late formative periods introducing major changes in the power
structures of pre-Columbian cultures. This encouraged the more intense and
rationalized use of the three basic resources of pre-Columbian agriculture—
labour, land and water—especially between A.D. 0 and 900 in Mesoamerica
and between A.D. 200 and 600 in the Andean area.

The new situation required urban centres of unprecedented size, power and
diversity: Teotihuacán in the central highlands of Mexico, Tikal in the Petén,
Monte Albán in Oaxaca, Tiahuanaco in the highlands of Bolivia, Pucara in the
northern basin of the Titicaca lake and, centuries later, Huari in the highlands
of Peru and several centres in the river valleys of Peru's northern and central
coast (Hardoy, 1965; Hardoy, 1973).

Almost all pre-Columbian cities grew spontaneously on the site of an
existing agricultural village or a religious centre. As a result, practically all
major classic and postclassic cities initially grew without a physical plan. They
expanded because of favourable ecological factors, essentially water and land
availability, and due to good locations which encouraged trade and increased
their religious importance (Hardoy, 1973). The defensive properties, of a site
were less important, at least during the classic period, although strategic
locations in relation to newly conquered territory were taken into
consideration.

When it became necessary to expand, remodel or rebuild a city, it was
almost certainly a king, a high priest or a regional head of state who gave the
order. Pachacuti, emperor of the Incas between 1439 and 1471, ordered the
renewal of central Cuzco; he dictated the proportions of the main square;
ordered the construction of several buildings around it, instructed that the
Huatanay river which crossed the site be channelled, and essentially decided
the street pattern that in some sections of the city remains to this day. The
Aztec capital that so amazed the Spaniards, was essentially the work of
Moctezuma I, king of the Aztecs between 1440 and 1469; he ordered the
expansion of Tenochtitlán and the construction of the main temple dedicated
to the cult of Huitzilopochtli, the most important deity in the Aztec pantheon;
and, it was probably he who decided the layout of the two great axes which

gave Tenochtitlán its unique physical form. Nezahualcóyotl, king of Texcoco between 1428 and 1472, transformed his capital into central Mexico's cultural centre. Together with Moctezuma I, Nezahualcóyotl decided to build a dyke to protect Tenochtitlán from flooding, construct an aqueduct to supply water to the fast growing urban population and improve access to the city by means of the several causeways which permitted the Aztec capital to become the commercial and administrative centre of Mexico.

The true designers and builders of these marvellous ceremonial centres and squares and the authors of many outstanding feats of engineering remain anonymous. Orders were given by members of an élite with absolute power. The anonymous architects, artists and artisans left examples of their imagination and skill in setting a monumental perspective, in the subtle use of steps and terraces to emphasize the progressive approach to a monument, in the proportions of a square or in the use of topography to produce visual surprises. The beauty of a simple frieze, the symbolic meaning of colour and figures in a fresco are lasting memories of cultures which produced some of the world's masterpieces of civic design and art. The people simply followed orders. They never had the opportunity to participate in the decisions of governments which became concerned with public welfare only when economic or defence needs made this necessary. Urban planning was undertaken at the highest level of government. The scope of these cities required meticulous planning to organize the labour, the food and the supply of building materials.[1]

Teotihuacán reached its maximum size, some 2200 hectares, and population, perhaps as many as 85 000 inhabitants, during the fifth and sixth centuries A.D. The layout of the central districts was a simple gridiron approximately 54 metres square, the streets oriented according to the design of two main axes forming a cross (Millon, 1973). In the centre of the cross was an architectural complex formed by a group of ceremonial buildings, the Quetzalcóatl temple, and a vast building, probably the market. The two axes, the two monumental pyramids known as the Temple of the Sun and the Temple of the Moon, the broad ceremonial avenue known today as the Avenue of the Dead, and most of the gridiron, were developed in an area partially occupied and first built centuries before.

Seven or eight centuries after Teotihuacán was abandoned by its inhabitants, a culture which probably did not know the meaning and age of its ruins built a humble village on an island in Mexico's central lake district, some 60 kilometres southwest of the site of Teotihuacán. The origins of Tenochtitlán are dated around 1325. Towards the middle of the fifteenth century, the Aztecs also designed two monumental axes (Ruiz, 1973); where they crossed a ceremonial complex was developed across a 16-hectare area surrounded by a low wall (Marquina, 1960). A large square used as a market and for civic activities was opened to the south and rapidly framed by royal palaces. When Cortés and his men arrived in 1519, the Aztec capital probably covered 1200 hectares and had some 220 000 inhabitants. Almost one-third of the city was built on solid ground and two-thirds over areas reclaimed from the lake through an elaborate process of flood control and land filling (Calnek, 1972). The two axes also guided the lines of the streets and navigable water channels. These simple principles of town planning were also used in other Aztec cities or in cities which fell under Aztec domination (Motolinia, 1941).

In Andean America, the Incas gained control of a territory of more than one million square kilometres and inhabited by some five to six million people between 1440 and 1495. It was a territory of sharp ecological and cultural differences, consisting of both regional states and local kingdoms. The control of the Incas over much of this territory was short and tenuous. The capitals of the local kingdoms were partially remodelled according to the urbanistic and architectural principles applied in Cuzco during the reign of Pachacuti I. In most of these towns, as well as in their new towns, the Incas introduced a great ceremonial and civic square surrounded by the administrative buildings, the temple of the Sun and the house of the Virgins (Gasparini and Margolies, 1977; Hardoy, 1973). They did not use rigid axes as in the towns of Mesoamerica and the only attempts to incorporate the gridiron were in Ollantaytambo and Chucuito.[2]

These examples reveal the essential nature of pre-Columbian urban planning was not concerned with the periphery of cities, with the low-density and unserviced suburbs. The housing of the poor classes was self-built with segregation, the élite living in or around the central square. Since little urban land was held privately there were few impediments to changes in land use. In some cases, as in Tenochtitlán, these guidelines were complemented by building ordinances regulating the heights and some of the characteristics of particular buildings.

The pre-Columbian city was an artificial environment built by an élite to administer and control the production, commerce, and religious and cultural life over a vast territory. Thus, town planning only reflected concern about the physical characteristics and the quality of the environment in the central districts of major towns where the élite and its immediate collaborators lived. The latter included artisans, who transformed obsidian, jade, turquoise, gold, feathers and other materials into goods consumed by the élite or exported, artists, fully dedicated to the town's embellishment, bureaucrats, merchants, lesser army officers, and the numerous servants of these classes. Town planning was not concerned with the periphery of cities, with the low-density and unserviced suburbs. The housing of the poor classes was self-built with perishable materials, not very different from rural shelters.

Urban land use, the variable quality of urban housing, the design of the different districts, the quality of public architecture, and the practice of town planning as a reflection of the will of a ruling élite, clearly showed the class differences of pre-Columbian societies. We cannot talk of urban or housing policies, only of attempts to regulate the physical growth of cities and of the spontaneous adoption by poor people of minimum standards of shelter. Planning was concerned with the development of coherent public work policies for the construction of ceremonial and civic buildings. Good organization was required to assure the supply of water, food and basic consumer goods which served the urban workforce. But, education and recreation was a privilege of the ruling élite; no organized health system has been recorded; there was no urban transport.

For the mass of population, progress, if any, came as a result of a filter-down process which began when the supply of food, services and goods for the ruling élite was expanded. Public investment was seldom intended to satisfy the needs of a growing urban population, with the exception of food and, occasionally, water. It was to maintain production, social controls and defence, in other words, to minimize the dangers of a change in the established order. The popular classes benefited only indirectly from public works. There was no popular representation in Government, nor was there any general interest in satisfying their aspirations and needs. Archaeology has revealed very little about popular uprisings during the pre-Columbian wars and there was no written record, but undoubtedly they existed. My hypothesis is that regional uprisings must have taken place when government policies failed to prevent famines, thereby hitting the rural population and especially the urban masses. Records of people selling themselves as slaves to avoid starvation are frequent from the last decades of the Aztec era.[3] Popular uprisings are more likely to have been caused by famines and pestilence than by inequality. In any event they must have been shortlived and do not seem to have produced changes in social, economic or political organization. On the contrary, the Aztec government increasingly concentrated power in the hands of one person, and both the Aztecs and the Incas were apparently distributing labour, and possibly land, among members of the ruling élite.

THE COLONIAL PERIOD

Between 1520 and 1580, hundreds and even thousands of urban settlements of all types were officially founded, or established spontaneously, in what is now Latin America. Seldom in history, and never in Latin American history, has a comparable process taken place over such an immense territory. Urbanization formed a key element in the Spanish and Portuguese discovery, conquest, colonization and administration of Latin America; the colonial city was the centre of power and domination. The conquest moved the centres of power and decision-making from the capitals of pre-Columbian cultures to Spain and Portugal. Thus ended the independent experiences of the indigenous cultures, experiences that through millenia had taken place with complete autonomy from parallel experiences in Europe, Asia and North Africa.

All of the European powers who participated in the conquest of America brought their own experience in the planning and construction of cities (Hardoy, 1978). Spaniards, Portuguese, French, English and Dutch already had centuries of urban experience when they moved to America during the sixteenth and seventeenth centuries. They built cities that in layout, architectural styles, technology, land-use patterns and even in criteria used to select the location of the new settlements, were similar to their own in Europe.

Spain introduced a city model that is easy to identify: a simple street pattern, almost always a gridiron, with the cathedral, the town hall and the Governor's house built around a square often surrounded by arcades (Hardoy, 1972). The low profile of the Spanish–American town was interrupted by the towers and domes of the churches. Its simple beauty was a consequence of the architectural unity achieved through the use of regular squares of different size and homogeneous building materials, stone and more often adobe bricks employed in facades coloured in light blue, pink, green, yellow, or most frequently, just whitewashed. This simple model was modified only when the topography was difficult or when a settlement developed spontaneously. Some mining centres, ports and rural settlements were very different in physical layout and architectural and urban conceptions.

The Spanish conquerors and governors responsible for early city foundation did not bring a city prototype from Spain. Between 1493 and sometime during the 1520s, they built dozens of new settlements, in the islands of the Caribbean, in Mexico, Central America and in the north-western coast of South America, which reflected European cultural ideas partially developed in new urban centres in the north of Italy, the south of France and occasionally in Spain (Kubler, 1972). But, neither the elements that formed the classic model of the Hispano–American city, nor its hierarchical order, had been synthetized in a single settlement in previous centuries. It was only gradually that the Spanish Crown sanctioned legislation influencing the layout of streets and land use, the relationships between climate, the width of streets and the location and orientation of buildings, the locations and proportions of city squares, the location of churches and public buildings, the selection of regions and sites for new settlements, the distribution of urban and rural lots and the election of public officers.

The instructions relating to the planning and construction of settlements were not codified until 1573.[4] These royal instructions of 1573 were preceded by the foundation of specific towns; discoverers, conquerors and royal administrators founded towns and settlements of different sizes in order to establish centres of supply and exchange and to confirm their institutional and political claims. The process of discovery, conquest and settlement was essentially the result of private initiatives, privately funded and implemented but requiring royal permission as legally the new lands were considered as territories of the Crown. Only rarely were major expeditions financed by the Crown and directly executed by its appointees. One was Columbus' second trip which resulted in the foundation of Isabela (1494) and six forts in the interior of Santo Domingo island. A second was Ovando's visit to the same island which resulted in the second and final foundation of Santo Domingo (1502) and of eleven small settlements before 1508. A third was Pedrarias Dávila's administration in the Darién (Castilla del Oro) which resulted in the foundation of Panamá (1519), the oldest surviving European settlement on the American mainland.

The Spaniards were the only ones to attempt to develop an urban prototype. The number of settlements they built in America were many times larger than the combined total built by all the other European powers. But although more Spaniards are likely to have moved to Latin America before the 1830s than all other Europeans put together, the number of Spaniards in any town was never very large. Once the location of the new town and its layout was decided, once the urban blocks were subdivided into four, six or even eight lots and allocated to the new settlers, it was the *Cabildo*'s (town council) responsibility to supply and maintain indispensable services, to control land uses and to maintain urban order. The *Cabildos* raised taxes to pay for essential services, such as the paving of central streets and the upkeep of the main public buildings. Payment of these taxes was essentially the responsibility of the owners of land and houses which meant the miners, merchants, high ranking officers of the colonial administration and the religious orders. If we exclude the latter, who were exempted from taxes, the other groups formed the colonial aristocracy from whom the members of the *Cabildo* were largely drawn. Naturally, the tendency was to postpone the raising of taxes or simply to ignore them.

The popular sectors were not represented in the *Cabildo* despite the fact that the functions of the *regidores* (town councillors) included several which directly affected the living conditions of the lower income groups, control of the city's supplies, the allocation of urban lots and land use, the regulation of prices and salaries, the enforcement of taxes, and the supply of water (Lohman Villena, 1975). A large share of the town's scarce resources financed civic and religious celebrations in order to enhance the councillors' prestige. Thus, it cannot come as a surprise that the general poverty and the decaying character of the colonial towns are reflected in impressions coming from travel books and chronicles of the seventeenth and eighteenth centuries.

In Renaissance Europe, mercantilism and the formation of nation states during the seventeenth century saw some cities develop into national capitals and attract new administrative, cultural and political functions. The organization of professional armies, which required the construction of garrisons in some towns and the development of new manufacturing and handicraft activities encouraged further urban growth: from the seventeenth century, Europe's main towns and ports began to expand more rapidly.

Overcrowding, bad sanitation and poor housing conditions in these cities led to a search for new solutions: groups of squares, long perspectives and occasionally parks were built; the growing number of horse-drawn carriages led to the design of 'rond points' and the widening and straightening of the narrow medieval streets; new market squares were built, water supply improved and garbage collected.

In Latin America, the situation was quite different. The original gridiron was sufficiently large to accommodate the population and few towns expanded physically during three centuries of colonial rule. Whether it was a new foundation on an unbuilt site, near the site of an indigenous settlement, by the ruins of pre-Columbian cultures or close to cultivated lands, the inevitable gridiron of regular blocks was laid out covering an area which today seems overextended. The excellent town plans of the seventeenth and eighteenth centuries shows that even Lima, the second largest city at the end of the colonial period, still had large unbuilt areas within the walled area (IEAL, 1960). Similarly, major ports such as Havana, Cartagena, Veracruz, Callao, Campeche, Santo Domingo and San Juan, where the Crown had invested large sums in the building of defensive walls, had lower densities than in the contemporary European towns and contained plenty of unbuilt areas, if few public open spaces.

The populations of the colonial cities grew very slowly: by the beginning of the nineteenth century, only Mexico City and Rio de Janeiro had more than 100 000 inhabitants and only Havana, Salvador, Lima, Buenos Aires and Santiago de Chile had over 40 000 inhabitants (Sánchez, 1975). Plagues haunted the urban populations and most growth was a result of internal migrations. The colonial town did not incorporate major technological innovations. The supply of water, garbage collection and waste disposal followed similar procedures to pre-Columbian cities. The improvements that horses, mules, oxen and carriages brought to transport were limited by the deplorable state of the roads. Perhaps the major improvement was the continent-wide network of hospitals and the introduction of sanitary standards.

In the Hispano–American colonial city, the ruling élite lived with their servants in large houses, built around or close to the main square. The houses of the wealthiest usually had two floors, the rooms opening on to two or three patios. Front rooms were often transformed into shops. The humbler houses of small merchants, minor officers of the Crown, certain artisans and some independent workers, surrounded the central district. The lower income groups, unskilled Indians and *mestizos* without regular employment, built their small houses still further away. Like the pre-Columbian city, the colonial city was largely self-built. What we could now call the professional building industry worked mostly for the élite. The rigid class structure of colonial society was clearly demarkated by dress, diet, housing, education, occupation and freedom of movement: at the top was the Spaniard, then the criole followed by the *mestizo*; at the bottom the Indian, the free African and the black slave.

In Brazil, the Portuguese found neither advanced urban cultures nor densely settled agricultural areas from which to extract tribute. Nor, until the beginning of the eighteenth century, did they manage to develop a mining economy comparable to those of the Spanish in Mexico and Peru. In the sixteenth and seventeenth centuries, the Brazilian economy was wholly dependent on agriculture worked by African slave labour. Concerned about the future of its colonies in India and south-east Asia and its trade along the African coast, Portugal neglected Brazil. Portugal had neither the population nor the capital to settle a coast 7000 kilometres long. To overcome these limitations, the Crown of Portugal resorted to the system of 'captaincies' first employed successfully in their Atlantic island colonies in the fifteenth century. Land grants, 250 kilometres wide and of unlimited depth, were made to private individuals who began to clear the forests, enslave the Indian population and develop agriculture. Numerous ports established before 1540, Olinda, Pôrto Seguro, Espíritu Santo, Igaraçu, Santa Cruz, Cabralia, Ilheus and São Vicente, developed into Brazil's first settlement network (Reis Filho, 1968; Geiger, 1963; Azevedo, 1956).

Most of the new settlements such as São Vicente and Pôrto Seguro were merely temporary trading posts; permanent settlements like Olinda were quite exceptional. In 1549, the Crown of Portugal founded Bahia (now Salvador) as the administrative capital; Rio de Janeiro was founded in 1565; Paraíba (now Jóão Pessoa) twenty years later. These three towns and fourteen smaller settlements continued to be inhabited at the end of the sixteenth century; all but São Paulo were coastal settlements (Azevedo, 1956).

The prosperity of Bahia and Pernambuco (now Recife), the two largest cities in colonial Brazil, depended on the success of the sugar plantation economy of the North east. But, in the eighteenth century, Brazil's economy entered into a new stage with the discovery of gold and diamonds in Minas Gerais. Mining introduced a new geographical dimension into Brazil's settlement pattern: hundreds of new settlements were established in the mountains of Minas Gerais and in the States of Bahia, Mato Grosso and Goîas. Thousands of settlers came from Portugal and other ports in Brazil to the new cities such as Mariana, Oûro Preto, Sabara, Diamantina and São João del Rei.

One of Latin America's greatest architectural and sculptural movements flourished in those towns during the eighteenth century. Its culmination was Vila Rica (now Oûro Preto). Medieval reminders are everywhere in Oûro Preto: in the location of its churches which take advantage of small elevations in the terrain; in the oblique view that the pedestrian has of the churches' facades; and in the formal irregularity of its square. Founded on undulating terrain, its spontaneous growth did not follow a regular form. By contrast,

1other spontaneous settlement, Mariana, was given a regular layout in 1740. The colonial towns of Brazil did not follow a simple model as in Spanish colonies. But, a medieval pattern did not predominate as several authors have suggested; the builders gradually incorporated a regular pattern when topography made it possible.

POST-INDEPENDENCE URBAN DEVELOPMENT

Latin America's population has been estimated to have been around 31 million in 1850 and 63 million in 1900 (Hardoy and Langdon, 1978). During those fifty years, major changes took place in the spatial structure of certain regions, as they developed into sources of raw materials and foodstuffs for Western Europe and the United States. In 1850, the colonial settlement pattern differed little in terms of hierarchy and function from that of 1600. But, in certain areas, the impact of European and especially British investment in railways, mining and industry, the introduction of modern farming techniques, cheaper oceanic transport, massive immigration from Europe, growing political stability and the introduction of sanitation in the major cities, very rapidly produced substantial changes.[5]

Between 1840 and 1910, 100 000 kilometres of railway were built in Latin America, mostly in Argentina, Mexico, Chile and Brazil. By linking the most fertile lands and the more productive and accessible mining areas to the ports, the railway network promoted regional specialization: beef and grain in the Argentine plains, beef and sheep in Uruguay, coffee in the state of São Paulo, grain and vineyards in central Chile, vineyards in the Cuyo region of Argentina. During this period, some of the highest rates of urban growth occurred in the major port cities such as Buenos Aires, Montevideo, Rio de Janeiro and Havana. Improved transportation along the São Francisco and Amazon rivers in Brazil, the Magdalena in Colombia and the Paraná, Uruguay and Paraguay rivers in the southern cone led to the rapid growth of ports such as Rosario and Santa Fé after 1870, Barranquilla between 1890 and 1920, Asunción after 1890, and Belém and Manaus by 1900.

Mining, the exploitation of forests and the opening of new land for cotton, sugar, cocoa, coffee, cattle and sheep production extended the frontiers and led to the foundation of many towns in northern Chile and Mexico, in Goîas, the Mato Grosso and Amazonia in Brazil, in Patagonia and the Chaco region of Argentina, Paraguay and Bolivia. During the 1860s and 1870s, the first phase of import substitution saw the establishment of industry in certain capital and port cities. The demand for unskilled workers in these now fast-growing urban centres attracted migrants from Europe.

By 1900, Buenos Aires had around 800 000 inhabitants and 690 000 people were crowded into an unhealthy Rio de Janeiro. Twelve other cities had populations of more than 100 000 inhabitants: Mexico City (345 000), Santiago de Chile (333 000 in 1907), Havana (329 000 in 1907), Montevideo (309 000 in 1906), São Paulo (240 000), Salvador (205 000), Valparaíso (162 000), Lima (142 000), Recife (113 000), Rosario (112 000), Guadalajara (101 000) and Bogotá (100 000) (Hardoy and Langdon, 1978; Morse, 1974; Sánchez, 1975). With the exception of Montevideo and Rosario, which had been established during the eighteenth century, all of these cities had been founded by the Spanish or the Portuguese between 1520 and 1580.

The growth of some of these centres towards the end of the nineteenth century was truly exceptional: Buenos Aires grew annually at 5.2 per cent between 1895 and 1900, Rosario at 7.2 per cent between 1887 and 1895, São Paulo at 12.5 per cent between 1886 and 1890 and Bogotá at 5.7 per cent between 1870 and 1884. Several smaller cities grew rapidly as a consequence of foreign immigration. Mortality rates were inevitably high given the poor sanitary conditions and overcrowded housing conditions; certain ports like Santos, Havana, Veracruz, Panamá, Rio de Janeiro and Guayaquil had a very bad reputation. Smallpox and bubonic plague were endemic, epidemics of yellow fever were frequent, tuberculosis was a major cause of death among poorly fed and poorly housed workers, and malaria and typhus worsened the situation. It is not surprising, then, then to find a temporary decline in the population of some Latin American cities, even among the twenty largest, between 1850 and 1930.[6]

Buenos Aires and Rio de Janeiro, the two largest cities of Latin America in 1900, illustrate the prevailing initiatives in urban planning and construction at the turn of the century. Their rapid growth after the 1870s was a result of the massive immigration of Italians and Spaniards to Buenos Aires and Italians and Portuguese to Rio de Janeiro. British, French and German capital built new electricity, telephone, water, sewerage, tram and suburban train systems as well as new docks and factories. Avenues of unprecedented width and diagonals cutting across the colonial gridiron were opened, ideas strongly influenced by Haussman's plan for Paris half a century earlier. Some of the best parks in Buenos Aires and Rio de Janeiro were planned by French landscape architects. Public buildings, private parks, opera houses, theatres and markets were rapidly incorporated into a townscape reflecting the contemporary architectural styles fashionable in Western Europe and especially in France.

Tramlines allowed the development of new housing districts for the growing middle classes. Meanwhile private entrepreneurs rapidly developed tenements for poor immigrant families near the docks, railway stations, the central commercial district and the early factories. This new conception of workers' housing was designed to make maximum use of narrow-fronted urban lots (Scobie, 1974). Dozens of rooms were built on both sides of narrow patios or a central corridor with common privies and wash basins. Sometimes sixty or seventy families crowded into these small lots and lived in appalling conditions. It was not surprising that death rates were so high in these districts.

During the 1920s, master plans were prepared for Buenos Aires and Rio de Janeiro. Although both plans were concerned with transport problems and with the sanitary conditions confronting the majority of the population, their emphasis was on the design of new avenues and the improvement of the central districts. Both plans encompassed the entire city, designated new parks and playgrounds, and established building codes and zoning regulations to restrict densities, control urban expansion and organize land use. On the other hand, no attention was given to social segregation, accentuated by soaring land prices, nor to the urban economy, to city finance, much less to the conditions of the poor. Both plans represent the peak of the classic French approach to town planning in Argentina and Brazil; their physical impact on the two fast-growing cities was negligible.

If the 1880s and 1890s represented a golden age for the builders of slums, the 1920s and 1930s gave unusual opportunities to land speculators. After his visit to Buenos Aires and Rio de Janeiro in 1929, Le Corbusier prepared sketches synthesizing his ideas for both cities. An artificial island platform was proposed for the new central business district of Buenos Aires, an idea which he replicated in the new scheme he prepared for Rio de Janeiro in 1936. An elevated highway supported by apartment blocks and offices crossed Rio de Janeiro from north to south and crossed the bay of Guanabara to the city of Niterói. Both schemes paid little attention to local incomes, local finances, local technology or local ways of life. They were rigid schemes irrelevant for cities which were largely self-built, where the incomes of most people were low and where consistent employment, housing and service policies were notable for their absence. Le Corbusier's imagination fired the first generation of modern architects in Argentina and Brazil with enthusiasm.[7] The fact that the plans relied on static control mechanisms and unreal standards, paid no attention to social realities, to costs, to possible conflicts between private and public interests or to the rate of urban growth did not impede their acceptance.

These two examples of urban renewal had a major influence in those Latin American cities which had tried to partially renovate their structures (Violich, 1944). In the 1890s, new avenues were opened in the central area of Santiago and in the 1900s, the French architect Dubois designed the Forest Park along the Mapocho river. In the 1930s, an Austrian architect, Carl Brunner, was asked to prepare plans for the capitals of Chile and Colombia. Léon Jaussely, a professor at the Paris Beaux Artes School, was hired by the City Council of Buenos Aires during the 1920s. French, German and Austrian architects and engineers were appointed as consultants in several countries while the first local town planners were trained in Paris, Berlin and Vienna.

During the 1930s, 1940s and 1950s, many cities established planning departments with broader functions. Ironically, it was at this time, that local government lost much of its power to higher levels of government. New autonomous national or provincial bodies assumed responsibility for most public services. By the 1960s, practically all Latin American cities, regardless of size or political system, depended upon national or provincial investment, subsidies and loans.

The 1950s and 1960s were the decades of agrarian reform, national planning, and foreign aid and investment. Such initiatives were intended to improve living conditions in the rural areas, integrate the rural population into national life, reduce geographical isolation and, thereby, slow rural–urban migration. Agrarian reform would bring about self-sufficiency in food and lead to increased exports. Unfortunately, it was quickly seen that major change could not be achieved through peripheral reforms. Legislation and the creation of ineffective government ministries could not solve problems which were rooted in centuries of exploitation. Disillusion soon replaced the optimism of the 'fifties and early 'sixties.

The urban population continued to grow rapidly; after the Second World War many of the largest cities doubled their population every decade. Latin America emerged as a region of very large cities. New urban plans were prepared, were sometimes approved, but were as ineffective as their predecessors. Land continued to attract investment given high rates of inflation, risky alternative opportunities, inadequate land-use controls and the absence of effective taxes.

Urban planning *per se* can modify neither social structure nor the power system. Planning is the instrument of the powerful; rarely in Latin America has it harnessed the people's inventiveness, resourcefulness and capacity for organization. Urban planning has largely failed to create a better human environment and has mostly had negative repercussions for lower income groups. The people themselves have become the modern builders of Latin American cities. They have lacked technical assistance and government credits, access to basic services is often illegal or totally lacking, the low-rise homes have been built with simple technology and often poor materials. Contemporary Latin American cities, like their predecessors, have been constructed by many builders, mostly anonymous, forced to find their own solutions in the face of government neglect and sometimes repression. The popular sectors have retained their capacity to undertake massive although humble works in a spontaneous way.

NOTES

1. The Aztecs employed slaves captured in military campaigns in the construction of their monumental works. This was, for example, the case in the Tenochtitlán's Main Temple built between 1461 and 1463. Stone, wood and clay often had to be imported from distant places.
2. Ollantaytambo was a small agricultural centre and garrison built on the banks of the Patacancha river whose main function was to protect Cuzco from attack along the

32 URBANIZATION IN CONTEMPORARY LATIN AMERICA

Urubamba valley. Chucuito was the ancient capital of the Lupaqa, built on the shores of Lake Titicaca. Both exhibit a simple layout of parallel streets in both directions.

3. Between 1452 and 1455 the central valley of Mexico experienced a widespread famine that caused the depopulation of Tenochtiltán (Duran, 1967).

4. The royal 'Ordinances for Population and Discovery' were signed by Philip II in 1573. The text can be found in Altamira y Crevea (1956). Thirty-six of the 148 articles were directly related to the location, foundation, planning, design and construction of colonial towns.

5. The changes were most noticeable and sudden in the central-eastern region of Argentina, the centre and extreme north of Chile, the central-south region of Brazil, Uruguay and Cuba, central and northern Mexico, and limited areas of Peru, Panama and Colombia. Elsewhere the isolation and stagnation of the colonial days remained almost unchanged.

6. However, the decline of several cities in Mexico after 1910, of Cuba before 1898 and of Bolivia was the result of internal conflict.

7. National chapters of CIAM (Congrés Internationale d'Architecture Moderne) were organized in both cities.

REFERENCES

Altamira y Crevea, R. (1956). *Felipe II, Hombre de estado*. Mexico.

Azevedo, A. de (1956). *Vilas e cidades de Brazil colonial: ensaio de geografia urbana retrospectiva*. São Paulo.

Calnek, E. (1972). 'Settlement pattern and chinampa agriculture at Tenochtitlán', *American Antiquity* 37.

Durán, F. D. (1967). *Historia de las Indias de Nueva España e islas de Tierra Firme*, Volumes II–XXVI. Editorial Porrua, Mexico.

Gasparini, G. and Margolies, L. (1977). *Arquitectura Inka*. Universidad Central de Venezuela, Caracas.

Geiger, P. P. (1963). *Evolução da rede urbana brasileira*. Rio de Janeiro.

Hardoy, J. E. (1965). *Urban Planning in pre-Columbian America*. George Braziller Inc.

Hardoy, J. E. (1972). 'El modelo clásico de la ciudad colonial', *Acts of the 38th International Congress of Americanists*. Munich.

Hardoy, J. E. (1973). *Pre-columbian Cities*. Walker & Co.

Hardoy, J. E. (1978). 'The theory and practice of urban planning in Europe between the XV and XVII centuries and its influence in Latin America.' In Schaedel, R. P., Hardoy, J. E. and Kinzer, N. S. (eds.), *The Process of Urbanization in the Americas from its Beginnings to the Present*. Mouton.

Hardoy, J. E. and Langdon, M. E. (1978). 'Análisis estadístico preliminar de la urbanización en América Latina entre 1850 y 1930', *Revista Paraguaya de Sociología* 42/43, 115–74.

Institute de Estudios de Administración Local (IEAL) (1960). *Planos de Ciudades de América y Filipinas Existentes en el Archivo de Indias*. Madrid.

Kosok, P. (1965). *Life, Land and Water in Ancient Peru*. Long Island University Press.

Krickeberg, W. (1961). *Las antiguas culturas mexicanas*. Fondo de Cultura Económica Mexico.

Kubler, G. C. (1972). 'The European gridiron plan', *Acts of the 38th International Congress of Americanistas*, Volume 4. Munich.

Lanning, E. P. (1967). *Peru Before the Incas*. Prentice Hall Inc.

Lohman, V. G. (1975). 'Los regidores del Cabildo de Lima durante 1535 hasta 1635.

Estudio de un grupo de dominio.' In Solano, F. (ed.) *Estudios Sobre la Ciudad Iberoamericana*. Madrid.

Lumbreras, L. (1969). *De los pueblos, las culturas y las artes del antiguo Perú*. Francisco Mondoa, Lima.

Marquina, I. (1960). *El Templo Mayor de México*. INAH, Mexico.

Morse, R. (1974). *La ciudad latinoamericana*, Vol. 2. SEP-SETENTA.

Motolinia, F. T. de B. (1941). *Historia de los Indios de la Nueva España*. Mexico.

Millón, R. (1973). *The Teotihuacán Map*. University of Texas Press.

Palerm, A. (1973). *Obras hidráulicas prehispánicas en el sistema lacustre del Valle de México*. SEP-INAH, Mexico.

Reis Filho, N. G. (1968). *Contribuição no estudo de evolução urbana de Brasil*. São Paulo.

Ruiz, S. L. de (1973). *Desarrollo Urbana de México–Tenochtitlán según las fuentes históricas*. SEP-INAH, Mexico.

Sánchez Albornoz, N. (1975). *The Population of Latin America*. University of California Press.

Sanders, W. T. and Price, B. J. (1968). *Mesoamerica— The Evolution of a Civilization*. Random House.

Scobie, J. R. (1974). *Buenos Aires. Plaza to Suburb 1870–1910*. Oxford University Press.

Violich, F. (1944). *Cities of Latin America*. Reinhold Publishing Corporation.

Urbanization in Contemporary Latin America
Edited by A. Gilbert with J. E. Hardoy and R. Ramírez
© 1982 John Wiley & Sons Ltd.

3

Regional urbanization and agricultural production in Argentina: a comparative analysis

JORGE BALAN

INTRODUCTION

This work examines the urbanization process as it affected two Argentinian provinces, Tucumán and Mendoza, between 1870 and 1914. These provinces, located one thousand kilometres from the centre of Argentine political and economic life in Buenos Aires, grew rapidly during this period. This growth was a response to the expansion of export-based cattle, sheep and agricultural production in the Pampas; activities which brought about rapid economic growth and profound changes in the nation's social structure. The growth of Tucumán and Mendoza was stimulated by the local expansion of the sugar and wine industries. These agro-industries were able to develop as a consequence of the growth of the national market stimulated in turn by export production. My aim in this chapter is to relate the process of urbanization in those two provinces to their major structural features: their peripheral national location and their rural structures dependent on the wine and sugar industries.

In the following section, I will set up several hypotheses which relate the present study to the current discussion about urbanization in Argentina and Latin America generally during the agricultural export phase. The following section describes the provinces as they were around 1870, their growth during the next four decades and the differences in the structure of rural production in the two provinces. In the penultimate section, I will analyse the process of urbanization in the two areas before drawing some broad conclusions in the final section of the paper.

THE PROBLEM

The principal features of Argentina's urbanization during the study period are well known. By the late 1860s, both population and economic activity had become concentrated in the urban areas; a process which agricultural export development strongly accentuated. The first national census, in 1869, showed that 28.6 per cent of the population was resident in settlements with more than 2000 inhabitants, a figure that had risen to 52.7 per cent by 1914. In 1869, there were 56 urban localities compared with 332 in 1914 (Recchini de Lattes, 1973: 12–14). The annual rate of growth in the level of urbanization was 0.82 per cent between 1870 and 1894 and 1.35 per cent between 1895 and 1914 (Lattes, 1978: 27).[1] Argentina exhibited a marked pattern of urban primacy; the city of Buenos Aires contained more than one third of the urban population in 1869. The growth of export agriculture and livestock raising in the following decades maintained this urban dominance and actually increased the proportion of Argentines living in Buenos Aires.

Other features of the urbanization process are less well known, even if they have been discussed in detail. The most important is that rapid urbanization during this period coincided with a strong increase in the rural population, a consequence of natural increase and rapid European immigration. The countryside was quickly populated and denser settlement, together with improved land transportation, encouraged the growth of a more complex urban network. The proliferation of new urban centres constituted the country's second urban revolution, roughly three centuries after the first. This revolution formed part of a wider process: rapid change in the spatial pattern of settlement and in the relationships between the rural and urban sectors.

The change in the relationship between the rural and urban sectors, the growth and differentiation of the towns serving a more densely populated countryside and the introduction of new rural activities were part of a wider process that had important regional effects. The few regional studies of this period have concentrated on the areas directly responsible for export expansion. Cortés Conde and Nisnovich (1972) compared the growth of towns and the urban population in two regions within the province of Buenos Aires, one on the coast, with good sea communications, the other inland. Their work showed that the growth of intensive agricultural activities in the inland area stimulated the rapid growth of towns serving the rural area. Urbanization in the coastal area was slower, the towns acting as links to export markets rather than diversifying to serve the rural market. According to these authors, it was the differences between cereal agriculture and livestock production which gave rise to the areas' distinctive urban structures. In similar fashion, Gallo (1970 and 1974) compares the effects of agricultural development with those of wool production in the province of Santa Fé, the 'gringo' pampa contrasted with the 'creole' pampa. These areas differed not only through the presence of

European settlers in the first but also in terms of social structure and urban form.

Regional variations in the process of urbanization have been little studied in Argentina until recently, and then mainly in the Pampa (Tulchin, 1978; Gallo, 1974, 1978; Cortés Conde and Nisnovich, 1972) or through comparisons of the distribution of urban population in the distant macro-regions of the country (Vapñarsky, 1969). But, before beginning our case study it is important to ask: what do we understand by the term 'regional urbanization'?

For a start, is it sensible to consider urbanization at the regional level? That is to say, up to what point is it sensible to consider provinces or groups of provinces in the Argentine of the late nineteenth century as distinct political and economic entities when they formed part of a relatively highly integrated spatial system? Given such integration, where are the geographical limits to be drawn in the study of the urbanization of a particular area? In the case of contemporary societies, the nation appears to be the most appropriate level of analysis (Balán, 1976). Nevertheless, a case can be made that subnational units such as regions or provinces are particularly appropriate in the understanding of processes linked to changes in agrarian structure, especially when those changes only occur in one part of a nation. At that regional level we can examine in detail the interaction between land use, urban-rural relations and the organization of rural production. This kind of analysis would seem to be particularly relevant to Latin American countries such as Argentina which experienced rapid agrarian growth and change in the period from the middle of the nineteenth century to the depression of 1913.

But, if the term regional can be defended, what do I mean by the term urbanization? Broadly, I mean both the spatial distribution of urban places (and changes in that distribution) and the division of economic activities between urban and rural areas. My definition covers, therefore, not only the distribution but also the relationships between activities and populations in rural and urban areas. This requires that I analyse both rural and urban activities in turn.

Having thus provided a working definition of, and a rationale for using, the term regional urbanization, it is more or less obvious where my analysis should begin: the comparison of agricultural and urban patterns in different parts of Argentina. There are three broad elements to such an approach (Balán, 1976).

First, we can start from the notion that different primary products give rise to different social forms of production, notably different densities of population and different kinds of labour force. These variations in the rural productive structure are especially important because of their effect on the demand for particular urban goods and services. Such demand originates both in the consumption of the agricultural population (obviously affected by the distribution of income) and as inputs into agricultural production (tools, storage, transport, etc.).[2]

Secondly, we can hypothesize that the division of labour between the city and the countryside and the pattern of urbanization which arises from agricultural development, depend upon the dominant mode of production, its articulation with other modes, its class characteristics and the roles which different classes play in the productive process. The transition from the slave plantation or the 'extensive' hacienda with their servile workforces to the capitalist agrarian enterprise, for example, is likely to explain the form, distribution and level of diversification of the urban system.[3]

Finally, factors external to the region which affect the process of urbanization ought to be included. These factors can be conceived in terms of the particular way in which the study region interacts with the wider economic and political context. Here the centre-periphery concept can be useful in demonstrating the extent to which the local economy is relatively autonomous in political and economic terms from outside influences. The more peripheral a region, that is to say where local power and control over production is weak, the more the dynamism arising from agricultural development will be channelled outside thereby preventing investment within the region. Such peripheral development is normally manifest in an undiversified urban system and an exploitative relationship between urban and rural areas.[4]

One general way of considering the level and nature of causation is through a recent reformulation of linkage theory (Hirschman, 1977). Hirschman suggests that different paths of development (or underdevelopment) for primary export producers are described by the different kinds of linkage arising from each kind of product. His revision incorporates a spatial component even if it was devised for national rather than regional analysis. The earlier form of linkage theory, limited to backward and forward production linkages, is now supplemented by linkages arising from consumption. Such linkages may be weak, strong or even negative; the last occurring when primary expansion destroys pre-existing artisan industries by increasing the prices of their inputs or by making available competing imports. In addition, the new formulation includes a fiscal linkage, the outcome of State action in extracting part of the surplus created by primary product expansion and directing it towards new activities. Finally, Hirschman depicts two groups of agents in control of these linkages; those internal to the primary production process and those external to it (other local capitalists or interests from outside the region). This schema provides a useful way of describing how certain things lead, or do not lead, to others and in that way allows a clearer description of how urban change proceeds from the expansion of primary production.

TUCUMAN AND MENDOZA: INITIAL CONDITIONS, AGRICULTURAL DEVELOPMENT AND CLASS STRUCTURE

The two provinces are often classed together in Argentine history (Rofman and Romero, 1973). Almost simultaneously, they developed agro-industrial sectors oriented to the internal market; a market that was expanding towards the end of the last century as a result of agricultural export development. Tucumán production soon replaced imported sugar and a few years later wine from Mendoza had similar success. The two new sectors rapidly came to dominate their respective regional economies developing from modest beginnings as a result of cheaper transportation, national market expansion and the protectionist policy of the national government (Fleming, 1976; Guy, 1980; Balán, 1978). Equally isolated geographically from the centre of national economic and political life in Buenos Aires, the two provinces established an active position in the interregional division of labour. They differed, therefore, from most other provinces outside the Pampa which were static and neglected. The agro-industrial character of their production made them exceptions to the general tendency of industrial concentration in the coastal region. The dominant sectors in each province were similar in size in 1913, even if growth in Tucumán came earlier (Table 3.1).

Table 3.1   Tucumán and Mendoza: Industries in 1895 and 1913

	Tucumán		Mendoza	
	1895	1913	1895	1913
Establishments	639	897	885	2 555
Capital (million pesos)	34.8	89.2	14.0	171.8
Employees	13 567	15 159	4 290	14 598
Sugar mills	36	30	—	—
Wine vaults	—	—	423	1,507
Production value of mills and wine vaults (million pesos)	21.0	95.2	5.9	67.1

Source: *Censo de las Industrias* (1913), Volume 4 of the Censo Nacional de Población, 1914.

The similarities between the two provinces derived from pre-existing forms of human settlement and the orientation of the regional economies. Sarmiento (1837) maintained that Argentine settlements lived on the basis of livestock production, with the exception of those in the Cuyo (Mendoza and San Juan) and Tucumán where agriculture was more important. The agricultural vocation which Sarmiento associated with a sedentary existence and with 'civilization', was viable beyond a certain demographic density. This threshold density and the opportunity to develop agriculture were both achievable due to the privileged positions of the provinces in interregional trade; Mendoza was located on the border with Chile, Tucumán was strategically placed with respect to Bolivia and northwest Argentina (Martínez, 1961; Masini Calderón, 1967; Guy, 1980).

The great difference today in the populations of the provinces did not emerge until after 1880. It appeared once the conquest of the desert made colonization possible to the south of Mendoza, but even then Mendoza remained an oasis economy. Population and economic activity was concentrated in the area to the north of the city irrigated by the rivers Mendoza and Tunuyán. Use of the rivers Atuel and Diamante after 1880 extended the productive area but did not alter the dense population distribution. The similarly dense population of Tucumán was also concentrated in a limited area; the relatively narrow northeast–southwest strip suitable for agricultural and intensive pastoral use. This fertile plain, 300 to 600 metres high and favoured by ample rainfall and abundant irrigation, was constricted by the mountains to the west and by aridity to the east (Santillán de Andrés, et al., 1966). The effective area of the Tucumán and Mendoza oases was similar around 1870. In Mendoza, the irrigated area just exceeded 100 000 hectares; in Tucumán, the agricultural strip occupied 200 000 hectares. The greater population of Tucumán in 1869, 109 000 compared to Mendoza's 65 000, meant that population densities were very similar. In addition, both areas' populations were concentrated in villages around the two provincial capitals, the only important urban centres.

Unlike the rest of the country, pastoral activity was intensive. It was intimately linked to an active interregional commerce that gave rise to a complex division of labour. In Mendoza, except for the least inhabited and unirrigated areas where extensive livestock rearing was practised, livestock fattening was concentrated in the alfalfa farms close to the main city. Traders brought livestock from the coast and from central Argentina for fattening in Mendoza and for eventual sale in Chile. In Tucumán, livestock breeding was concentrated in the mountains and the fattening took place in the plain. The hides were a basic input of the tanneries which exported them or sold them to local industries.

Even if both provincial economies were agricultural they differed in terms of their suitability for agriculture. Tucumán, with a subtropical climate, produced cane, tobacco, rice and citric fruits, as well as maize, wheat and meat the principal local staples (Granillo, 1872). Mendoza, with a temperate climate, was ideal for alfalfa, wheat, fruit trees and wine (Lemos, 1888), products that formed part of the province's trade with other regions. Maize and wheat were the principal staples for local consumption, the first consumed by the indigenous population, the second by the Spanish element. The indigenous population, which had been subject to forced migration to Chile during the colonial period, was in the minority. By contrast, the pre-Hispanic element was dominant in Tucumán, thanks to the activities of the Jesuits and the limited amount of crossbreeding.

But the most important difference between the two provinces lay in their wider regional environments. Tucumán was a densely populated area located in the oldest and most densely settled part of the country. In spite of population decline, its provincial neighbours, Santiago del Estero to the south and Catamarca to the west, still contained large rural populations. To the north, the road to Bolivia crossed other densely populated agricultural areas. Mendoza by contrast, was a true oasis, the gateway to Chile but of little importance within its macroregion. This region was quite sparsely populated and its towns either replicated Mendoza's livestock activities, as in the case of San Juan, or complemented them, as in the case of San Luis. In these provinces there was no equivalent to the peasant agriculture of the north-west.

This difference was of immense importance to the later development of the sugar and wine industries. Tucumán had a regional market of some importance for its production; aguardiente and sugar were in much greater demand than the wines and fruit of Mendoza. Nevertheless, even at this time it was clear that the most important market for provincial production lay increasingly in the coastal area. The Tucumán sugar industry relied on a local peasant labour force (Balán, 1976a). In Mendoza, the shortage of local labour made European immigration the only (and preferred) source of manpower.

The sugar plantations of Tucuman began to expand in the 1870s (Table 3.2). Even if the figure for 1874 is underestimated, the increase in four decades is

Table 3.2   Tucumán: Cultivated area by major product 1894–1914 (percentages)

	1874	1882	1895	1905	1914
Sugar cane	5	14	53	44	70
Maize	42	40	35	33	27
Wheat	30	37	1	5	*
Rice	7	7	*	2	1
Tobacco	2	2	3	3	*
Alfalfa	7	7	5	4	*
Others	7	4	3	8	1
Hectares	48.400	51.600	105.444	121.364	130.264

*Less than 1 per cent.
Sources: 1874, Juan M. Terán, 'Cuadro estadístico de la Provincia de Tucumán.' In *Informe del Departamento Nacional de Agricultura*. Buenos Aires, 1975.
1882, *Registro Estadístico de la Provincia de Tucumán*. Tucumán, 1882, p.78.
1895, Antonio Correa y Emilio Lahitte, *Investigación parlamentaria sobre agricultura, ganadería, industrias derivadas y colonización*: Anexo G. Buenos Aires, Cámara de Diputados de la Nación.
1914, *III Censo Nacional*.

impressive and that up to 1895 truly spectacular. The tendency to agricultural monoproduction was clear; maize, traditionally the major product, maintained its area but other products such as rice and tobacco almost disappeared. With the advance of sugar cane, the province became a net importer of maize.

Cane began to be cultivated close to the city, following the water courses that ran from the mountains towards the river Sali (Figure 3.1). Its

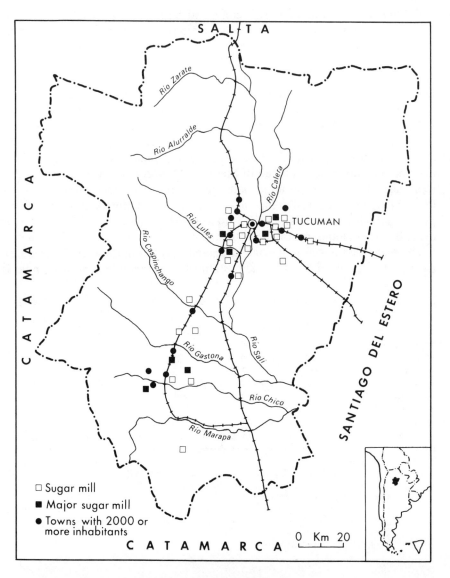

Figure 3.1   Distribution of sugar mills in the Province of Tucumán, 1881

expansion, limited, of course, by environmental conditions, followed the road towards Córdoba in the south and dictated the routes of the new railways. The newer sugar mills took advantage of rail access to locate further away from the city (Bosonetto, 1951). In 1881, 28 of the 34 sugar mills were located around the departmental capital and another five were in nearby Famailla; most of the mills established after that date were located more than 25 kilometres from the city along the main Tucumán–Coast railway (Figure 3.1).

Sugar expansion took place in the most densely settled and cultivated areas of the province. Unlike the rest of Argentina, there were numerous small properties and relatively few big estates. Most of these farms began to cultivate sugar or increased its production. The relative or absolute decline of other products was due in part to the shortage of land but more to the desire to devote capital and labour to the most profitable activity then available. The large estates maintained a measure of diversification, only cattle were physically displaced to the hard pastures of the higher land.

Wine cultivation began to grow rapidly in Mendoza in the 1880s, even if the data tend to underestimate the cultivated area in the earlier decades. Expansion of the cultivated area (Table 3.3) was as dramatic as that of sugar in Mendoza. If the total area cultivated at the end of the period was less than that devoted to sugar, this can be explained by the greater investment required to establish the vines. The major contrast with Tucumán was that alfalfa, which was used to fatten cattle, maintained its dominance in terms of cultivated area despite two depressions induced by Chilean policy (Fleming, 1976).

Table 3.3 Mendoza: Cultivated area by major product, 1888–1914

	1888	1903	1914
Wine	8	16	32
Wheat	8	6	1
Maize	5	6	6
Barley	1	—	1
Alfalfa	78	71	61
Total	100	99	101
Hectares	88 000	163 000	230 000

Source: Recalculated from data in Fleming (1976), p.113.

The vineyards, like agriculture in general, were originally concentrated close to the city near to the river Mendoza. They tended to expand towards the east and south along the Mendoza, Tunuyán, Diamante and Atuel valleys (Figure 3.2).

The incorporation of new agricultural land through irrigation led to a general expansion of both crops and livestock; traditional crops such as alfalfa and wheat increased their hectarage as did livestock rearing and fattening. At the beginning of the century, cattle-raising was concentrated almost exclusively in the departments of the south; higher land prices due to better transport links with the coast led to more intensive land uses on the irrigated land close to the capital. Production of alfalfa complemented the production of wine. In the annual cycle, the cultivation of alfalfa and the fattening of

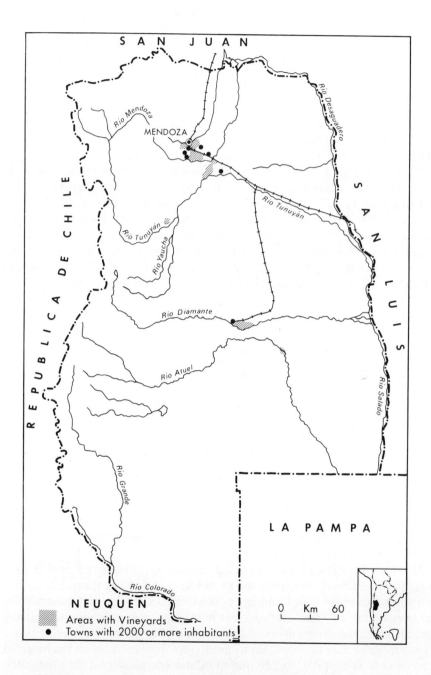

Figure 3.2   Distribution of vineyards in the Province of Mendoza, 1880s

cattle-generated profits and cash flows (notably from cattle exports to Chile) that financed part of the expansion of vineyards. These financial flows were channelled through foreign-exchange agencies and later through local, national and foreign banks. In the longer term, the cultivation of alfalfa required the levelling and improvement of land unsuitable for the vine. In this way, traditional activities played a role in the expansion of viticulture, while the supply of new land and the continuing demand for its products ensured its prosperity. Even the traditional cultivation of wheat, and its production into flour for local and export markets, remained active for several decades despite competition from the pampa.

In the two provinces a division of labour developed between agriculture and industry. In 1913, the sugar mills bought almost half the processed cane from independent cultivators while the *bodegas* bought 62 per cent of processed wine from them.[5] While the exact figures varied year by year, the tendency was for the cultivators' share of sugar production to increase in Tucumán and for their share of wine production to remain around 50 per cent in Mendoza. In both places non-industrialized agriculturalists could survive. In 1914, there was a limited number of big sugar producers and a large number of small holders; 41 owners had more than 100 hectares (including the mills) and more than 3000 had less than 10 hectares of cultivable land. The grape producers were more evenly distributed. A large grape producer tended to become the owner of a *bodega*; there was no technological barrier to mobility as in the sugar business.

A further difference was evident in the land cultivated by the sugar mills and the *bodegas*. The mills with large areas of land devoted to sugar, tended to subdivide part of their land into quite large 'colonies' which they rented to people with some capital who were known to the mill. These people would manage the cane cultivation and the labour force. The mills kept the rest of the land to manage directly. The *bodegas* with extensive vineyards worked them almost exclusively through the system of wine contractors; a system used initially to plant the vines but which developed into the principal form of permanent labour. The units worked were small enough for a worker and his family to manage, with additional labourers employed only at the time of the harvest.

In short, the large sugar producers and the *colonos* of the mills represented a limited stratum of powerful capitalist cultivators. Excluding the cane produced directly, the mills bought threequarters of their cane in 1914 from 200 to 300 proprietors and renters. The *bodega* owners, by contrast, bought grape juice from the farmers or dealt with renters who delivered it in a much less concentrated form. The Mendoza vineyard produced a much larger rural middle class than that produced in Tucumán.

Permanent labour for the vineyards came mainly from contractors; renters who used their families' labour. The small wine and cane producers were direct workers. But, in the case of cane there was also a large, year-round, salaried labour force supplemented by large numbers of additional workers at harvest time. The regular wine workers were limited in number and received higher wages. In both cases, the harvest was the peak employment period. The vintage was concentrated into six busy weeks employing resident family labour as well as transitional male, female and child labour. In Mendoza, local labour was fully occupied, whereas in Tucumán additional labour was contracted through the organization of seasonal migrations from the neighbouring provinces and from the Chaco. Sugar cultivation paid its labourers much less than the wine growers paid theirs. The sugar harvest cost much more than the vintage so that the sugar producers were forced to look for cheaper sources of labour. These differences meant that the rural proletariat were better paid in Mendoza than in Tucumán. In addition, a higher proportion of these wages were spent in the wine region than in the sugar area.

Patterns of social stratification were as different in the agricultural sectors of the two regions as in the case of industry.[6] In the second decade of the century, some 30 mills in Tucumán were producing a total of more than 300 000 tonnes of sugar. Variations in size were important but all used similar technology. Most mills also distilled alcohol and some had begun to install sugar refineries. Some mills marketed their production directly. The 30 mills constituted nearly 5 per cent of the nation's industrial capital. With four exceptions all were owned by Argentines many of whom were natives of Tucumán even if few still lived there. Nineteen were public companies established at the end of the century with their head offices in Buenos Aires.

The census of 1913 recorded 1500 bodegas in Mendoza with a total production of some four million hectolitres. This was a much more heterogenous grouping than the 30 sugar mills. In the previous ten years some enormous producers had emerged but most were very small having a capacity of less than one thousand hectolitres. According to the Census of *Bodega* Owners in 1913, the principal companies produced one-fifth of Mendoza's wine and the twenty largest enterprises, two-fifths. A few years previously, the commercialization of wine between *bodegas* had begun the so-called market of transported wine (*vino de traslado*). The companies engaged in this business quickly replaced the buyers and blenders from the coast. Before 1900, only two or three Mendoza *bodegas* were capable of directly marketing their production, whereas in 1913 most of Mendoza's production reached the coastal market through the branches of locally based enterprises. While the origin of the industry and its development up to 1895 was in the hands of long-established Mendoza residents, from then on the shares of recent immigrants, and Buenos Aires and international companies increased.

Industrial employment showed similar differences to that apparent in agriculture. The wine producers needed a larger labour force during the harvest but kept their workers on during the year. The mills closed for several

labour force brought in specially for the harvest, a force that was accommodated and supervised by the mill itself. This characteristic, together with its extensive land holdings (due to other factors which cannot be discussed here) meant that the mill tended to self-sufficiency; even though physically close to the city its links with other sectors in the region were limited. By contrast, the more specialized *bodega*, not trying to compete with the wine producers nor provide housing or grow food for its permanent workforce, was much more integrated into the local economy.

THE PROCESS OF URBANIZATION

What impact did the development of the wine and sugar industries have on the patterns of urbanization in Mendoza and Tucumán? The question can be answered by focusing on two different elements of the urbanization process. First, I will analyse the available data on urban growth and its spatial distribution in the context of the dominant form of production and the social structure linked to it. Secondly, I will discuss urban diversification in each province.

Before analysing the data on urban and rural population, it is important to note the difficulties posed by the Argentine census information. The national censuses of 1869 and 1895 considered urban areas to be those so designated by the provincial census commissions. In 1914, a similar procedure was followed, even if they employed trained personnel and based their final decision on the occupations of the local populations. These definitions are consequently of only limited use. Another possible criterion, even if its failings are well known, is to define as urban those centres with more than 2000 inhabitants (Recchini de Lattes, 1973). The slight advantage of this method is that levels of urbanization can be compared at different times and places.

Table 3.4 shows how Argentina's population grew rapidly from 1870 to 1895 and still faster up to 1914. The rate of urban growth was very high but was accompanied by a slower, but still considerable, increase in the rural areas. The nation's population grew faster than the rate of natural increase as a result of immigration from Europe. Mendoza's population, which grew more slowly than the national rate before 1895, expanded more rapidly later. In Tucumán, the population grew more rapidly before 1895 than after but in both subperiods expanded more slowly than the national population. The difference between the two areas was the result of different economic experiences; the sugar industry expanded most rapidly before 1895, the wine industry after 1895.

Table 3.4 also shows the growth of population in the macroregions of which Mendoza and Tucumán form part.[8] Mendoza dominated the Cuyo macroregion, but in a different way and to a more limited degree than Tucumán's domination of its neighbouring provinces. In Cuyo, the older wine

Table 3.4   Argentina: Annual rates of provincial population growth 1870–1914

	1870–1895			1895–1914		
	Total	Urban	Rural	Total	Urban	Rural
Cuyo	1.7	3.2	1.4	3.0	4.8	2.5
Mendoza	2.2	4.3	1.6	4.3	5.4	3.8
San Juan	1.3	0.9	1.4	1.8	4.0	1.4
San Luis	1.6	3.4	1.3	1.8	3.9	1.2
Northwest	1.4	0.0	1.5	1.5	5.2	0.9
Tucumán	2.6	2.8	2.5	2.2	6.4	0.1
Catamarca	0.1	–3.5	1.5	0.6	2.7	0.3
Santiago	0.7	–2.0	1.0	2.5	6.2	2.0
Total Country	3.0	3.9	2.6	3.5	5.0	2.1

Source: Estimates from Alfredo E. Lattes, 'Aspectos demográficos del proceso de redistribución espacial en Argentina.' In *Politicas de Redistribución Espacial de la
Población en la Argentina, 1930–1973*. CEDES, 1979.

region of San Juan grew more slowly than did Mendoza while San Luis was a livestock region which did not compete with the growth of Mendoza. Both San Juan and San Luis lost population through migration to Mendoza. But this migration was very limited compared to the way in which Tucumán literally drained its neighbouring provinces; a tendency which accelerated between 1870 and 1895.

Throughout the country and in both provinces, urban areas grew more rapidly than the countryside. But, there were important differences between the provinces in the two subperiods considered here. From 1869 to 1895, Mendoza's urban areas were growing much more rapidly than its rural areas whereas both rates were similar in Tucumán. In the following period, urban Tucumán grew rapidly and the rural population stagnated; in Mendoza, urban growth accelerated but so did that of the rural areas. From one period to the next a major change affected the populations of Tucumán's neighbours; the cities of Catamarca and Santiago del Estero lost people to Tucumán during the period of sugar expansion. In the following decades, the slower growth of the sugar industry together with other local phenomena encouraged the renewed growth of the cities of Santiago, and to a lesser extent those of Catamarca.

The capitals were the only real cities in both provinces in 1869. Both were the seats of provincial government and the centres of political and military control. Both were typical *entrepôts* trading in provincial products, goods from other regions for the home market, and products passing through the region destined for other areas. Thus, Mendoza was the major centre for Chilean traffic and Tucumán for the trade with Bolivia and northwest Argentina. Manufacturing was limited to the processing of a few local products. In Tucumán, apart from the sugar plants and the distilleries, there were tanneries, saddlers, carriage works, wool weavers and cigarette makers; in Mendoza, besides the *bodegas* there were flour mills, fruit conservers and a few local artisans. Primary and secondary activities were closely related which, together with the cultivation of land right to the limits of the built-up area, gave life in both places a strong rural flavour.

The rate of urban growth in both cities was spectacular. Tucumán's 17 000 people in 1869 had doubled by 1895 and trebled to reach 100 000 by 1914. Mendoza, which had only recently recovered from the effects of the 1861 earthquake, grew from 9000 to 28 000 and then to 59 000 between the three census dates. By 1914, the urban area could justifiably be said to include three neighbouring towns, Godoy Cruz, Guayamallen and Las Heras, the first of which contained 10 000 people.

Rapid urban growth was accompanied by the installation of many new services. Electricity, running water, drainage, street paving, public transport and street lighting were all introduced in the two capitals. This improvement in urban services was characteristic of most interior cities and reflected earlier improvements made in the national capital (Scobie, 1974; Ricci, 1967). Street paving began in the 1850s and advanced rapidly in the 1880s; kerosene street lighting which had been introduced in the 1870s was replaced by electric lighting in the 1890s; the first horse-drawn trams were introduced in the early 1880s and replaced by electric trams at the turn of the century. By the late 1890s, both cities had begun to install water systems and from 1910 the central areas began to get sewers. Mendoza began to construct a system of canals in the 1880s to regulate its water flow and Tucumán improved its drainage to prevent the flooding that was regularly caused by rainstorms.

The provincial governments initiated most of these public works. Even if the municipalities had adequate budgets the major works were financed or assisted by the provincial administrations. These provincial budgets increased rapidly in real terms (seven times in Tucumán and nine times in Mendoza in four decades) and were dispensed by urban-oriented administrations. Needless to say, expenditure favoured mainly the capital cities and the main economic activities (Balán and López, 1977). Administrative costs absorbed around four-fifths of the budget with one-half of the salary bill going to the large police force. Even if provincial government employees sometimes worked outside the capital they formed part of a highly centralized bureaucracy. In Mendoza, the most productive investments were those in the irrigation system (helped by funds from the national government), in the provincial railways and to a lesser extent in the roads. Urban improvements were concentrated in the two capitals and included expansion of the education system, particularly once the provincial governments decided to support secondary and specialized schooling.

The two capitals were the only settlements with more than 2000 inhabitants before 1890. In 1914, seven other settlements had reached this size in Mendoza and seventeen in Tucumán. These 'towns' posed no threat to the autonomy of the capitals, however, because so many were located close to them; Figures 3.1 and 3.2 show that only two settlements in Mendoza and five in Tucumán were more than 25 kilometres from their respective capital. In 1914, both capitals contained more than two-thirds of the urban population: Mendoza contained 21 per cent of the provincial population; Tucumán, 28 per cent. Most of the small urban centres had been founded before the period of sugar and wine expansion. In Tucumán, some emerged in the vicinity of the large sugar mills, indeed eight bore the name of the mill. In Mendoza, no urban centre was dependent on a single *bodega* but many were totally oriented to wine production. Few of these urban centres were departmental capitals. This reflected the fact that they had developed from an economic base rather than from their administrative functions.

Urban settlement in Mendoza was much more widely dispersed than in Tucumán and many settlements with less than 2000 people were considered to be towns by the Mendoza census authorities. In part, the different urban pattern was a result of different patterns of migration into the two provinces. In 1914, migrants represented only 10 per cent of the Tucumán population and 16 per cent of the urban population; in Mendoza migrants constituted 32 per cent of the provincial population and 34 per cent of town dwellers.

The upper classes in both provinces lived predominantly in the cities even if the large landowners also had a home and sometimes a luxurious home, at the mill or *bodega*. Where the provinces differed was in the distribution of the middle-class population. In Tucumán, few middle-class people lived in the rural areas, but in Mendoza large numbers were engaged in wine cultivation and production, something which made local politics much livelier in the latter (Peck, 1977; Denis, 1969). These groups pressed local government for service improvements and represented a substantial market for private goods and services.

The differences in agrarian structure were reflected in the industrial structures of the two departments. Table 3.5 shows that in 1913 the sugar mills and the *bodegas* dominated the permanent industrial work force; three out of five industrial workers in Tucumán and one in two in Mendoza. But the rest of the industrial sector was more diversified in Mendoza; numerous workers were employed in the conservation industry, in flour mills, and in the printing industry. In addition, the growing wine industry stimulated the development of several new activities, notably the production of boxes made of wood from the newly established poplar plantations.

But, if Mendoza had a more diversified industrial structure, neither province experienced strong industrial growth as a result of agricultural expansion. In Mendoza, agricultural tools and machinery were all imported as were corks, bottles and barrels. Integration had developed up to the production and commercialization of wine and spirits but not beyond. The

Table 3.5   Tucumán and Mendoza: Personnel by industry 1913

	Tucumán (a)		Mendoza (b)	$\frac{(a)}{(b)} \cdot 100$
I *Foodstuffs*	10.675		9.676	110
Sugar mills		9.074	—	
Wine vaults		—	7.530	
Distilleries		146	365	
Conservation plants		—	179	
Flour mills		8	137	
Bakeries, etc.		901	931	
Milk products		164	242	
II *Clothing*	849		967	88
III *Construction*	2.023		2.054	98
Sawmills and carpentry shops		560	338	
Forestry		714	459	
Construction companies		153	373	
Brick and tile factories		250	240	
Iron works and blacksmiths		77	310	
IV *Furniture and Carriage Works*	486		687	71
Carriage works		250	321	
Saddleries		155	171	
V *Metallurgy*	262		499	53
Foundries		104	52	
Metal shops		49	266	
VI *Chemicals*	193		99	195
VII *Printing*	154		274	56
VIII *Various*	517		345	150
Wireworks		154	227	
Tanneries		180	19	
SUBTOTAL (excluding sugar mills and wine vaults)	6.085		7.068	86
TOTAL	15.159		14.598	104
POPULATION IN 1914	332.933		277.535	120

Source: *Censo de las Industrias* (1913), Volume 4 of the Censo Nacional de Población, 1914.

same was true in Tucumán. The sugar mills had diversified to the point where some had introduced refining capacity and most packed and marketed their own sugar and alcohol, but few inputs were produced locally. Only the production of carts was a real exception. If inputs to the mills and the *bodegas* were mainly imported, so too were most consumption goods. Only basic foodstuffs were produced locally.

In summary, industrial production was somewhat larger and more diversified in Mendoza but was limited in both provinces. Most manufactured products were made in or shipped from Buenos Aires.

CONCLUSION

The basic differences between the two provinces derived from the linkages which developed at the local level between urban and rural activities. The first difference lay in the fact that urban development was more balanced in Mendoza than in Tucumán. In the latter, rapid urban growth was followed by a slowing of rural growth, whereas in Mendoza rural growth continued. Second, rural Mendoza was more deeply penetrated by urban values and institutions, and had greater contact with the outside world, a direct reflection of its greater specialization and more accentuated division of labour between urban and rural areas. Lastly, the local Mendoza economy was more dynamic than that of Tucumán; possibilities for investment, growth and diversification were greater and there was greater autonomy for local groups. If these differences are not always easy to quantify, together they present a clear picture of different patterns of urbanization.

The question is how best to explain these contrasts while accounting for essential similarities in the form and function of the capital cities? The differences noted above and the fact that it was richer did not make Mendoza's urban economy more diversified than that of Tucumán. Both cities were service centres linked to a densely populated and integrated rural area, both were the seats of highly centralized machines for political and administrative control, both were the apexes of narrow economic and political pyramids. Both cities contained a middle class of small businessmen, government employees and professional workers who adopted the values of the 'decent people' at the top of the pyramid.

There are clear reasons for the greater dynamism of rural Mendoza, notably continued national demand for its products and the opening up of new land. But, it is also vital to recognize the effects on Mendoza's economy of the different social structure of the wine region. The establishment of a stable workforce, organized into family units unconnected with the peasant economy, the opportunities offered by relatively high incomes for social mobility, the slow maturing of the investments in the vineyards, and the opening up of new areas of land are the main factors underlying the emergence of the rural middle class in Mendoza. In Tucumán, the partial and temporary proletarianization of a good part of the provincial labour force, the seasonal in-migration of labourers from areas with diverse patterns of peasant organization, encouraged a social and productive structure which was spatially and functionally closed off from the local environment, placing almost a physical limit on urban expansion at the local level. This process was further encouraged by the displacement of peasant farmers by the expansion of the area under sugar and their migration to the city of Tucumán.

These structural differences were not reflected in the growth, autonomy or diversification of the main cities. The wider rural market in Mendoza and the less concentrated ownership pattern in the wine industry failed to stimulate links with the industrial sector. Vertical integration in the industry was marked, from the growing of the grape to the marketing of the wines and spirits, but no other forms of diversification were apparent. Similarly, in Tucumán, the sugar mills increased their productivity, they began to refine the product and to produce alcohol. But, the sugar industry did not stimulate the establishment of a machine-goods industry nor was the market offered by thousands of sugar workers sufficient to stimulate a dynamic and diversified consumption-goods industry.

The essential similarities in the form and function of Mendoza and Tucumán and their failure to stimulate a genuine process of regional development would seem to be best explained by the ways in which the two provinces were inserted into the national economy. But a simple centre-periphery dichotomy is too simple to explain these developments. Their peripheral location did not prevent the emergence of the wine and sugar industries nor did the participation of 'Porteño' and international capital undermine local groups who continued to control those industries; it only prevented their industrialization and limited their urban growth. Clearly, the answer lies in the way in which the Argentine national economy functioned. The development of the provincial export economies created two-way links, manufactured goods were exchanged for sugar, wine and spirits. The limited size of the local markets and the competitiveness of national and especially international industry, prevented the emergence of a dynamic local industrial sector.

But this explanation does not explain why the form of insertion in the national economy was not modified by local power groups or by the provincial governments. As I have discussed elsewhere, both were influential in the promotion of the wine and sugar industries, a development which considerably increased their prosperity and their political independence (Balán and López, 1977; Balán, 1978). The links between the agro-industries and the provincial governments crystallized when those industries began to sell to markets outside the home provinces and therefore could be easily taxed. But, the political authorities could not dispense these taxes freely because of the way the provincial economy was linked with an open capitalist system and because of the way the regional bourgeoisies were inserted into the national political system (Botana, 1977). On the one hand, that insertion placed certain constraints on the form of public expenditure; local political demands encouraged the centralization of budgetary control and the strengthening of the provincial cities as centres of administrative and political control. Such demands emanated, in large measure, from the political game between the provinces and the national executive which required that control be maintained over the electoral process. The result in both provinces was similar: the growth of the public bureaucracy, concentrated in the two capitals, and restrictions on the autonomy of municipal government. On the other hand, such insertion limited the kinds of pressures that the provincial authorities could exercise at the national level. There was no way that the provinces could confront the essential interests of the agricultural export sector. Protection of local agro-industries, even if resisted, were easier to achieve than protectionist measures of other kinds. In these two ways, the peripheral insertion meant not only external pressures but also limitations on internal policies, both provincial governments and regional élites were limited in what they could do within the provinces. In other words, the provincial élites showed no tendency towards regionalism beyond defending those economic sectors that were vital to the health of the provincial economies.

NOTES

1. Annual change in the level of urbanization (urban population divided by the total population).
2. The approach has been used consistently by economic historians interested in economic expansion in frontier areas, especially in Canada and Australia (Baldwin, 1956).
3. The difference between the approach of 'export staple' theory and marxian analysis has been suggested by Morse (1973). In another context, Hirschman's 'micro-marxism' concerns a similar kind of analysis (Hirschman, 1977).
4. The relationship between centre and periphery, metropolis and province, has been extensively discussed in the 'internal colonialism' literature (Balán, 1977; Walton, 1975) even if little emphasis has been placed on the differences between peripheries or between those national contexts that permit greater or lesser dynamism of provincial economies (Roberts, 1976).
5. There seems no satisfactory word in English to describe the *bodega*. It is a term which includes not only the place where wine is stored and blended but also where it is produced. Hence the direct translations such as wine vault or cellar are unsatisfactory though the American English term winery comes close.
6. The literature has practically ignored the theme of the labour force in Mendoza. The present discussion is based on contemporary accounts (Lemos, 1880; Galanti, 1900; Argentina, 1919; Marianetti, 1927) and on descriptions found in the files of the El Trapiche *bodega*. On labour in the Tucumán sugar industry see Balán (1976a) and Guy (1978).
7. The description of the San Pablo sugar mill is based on the Inventory and Accounts of the Nougués Brothers for the years 1875 to 1897. These were kindly made available by Mr. José María Nougués. Even if the mill was not entirely typical it does demonstrate many of the same characteristics described for other sugar mills. Information on the El Trapiche bodega was made available by Engineer Raúl Benegas in the form of the records of the company and its founder. The data mentioned in the text are based on the Inventory and Accounts for 1900. El Trapiche was typical only of the largest and most integrated *bodegas* of the period and not of the vast majority of small wine producers.
8. The north-west region of which Tucumán forms part includes provinces other than the two included in Table 3.4.

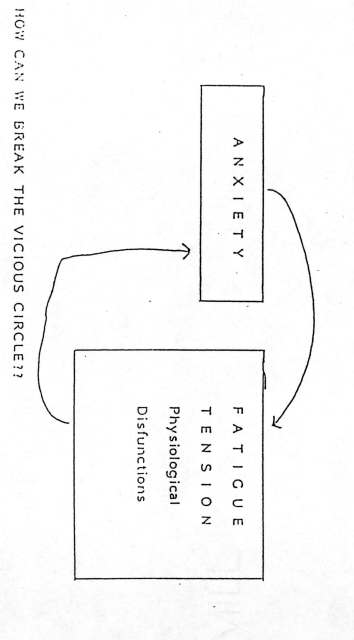

HOW CAN WE BREAK THE VICIOUS CIRCLE??

ANXIETY

FATIGUE
TENSION
Physiological
Disfunctions

THE VICIOUS CIRCLE

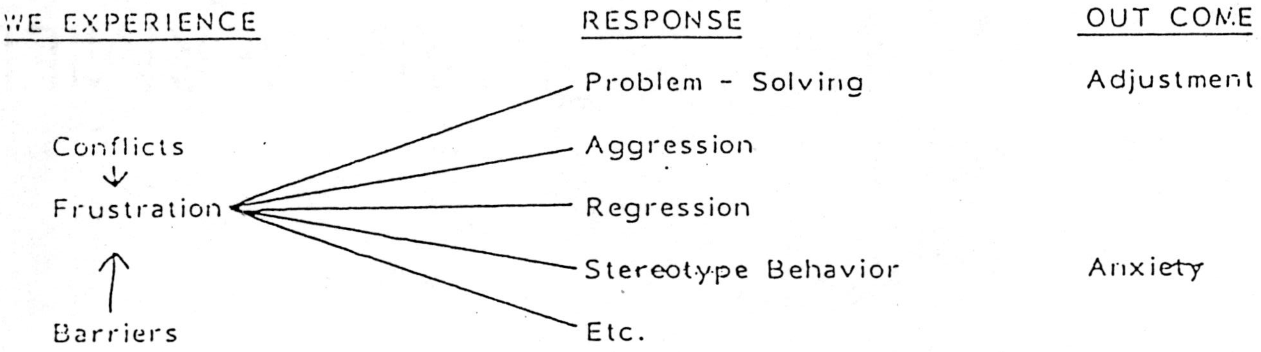

WE EXPERIENCE

Conflicts

Frustration

Barriers

RESPONSE

Problem - Solving

Aggression

Regression

Stereotype Behavior

Etc.

OUT COME

Adjustment

Anxiety

ANXIETY RESULTS IN

Fatigue
Tension

REFERENCES

Argentina (1919). 'Mendoza; legislación obrera desde 1906.' In *Crónica Mensual del Departamento Nacional de Trabajo*, **III**, 15.

Balán, J. (1976a). 'Migraciones, mano de obra y formación de un proletariado rural en Tucumán, Argentina, 1870–1914', *Demografía y Economía*, **X**, 201–34.

Balán, J. (1976b). 'Regional urbanization under primary sector expansion in neocolonial societies.' In Portes, A. and Browning, H. L. (eds.), *Current Perspectives in Latin American Urban Research*. University of Texas Press.

Balán, J. (1977). 'Urbanización y fuerza de trabajo en America Latina: la tésis del colonialismo interno'. In *Urbanización, estructura urbana y dinámica de la población*. PISPAL, Santiago.

Balán, J. (1978). 'Una cuestión regional en la Argentina: burguesías provinciales y el mercado nacional en al desarrollo agroexportador', *Desarrollo Económico* **69**, 49–87.

Balán, J. and López, N. (1977). 'Burguesías y gobiernos provinciales en la Argentina. La política impositiva de Tucumán y Mendoza entre 1873 y 1914', *Desarrollo Económico* **67**, 391–435.

Baldwin, R. E. (1956). 'Patterns of development in newly settled regions', *Manchester School of Economics and Social Studies* **24**, 161–79.

Bosonetto, J. C. (1951). 'Distribución de los ingenios azucareros tucumanos.' In Rohmeder, G. (ed.), *Geographia et varia: homenaje al Dr. Federico Machatschik*. University of Tucumán.

Botana, N. R. (1977). *El orden conservador, la política argentina entre 1880 y 1916.* Sudamericana, Buenos Aires.

Cortés Conde, R. and López de Nisnovich, N. (1972). 'El desarrollo agrícola en el proceso de urbanización: funciones de producción, patrones de poblamiento y urbanización.' In Schaedel, R. P. *et al.* (eds.), *Urbanización y Proceso Social en América*. Instituto de Estudios Peruanos.

Denis, P. Y. (1969). 'San Rafael, la ciudad y su región', *Boletín de Estudios Geográficos* **16**, 64–5 and 133–430.

Fleming, Jnr., W. J. (1976). Regional development and transportation in Argentina: Mendoza and the Gran Oeste Argentino Railroad, 1885–1914. Indiana University doctoral dissertation.

Galanti, A. N. (1900). *La industrial vitivinícola.* Oswald, Buenos Aires.

Gallo, E. (1970). Agricultural colonization and society in Argentina: the Province of Santa Fé. University of Oxford doctoral dissertation.

Gallo, E. (1974). *El 'boon' cerealero y cambios en la estructura sociopolítica de Santa Fé* (1870–1895). Centro de Investigaciones, Instituto Torcuato Di Tella, Documento de Trabajo 88.

Granillo, A. (1872). *Provincia de Tucumán: série de articulos descriptivos y noticiosos.* Imprenta de La Razón, Tucumán.

Guy, D. J. (1978). 'The rural working class in nineteenth-century Argentina: forced plantation labour in Tucumán', *Latin American Research Review* **13**, 134–45.

Guy, D. J. (1980). *Argentine Sugar Politics: Tucumán and the Generation of Eighty.* Arizona State University Press.

Hirschman, A. O. (1977). 'Enfoque generalizado del desarrollo por medio de enlaces con referencia especial a los productos básicos', *El Trimestre Económico*, **44**, 199–236.

Lattes, A. E. (1978). 'La dinámica de la población rural en la Argentina entre 1870 y 1970.' Paper presented at the Symposium on Internal Migration and Development, Cuernavaca.

Lemos, A. (1888). Mendoza: memoria descriptiva de la provincia, Los Andes, Mendoza.

Marianetti, B. (1927). Los trabajadores de la industria vitivinícola. University of Mendoza doctoral dissertation.

Martínez, P. S. (1961). *Historia económica de Mendoza durante el virreinato (1776–1810)*. Instituto Gonzalo Fernández de Oviedo, Madrid.

Masini Calderón, J. L. (1967). *Mendoza hace cien años*. Teoría, Buenos Aires.

Morse, R. M. (1973). 'Patrones de la urbanización latinoamericana: aproximaciones y generalizaciones tentativas.' In Morse, R. M. (1973). *Las ciudades Latino-Americanas II Desarrollo económico*. SepSetentas, Mexico.

Peck, D. M. (1977). Argentinian politics and the province of Mendoza. University of Oxford doctoral dissertation.

Recchini de Lattes, L. (1973). *Aspectos demográficos de la urbanización en la Argentina*, 1869–1960. Editorial del Instituto, Buenos Aires.

Ricci, T. R. (1967). *Evolución de la ciudad de San Miguel de Tucumán*. Universidad Nacional de Tucumán.

Roberts, B. R. (1976). 'The provincial urban system and the process of dependency.' In Portes, A. and Browning, H. L. (eds.), *Current perspectives in Latin-American Urban Research*. University of Texas Press.

Rofman, A. and Romero, L. A. (1973). *Sistema socioecónomico y estructura regional en la Argentina*. Amorrortu, Buenos Aires.

Santillán de Andrés, S. E. *et al.* (1966). La real distribución de la población de la provincia de Tucumán, Universidad Nacional de Tucumán.

Scobie, J. R. (1974). *Buenos Aires: plaza to suburb*, 1870–1910. Oxford University Press.

Tulchin, J. S. (1978). 'El crédito agrario en la Argentina, 1910–1926', *Desarrollo Económico* **71**, 381–408.

Vapñarsky, C. A. (1976). 'On rank size distribution of cities: an ecological approach', *Economic Development and Cultural Change* **17**, 584–95.

Walton, J. (1975). 'Internal colonialism: problems of definition and measurement,' In Cornelius, W. A. and Trueblood, F. M. (eds.), *Latin American Urban Research* **5**. Sage Publications.

Urbanization in Contemporary Latin America
Edited by A. Gilbert with J. E. Hardoy and R. Ramírez
© 1982 John Wiley & Sons Ltd.

4

Working in the streets: survival strategy, necessity, or unavoidable evil?

RAY BROMLEY

This essay is concerned with some of the theoretical, moral, and policy issues associated with the low-income service occupations found in the streets, parks, and other public places of most Third World cities.[1] These 'street occupations' range from barrow-pushing to begging, from street trading to night-watching, and from typing documents to theft. They are often grouped together in occupational classifications, and socially they are generally held in low esteem. The street occupations are frequently described by academics and civil servants as 'parasitic', 'disguised unemployment', and 'unproductive activities', and are conventionally included within such categories as 'the traditional sector', 'the bazaar economy', 'the unorganized sector', 'the informal sector', 'the underemployed' and 'subproletarian occupations'. It seems as if everyone has an image and a classificatory term for the occupations in question, and yet their low status and apparent lack of development significance prevent them from attracting much research or government support.

This discussion of 'street occupations' is based mainly on research in Cali, Colombia's third largest city with about 1.1 million inhabitants in 1977.[2] The research was conducted between mid-1976 and mid-1978, and the present tense is used here to refer to that period. The occupations studied in the streets and other public places of Cali are remarkably diverse, but they can be crudely described under nine major headings:

Retail distribution (the street trading of foodstuffs and manufactured goods, including newspaper distribution);
Small-scale public transport (the operation of *motocarros*—three-wheel motorcycles used to carry passengers and cargo, horse-drawn carts, handcarts, and the work of porters);

Personal services (shoe-shining, shoe repair, watch repair, the typing of documents, etc.);

Security services (night-watchmen, car-parking attendants, etc.);

Gambling services (particularly the sale of tickets for lotteries and *chance*— a betting game based on guessing the last three digits of the number winning an official lottery);

Scavenging (door-to-door collection of old newspapers, bottles, etc., searching for similar products in dustbins, rubbish heaps and the municipal tip, and the bulking of recuperated products);

Prostitution (or, to be more precise, soliciting for clients);

Begging;

Theft (including robbery with violence).

Of these nine groups, 'retail distribution' is the largest, accounting for about 32 per cent of the workforce in the street occupations, followed by small-scale public transport and gambling services, each accounting for about 16 per cent of the total workforce. The six remaining categories each account for 2 to 10 per cent of the total workforce.

With the exception of small-scale public transport, all of these occupations can be conducted in private locations as well as in public places. Private locations are generally considered more prestigious; they give a business a certain stability and security which is not available to the persons who work in streets, parks and other areas of public land. Those who work in public places may try to obtain a degree of stability by claiming a fixed pitch and by building a structure there to give them some protection, but their tenure is almost always precarious and the overall level of investment in 'premises' is likely to be very limited under these circumstances. Thus, the street occupations are classically viewed as 'marginal occupations', as examples of how the poor 'make out', or as the 'coping responses' of the urban poor to the shortage of alternative work opportunities and the lack of capital necessary to buy or rent suitable premises and to set up business on private property.

Even though they are an integral part of the street environment and interact strongly with the street occupations, four major groups of economic activities are not considered as street occupations *per se*: off-street private shops, supermarkets, market stalls, etc. which open onto the street; the government and company employees who are responsible for building, maintaining and cleaning the streets; the police and soldiers who are responsible for law and order on the streets; and, the operators of larger-scale public transport vehicles such as buses, trucks and taxis. These occupations are considered here in terms of their relation to the street occupations but not as part of the street occupations. All of them have a strong off-street base, most have working regimes and relationships rather different from those prevailing in the street occupations, and many have much higher levels of capital investment in premises, equipment or merchandise.[3]

Because they are neither practised in conventional (off-street) establishments, nor in the homes of the workers, the street occupations are usually severely underrepresented or excluded altogether in statistics based on sample surveys of establishments or households. In spite of their underrepresentation in most official statistics, however, their highly public location ensures them a prominent place in the urban environment and popular consciousness. Even if he has no direct dealings with those who work in the street occupations, a member of the general public can hardly fail to be aware of their existence.

The streets of the city serve a wide variety of interrelated purposes: as axes for the movement of people, goods and vehicles; as public areas separating enclosed private spaces and providing the essential spatial frame of reference for the city as a whole; as areas for recreation, social interaction and the diffusion of information; and as locations for economic activities, particularly the 'street occupations' (Anderson, 1978a, 1978b). Within the functional complexity of the street environment, not only are the street occupations strongly influenced by changes in other environmental factors but also contribute to general environmental conditions. Thus, for example, street traders and small-scale transporters depend upon the direction, density, velocity and flexibility of potential customers' movements, and are immediately affected by changes in traffic flows and consumer behaviour. At the same time, they influence patterns of movement and overall levels of congestion.

Average incomes per worker in the street occupations in Cali in 1977 are only equivalent to about U.S. $3 per day, and are roughly comparable to the sums paid to unskilled urban wage-workers in casual employment (those without long or indefinite term contracts). The actual distribution of incomes in the street occupations is highly skewed, with the majority of workers having incomes below U.S. $3 per day, but with a minority having incomes far in excess of this mean value. On a 'good day', a prosperous street trader with a large capital stock of merchandise may make $30 or more in profit, and a skilful street thief might make much more than that. The success of a few of the most prosperous, skilful or simply lucky people working in the street occupations, however, should not blind us to the bare economic subsistence of the great majority of the participants in these occupations. Most of the street occupations are intensely competitive.

Improvements in profit levels and incomes tend to lead to additional workers entering occupations, and/or to increased competition from larger, more capital-intensive enterprises based in off-street locations, forcing average incomes down again to their previous level.

As well as low status and low average incomes, the street occupations are characterized by relatively low inputs of capital in relation to labour, and by low 'formal' educational requirements. Most street enterprises operate with a total working capital equivalent to less than $100 in terms of equipment and/or merchandise. Indeed, some porters, watchmen, scavengers, beggars and thieves incur no monetary expenditures in order to be able to work, beyond the costs of their normal clothing, food, and transport to a workplace. Even the most elegant and well-stocked street stall is unlikely to have a value of more than $1200, and the most expensive small-scale public transport vehicle, the *motocarro*, has a maximum capital cost of about $560. Basic literacy and numeracy are generally useful to participants in the street occupations, but even these relatively low educational standards are rarely required. Instead, the occupations are characterized by skills learnt outside the government educational system, such as hard bargaining, quick wittedness, manual dexterity, good memory, an engaging personality, and physical endurance. On-the-job experience and effective utilization of social networks are particularly important in the street occupations, together with such difficult to alter variables as 'an honest face', and physical toughness or beauty.

The most basic need of the urban poor is an income in goods and/or money to provide for food, drink, housing, clothing, and other necessities. An income may come from government or private charities, from investments, moneylending and renting, from windfall gains, or from work. For the poor, work is the normal way to obtain an income, and for an estimated 24 000– 36 000 people in Cali, some or all of their work is in the street occupations.[4] Ideally, work should be both enjoyable and rewarding, yielding an income and a sense of personal achievement and satisfaction. Instead, to most people, including those working in the street, work is boring and exhausting, and even dangerous or degrading. Furthermore, work opportunities are usually scarce and insecure, and work is often inadequately remunerated, leading to poverty and deprivation. All of the occupations under consideration here have some of these negative work characteristics and together the street occupations form a complex of low-status, poorly remunerated, insecure forms of work. Although many who work on the streets comment that their occupations are less exhausting than heavy manual labour like cutting sugar cane and carrying bricks on construction sites, the street occupations usually require long hours and uncomfortable conditions. The 'curse of Adam' weighs heavily on the urban poor, and most perceived advantages in street occupations reflect even worse conditions in alternative occupations. Thus, 'according to Genesis iii, 19, when Adam was expelled from the Garden of Eden, it was with the admonishment: "you shall gain your bread by the sweat of your brow" . . . It has remained the case that those who perform the most monotonous, and most soul-destroying labour gain the least from it, live in the worst surroundings, eat the poorest foods and suffer the diseases and injuries which such work in such conditions is likely to inflict upon them' (Banks, 1977: 16).

WORK, EMPLOYMENT AND THE SERVICE SECTOR

Work is defined here as *any activity where time and effort are expended in the pursuit of financial gain, or of material gain derived from other persons in exchange for the worker's labour or the products of such labour.* In other words, work is the labour involved in producing goods and services for exchange, and it is 'income-generating'. The category of 'work', thus defined, excludes the equally important category of 'expenditure-reducing' activities which can be described collectively as 'subsistence-labour' (for example, growing food for household consumption, self-help house construction and repair, unremunerated housework and childminding, voluntary unpaid help given to friends and neighbours, and walking or cycling to places of work or recreation so as to avoid paying transport fares).

Any form of work which is regularly performed by a given person may be described as an occupation. Under this definition, such classic lumpen-proletarian occupations as begging, prostitution and theft can all be viewed as work, and hence can be analysed together with the remaining street occupations. Naturally, however, the presence of these illegal or illegitimate (not illegal, but considered shameful or a public nuisance by most authorities) occupations in the category of street occupations emphasizes the high degree of differentiation which exists within this category. Of course, illegality and illegitimacy extend much further than begging, prostitution and theft; some traders deal in illicit merchandise, various forms of street gambling are illegal, and substantial numbers of persons working in transport and gambling services and the overwhelming majority of street traders do not possess the licences and documents required by official regulations.

However, before we consign the street occupations to the dustbin of immorality, it is worth considering how much corruption and tax evasion occurs in government and big business, and the extent to which élites make laws to further their own interests. Illegal and illegitimate income flows are received by both rich and poor, and arguably the poor have greater moral justification for breaking the laws and norms of society than the rich. The poor did not make the laws and norms that they are expected to live under, and they can legitimately claim that their own poverty, combined with the presence of wealth and conspicuous consumption around them, led them to break these laws and norms. The poor are often acutely conscious that their own income must be earned by work, whilst the rich have inherited wealth and access to unearned income through investments, usury, and renting out property. The problem of poverty is not just a shortage of income and wealth, but more importantly, a shortage of *bona fide* income opportunities. Illegal and illegitimate opportunities help to make up some of this deficit.

In this analysis, the term 'work' has a different meaning to the term 'employment'. 'Employment' is used to denote a relationship between two parties, an 'employer' and an 'employee', the former paying the latter to work on the former's behalf for a substantial period of time (at least a working day) or for lesser periods on a regular basis. When there is a direct two-tier employer–employee relationship based on some form of contract (an oral or written agreement), there are two main forms of working relationship:

'on-premises working', when the employee works at a site owned, rented, or operated by the employer; and, 'outworking', when the employee works away from the employer, usually in his own home, in the streets, or in some door-to-door operation. An employee may be paid wages per unit of time worked, per unit of 'output', or by some combination of the two. When payment is partly or entirely per unit of output, the employee is effectively paid a commission, and this mode of remuneration is known as piecework. When work is remunerated wholly or partly by the unit of time worked, whether as 'on-premises working' or 'outworking', it is generally recognized as a form of employment. When it is remunerated solely per unit of 'output', however, it is usually only viewed as employment if it is conducted 'on premises'. When conducted off-premises, piecework is conventionally viewed as a form of self-employment, and this is certainly the conception embodied in Colombian labour legislation and in the perceptions of most middle- to upper-class Colombians. In contrast to such views, and in keeping with our definition of employment, we view 'outwork on a piecework basis' as a form of employment remunerated at a piece rate. The fact that it is not officially or widely recognized as such means that it may be viewed as 'disguised wage-working', as distinct from the more widely recognized forms of wage-working which take place 'on-premises' or which involve off-premises work remunerated per unit of time worked.

When a worker is not employed by someone else, two alternative working relationships are commonly found; 'dependent working' and 'self-employment' (Bromley and Gerry, 1979: 5–11). Although dependent workers are not employees, even on a piecework basis, and they do not have fixed margins and commissions, they do have obligations which take a contractual form and which substantially reduce their freedom of action. These obligations are associated with the need to rent premises, to rent equipment, or to obtain credit, in order to be able to work. Although the appropriation of part of the product of the worker's labour is not as clear and direct in the dependent working case as in the disguised wage-working case, there is normally an appropriation process through the payment of rent, the repayment of credit, or purchases and sales at prices which are disadvantageous to the dependent party in the relationship. In contrast, true self-employment has no such relationships; the workers work on behalf of themselves and other persons that they choose to support. Self-employed workers must rely, of course, on inputs provided by others, on the receipt of outputs by others, and on a system of payment. However, the bases of their self-employment are that they have a considerable and relatively free choice of suppliers and outlets, and also that they are the owners of their means of production. They are dependent upon general socioeconomic conditions and on the supply and demand conditions for their products but they are not dependent upon specific firms for the means to obtain their livelihoods.

In the streets of Cali, true self-employment is a much less common phenomenon than might at first glance seem apparent, and there are signs that it is diminishing in significance in the face of expansions of disguised wage-working and dependent working (Birkbeck, 1978a; 1979; Bromley, 1978; Gerry, 1978; Gerry and Birkbeck, 1981). Estimates of the proportions of those working in the street occupations falling into the different categories of working relationship suggest that only 40–45 per cent are in true self-employment.[5] A further 40–45 per cent of those working in the street occupations are disguised wage-workers, 10–15 per cent are dependent workers, and only about one per cent are overtly wage-workers.

Disguised wage-workers and dependent workers have a variety of obligations to employers, contractors, suppliers, property owners, and usurers, yet do not have the employees' rights specified in government labour legislation. They are 'disenfranchised workers'. Thus, for example, *motocarro* drivers notionally own their vehicles, but a substantial minority are buying them on hire purchase, or have borrowed money for the full purchase, so that they are really dependent workers. Similarly, most night-watchmen who work on the streets watch over a single property, or a group of neighbouring properties, guarding the property of the same owner(s) night after night. Though they are officially viewed as self-employed, they are paid a fixed sum by the owner(s) every day, week or month, and their working relationship is effectively one of disguised wage-working. As a further example, those street traders who have kiosks or fairly sophisticated mobile stalls are usually renting the units or buying them on some form of credit (dependent working), or, as in the case of soft-drinks company kiosks and ice-cream company carts, they have been lent these units by companies on the condition that they sell company products on a commission basis (disguised wage-working). Even in the street trading operations requiring least capital and yielding the lowest incomes, such as door-to-door newspaper selling by small boys and small-scale fruit and vegetable selling in the street markets, dependent working relationships are formed when, because of their own poverty, the sellers have to obtain the merchandise on credit from other sellers or wholesalers. The condition of this credit is that they must sell that merchandise and pay for it before they can have another lot of merchandise on credit.

The low status and economic dependence of many of the people working in street occupations, combined with the intensely competitive, individualist mentality associated with most of these occupations, contributes to a lack of political and economic organization at the level of the ordinary workers. The street occupations are fractionalized by the high socioeconomic differentiation within and between occupations, low general levels of education, insecurity, instability, official ignorance and persecution, and conflicting loyalties to a variety of different 'masters'. Although trade unions and co-operatives exist, these associations are usually small, unstable, and relatively ineffective. Worse still, they are frequently corrupt and/or personalistic, there are often several different rival organizations within a single occupation, and only a small proportion of the total workforce belongs to any organization. Even among lottery-ticket sellers, the most unionized group in the street occupations, only half of the total workers are paid-up members of trade unions or occupational associations, and these are divided between five different organizations (Gerry, 1978: 6). Only about one-eighth of street traders are in unions and associations, and they are split between six different organizations (Bromley, 1978: 1167). Among most of the other street occupations, the proportion of workers in such organizations is even lower, and several occupations have either never had a 'formal' organization, for example, theft, begging, and knife-grinding, or have only defunct organizations which no longer hold meetings or collect subscriptions, for example, shoe-shining and garbage scavenging. Viewing the street occupations as a whole, worker solidarity is ephemeral or nonexistent, and group interests tend to be subordinated to individual concerns and ambitions.

Having viewed the classification of street occupations as work, and the variety of working relationships found in the streets, it is logical to go on to discuss the utility and validity of classifying the street occupations into the service or tertiary sector. In classifying work and economic activities, it has become customary to identify three major economic sectors: 'extraction' (primary production), 'manufacturing' (secondary production), and 'services' (occasionally described as tertiary production) (Fisher, 1933; 1939). Of these three sectors, the third is by far the most heterogeneous, and many attempts have been made to subdivide it into smaller groups (Foote and Hatt, 1953; Gottmann, 1970). All of the street occupations fit loosely into the service sector, and the diversity of occupations found in the streets reflects some of the diversity and internal contradictions in this sector. The term services ranges from the highest levels of government, education and research, to such low-status workers as watchmen, porters, and scavengers. The category of services also includes work in such diverse institutions as the church, the fire brigade, the police, and the armed forces, so that the general character of the service sector is really that of the 'everything else sector' after extraction and manufacturing have been separated out from the total range of economic activity. Within the broad category of services, I include begging and theft, occupations which are usually viewed as 'parasitic' in that the worker serves himself at the expense of the victim (Hirst, 1975: 225). We should not forget, however, that the beggar may provide a service to the donor by giving him some moral satisfaction, and that the thief may serve a 'fence' by supplying him with cheap stolen goods.

Most people's attitudes to services tend to be coloured by whether or not they consider services to be 'productive'. The word productive has a good connotation, whilst the word 'unproductive' is little short of insulting. In some circles, productive is used only to describe the extraction or manufacture of goods, and in this sense, services are clearly not productive. In other circles, productive is used to describe any activity which 'creates surplus-value' or even simply 'adds value', and there is no distinction between primary, secondary and tertiary sectors in terms of their innate productivity or nonproductivity.[6] In a sense, this is merely a terminological debate. Whether or not services can be *produced* like goods, some services must be *provided*, if only to sustain the output of the primary and secondary sectors. No economy could function for long without transport or commercial distribution, and some services are clearly 'essential', whether or not they are defined as productive. In contrast, the production of such superfluous goods as electric toothbrushes and plastic beads can hardly be described as satisfying any basic human need, or as making any major contribution to the economy. Production may not only be 'superfluous', but also 'antisocial', in that for some forms of production the social costs clearly outweigh the private benefits and social benefits are virtually nonexistent. Forms of extraction or manufacturing which cause severe environmental damage, or which produce dangerous materials, may be productive in terms of both material output and profit, but are still socially very undesirable. There is a growing awareness that our concern to increase production should be tempered by periodic consideration of *what* we are producing and for *whose* benefit. Thus, for example, the work of slaves or serfs, or even of low-paid wage-workers, to enrich their employers is not necessarily productive for society as a whole, but only for a privileged minority. The creation of material wealth is a less important objective than welfare; so-called unproductive work may be desirable if it contributes to the welfare of members of society other than the worker, or even if it simply contributes to the welfare of the worker without prejudicing the welfare of others.

THE DIVERSITY OF STREET OCCUPATIONS

The typology of street occupations in Cali shows considerable variety of types of work within the broad category of the street occupations. Further variety is emphasized by the consideration of the nature of work, and the 'rag-bag' character of the general descriptive category of services. Most street occupations provide some wanted services, as evidenced by the fact that the public is prepared to pay for these services. Of course, we may feel that some of these services, such as prostitution and the sale of gambling opportunities, should not be offered to the public, but we should recognize that they are available off-street as well as on-street, and that even worse social problems may result from their indiscriminate repression. The lessons of the 'Prohibition Era' in the United States are as valid today as they were in the 1920s. Furthermore, of course, the repression of any income opportunity may endanger the livelihoods of its workers, and also the income flows and accumulation patterns associated with it. Thus, for example, a complex set of 'moral dilemmas' faces anyone seeking to formulate policies towards the sale of lottery and *chance* tickets. Not only is it necessary to bear in mind the welfare of approximately 4700 sellers and their dependents, but also the facts that the lotteries are government organized to generate revenues to finance part of the social welfare system, and that *chance* is organized by capitalist enterprises employing disguised wage-workers and also paying taxes to local government (Gerry, 1978). Further dilemmas arise when one tries to assess the overall effects of gambling on the gambler and his/her household, and the degree to which the 'ethic of the windfall' implicit in gambling may strengthen individualistic and competitive traits amongst the poor, reducing the potential for worker solidarity and class conflict.

For those services which are offered both on-street and off-street, the street occupations play an important role by increasing levels of competition in the economy, and hence reducing the likelihood of the formation of oligopolies working against the interests of the consumer. In two price surveys conducted by the author in Cali, for example, street vendors were shown to sell most basic foodstuffs in small quantities at prices significantly below those of supermarkets, with the sellers in the street markets generally recording the lowest prices in the whole city.[7] Thus, some street occupations contribute towards lowering the cost of living in the city, and particularly towards holding down the prices of foodstuffs for the urban poor, who buy a greater proportion of their food in the streets than better off social groups. By holding down the cost of living for the urban poor, these street occupations contribute to holding down the costs of wage labour for capitalist enterprises (Oliveira, 1972; Williams and Tumusiime-Mutebile, 1978). Street retailing also plays a role in encouraging consumption, both by selling at relatively low prices and by making items available in a wider range of locations and for longer time periods on each day of the week. Further encouragement to consumption is given by the cheapness of many transport services, including such small-scale transporters as *motocarros* and handcarts, which enable the consumer to get the goods home at relatively low costs. It should be evident, therefore, that most of the street occupations are eminently functional to the socioeconomic system as a whole. They are not simply 'marginal occupations' of no significant social or economic significance beyond providing subsistence to those who work in them.

Three street occupations stand out from the others as not clearly offering a service to the general public; scavenging, begging and theft. Scavenging as a street occupation is distinct from the municipal collection of refuse, and is oriented mainly towards the recuperation of paper, metal, glass, bone, cloth, and other products which can be sold to artisans and industrial establishments. As an occupation, it serves manufacturing industry directly by collecting (or, in a sense, extracting) useful materials, thereby reducing industrial costs and national imports. Potentially, the benefits of scavenging can be passed back to the consumer in terms of cheaper manufactured goods and even increased manufacturing employment. Scavenging is not parasitic, but rather symbiotic, to some extent benefitting all parties involved though providing the scavenger with only a low income and a rather degrading and frequently unhealthy job. Begging is a very different case, in that it is genuinely parasitic, but as there is no victim, it cannot be considered seriously antisocial. Theft is yet again a different case, being parasitic, having a clear victim, and hence, given that almost everyone is at risk, being decidedly antisocial.

UNDEREMPLOYMENT: CONCEPT AND REALITY

In Colombia, any discussion with an academic or civil servant on the characteristics of the street occupations is likely to be cut short by a kindly 'Ah yes . . . you mean underemployment'. All work in low-income services, and often also the work of artisans and peasant farmers, is lumped together as underemployment, and the street occupations are considered classic examples. The implicit assumption is that the workers are doing something, but not much, and that they are in some sense 'less employed' than those who work in government, public services, factories, or capitalist agriculture. When one asks what underemployment means, answers are usually tautologous or contradictory, revealing the different meanings attached to the popular usage of the word employment as well as general confusion about under-employment. Four main approaches are taken, individually or in combination, to the definition of underemployment: that the workers work less hours than they wish to or ought to according to some élite-defined norm; that the workers have very low productivity in terms of the amount of work completed per unit time; that the workers are inadequately remunerated for their labour; and, that the workers do not have a 'normal relationship' with an employer (in other words, that they are not on-premises wage employees). The variables embodied in the four approaches are not necessarily mutually correlated, and none applies exclusively to those occupations which are usually described as underemployment.

Underemployment is a decidedly derogatory term mainly used by the upper and middle classes to describe the work of the poor. Those who work on the streets do not usually describe themselves as underemployed, but rather stress the long hours that they have to work to earn a subsistence income, their shortage of capital, and the hard or tedious nature of their work. If under-employment simply means low incomes, clearly the street occupations reflect underemployment. If underemployment means low productivity per worker because of low capital investment and intense competition between workers, then again the street occupations reflect underemployment. However, these two criteria for defining underemployment are simply the criteria for defining poverty; low incomes and little or no capital. If, instead, we look at how much those who work in the streets actually work, there is no evidence that they work less than those in most other occupations. Most people working in the streets work relatively long hours and a seven-day week. Although some sellers of goods and services spend substantial periods between sales waiting for the next customer, such slack periods are also found in most government and private offices and in many off-street commercial enterprises. A few years ago, a Communist Party member of Cali's Municipal Council suggested that many Municipal offices were being refurnished at public expense 'so that bureaucrats can have larger desks to stretch their newspapers over'!

One remarkable feature of many street occupations is the high return they can give to very small amounts of capital invested. One hundred pesos loaned to a retailer at the beginning of a day can yield 150–200 pesos at the end of the day, enabling the retailer to pay back the loan with an exorbitant 5–10 per cent interest with the balance for his/her own subsistence. Thus, large numbers of workers can make an income around, or somewhat above, the national minimum wage with an extraordinarily low capital investment.[8] Capital is used very efficiently, though, of course, this efficiency is conditional on the low cost and high availability of labour, and upon the donor of credit limiting the number and size of loans so as to be able to closely supervise the recipients and avoid frequent nonrepayment.

On-premises wage-working governed by written contracts and official labour and social-security legislation is only available to a minority of the labour force in Colombia and most other Third World countries. However desirable regulated, protected on-premises wage employment and its associated bonus payments, holiday pay, redundancy pay, family benefits and social security, may be, it is necessary for governments to spread their attention more widely so as to cover short-term wage-workers, disguised wage-workers, dependent workers and the self-employed. To simply consign all of these forms of working away as underemployment which will eventually disappear, is to ignore the worst forms of poverty and exploitation associated with work.

The urban poor are loosely tied into a vicious circle of low capital, low training, shortage of remunerative work opportunities, and low incomes. Only a minority with considerable luck, talent or initiative can break out of this situation, and the success of a minority is often conditional on the relative stagnation of a great majority. The vicious nature of the circle within which the urban poor usually work, is accentuated by a variety of exploitative contractual relationships, and by the lack of effective organizations and participatory structures. The application of the term underemployment to a wide variety of the occupations of the urban poor can have serious negative effects, both in lowering the status of the occupations concerned, and in tending to throw the blame for low incomes and productivity caused by poverty, upon the poor themselves; in effect, blaming the poor for being poor.

OFFICIAL INTERVENTION IN
THE STREET OCCUPATIONS OF CALI

It is not surprising, and in total accordance with the legal system, that clearly illegal activities such as theft, trading in contraband goods, and the sale of prohibited gambling opportunities, are persecuted occupations in Cali. Indeed, many complain that these occupations are not persecuted enough. It is also hardly surprising that such occupations as prostitution and begging, viewed as 'disreputable' by most of the population, are officially regulated and suffer from periodic police harassment. In the case of prostitution, however, official attitudes are decidedly ambiguous, and there are many complaints that upper-class prostitutes and the organizers of prostitution are free from harassment, while the lower-class prostitutes are frequently persecuted.

The intervention of the authorities in occupations which are not clearly criminal, immoral, or antisocial according to conventional élite-defined standards, is much more complex and diverse. In general, the concern is to regulate activities by introducing checks and controls on prices, standards and locations, and by regulating entry to these occupations. Government personnel are appointed to make these checks, and penalties are prescribed for offending workers. Thus, for many street occupations, for example, shoeshining, the operation of a street stall, and the commercial use of a *motocarro*, a horse-drawn cart or a handcart, registration procedures have been introduced and regulations have been made as to when, where and how these occupations should be practised. Hundreds of pages of official regulations (M.S.C., 1971; G.V., 1976) specify the municipal, departmental and national governments' regulations on street occupations, and substantial bodies of police and municipal officials are expected to administer these regulations. In reality, however, these regulations are excessively complex, little known and ineffectively administered, resulting in widespread evasion, corruption and confusion. Thus, for example, in one of the poorest squatter settlements on the extreme eastern periphery of Cali, the inhabitants were subjected to harassment from the local police for a three-month period in 1978. The inhabitants of the settlement include a number of street thieves, and the period of harassment began when four of the inhabitants who had been arrested and locked up in the local police station paid a bribe of 500 pesos to the police on duty so as to secure their own liberty.[8] From then on, until there was a change of personnel at the police station, the police visited the settlement two or three times a week, each time 'detaining' someone and extracting a bribe of 100–200 pesos so as not to make a 'legal arrest'. This harassment was partly directed at known offenders, even though there was no evidence of any specific act which might merit arrest, but also at anyone else against whom they could find the slightest pretext for detention. In most cases, the detainees were never even taken to the police station, and in others they were released immediately upon arrival (after payment), without the case being recorded.

A more complex example of corruption associated with the regulation of the street occupations is the case of the *Calle Trece-Bis* street market, close to the main shopping area of central Cali (Bromley, 1978: 1170). This street market functioned without official permission and against the wishes of virtually all higher-level municipal officials from 1972 until July 1978, and it has been active again since October 1978. When the market has been functioning, the traders have made a daily collection so as to gather together the necessary funds to pay off each shift of police patrolling the area; a routine bribe to enable the market to continue its activity. In the period from July to October 1978, the street market was temporarily 'eradicated' in a very determined municipal campaign to control street activities in that section of the city, an area bisected by the inner ring road, and highly visible to passing tourists and rich Caleños. After a change in municipal administration, however, the political will for 'eradication' was sharply reduced, and despite the hardships caused by the recent persecutions, most of the traders returned to their previous locations. In general, those who administer law and order on the streets complain that there are so many people working in the street occupations, and that there is such widespread ignorance and disrespect for the official regulations, that controls must be very selective. The main objective usually is to reduce the numbers of people working in priority areas; the central business district, the upper-class shopping centres and residential zones, and the main tourist zones.

Although there are occasional cases of assistance by the authorities to street occupations, as when help was given in improving street stalls and providing uniforms for street vendors and shoeshiners at the time of the Pan American Games in Cali in 1971, official intervention in the street occupations is essentially negative and restrictive. This contrasts with declared government policy that 'off-street occupations' should be supported in the hope that they will absorb labour from the street occupations. This reasonable objective has not been achieved because insufficient investment funds have been mobilized, and because investment has tended to be concentrated in areas which generate relatively few income opportunities. In the meantime, the street occupations have tended to be persecuted and opportunities to improve working conditions in these occupations have generally been neglected.

The street occupations conflict strongly with prevailing approaches to town planning. Although Cali has a warm, dry and congenial climate for the open air activities, city planners have usually reserved the streets for pedestrians and motorized transport, and concentrated economic activities into buildings. In general, no special provision has been made for street occupations, and restrictions on *motocarros*, nonmotorized transport and the sale of goods and services in the streets have been partly intended to reduce the incidence of these occupations. Cali is officially twinned with Miami and has strong links with other North American cities. Urbanistically, Cali is being planned along North American lines, and the street occupations are, from the planners' point of view, an unfortunate embarrassment to such plans.

WOMEN AND CHILDREN IN THE STREET OCCUPATIONS

Among the urban poor, conventional official definitions of the 'labour force' and the 'economically active population', which are based upon the idea that neither children nor housewives earn an income, are simply irrelevant. When personal incomes are low, and when the membership of households is often unstable, there is a strong pressure on all household members to seek work opportunities. Work is a form of personal security as well as a contribution to the household budget, and women and children cannot assume that they will be supported by an adult male breadwinner. Instability and insecurity of work and income opportunities are endemic among the urban poor, and reliance on only one breadwinner increases the risk of disaster (McGee, 1979; Rusque-Alcaino and Bromley, 1979). An adult male breadwinner may be the victim of theft, arbitrary arrest or the eradication of job opportunities (Cohen, 1974), or he may choose to abandon family responsibilities and to spend his money on himself. As poverty may also contribute to family breakdown, or heavy reliance on tobacco, alcohol, drugs or gambling as potential escapes from a humdrum reality, it is especially important for each member of a poor household to have his/her own potential income opportunities.

About 70 per cent of those working in the street occupations in Cali are males, at least three-quarters of these falling into the 18–55 age range. Between 14 and 17 per cent of those working in the street occupations are aged under 18, about three-quarters of these being boys.[10] Some occupations, for example, virtually all work in transport and security services, shoeshining, and most forms of street theft, are almost exclusively male preserves. In general, therefore, males and adults predominate in the street occupations, though females and children are numerically quite significant. Only prostitution is almost exclusively a female preserve, though women predominate in many forms of retailing, particularly the sale of fruit, vegetables and cooked foodstuffs. Child workers are mainly concentrated in scavenging, newspaper selling and other small-scale retailing, shoeshining, and petty theft.

In general, women and children are especially concentrated in the least remunerative or lowest status street occupations and have less access to capital than men. Particular occupations are age and sex specific, and although this division of labour may at times be convenient, it mainly acts to reduce the range of work opportunities and the potential income available to women and children. Children working in the streets have great difficulty in obtaining and keeping any significant capital equipment or merchandise for their occupation; most young women without access to significant capital are aware that prostitution may be potentially their most remunerative form of work.

CONCLUSIONS

This rapid summary of the characteristics of street occupations, based on the example of Cali, has emphasized the diversity of these occupations and the impossibility of applying a uniform set of policies to all street occupations. These occupations deserve greater attention and respect than they have received. The present predominance of negative policies should be changed. Most potential improvements to the working conditions in street occupations are relatively inexpensive, and some would actually save government money by reducing the number of regulations and the costs of enforcing these regulations. There is no reason, therefore, why a 'humanization' of the street occupations should hold up vital investments in agriculture, manufacturing and public services. An improvement of street working conditions will not greatly increase the number of workers in these occupations nor lead to accelerated rural–urban migration if appropriate investments are made in agriculture, manufacturing, and public services, and if investment funds are to some extent diverted away from the largest cities towards smaller cities and rural growth centres.

For substantial numbers of the urban poor, working in the streets is a survival strategy. The great majority work in legal occupations, though they may contravene minor bureaucratic regulations, and the legal street occupations are often their only alternative to parasitic or antisocial occupations or to destitution. It is important to realize that many of the negative features of the street occupations are reflections of a much wider social malaise which cannot be resolved simply by regulating and persecuting the street occupations. Gross poverty and social inequality are institutionalized in Colombia, and it is unreasonable to blame the poor for their own situation and to fail to tackle the conditions which underlie their poverty.

Many of the street occupations, and particularly those concerned with public transport and food retailing, are important to the functioning of the urban socioeconomic system. Indeed, in some cases where significant capital investments are required or where official controls are exercised overzealously, there appears to be a shortage of service provision resulting in increased costs and inconvenience for the consumers of those services. Thus, for example, in Cali there are serious deficits in public transport and food retailing facilities in some sectors of the city and these deficits raise living costs and reduce the numbers of work opportunities available. More generally, the removal of street traders would encourage price speculation in the shops and supermarkets and might reduce the sales of some agricultural and manufacturing enterprises; the removal of street newspaper-sellers would severely damage the sales of the press and would bankrupt some of the newspaper companies; the abolition of street sales of lottery tickets would reduce government revenues and lead to the closure of several social welfare institutions; the elimination of scavenging would lead to increased imports and higher costs for Colombian manufacturers.

A few street occupations, of course, are decidedly antisocial and/or parasitic and are obviously undesirable. These occupations require control, and efficient control may reduce their incidence, but there is no evidence that they can be eliminated. Any hope of their disappearance must depend on general improvements in social conditions and the creation and improvement of alternative work opportunities, not simply on the repression of those involved.

In summary, therefore, working in the streets is a description of a very wide range of service occupations. Almost all can be described as survival strategies for those who work in them; many can be described as necessities for those they serve, and for the efficient functioning of the contemporary national economy; a few can be described as unavoidable evils. In policy terms, the most urgent requirement is to generate more work opportunities both outside the street occupations and in the more necessary street occupations, and to improve the general range of income opportunities available to the urban poor. It is also necessary to adopt a more positive series of policies towards those street occupations which are not clearly antisocial or parasitic, simplifying rules and regulations, administering them more equitably, providing workplaces and sources of credit and training for workers, and encouraging the formation of workers' organizations without coopting them into a web of governmental paternalism. Unfortunately, of course, there can be no assurance, either in Colombia or in most other Latin American countries, that the sort of government which would adopt such policies will assume power in the near future. Under such circumstances, increased worker consciousness and the mobilization of those working in the street occupations in alliance with the more conventional 'proletariat' of unionized wage labour, may represent the only means of achieving greater bargaining power to enforce more favourable government policies and to break the present dependent links with employers, contractors, suppliers, usurers, and the owners of sites and equipment.

NOTES

1. The author is indebted to Chris Birkbeck and Chris Gerry for critical comments on an earlier draft. The research was financed by the U.K. Ministry of Overseas

Development, and was conducted in association with the *Servicio Nacional de Aprendizaje, Regional Cali.*

2. In the 1973 census, Cali was recorded as having 923 446 inhabitants (DANE, 1975); the projection to 1.13 million inhabitants in 1977 is based on an estimated growth rate of 5 per cent per annum.

3. In public transport, for example, there is a sharp distinction between the vehicles used in small-scale transport, none of which cost more than U.S. $560 new, and those used in larger-scale transport, none of which cost less than $4000 new, and most of which cost over $20 000 new. This distinction is paralleled by the much heavier involvement of government regulation, subsidies and credits, and of capitalist companies employing wage-labour in the larger scale forms of transport (Birkbeck, 1978b).

4. Estimates of the numbers working in the street occupations are based on a combination of different sources and research methods: official registers, particularly of transport vehicles and *chance* sellers; street counts at different times of the day, week and year in all concentrations of people working on the streets, and in sample residential neighbourhoods; estimates given by knowledgeable individuals, particularly the more experienced workers, union leaders, administrators and policemen; calculations derived from estimates of supply, demand and/or turnover. Estimates were made for each occupation and then summed to produce a general total for the city.

5. These estimates are based on the same sources as the estimates of numbers of persons working in the street occupations, though they have a lower level of accuracy. Most of those workers who are in true self-employment work on their own, but a few are involved in partnerships and a very small number actually employ others as wage-workers.

6. For a useful review of these issues, see Hirst's (1975: 221–30) discussion of Marx (1969: 155–75, 387–8 and 399–401).

7. The main survey was conducted on Friday, 3 September 1977, and the other survey was held on the following day. A 'shopping basket' of basic foodstuffs was purchased in a wide variety of different sectors of the city and types of establishment, according to a prearranged sampling scheme. All purchases were made by the same person, Carmen Rosario Asprilla, and the author is indebted to her for her assistance with the survey. She is a relatively poor black person who has been resident in Cali for several years. Once the purchases had been made, all products were weighed and details of quality were noted.

8. During the first part of 1977 the minimum wage was equivalent to $1.61; it later rose to $2.00 per day.

9. In 1978 the dollar was worth approximately 41 Colombian pesos.

10. Estimates of the proportions of males, females, adults and children in the street occupations are based on the results of the street counts mentioned in Note 4, and on general observations at points of concentration of the street occupations. The main count was made on the afternoon of Tuesday, 13 September 1977, but further sample counts were made at different times of the day and night, on all of the different days of the week, and in all of the months of the year.

REFERENCES

Anderson, S. (1978a). 'People in the physical environment: the urban ecology of streets.' In Anderson, S. (ed.), *On Streets*. MIT Press, 1–11.

Anderson, S. (1978b). 'Studies toward an ecological model of the urban environment.' In Anderson, S. (ed.), *On Streets*. MIT Press, 267–307.

Banks, J. A. (1977). 'The abiding curse of Adam', *Times Higher Education Supplement*, 25 Nov., 14.

Birkbeck, C. (1978a). 'Self-employed proletarians in an informal factory: the case of Cali's garbage dump', *World Development* **6**, 1173–85.

Birkbeck, C. (1978b). 'Small-scale transport and urban growth in Cali, Colombia.' In Denevan, W. M. (ed.), *The Role of Geographical Research in Latin America*. Conference of Latin Americanist Geographers, Publication 7, Muncie, Indiana, 27–40.

Birkbeck, C. (1979). 'Garbage, industry, and the "vultures" of Cali.' In Bromley, R. and Gerry, C. (eds.), 161–83.

Bromley, R. (1978). 'Organization, regulation and exploitation in the so-called "urban informal sector": the street traders of Cali, Colombia', *World Development* **6**, 1161–71.

Bromley, R. and Gerry, C. (eds.) (1979). *Casual Work and Poverty in Third World Cities*. John Wiley.

Bromley, R. and Gerry, C. (1979). 'Who are the casual poor?.' In Bromley, R. and Gerry, C. (eds.), 3–23.

Cohen, D. J. (1974). 'The people who get in the way', *Politics* **9**, 1–9.

DANE (Departamento Administrativo Nacional de Estadística) (1975). *XIV Censo Nacional de Población y III de Vivienda: Resultados Provisionales*. Bogotá.

Fisher, A. G. B. (1933). 'Capital and the growth of knowledge', *Economic Journal* **43**, 379–89.

Fisher, A. G. B. (1939). 'Production, primary, secondary and tertiary', *Economic Record* **15**, 24–38.

Foote, N. N. and Hatt, P. K. (1953). 'Social mobility and economic advancement', *American Economic Review* **43**, 364–78.

Gerry, C. (1978). 'Employment and income stability in the gambling sector: a study of lottery-ticket selling and allied occupations in Cali, Colombia.' Unpublished manuscript. Centre for Development Studies, University College of Swansea.

Gerry, C. and Birkbeck, C. (1981). 'The petty commodity producer in Third World cities: petit bourgeois or disguised proletarian?.' In Elliot, B. and Bechhofer, F. (eds.), *The Petite Bourgeoisie: Comparative Studies of the Uneasy Stratum*. Macmillan.

Gottman, J. (1970). 'Urban centrality and the interweaving of quaternary activities', *Ekistics* **29**, 321–31.

G. V. (Gobernacion del Valle) (1976). *Código de Policía del Valle del Cauca*. Imprenta Departamental.

Hirst, P. A. (1975). 'Marx and Engels on law, crime and morality.' In Taylor, I., Walton, P. and Young, J. (eds.), *Critical Criminology*. Routledge and Kegan Paul, 203–232.

McGee, T. G. (1979). 'The poverty syndrome: making out in the Southeast Asian city.' In Bromley, R. and Gerry, C. (eds.), 45–68.

Marx, K. (1969). *Theories of Surplus Value, 1*. Foreign Languages Publishing House.

M.S.C. (Municipio de Santiago de Cali) (1971). *Compilación de Disposiciones Legales sobre Urbanismo, Saneamiento y Otras Materias*. Cali.

Oliveira, F. (1972). 'A economia brasileira: crítica à razão dualista', *Estudos Cebrap* **2**, 3–82.

Rusque-Alcaino, J. and Bromley, R. (1979). 'The bottle buyer: an occupational autobiography.' In Bromley, R. and Gerry, C. (eds.), 185–215.

Williams, G. and Tumusiime-Mutebile, E. (1978). 'Capitalist and petty commodity production in Nigeria: a note', *World Development* **6**, 1103–4.

Urbanization in Contemporary Latin America
Edited by A. Gilbert with J. E. Hardoy and R. Ramírez
© 1982 John Wiley & Sons Ltd.

5

Low-income housing and the State

ALAN GILBERT AND PETER WARD

Integral to any interpretation of low-income settlement is an implicit or explicit conception of the State and the model of socioeconomic development. According to the writer's ideological perspective, low-income settlement is a route towards middle-class respectability, towards impoverished petty bourgeois values or to outright immiseration. Such broad generalization, however, has its dangers: it is difficult to believe that any single perspective encapsulates the wide variety of situations that face low-income settlers in Latin American cities. And yet, most studies have done just this.

Until comparatively recently, most housing studies in Latin America emphasized the opportunities that 'irregular' or 'spontaneous' housing offered to low-income urban populations.[1] Stimulated by the pioneer work of Mangin (1967) and Turner (1968) in Lima, most studies demonstrated that the chance to build a home in an emerging peripheral settlement was a major opportunity to adjust to, and to benefit from, urban life. Such an emphasis was in marked contrast both to studies which had emulated Lewis (1966) and his concept of the 'culture of poverty' and indeed to studies of a similar vintage which were to form the basis of the 'marginality' perspective. Both sets of work tended to emphasize the problems facing the poor and their essential exclusion from normal city life. As such, low-income housing was an inevitable and undesirable outcome of this marginality. More recently, Marxian writers have tended to emphasize the less positive side of low-income settlement; they have portrayed peripheral housing areas as an inevitable and indeed necessary feature of dependent capitalist development (Pradilla, 1976; Burgess, 1978).

We are doubtful whether generalization of this order is helpful in the analysis of low-income housing in Latin American cities. Even if it is clear that Latin America's urban poor are faced by a hostile and discouraging economic environment, many nevertheless gradually improve their material situation. Whether this represents a minority or a majority of the poor depends upon two essential elements. Firstly, it depends upon the level of material prosperity in a city; we have no doubt that the poor are likely to gain some benefit from higher levels of economic prosperity in the medium term. Secondly, it depends upon the policy that the State adopts towards the poor and to modifying their environment. This is probably the most critical element as it determines the proportion of national and urban resources made available to low-income groups. It is true that such groups are not easily helped in a slowly expanding economy; it is equally true that such groups do not benefit from economic growth under repressive, authoritarian regimes. The nature of the State and the role that it plays within the economic and social system is clearly critical here.

In this paper we examine a limited, but vital, aspect of the relationship between the State, the urban economy and low-income populations: the allocation of land. Access to land is, of course, a critical input to the construction and consolidation of a home. If lots are scarce or expensive, if tenure is insecure, if the State is hostile to the undesirable 'blots on the landscape' that low-income settlements are often perceived to represent, then the opportunities to establish and consolidate a home are likely to be limited. On the other hand, if the State should seek to ease the process of low-income settlement, making plots available, servicing settlement in an efficient and prompt fashion and restricting the opportunities for land speculation, low-income housing conditions are likely to improve.

But how does the Latin American State address the issue of land availability and settlement servicing? At particular times, and in particular places, the State permits the illegal occupation of public land. Indeed, it is clear from accounts of Lima (Collier, 1976; Dietz, 1977), Cali (Nalven, 1978), Valencia (Gilbert, 1981b; CEU, 1977), Rio de Janeiro (Leeds and Leeds, 1976) and Santiago (Cleaves, 1974; Kusnetzoff, 1975; Lozano, 1975) among others that the State has not only permitted, but has actually encouraged the process of illegal land occupation. Elsewhere, or at other times, invasions have been vigorously opposed. In Rio de Janeiro after 1964 (Portes, 1979; Valladares, 1978), in Santiago after 1973 and in Bogotá the State has acted firmly to remove settlers from invaded land.

Given such variations in State action, how best can we seek to explain the response to low-income invasions and land settlement? A comprehensive explanation requires examining the following elements. First, we must understand the nature of the State, whom it represents and for what it stands. What is its role in the society of which it forms a key part? What role do the poor play in the political and economic system? To what extent do they threaten political stability? What is the relationship between the various fractions of the classes dominating State policy making; are the agricultural, industrial and commercial bourgeoisie in alliance or in conflict? Is the State attempting to modernize and foster economic development; is it authoritarian or participative, open or repressive? Secondly, we must understand the role that land and construction play in the urban economy. Prima facie, the more important land speculation and the building industry are to the process of capital accumulation and economic growth, the more critical the issue of land will be in the determination of State policy. Thirdly, we must analyse the role of the poor in the wider urban economy. Is cheap labour so necessary to man industrial and commercial enterprise that cheap land is made available to the poor? Given the choice between a repressive land policy and a housing crisis for the labour force of capitalist enterprise, is land given up so as to maintain the pace of economic growth?

The length of this paper and the complexity of the two cities we are discussing preclude a comprehensive analysis of this kind. Here our aim is more modest. In the first section we examine different theoretical approaches to the issues of low-income settlement and the role of the State. Our aim is to examine how low-income housing contributes to the stability of the socio-economic system and to analyse the form of State policies towards this sector. This aim requires that we consider the nature of the State so as to understand its attitude to low-income housing, its relationship with powerful interest groups and its broad social and economic role in Latin American societies. In the second section, we examine State policy towards the land issue in two metropolitan areas, Bogotá and Mexico City, where we have carried out detailed investigations as part of a major research project.[2] We seek to explain basic patterns in the State's response to the land issue during the past twenty years, any changes that have occurred in those patterns, and the reasons for those changes taking place. Finally, we draw certain conclusions from these case studies which may contribute to our understanding of the State in Latin America, the process of land allocation and the prospects for improving the situation of the poor.

LIBERAL, MARGINALITY AND MARXIAN PERSPECTIVES ON THE STATE AND LOW-INCOME HOUSING

How land is allocated and how the poor are treated by the State can be interpreted from a variety of perspectives. As we have suggested above, the literature offers three broad approaches to understanding the presence of low-income settlement and the differential response of the State.

Many liberal theories explain low-income settlement as a temporary phenomenon; a dysfunction brought about by rapid population growth, imbalances in the distribution of resources and income, and national poverty during the inevitable transition period before economic development policies take effect and lead to a 'trickle-down' of benefits to the population at large (Inkeles, 1969; Millikan and Blackmer, 1961). While this transition occurs, or even if poverty is expected to persist, the worst aspects of poverty and low-income settlement can be reduced by appropriate action. The onus for this action falls on the State which is responsible for the introduction of progressive taxation, effective town planning and housing policies, and, most of all, for the raising of *per capita* income. To the liberal, the market economy must be controlled by the State and the worst forms of inequality removed.

A major weakness of this perspective in a Latin American context is that it tends to overvalue the influence and indeed the good faith of the State. Its proffered solutions depend upon a wholly autonomous, socially conscious, efficient and powerful State dedicated to redressing societal problems. Unfortunately, few of these adjectives are appropriate to the capitalist State in Latin American cities. Implicit in this liberal perspective is a view of the State based on either representational politics or a Weberian bureaucratic/managerialist interpretation (Saunders, 1980). Pluralism or representational politics sees the State as a set of political institutions with a high degree of autonomy from other elements in society. The State should ideally represent all groups in society and resolve differences between those groups in the general interest. It is quite clear that certain critical elements in this description are invalid in most Latin American countries. The State does not represent large groups in society in a responsible way: there are 'systematic disadvantages enjoyed by the great mass of the populaton not merely in lacking material resources, education and leisure but, more importantly, in assimilating values and personal resources conducive to social success' (Dowse and Hughes, 1972: 143). Not only are the poor disadvantaged in their political participation but systematic efforts are made by some Latin American states to fragment, channel, and control the views of the poor.

Even without representation, as in say a dictatorship, it may still be argued that the State will act in the general interest providing the State is autonomous from powerful interest groups. This view is implicit in certain strands of managerialist thought (Pahl, 1975), which argue that major decisions are in the hands of managers who allocate urban resources according to rational criteria. They are considered to have a large measure of autonomy from partisan political and indeed from popular pressures. Resources are allocated according to rules established within the State bureaucracy. These 'urban managers' or 'gatekeepers' are accredited with much greater importance than in other theories of the State. One problem with this approach is its indeterminancy; what factors determine the values and goals of the officials (Dunleavy, 1980)? A further critical problem is that the decisions made by gatekeepers are often determined, or at least critically bound by, the decisions of other actors on the urban scene. Thus, the form of housing policy adopted by an urban manager will depend in large part upon whether or not he is permitted to subsidize low-income populations and upon the size of his budget. Insofar as other individual groups outside the bureaucratic structure make these decisions, the gatekeeper decides only who enters the gate rather than how many people are permitted to enter (Harloe, 1977). While a management function clearly exists, and can be of considerable importance within the activities of the State, managerialism must be supplemented by some other theoretical perspective if it is to explain the dynamic of urban resource management.

The general consequence of this approach to State action on low-income housing is to credit the State with a stronger willingness and ability to remedy the problems inherent in Latin American cities. The emphasis here is clearly on the State to remedy problems in the belief that structural limitations can be overcome or bypassed. As a result, while such approaches often present sensible strategies for improvement, few Latin American States are disposed to accept them.

By contrast, marginality theories emphasize the position of low-income settlement and its inhabitants as a residual element in society. Early functionalist interpretations observed a population excluded from most of the 'normal' or 'mainstream' functions of society; lacking well-paid or productive work, adequate diets, health care or education, many steeped in rural or traditional values, speaking their own languages, not voting nor participating in politics, outside the market for manufactured products (Nelson, 1969: Peattie, 1974). Several of these views were modified as the result of empirical studies which showed this characterization to be erroneous. They were followed by another more radical view that explained the marginal mass as a permanent and growing sector of the urban population. Unlike their nineteenth-century English counterparts, this marginal mass did not constitute an 'industrial reserve army' ready to be integrated in times of economic expansion. Rather they were afunctional to an increasingly capital-intensive and technological industrialization process requiring a skilled labour force (Quijano, 1974; Nun, 1969). As a consequence, incomes remained low, and since governments were unable to improve the situation of this group, petty services, unemployment and shanty housing proliferated. Many States, especially those which adopted the earlier functionalist explanation of poverty, developed policies aimed at 'integrating' the poor and educating them to adopt what were accepted as 'modern' patterns of behaviour. In the housing sector, programmes often sought to eradicate low-income settlement and to relocate their inhabitants in State-sponsored housing projects. Such action favoured urban élites: ideologically, it perpetuated the 'myth' that the poor were responsible for their own poverty and reduced pressure for redistributive policies; practically shantytown eradication conveniently freed valuable sites for urban redevelopment (Perlman, 1976; Portes, 1979).

The weakness of this perspective is that it fails to account for the amount of employment and degree to which incomes rise during periods of rapid industrial growth. Evidence from both Peru and Brazil for the 'fifties and 'sixties has demonstrated that there is little sign of increasing marginalization: in both countries manufacturing employment and the incomes of low-income groups improved generally during this period (Roberts, 1978; Webb, 1975; Kowarick, 1975). While there are reasons to doubt whether this trend was true in the 'seventies, there is no inevitability that manufacturing expansion will either harm low-income groups or generate marginality. The indications seem to be that the integration of labour into the modern sector is the predominant trend.

Marxist theories, such as those of the CEBRAP school, modify the marginality argument in several important respects (Roberts, 1978: 164–70). Rather than being superfluous and dysfunctional to the capitalist economy, they argue that the poor are necessary to the process of capital accumulation. Continued accumulation of capital depends upon the cheapening of the cost of labour reproduction which operates in two principal ways. Firstly, the presence of a large labour pool looking for work depresses wages through weakening the bargaining power of the existing labour force: the classical Marxist notion of the 'industrial reserve army'. This is especially useful to those industries that are not heavily dependent upon advanced technology and which do not require highly-skilled personnel. Recent research has indicated that cheap services (such as cleaning, surveillance, transport, repairs and 'outwork') are intimately related to the productive sector. They cheapen the overall cost of labour and thereby contribute to the creation of surplus value (Oliveira, 1972; Kowarick, 1975; Bromley and Gerry, 1979). Secondly, labour must be reproduced not only biologically but socially, that is to say fed, housed, educated and kept healthy. From this viewpoint, low-income settlement satisfies the housing requirements of labour and minimizes the need for the State to invest in nonproductive activities like house construction. Relatively cheap housing opportunities are generated through informal channels: invasion, illegal land sales and self-help. This, many Marxists would argue, constitutes a double exploitation of labour: first in the workplace, second in the home environment (Oliveira, 1972).

The State's role is both to directly support capital accumulation and to maintain social stability. With respect to low-income housing the State may encourage the regularization and incorporation of such areas so as to permit the easier penetration of capitalist enterprise. By increasing the consumption of cement, bricks and other building materials produced in large-scale plants and by increasing the opportunities for capitalist construction companies it may accelerate the pace of economic growth. At the same time, it seeks to mediate, and in some ways perhaps improve the situation of the poor, so as to maintain stability in the social and political system. Both roles serve to maintain the capitalist system, thereby increasing income inequality and failing to resolve the housing situation of the poor.

The contradictions in this perspective are twofold. Firstly, why are low-income settlements so often destroyed if it is so clearly in the interests of the dominant capitalist classes to maintain them? A possible answer is that different interests press the state, or operate through it, for different policies. Building interests may be pressing for the demolition of high-value commercial land, industrial interests may favour the maintenance of low-income settlements. These pressures may act on different levels of the State. Thus, national States may respond to industrial interests, vaguely sympathetic to spontaneous settlement because of the cheap labour it offers, by failing to formulate a consistent housing policy. Meanwhile, local State policy may respond to élite residential groups and the construction industry whose best interests are served by demolition. Such action would be favoured when the poor have occupied high-value land awaiting redevelopment, when they have blocked prestige public-works programmes and when the poor have established themselves close to middle- and high-income housing areas, threatening to lower land and property values by their presence (Gilbert and Gugler, 1982: Ch. 5). Secondly, if the main function of low-income settlement is to encourage the cheap reproduction of labour, why is there increasing penetration by the State and the capitalist sector into such settlements through the introduction of costly building materials, prefabricated parts, elaborate regulations and rising taxes? We shall return to several of these points below.

Critical to the Marxian argument is the view of the State. Two broad interpretations exist, the 'instrumentalist' and the 'structuralist' views. The instrumentalist view, most associated with the work of Miliband (1969; 1977), assumes that the State intervenes directly or indirectly as the instrument of the dominant capitalist class to ensure that its interests are maintained or extended. It does this because functionaries within the State apparatus are drawn from similar social and educational backgrounds to élite groups; this common background determines their range of sympathies and their responses to problems (Dowse and Hughes, 1972: 144–54). The State adopts a normative view of society that comprises the ideas and values of the dominant classes and imposes this order through its institutions, the Church, mass media and, of course, the education system. The Miliband approach has the advantage of being testable insofar as one can discover the degree of overlap between private and public sector personnel, and insofar as such overlap systematically advances the interests of the dominant class. It is important to recognize that despite the basic assumption that the capitalist relation is all important, much of the explanation is derived from straightforward analysis of the interactions between social and political groups. To this extent, its conclusions often differ little from those of non-Marxist political analysis.

The structuralist view of the State developed by Poulantzas (1973) and built upon the concept of social structure as defined by Althusser argues that the State responds to conditions of class conflict and aims to maintain and reproduce the capitalist structure. At an economic level the State organizes the labour process, at an ideological level it obscures class conflict, and at a political level it helps to disorganize the dominated classes. In this approach, the capitalist class and the State are separable: the State is 'relatively autonomous' from the capitalist class in that it takes independent action. It is no longer necessary for the capitalist class to dominate the State apparatus because they control the structure to which the State responds. The major difficulty with this approach is that it is untestable (Saunders, 1980: 184–7). It explains both State action at the behest of élite groups and the failure to take such action in the same terms. The mere continuance of the capitalist system is proof of the action of the State: without such action the system would have succumbed.

These two interpretations of the State are invariably presented as alternatives: structuralists argue that instrumentalist theories focus excessive attention upon interpersonal relations and individual agents at the expense of an understanding of the structural constraints within which they act.[3] It may well be, however, that the two perspectives are not so different after all (Bell, 1981; Holloway and Piccioto, 1978). Instrumentalism does not claim that the State is a rigid class instrument, bound to express on every occasion the interests of the dominant class. Like structuralism, it recognizes the need for flexibility, the problem of legitimation, the real power exercised by the dominant classes and the separation and distinct nature of political activities and political struggle. At root, Poulantzas seems to suggest that the instrumentalist state invariably protects both the long- and short-term interests of the dominant classes, while structuralism assumes that their long-term interests will be protected while admitting that their short-term interest is sometimes sacrificed to maintain stability (Poulantzas, 1973: 190–4). Instrumentalism and structuralism appear to differ primarily in their respective emphasis; the former on agents and volition, the latter on structures. In both, the dominant classes are assured hegemony but in instrumentalism this occurs because of its own activity (for example, control of the media and patterns of élite recruitment) whereas in structuralism the system operates in such a way that they benefit automatically. In both cases, although for different reasons, the State is to be found in a situation of relative autonomy, conceptualized as a dislocation between political and economic forces.

As we shall exemplify below, neither perspective adequately explains the State's reaction to the issue of land in Bogotá and Mexico City. Indeed, we agree generally with Saunders (1980: 180) when he suggests that a satisfactory theoretical explanation of the State must embrace different elements from several strands of analysis. We also agree with him that the concept of relative autonomy, while vital to understanding, can be established only after empirical analysis. It cannot be established theoretically because institutions, and even individuals, have their own internal dynamic and have an important impact upon local and national decisions. Put simply, while we believe that the State acts to maintain the overall conditions for capital accumulation, we find no consistent route by which this can be achieved. While we eschew many assumptions contained in pluralist perspectives, there seems little doubt that political institutions often possess a high degree of autonomy and their position of externality and superiority allows the regulation and mediation of conflict within civil society.

Whatever our doubts about the appropriate theoretical explanation of the role and nature of the State we are certain that the general tolerance of low-income housing in Latin American cities is not incidental to the survival of both the Latin American State and dependent forms of development. Although we question whether the low-income housing sector is necessary to the process of capital accumulation in all Latin American countries, it is certainly not DYSFUNCTIONAL. It seems clear that whatever the problems that face the urban poor, Latin American housing systems are effective in maintaining existing economic and social systems. They are effective as safety valves because through land invasion and illegal subdivision the more fortunate poor receive land on which they can consolidate their homes. Low-income settlement provides them with flexibility and creates a base from which they can seek work, raise their families and improve their absolute living standard. Though the conditions in which they live are sometimes hostile and rarely conducive to a comfortable existence, comparison with rural conditions or with the lives of their parents normally favours their situation. As such, only where conditions deteriorate markedly are they likely to react politically en masse.

In addition, other more privileged groups in society gain certain benefits from the development of low-income housing. Élite residential groups are served in the sense that low-income settlement often indirectly maintains the sanctity of private property. If invasions can be confined to public land and illegal subdivisions are kept to certain clearly demarcated areas, then high-income residential areas are not directly threatened. Indeed, by offering the poor some stake in the property system, low-income settlement upholds the property concept throughout the city and maintains the inequality of land holding. Élite construction companies and landowners are not averse to the system insofar as they may participate in the sale of land to the poor. Owners of land near to low-income areas may illegally subdivide their property as they will be unable to sell the land to the developers of middle-income settlements. Construction and building interests may make profits either through the sale of plots or through the eventual sale of building materials to the poor.

Industrial and commercial interests benefit to the extent that the labour force is housed cheaply and, therefore, is less likely to demand higher wages. Sales are helped by purchases made in these settlements and by the subcontracting that further reduces company production costs. Companies might gain still more from a better housed population with a higher disposable income, but they are not threatened by the system and gain certain benefits from it.

Politicians are directly served by an increasing constituency and by greater opportunities for patronage (Collier, 1976; Nelson, 1979). It is only when the process gets out of hand because services cannot be provided or because land becomes too expensive that politicians are likely to lose the poor's support.

Only the State bureaucracy is directly threatened because it is required to respond to many of the problems created. Infrastructure, services and regularization need to be laid on at a price the poor can afford. If the State cannot satisfy the demand, it may come under pressure from a variety of sources. Nevertheless, even when its action is insufficient it gains in a variety of ways. It can tap international lending sources to provide additional services, it can increase its fiscal base because of increasing cadastral values in the low-income settlements, and the whole demimonde of the settlement creates opportunities for bureaucratic expansion and empire building. At the very least, the proliferation of low-income settlement creates jobs for professional architects and planners.

We interpret the continued existence of low-income settlements, therefore, to the compatability of these areas to the continuance of the urban system. Of course, that system does not remain stable; economic structure changes, the political power balance shifts, urban development and the very process of low-income settlement modifies the macroenvironment. As a result of these changes new responses are called for, most notably from the State. We believe that the changing policies which have characterized Latin American State policies to low-income settlement are a consequence of these structural changes and consequent power shifts. While conventional wisdom plays its role in moving State policies, more often than not such wisdom is used by dominant groups to further their own interests. The current line in the World Bank in favour of legalizing and upgrading low-income settlement will only be taken up where the most powerful groups in the society believe it to be in their best interests. This tendency is clearly apparent in our two case studies.

Each study begins with a brief description of the growth, economy and nature of low-income settlement in each city. Next, we select for closer analysis a critical area of government decision-making, policy towards the growth of low-income settlement. Clearly, there are many other areas of policy that could, and should, be examined and we recognize some degree of artificiality in the selection of a single dimension of the housing problem. Other areas such as the emergence of a policy to finance low-cost housing production, the process of adoption of self-build technologies and policies, the arrangements for servicing rich and poor barrios, would also provide insight into the interests that inform and shape Government intervention. Ideally, we would wish to examine all of these aspects against the political economy of each city but that task demands greater space than the confines of this chapter allow.

MEXICO CITY

Mexico City has grown rapidly during the twentieth century. By 1940, it had 1.8 million people approximately 8 per cent of the national population (Bataillon and D'Arc, 1973: 161). The disruption of international trade caused by the Second World War stimulated Mexican industrial development and attracted both national and foreign investment (Eckstein, 1977: 6–17; Wionczek, 1971: 147); between 1940 and 1970 the industrial sector grew annually by 8 per cent. In turn, this expansion boosted the rate of national economic growth: the gross national product grew at 6.8 per cent per annum during the 'forties and 5.8 per cent during the 'fifties. Mexico City attracted considerable industrial investment because it offered a central location, access to the increasingly centralized Federal Bureaucracy, agglomeration economies, an ample supply of labour and, from 1955 onwards, major tax incentives in contiguous municipalities. Needless to say, rapid industrial expansion attracted migrants and fuelled a dramatic increase in the city's population: 3.1 millions in 1950, 5.2 millions in 1960, 8.7 millions in 1970 and over 16 millions today.

Gradually, the pace of industrial growth slowed and manufacturing's share of the labour force fell slightly during the 'sixties to 34 per cent in 1970. By contrast, the labour force employed in services increased from 22 per cent in 1960 to 29 per cent in 1970 (Muñoz *et al.*, 1973: 210). Although the city is much more prosperous than most other parts of Mexico, much of the population is poor. In 1974, an estimated 70 per cent of the economically active earned the minimum wage or less, enough for subsistence but litle more (BIMSA, 1974).

Until 1950, the growth of the city was limited mainly to the four central delegaciones (Figure 5.1). Suburbs then developed to the limits of the Federal District after which housing sprawled into the neighbouring State of Mexico. Netzahualcóyotl, a municipality created from the former Lake Texcoco in 1964, had more than 600 000 people in 1970 and now has around two million. Much of the population in this area is housed in self-built dwellings located in what are known as colonias proletarias. These colonias grew from housing a mere 14 per cent of the population in 1952 to between 40 and 50 per cent by 1970 (Ward, 1976c: 330; COPEVI, 1977: 61–2).

Administration in Mexico City is divided between the Department of the Federal District and the Government of the State of Mexico. The country has a federal political system so that each State elects a governor for a six-year term together with deputies who serve for three years in the State legislature. Posts in the State government bureaucracy are appointed according to a system of personal patronage as are nominations for many of the lesser elected posts in the form of municipal presidencies (Smith, 1979). Governors in particular possess very wide powers of authority but are heavily dependent upon the

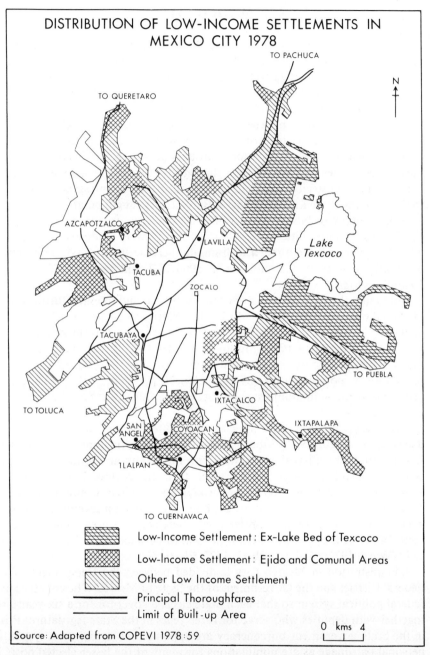

Figure 5.1   Distribution of low-income settlements in Mexico City, 1978

federal executive for funds (Fagen and Tuohy, 1972). Resources are tightly controlled by the national president who channels them through his ministries and decentralized agencies. This has meant that land allocation and land-use planning in the State of Mexico have been strongly influenced by the Governor and his close associates but access to the resources necessary for infrastructure have invariably required the support either of a ministry or of a decentralized agency. Until 1970, planning in the State was the responsibility of a low-ranking department located in the capital Toluca (some 65 kilometres from the Federal District). Later, responsibility was shared with another State institution (AURIS).

The Federal District is something of an anomaly. Here the President, in his own back yard, has traditionally kept tight control. Authority is invested in the Mayor who heads the Federal District Department (DDF). This post is non-elective: he is a Presidential appointee and holds high-ranking ministerial status. Resources for the Federal District are considerable compared with those available to the states. The President and Mayor between them appoint secretaries, director-generals, commission heads and submayors (*delegados*) on a personal patronage basis. A planning department has long existed in the Federal District but its role has been limited; it has never provided a firm blueprint for city development. The underlying weakness of planning is further compounded by the multiplicity of agencies, departments and commissions which help to plan the city (Ward, 1981b): no single body has responsibility for planning the whole area.

In Mexico City, most low-income settlements have developed illegally, usually in one of two ways. First, illegal sub-divisions have been promoted either by individual landowners or, more usually, by real-estate companies. Land is subdivided and 200 square-metre lots are sold off, almost invariably with only the bare minimum of services: electricity, a few standpipes and perhaps kerbstones to delineate the streets. They are illegal because they infringe the city building and land-use regulations and because their land ownership status is confused. These colonias have proliferated in Mexico City especially to the north and east of the city. Second, land 'cessions' have occurred largely where *ejidatarios* or their leaders have subdivided and sold-off plots of land allocated to them under the Agrarian Reform programme. By law, the *ejidos* are inalienable so that the widespread cession of this land in the west, north-west and south of the city for urban development is again illegal.

One other form of illegal urban development, the invasion of land, has been relatively rare. Such invasions have normally occurred where ownership is unclear or where private landholders or *ejidatarios* have been prevented from selling plots.

State involvement in the development of low-income settlement

It is important to recognize that either the presence or the absence of State action may encourage low-income settlement. Any evidence of overt intervention on behalf of specific interest groups must be balanced by an awareness of what actions the State could have taken but which were deliberately neglected. We have also to account for inconsistencies in the State's response: for many years contrasting policies were followed in the Federal District and the State of Mexico; in 1966, 1970 and 1977 major policy changes took place in one or both areas.

(a) Low-income subdivisions

These subdivisions occupy the saline, dried out marshlands of Lake Texcoco. Originally national property, the land was sold off in the 1920s for agricultural land improvement. Later, the State tried to regain ownership after it became apparent that no improvement had taken place, but lost the Supreme Court case (Guerrero et al., 1974). During the 1940s, large areas were bought up by a few private companies as it was apparent that this land would eventually be turned over to urban and specifically low-income residential use. In one area of what later was to become the municipality of Netzahualcóyotl, 62 square kilometres were subdivided into 160 000 plots by 34 companies. The reasons why this land, and that in the municipality of Ecatepec, was available for low-income housing are: that the environment was wholly unattractive to higher income groups whose attention was attracted by the more profitable developments in the south and south-west of the city (Unikel, 1972); that the area was unsuited to heavy industrial development; and that rapid population growth had increased the demand for cheap accommodation especially as the imposition of rent controls in 1942 and 1948 had cut the supply of rented rooms in downtown tenements.[6]

There is considerable evidence to suggest that the State government actively supported the real-estate transactions. Firstly, in 1952 the then Governor of the State of Mexico authorized the creation of Juntas de Mejoramiento Cívico, Moral y Material, ostensibly to coordinate the installation of services in the region, but actually to take responsibility for the promotion of settlement. Not surprisingly, the Juntas ignored the question of services. Our data suggest that certain members of the State executive acted directly on behalf of the companies with whom they had a close personal interest.[7] Secondly, the State took no action against the common abuse whereby companies sold the same plot to more than one individual. This practice was encouraged by the way many purchasers waited for the installation of services before they tried to occupy their lot as well as by contractual clauses which allowed the company to resell the lot whenever payments fell behind time. Thirdly, the State authorities scarcely bothered to disguise their support for the real-estate companies; even in the 'sixties when many settlers began to organize themselves into 'defence' associations to demand that companies install the services they had promised and to petition for investment by the State. Residents drew attention to the way in which companies flaunted very comprehensive State statutes designed to regulate residential subdivision (*Ley de Fraccionamientos* of 1958). Federal, State and Municipal control of subdivisions was nonexistent: no attempt was made to make the subdividers comply with the regulations and no sanctions were brought against them (Guerrero *et al.*, 1974: 27–28). In several cases, authorizations were given for further subdivisions even when the companies had failed to comply with the conditions governing previous developments. Frequently, too, extensions were given to companies which had failed to meet the initial deadlines set for service installation. It was not until the early 1970s that any attempt was made to penalize the developers. Nor did the authorities ever attempt to compete with the developers by expropriating land and providing serviced lots even though the housing agency and international journals were recommending such a course of action (INVI, 1958; Frieden, 1965–6).

(b) *Ejidal lands*

The authorities have been rather more circumspect with *ejidal* land because new land uses often threaten the interests of those who live or work on those lands. Those who gain their livelihood from *ejidal* land are almost invariably communities whose rights are protected by the Constitution and by the joint strength of the campesino movement (CNC), the ruling party (the PRI) and the Ministry for Agrarian Reform (SRA). It is possible to turn whole *ejidos* or parts of *ejidos* over to urban development but only when it is deemed to be 'in the public good'.[8] Such action can be implemented in a number of ways.

Firstly, *permutas* can be arranged where *ejidal* lands required for urban or economic development are exchanged for equivalent agricultural lands elsewhere; a process twice adopted by President Miguel Alemán (1946–52) to promote land development in Mexico City. Large portions of two *ejidos* in the south of the city were exchanged to provide land for the national university. The area used was largely scrub land and this action could justifiably be held to have been in the public interest. However, one large section of the same *ejido* (some 794 hectares) was made over to an individual who soon began to develop a luxury housing estate; Jardines del Pedregal de San Angel and later the middle-income project of Villa Olimpico were developed here (COPEVI, 1976: F 74). A further abuse of executive power was the *permuta* that later led to the upper-middle-income housing estate in 'Satellite City', 15 kilometres north-west of the downtown district.

Secondly, low-income settlement often emerges through connivance between the *ejidal* community and officials in the Agrarian Reform Ministry. A proposal is made to create, or extend, an *ejidal* urban zone. Plots are ceded to would-be owners who pay the *ejidatarios* while the officials from the Agrarian Reform Ministry authorize certificates of cession. Once a low-income settlement is established, however, the mechanism for official land transfer founders and the matter can only be resolved through expropriation, compensation of the *ejidatarios* and the transfer of land title to the occupiers.

One study reports that 30 per cent of all low-income settlement in Mexico City has developed on *ejido* or communal land (COPEVI, 1977: 62). The very scale of this development suggests direct complicity between the *ejidatarios* and the Agrarian Reform Ministry with the latter protecting, or even initiating, the illegal land sales. The strength of the peasant movement and their power base within the Ministry, makes it very difficult for other groups, or even executive officers at the level of Governor, to intervene. In addition, the administration's need for electoral legitimacy, achieved to a considerable extent through the CNC and the Agrarian Ministry, precludes any action that might alienate the grassroots.

Finally, the pace of the recent regularization of low-income settlement on *ejidal* land, and the compensation that *ejidatarios* receive for their 'loss', has stimulated and guaranteed further developments. The establishment of CoRett in 1973, an agency with wide-ranging powers to regularize existing settlements, to create new urban reserves from *ejidal* land, and to sponsor subdivisions, constituted a major threat to the lucrative business of illegal land sales. The response was a sharp reduction in CoRett's charter; forthwith it was to deal only with land regularization and compensation for *ejidatarios* (*Diario Oficial*, 3 April 1979).

(c) *Land invasions*

Although invasions are comparatively rare in Mexico City, several notable cases have occurred in recent years (Montaño, 1976; Cornelius, 1975; Ward, 1976c). Although the State usually upholds the principle of private property and takes firm action against its violation, it is important to recognize that at certain political conjunctures land invasions may be permitted and even actively promoted. For example, several land invasions took place during the 'fifties and 'sixties when hard-line Mayor Uruchurtu (1953–66) prohibited low-income subdivisions. Faced with no alternative, landlords either ignored the invasions or agreed informally to 'sell' lands to the squatters (BNHUOPSA, 1966; INVI, 1958).

Other successful invasions have been the result of political in-fighting; certain politicians have sponsored the illegal capture of lands belonging to opposition groups. No lesser figure than President Echeverría (1970–6) promoted an invasion of land belonging to the newspaper co-operative Excelsior in July 1976 and used the action to oust the editorial staff. Other considerations also motivate the incitement of an invasion: the wish to create a political clientele among the invading community; the possibility of illicit financial gain; the opportunity to increase agency responsibility by initiating 'problems' that can subsequently be resolved by that agency.

State action to control and regularize low-income settlement

Since 1941, the Federal District has had adequate statutory powers to ensure that any form of residential land development be properly authorized, registered and serviced prior to public sale (*Diario Oficial*, 31.12.1941). In addition, fiscal powers have been such that subdividers have been subject to both land taxes and to taxation of their profits. These measures were intended to reduce the profitability of subdividing land but were not applied until 1953 when Mayor Uruchurtu introduced his ban on further subdivision. Under his administration many applications for subdivisions were refused. One application to develop a middle-income residential subdivision on an *ejido* in the extreme south-west of the city was quashed by the Mayor's Office in 1959 on the grounds that it was impossible to extend services to the area. This decision was made despite clear support for the scheme from the *ejido* commission and from the Agrarian Reform Ministry which argued that the land constituted an urban *ejidal* zone.[9] Not all such applications were opposed, especially those supported by the President, but the ban was imposed quite rigidly as far as low-income residential development was concerned. This fact has led many writers to argue that its principal impact was to shift, prematurely, the development of subdivisions outside the Federal District into the State of Mexico where the law did not apply (Cornelius, 1975). This interpretation, however, fails to account for the substantial development of low-income subdivisions in the east and north-east regions of the Federal district. Some of these areas appear to have been authorized for settlement prior to the ban, while others were invasions where the landlord chose to 'turn a blind eye' (INVI, 1958; López, 1978). But, other subdivisions involved *ejidal* land sales in which the Mayor could only threaten to refuse services or to encourage the local police force to pressurize residents (Durand, 1978; Ward, 1976a). Large land invasions were rare during this period and the few exceptions occurred through accretive growth on land whose ownership was uncertain (Ward, 1976c).

Significantly, Uruchurtu's downfall was precipitated by the bulldozing of a low-income settlement in the south of the city. During the next ten years his successors were careful to adopt a more relaxed attitude towards settlement creation and were more favourably disposed to granting permission for basic community services to be installed (Cornelius, 1975).

As we have observed in the adjacent State of Mexico no effective controls were imposed upon real-estate companies during the 1950s and 1960s. Their developments, however, could not continue indefinitely. By 1970, the population living in the low-income settlements of Netzahualcóyotl and Ecatepec had risen to almost 900 000 (Garza and Schteingart, 1978: 69). Most lived without basic services, in isolated districts that were virtually inaccessible to public transport during the rainy season. Public utilities such as schools, markets and clinics were totally inadequate and levels of gastric disease and infant mortality were very high (Fox, 1972). Land tenure was unclear and there were frequently several claimants to a single lot. Moreover, the late 1960s were marked by growing social unrest and local community leaders, who had previously fought one another for the right to represent the informal constituencies, now formed themselves into a common movement. The MRC (*Movimiento Restaurador de Colonos*) called a strike on all further payments to the subdividers and both residents and companies turned to the government for help. The conflict posed an acute political dilemma for the incoming Echeverría administration, which was particularly concerned to promote a closer link with disadvantaged groups and to take a more interventionist stance on their behalf (Tello, 1978). The solution was highly political. It proposed to create a Trust (Fideicomiso) in which the companies were to receive the sums owing to them less 40 per cent, the residents a discount of 15 per cent and legal title to their plots. In addition, service installation would begin immediately though charges would be levied on the residents over the following ten years. The agreement was accepted by all parties though it has been strongly criticized for favouring the companies; the latter were exonerated from responsibility for their illegal transactions, retained a large part of their profits and escaped the burden of paying for services (Guerrero *et al.*, 1974; Martin de la Rosa, 1975; Ferras, 1978). Nevertheless, the agreement marked the end of company-sponsored low-income subdivisions. The companies recognized that the State would no longer tolerate their indiscretions and legislation was introduced to tax profits which made only higher income subdivisions and the development of condominiums a profitable enterprise. It was not until 1977, however, that the State of Mexico took action that ceased to compensate developers; perhaps the only direct attack upon the interests they had previously protected.

In general, however, the Echeverría administration was very inconsistent in its attitude to the expansion of low-income settlement; new regulatory agencies and legislation on human settlements went hand in hand with the emergence of a large number of new settlements—mostly *ejidal* subdivisions and invasions. In part, permission for the new settlements was given in return for the political support that residents were expected to offer to the President (Cornelius, 1975; Ward, 1981a). Although some evictions occurred, they usually affected inner-city rental shantytowns where the land was required for redevelopment or where squatters had invaded lands belonging to someone influential.

Today, Mayor Hank González (formerly Governor of the State of Mexico) is vigorously preventing the development of unauthorized low-income settlement in the Federal District. As a large landowner himself, he has a strong motive for protecting private property. He has evicted settlers in several large new invasions and has issued local mayors (*delegados*) with precise instructions about the need for greater surveillance of vacant lands, about how to intervene quickly to prevent unauthorized settlement consolidation, and the necessity for ready access to the police to secure evictions. In addition, the Urban Development Plan (DF, 1980) has introduced policies to increase land-use densities and to control growth in the south of the city. One outcome of these policies has been to increase the demand for *ejidal* land; land of course which comes under the jurisdiction of other State agencies.

Unlike Bogotá, there is little evidence to suggest that either infrastructural provision or regularization procedures have been used as a constraint on the formation of low-income settlement. Recently, however, various changes have occurred in the organization and behaviour of the infrastructure and regularization agencies. Since 1973, household electricity supplies in the Metropolitan Area have been the responsibility of a single State enterprise (*Cia de Luz y Fuerza SA*). Its criteria for supplying a *barrio* are: a minimum lot occupancy of 60 per cent, a settlement layout that allows reasonable vehicle access, and home construction of more than makeshift materials. Legalization is no longer necessary as the company is striving to reduce illegal line tapping. Once the criteria have been satisfied, servicing is a matter of waiting: if the interference of politicians is not unknown (Montaño, 1976; Ward, 1976a), queue jumping is, today, uncommon. Responsibility for water and drainage is administratively complex and has changed over time. In brief, a ministry is responsible at the national level but a General Directorate is in charge within the Federal District. Regularization was a prerequisite until 1965 when Uruchurtu agreed to service *de facto* owners who paid land taxes; a policy that was extended by his successor (Cornelius, 1975). Echeverría and López Portillo further relaxed this requirement though their policies differed markedly. The former was less concerned with the systematic supply of household water and concentrated on partial solutions such as water lorries, communal tanks and street hydrants. In contrast, his successor intends to supply a further 1.2 million Federal District people with water and two million with drainage between 1978 and 1982 (DDF, 1979). Costs are to be recovered from *barrio* residents and therefore land regularization (and concomitant integration into the tax base) is being promoted simultaneously. As in the past, however, settlement servicing still depends upon the capacity of the company, the location of the settlement and its links with decision makers. Positive outcomes are most likely where access is relatively easy, the cost is not excessive, and relations with the local community are cordial. We are aware of only one case where a contour has been delineated above which a settlement will not be serviced.[11] Nevertheless, settlement demolition is still frequently justified on the grounds that the settlement is too difficult to supply with water or drainage.

Regularization in Mexico transfers ownership from the original owner to the *de facto* owner. Regularization policies have had no impact upon the rate of formation of low-income settlement but the increasing pace of implementation does reflect recent changes in attitude. As might be expected, regularization was relatively rare under Uruchurtu and the pace quickened after his demise in 1966 (Cornelius, 1975). The emergence of land tenure as a major issue of conflict from 1969 onwards led to the creation of several regulatory agencies between 1970 and 1973.[12] These agencies had relatively little success in terms of general programmes and most of their attention focused on the largest and most conflictive settlements, particularly those in the Federal District. In the absence of strict land-use controls, the combined effect of a more enlightened State attitude towards low-income settlement, the regularization of larger numbers of settlements, and the practice of compensating those responsible for illegal land sales, was to stimulate settlement formation. Only since 1977, have the State and Federal District authorities adopted stricter controls.

In summary, while the authorities in Mexico City have displayed an increasingly enlightened attitude towards servicing low-income settlement and a greater willingness to intervene on their behalf, it is almost always a *post-hoc* response and not a constraint aimed to prevent their expansion.

The changing policy response

It is clear that the existence of low-income settlements in Mexico City has not been dysfunctional to the interests of most groups in Mexico City. Firstly, land developers in the State of Mexico were favoured, at least until the early 'seventies, by their retention of disputed landholdings. They were permitted to subdivide or sell this land without complying with the planning regulations and were reputed to have made vast profits (Guerrero *et al.*, 1974). Several companies subsequently moved into legal middle and upper income residential developments. The State has systematically failed to prevent the development and sale of *ejidal* land. The political strength of the economic interests involved in the business and the electoral importance of the *ejidatarios* and the low-income settlers have been such that the powers of the only agency (CoRett) ever established to rationalize the process were quickly curtailed. It was only in the Federal District, under Uruchurtu, that sustained pressure was exerted on real estate interests; here the small landowners involved had insufficient influence to prevent legislation prohibiting low-income subdivisions.

Secondly, national interests have been served to the extent that labour for the booming Mexico City economy has been housed without substantial recourse to the exchequer; self-help has cut the need for expenditure on public housing. Although the State has promoted some public housing schemes for low-income groups, these have been designed largely to pacify other interests such as the construction industry (COPEVI, 1977: 83), or more recently the very powerful Confederation of Mexican Workers (in the case of INFONAVIT). The land that has been allotted to low-income subdivision had few other competing uses and the inconvenience of its distance from employment centres has been partly overcome by heavy subsidies to public transport.

Thirdly, the State bureaucracy has benefited in a variety of ways. Graft has been prevalent, State officials have received illicit payments for authorizing subdivisions, other functionaries have received kick-backs for favours given to leaders, for the resettlement of families and for arranging regularization. The massive expansion of personnel involved in settlement issues has provided jobs and empires within the bureaucracy and increased its powers of patronage and political manipulation; the *leitmotif* of the Mexican political system (Grindle, 1977; Smith, 1979; Ward, 1981a). Politicians and local leaders have at various times used low-income settlements to advance their particular interests. The ruling party (PRI) depends upon the cooperation of local leaders to ensure that demands upon the system are kept to a manageable level and to mobilize the electorate (Cornelius, 1975; Montaño, 1976). For local leaders trying to carve out a political career and for opposition militants and their factions, low-income settlements present an important sparring ground where personal support is generated. In Netzahualcóyotl, several officials and politicians have used the area as a springboard for their careers. At a broader level, the process has allowed the Mexican State to maintain high visibility at relatively low cost (Cornelius, 1975). Through extended patron–client links the State has successfully controlled the urban poor. The decision whether to sanction an illegal settlement, install basic services and regularize land tenure has given rise to the 'game' whereby residents support the PRI in return for ongoing community assistance. In the past, the Mexican State has been very successful in containing popular demand making and mobilization to a level that Castells would call 'Trade Union consumerism' (Castells, 1977; Montaño, 1976). Of course, there is always the danger that a wider social movement might take hold and transcend community and local issues, as happened with the MRC payments strike in Netzahualcóyotl, but so far this level of escalation has normally been restrained.

Finally, it is important to recognize that low-income groups have benefited from the process even if they have suffered from prolonged insecurity of tenure, inadequate services, the loss of leisure time taken up in house building and neighbourhood improvements, and the high cost of paying for land, regularization, taxes and bribes. However, at the end of the day, residents possess a plot which acts as a hedge against inflation, constitutes solid equity, and can be used to generate income through renting or sharing. Almost uniformly, 'owner' residents whom we interviewed expressed satisfaction with their investment, despite the innumerable difficulties they had encountered.

If, therefore, the expansion of low-income settlement has benefited so many in Mexico City and functioned in the general interest, how may we account for the following anomalies: firstly, why was there such a contrast of policy on either side of the Federal District during the 1950s and 1960s and specifically why was Mayor Uruchurtu so antagonistic towards them? Secondly, after the relaxing of controls upon low-income settlements in 1966 and the shift towards a more enlightened approach to servicing, how can we explain the imposition of restrictions in the State of Mexico from 1973 onwards, and in the Federal District from 1977?

In the case of Uruchurtu it is difficult to gather adequate information since he held office some two decades ago. However, his perspective appears to have been shaped by an overriding concern that the Federal District should not be overwhelmed by shantytown sprawl and, more specifically, by the enormous costs that the treasury would incur in any systematic attempt to service such areas. That he was able to pursue an anti-settlement policy may be explained by the absence of a powerful and coordinated group of low-income land developers within the Federal District; by the 'safety valve' that the expansion of *barrios* in the adjacent State of Mexico offered and, lastly, by the opportunities for settlement on *ejidos* or on those lands for which development permissions had already been authorized. Significantly, opposition mounted only after his refusal to install services, and, most importantly perhaps, once his policies began to threaten the more powerful groups involved in speculative land development in the south of the city. Doubtless, other issues were involved but the *cause celebre* that brought his downfall was the bulldozing of a low-income area. That his policies had become dysfunctional is indicated by the more circumspect and conciliatory approach of his successors.

The present mayor (Hank González) has also rigidly opposed further expansion of low-income settlement in the Federal District. In this case, however, we can be more specific about the interests that he represents. A leading figure in real estate in both the Federal District and in the State of Mexico he is a vigorous protector of private property and has acted firmly to prevent the invasion of public or private land. He has been concerned to develop various transportation and infrastructure projects, in part to extend patronage to the construction sector interests that support him. Large allocations of Federal District resources have been earmarked for these schemes, often to the detriment of programmes that Federal District housing agencies would otherwise have promoted.[13] Nevertheless, considerable attention has been paid to many of the problems facing those who live in the low-income settlements that were established prior to 1977. Water and drainage have been supplied, land regularized and public services installed. Unlike his predecessors, however, González' approach has been to ensure that the costs of the improvements are recovered from the beneficiaries (Ward, 1981a). Possible opposition to the Mayor has been offset by the opportunities for densification in existing settlements and by the continuing provision of low-cost land outside the Federal District. As was the case under Uruchurtu, these alternative opportunities have functioned as safety valves.

The sharp change in policy in the State of Mexico from one of implicit State support and complicity in company-sponsored subdivisions to one that has essentially frozen further expansion, and on recent occasions, has actually embargoed their plans, can be explained in terms of the political responses of these settlements. The numbers of people involved, the scale of resources required for *post-hoc* servicing, the intense social unrest that was moulded into a broad based social movement in Netzahualcóyotl and Ecatepec presented the State with a major crisis of political instability. The friendly Frankenstein created by the companies and ignored by the authorities until the early 1970s, began to change its nature. Hence, the attempt to promote a consensus, followed by programmes to install the necessary water and drainage networks. At another level, the State acted more subtly, encouraging penetration of the resident organizations and their eventual cooptation by the CNOP wing of the ruling party (Cisneros, nd). Nevertheless, even though State intervention demonstrated a determination that a similar situation should never again arise, it is important to recognize that the provisions which terminated this era of company subdivisions were, on balance, favourable to those companies.

A growing technical awareness has also been a factor that has contributed towards the change of policy. The emergence of interest in the planning of human settlements, the growth of policies aiming to legalize existing settlement and the early promotion of site-and-service type alternatives by agencies such as AURIS and INDECO were all, in part, a response to the emergence of self-help as an international conventional wisdom during the 1970s. López Portillo's administration took many of these proposals much further within its more streamlined federal bureaucracy. The creation of the physical planning ministry (SAHOP) responsible for the preparation of urban development plans at the national, State and municipal level consolidated federal intervention on settlement issues under the umbrella of a single agency. It is clear that many of the contemporary policies—upgrading, the provision of sites and services, the emphasis upon community participation schemes— all have their origins in international planning practice. However, these ideas have been in existence for over a decade. We believe that their adoption in Mexico reflects State needs rather than a new-found technical appraisal of the problem. Community participation schemes on a scale such as those currently promoted under the *Ejercito de trabajo* programme in the State of Mexico significantly lowers costs and allows the state to spread its limited resources more widely. Elsewhere, we have argued that social control underpins the form that community-state relations take, and that a primary motive for legalizing land title appears to be the amount of money that the poor can contribute to the city's taxes. An aggressive tax programme seeks to charge for the installation of services and to raise land and valorization taxes, stamp and contract duties and so on.

This case study affirms our general conclusion that the interests of the poor rank low on the decision-making agenda and that, on balance, the private sector has done well out of the expansion of low-income settlement, particularly in the State of Mexico. Only when social unrest brought about by housing conditions reached such a level that it threatened to disrupt stability did the State adopt a firm stand against low-cost real estate interests. For its part, the state benefited greatly from the presence of low-income settlements and the political support they offered. Today, it appears to be concerned to adopt policies which will enhance tax revenues, achieve higher densities and promote community participation. We expect future Mexico City administrations to become increasingly involved in policies of this sort as they attempt to gain greater control over civic processes.

BOGOTÁ

Since 1938, Bogotá's population has grown from 350 000 to over four million people. As a consequence of the commercialization of agriculture, State policies favouring urban and industrial development, and rapid demographic growth, large numbers of people have moved from the countryside to the major cities. Bogotá has benefited greatly from this process. In 1973, over 70 per cent of the city's inhabitants had been born in other parts of the country; in that year it contained 13.6 per cent of Colombia's population compared to only 4.1 per cent in 1938. Bogotá's rate of economic growth has tended to exceed that of most other large cities. Its national share of industrial employment grew from 26.5 per cent in 1958 to 29.0 per cent in 1975 while its share of building construction in the largest seven cities increased from 36.0 per cent in 1954 to 54.4 per cent in 1978 (DANE). The major cause of this trend has been the increasing dominance of State in the political and economic life of the nation and Bogotá's position as national capital. Ever since the late 'thirties, the Colombian State has adopted a more interventionalist role in the national economy and the 'National Front' political coalition which operated from 1958 to 1974 accentuated this trend.[14] Bogotá has increasingly become the centre of Colombian political and economic life. While Colombia is blessed with a number of dynamic, industrial and urban centres, those cities are highly dependent on decision makers in Bogotá (Gilbert, 1975). Regional decisions are heavily influenced by national policies and regional political élites have tended to become national élites and to operate from the national capital.

Between 1960 and 1975, Bogotá's *per capita* income increased 30 per cent in real terms (Svenson, 1977). The booming economy has meant that the city's *per capita* income is higher and its unemployment rate lower than those of most provincial cities (Lubell and McCallum, 1978). Nevertheless, the capital is still a poor city with a shortage of well-remunerated jobs. In 1973, the labour force of 831 000 contained 82 000 domestic servants (DANE, 1978); 20 per cent of poor male workers still work over 60 hours per week (Mohan and Hartline, 1979). According to the 1973 census, 62 per cent of all income earners were earning in 1978 dollar equivalents less than 70 dollars per month. The social consequences of this poverty are obvious, one-fifth of all 7 to 9 year-olds do not go to school, malnutrition among the young is rife, the incidence of infectious diseases is high and one-third of the population make no use of the health services (Bogotá, 1977). In terms of housing, poverty has an inevitable consequence: in 1973, an average of 1.6 persons were living in every room, 27.6 per cent of houses had more than two persons per room, half the population were renting accommodation and among the families who rented only one-third occupied more than 110 square metres (DANE, 1977).

Like other cities in poor countries, Bogotá is also an unequal place. This is well demonstrated by the acute level of residential segregation in the city. The poor live mainly in the south and north-west, the rich in the north, with middle-income groups living in between (Figure 5.2). Needless to say, the affluent suburbs are well planned, with green zones, good services, wide, paved roads and street lighting. The low-income *barrios* are poorly serviced and are located closest to the centres of pollution, flooding and heavy traffic. There is also an important difference with respect to their legal position. The upper- and middle-income sectors live in architect-designed houses located in fully serviced urbanized areas which comply with the city's planning regulations. Most of the poor live in settlements which fail to satisfy the planning regulations and are therefore technically illegal. Such illegality means that services are harder to acquire and there is some danger that the settlers may be removed by the local authorities should circumstances recommend such an action.[15] The difference in legality derives from the nature of urban planning and land sales in Bogotá. Up to 1972, the planning norms were set beyond the standard of servicing and housing that most poor families could afford. Because the poor could not buy homes in the conventional housing market another form of land market developed; the so-called 'pirate' urbanization system. Entrepreneurs offer the poor cheap lots and credit, usually over a period of four years, with which to buy the land in their subdivisions but fail to provide sufficient services or wide enough roads to satisfy the planning standards. In 1973, Arias calculated that 59 per cent of all Bogotanos were living in such areas, even if some of these areas, by then had been made legal. Since 1972, attempts have been made to slow the proliferation of such settlements (a programme we consider below), but it is still true

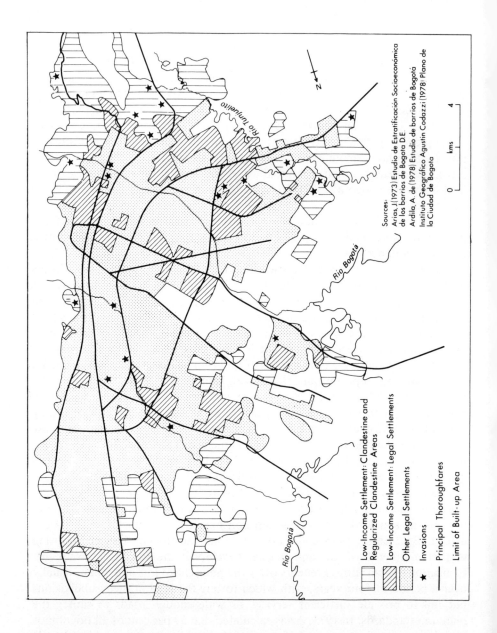

Figure 5.2   Distribution of low-income settlements in Bogotá, 1978

A second form of illegal settlement, the land invasion, exists but is comparatively rare. A major survey carried out by ICT in 1972 found that only 0.7 per cent of Bogotá's housing was located in areas currently defined as invasion areas (ICT, 1976). While this survey excluded certain areas which had been formed through squatting and later legalized, it is certain that invasions have occurred infrequently in the city. Our own count records an absolute maximum of 21 major invasions in the city, a small number in comparison with Bogotá's 800–900 settlements.[16] This phenomenon is not typical of the whole of Colombia; certain cities have experienced many invasions and others almost none at all (Gilbert, 1981b). Why this should be the case is discussed in the next section.

State involvement in the development of low-income settlement

The evolution of low-income settlement is much simpler to describe than in Mexico City. Most of the city is contained within one administrative area and only the neighbouring municipality of Soacha to the south-west forms part of the metropolitan area. Secondly, Bogotá lacks *ejidal* land, specific State agencies do own land but treat it as if they were private companies.[17] Bogotá is simpler than Mexico City, then, because we are dealing with only one urban authority and with one kind of land tenure. The essential issues in Bogotá, therefore, relate to: why the State has acted to prevent land invasions, why low-income settlement has occupied particular sectors of the city, rather than others, the extent to which State has specifically encouraged the development of low-income settlement; and the motives underlying state involvement in the low-income housing market.

Why have there been so few invasions in Bogotá when invasions are so common in other Colombian cities? Since the law is essentially the same throughout the country the difference rests in the way in which the law is actually applied. In Barranquilla or Cúcuta, for example, the police are seldom called to remove invasions (Foster, 1975), in Bogotá the police not only respond to the calls of landowners but anticipate invasions.

There are several reasons why invasions have been discouraged in Bogotá (Vernez, 1973). Firstly, the poor have the alternative of the pirate urbanization. Whatever the advantages of land invasion in terms of cost, a pirate urbanization is physically safer and tenure is more or less assured. Given that there is no tradition of invasion as in some other cities, pirate urbanization serves as a safety valve by offering large numbers of people land at relatively low prices. Secondly, politicians have not on the whole sought to encourage land invasion in Bogotá. Only one opposition Communist group has consistently sought political support through the invasion process, encouraging low-income tenants to occupy lands where there is some dispute over title. The major reason why politicians have not encouraged land occupation is that land has a high market value in Bogotá and the State agencies which hold land protect it as firmly as most private owners. In addition, the political system in Bogotá has developed other forms of patronage and ways of winning electoral support. For example, the fact that the servicing system is superior to that in most other Colombian cities, means the the low-income settlements can be provided with infrastructure and politicians can be seen to be active in this servicing process. Thirdly, these tendencies have been accentuated by the fact that Bogotá is the national capital and, in a country which has until recently suffered from civil violence, the authorities have been determined to maintain order in the capital. The so-called *Bogotazo* of 1949 is a constant reminder to Bogotá élites of the dangers of working class unrest and 'anarchy'.[18]

This brief résumé of the reasons why invasions are rare leads on to the observation that the few successful invasions in the city have been achieved only at high cost to the settlers. The repression applied to invasions such as El Quindío and especially Policarpa Salavarrieta was harsh, resulting in confrontations with the police and a certain number of deaths (Cardona, 1969). In recent years, the only invasions to be permitted have been those on land where there was some genuine doubt about the owner's legal title. Thus, in Nuevo Chile, although the original invaders were arrested they were eventually allowed to return to the site as the owners lacked adequate legal proof of ownership. In this case, though not in Policarpa, the service agencies have even been prepared to work with the *barrio* to provide services. But, if the response to existing invasion areas has become less repressive, the general environment facing new invasions has become more hostile. Indeed, since the passing of the Security Statute under the Turbay administration, the powers afforded to the authorities are such that it is very risky to engage in land invasion; a recent land invasion in Patio Bonito resulted in the arrest of 86 persons (El Tiempo, 1980).

Unlike its hostile reaction to invasion, the State has covertly accepted pirate urbanization. Although the overt reaction has generally sought to discourage the process, individual agents within the State have not. The difficulty in Bogotá is to determine the extent to which the State has followed a specific policy towards low-income housing formation. As an objective fact, over half of the city has developed in some sense illegally. On the one hand, this means that the State has attempted to control such urban growth through legislation, on the other, it is a clear indication that it has failed to apply its own laws and regulations. As we argued above, Latin American States are likely to encourage low-income settlement rather than to consistently discourage it because any other reaction will cause greater problems. Low-income settlement growth is conducive to rapid commercial and industrial development whatever problems it may cause. On the whole, therefore, the State has covertly supported its growth, or merely failed to act decisively to control it.

State action to control and regularize low-income settlement

The difficulty in explaining the State's response to low-income housing is simply that there has been no consistent policy on the part of the authorities. Certain agencies have regularly opposed the servicing of illegal settlements, while others have allowed it: some agencies have sought to regularize and ease the legalization of low-income settlements, others have opposed such a development. As a result, State policy has been somewhat unpredictable and opportunistic; a consequence of the fractionalism within both politics and administration in Bogotá. Because of this fractionalism there is not one State but many, the different parts of which are competing and undermining the actions of others (Gilbert, 1978). The result is that it is difficult to describe simply the principal policies of the State. Perhaps only two broad general statements can be made. The first is that overall strategy has clearly been to permit the expansion of low-income housing through pirate urbanization. Occasional demolition of low-income settlement has occurred but this has normally been associated either with the prevention of land invasions or with the clearing of land for commercial development or public works. The second is that there has gradually been an effort on the part of certain elements of the State to control, service and regularize these settlements. This second effort has been only partially successful because other groups both within the State and outside have sought to prevent effective regularization or more accurately have sought to prevent the introduction of measures which effective regularization both requires and implies.

The only way in which State policy can be understood is to examine the major elements which impinge on the development of low-income housing, to examine how effectively these elements have performed their overt and covert functions and to examine how policy has changed through time. In Bogotá, the main institutional elements which affect the development of low-income housing are: the city planning authorities who control land use, building standards and the extent of urban expansion; the service agencies which provide or fail to provide key services such as water, electricity, sewerage and transport; the national agencies in charge of regulating low-income housing developments; and local and national politicians who act as intermediaries between the low-income populations and the State agencies and indeed who often serve as representatives of those agencies. We shall consider each group's response to low-income housing during the past twenty years, and shall delay until the next section an explanation of changes in policy.

(a) *The city planning authorities*

Within the Special District of Bogotá, planning is the responsibility of numerous agencies. National agencies such as INDERENA have token responsibility but do not intervene in practice. Other national agencies such as ICT, the housing institute, or the National University have no formal planning responsibility but by their actions critically affect land use in the city (Lubell and McCallum, 1978). At the regional level, CAR has responsibility for planning in Bogotá but in fact has never interfered, confining its activities to the area outside the Special District. At the local level, planning is in the hands of the City Planning Department (the DAPD), the *Junta de Planificación*, the service agencies, the Institute for Urban Development, and various committees which ostensibly coordinate action between these agencies.

The urban perimeter is a device to slow the physical expansion of the city by imposing a limit on the area within which the service agencies will provide infrastructure and the planning authorities will legalize barrios. In fact, despite the efforts of the water authority to uphold the policy in particular parts of the city (see below), the perimeter has not been successful in this aim. Rather, development of low-income housing has consistently gone beyond the perimeter and the perimeter has later been modified to take account of the expansion (Losada and Gómez, 1976). Extensions to the perimeter have sometimes served a political function, as favoured *barrios* have been included in the serviceable area, but there has been no consistent tendency in this respect (Zorro and Gilbert, 1982). Indeed, the main changes have occurred as belated reactions to the existence of extensive areas of low-income housing beyond the perimeter. The existence of the perimeter has been important insofar as it has limited the availability of serviceable land and thereby increased the price of land within the perimeter and lowered the price beyond. Until recently, it has also had some effect on slowing expansion of low-income housing in directions where the water authority refused to service. Recent changes in the capacity of the water authority, however, have made the urban perimeter less meaningful and recent attempts to revise the zoning ordinance have included a proposal to abolish the perimeter altogether. Perhaps most important is that the continued existence of the perimeter has limited the availability of land which can legally be occupied by low-income housing; a factor that has undermined efforts to legalize and regularize low-income housing. This tendency has been magnified recently by the fact that the zoning decree of 1975, which extended the urban perimeter to include large areas of low-income housing, has been revoked, automatically placing much serviced and non-serviced housing outside the urban perimeter.

The zoning laws, the first of which appeared in 1944, lay down the areas which can be dedicated to a particular kind of development: industrial, commercial, high-density residential, low-density residential, etc. The main effects of the zoning legislation have been to increase the incidence of illegal low-income housing and to accentuate residential segregation. Given that there is now a shortage of urbanizable land in the city, land owners and construction companies are liable to exert considerable pressure on the authorities to modify the zoning ordinance. These interest groups pressure the authorities to shift land from the high-density (low-income) category to middle- or low-density designations. The result of such a shift is to raise the value of the land. As a consequence, the amount of land available for the legal development of low-income settlements is very limited, a fact which both increases the value of land in those settlements and encourages the emergence of pirate urbanizations.

A series of standards regulates the construction of individual buildings, the levels of services required in a legal urbanization, the required street width and the public areas. Here is not the place to go into detail (see Losada and Gómez, 1976: 43–7) but it can be argued that the gamut of complicated rules and regulations made it virtually impossible before 1972 for low-income housing to develop legally. The 1945 regulations required sewerage, water, paving and pavements. This ruling was modified in 1961 when the first effort at 'institutionalizing subnormality' was made (Zorro Sánchez, 1979; 42); henceforth only water standpipes, public lighting on wooden poles, and the construction of private latrines were required (Acuerdo 30 of 1961). Even these stipulations were beyond the means of many urban developments which meant that until the standards were further reduced in 1972, generalized illegality continued.

The change brought about in 1972 (Acuerdo 20) and the regulating decrees of the following year (Decrees 1259 and 1260) were potentially radical in the treatment they afforded low-income housing areas. The introduction of the so-called minimum standards had two related goals. The first was to improve the situation of existing *barrios* in three stages: rehabilitation of the *barrio*; its legalization and formal incorporation into the urban plan once the minimum standards had been achieved; its regularization through the complete provision of services and urban infrastructure. The second aim was to ease the legal development of new low-income areas thereby undercutting the demand for unserviced lots in the private urbanizations.

The outcome of this change from 'blind rejection' of low-income housing to its 'toleration' and even encouragement is debatable. The Planning Department claims that in the five years to April 1979, 36 minimum standards urban developments were approved covering 375 hectares; between December 1974 and February 1977, 24 per cent of land in Bogotá has been developed under minimum standards compared to around 30 per cent in pirate urbanizations (DAPD, 1978). These data suggest that if the new legislation has failed to stop the pirate urbanization it has at least slowed expansion. In addition, it has raised the level of services supplied by pirate urbanizers as they attempt to comply with the spirit of the new standards and thereby avoid intervention by the Banking Superintendency (see below). The new standards have undoubtedly eased the legalization and servicing of existing *barrios*.

On the other hand, the achievement has been more limited than some planners had hoped. A major limitation has been that the continued existence of the urban perimeter and the limited amount of land zoned for high-density/low-income housing has meant that the price of minimum standards lots has been high. Indeed, Carroll (1980) has shown that both the prices charged, and the profits made, by the minimum standards urbanizers have been consistently higher than those of pirate developers. As a result, the limited number of minimum standards *barrios* have been occupied by middle-income groups rather than by the poor. A further criticism is that some new pirate urbanizations have developed beyond the boundary of the Bogotá Special District into neighbouring municipalities. It is difficult to calculate the extent of this development but this is clearly the trend of the future. Given the shortage of building land in the Special District all housing developments will eventually spread into the neighbouring municipalities. The problem is, of course, that these municipalities do not have minimum standards decrees so that the pirate movement will continue unchecked. The criticism that can be levelled against the Bogotá authorities is that they introduced the new regulations far too late.

(b) *The servicing agencies*

In Bogotá, the willingness and ability of the major utilities to service low-income *barrios* has been an important influence on the latter's development and ability to consolidate. Of these utilities by far the most influential has been the water and drainage authority (EAAB). The EAAB is critical in the sense that it supplies the most 'lumpy' infrastructure required by the *barrios*. While the *barrios* can rob electricity and if necessary build a community hall, self-help with respect to water and especially to drainage is more difficult. As such, the degree of consolidation of a *barrio* is critically dependent on the attitude of the EAAB. In addition, it has been the EAAB which more than any other single institution in Bogotá has determined the limits of the urban perimeter. The water authority has surveyed the city and decided that certain areas were too expensive to supply and these have been placed beyond the urban perimeter. Until recently, two broad areas fell into this category, high *barrios* which could not be supplied with water without pumping and those below the level of the River Bogotá which could not be drained without pumping. The authority was extremely strict on this issue on the grounds that supplying these areas would undermine the financial viability of the enterprise and thereby the support it received from multilateral funding agencies. Whenever there has been pressure to go beyond the urban perimeter the EAAB has required that money be provided from other sources to finance it. Thus when one *barrio*, Casablanca, managed to find money to purchase a pump and materials, the water authority was prepared to supply the water.[19] Similarly, when the EAAB became convinced that pumping was a viable procedure, the funds to supply all the high altitude *barrios* in the city came from foreign sources as part of the *Plan de barrios periféricos* which began in 1974.

Within the urban perimeter, however, the EAAB has like the electricity authority (EEEB), been much less strict. In fact, Fuentes and Losada (1978) demonstrate that many illegal *barrios* have been supplied with official water and sewerage. Both agencies find it more practicable to service the illegal settlements than to suffer from contraband links to the mains. In the 'sixties, it was common for the electricity company to cut illegal lines but since 1967 an attempt has been made to supply and charge all *barrios*. The difficulties have come not from the low-income areas which have preferred this policy, but from the other service and planning agencies. Relationships with the planning department and with the Banking Superintendency (SIB) have sometimes been tense especially since the two agencies have even been prepared to service invasion areas. While relations with Policarpa Salavarrieta have not been regularized due more to the attitude of the *barrio* than to the reluctance of the EEEB and EAAB, Nuevo Chile which was formed in 1973 has collaborated easily and successfully with the two agencies (El Tiempo, 1979).

Both the water and the electricity agencies have sought to service as many low-income areas as possible. The limitation has been the urban perimeter on the part of the water authority and the capacity of both agencies to service large areas of the city. On straight commercial criteria both agencies have supplied higher-income areas before low-income areas. Since water and electricity pricing partially subsidizes low-income areas both agencies prefer to service high-income areas which pay the full commercial rate. Both agencies have also sought to ease the servicing of these *barrios* through loans and have been prepared to ignore the rules of other local authorities such as the planning department.

The attitudes of the servicing agencies have undoubtedly eased over time. The attitude towards illegal low-income settlements was much more relaxed in the 'seventies than in the 'sixties. This relaxation has been the result of certain political factors which we discuss below but also due to the enormous expansion in the capacities of the two utilities. Indeed, it now seems possible that the urban perimeter will be abolished altogether.[20] The other service agencies in Bogotá have had a much more limited capacity to service the *barrios* than the EEEB and EAAB and on the whole they have allocated their services in a much more partisan political fashion (see Gilbert, 1981b, for more detail). This has meant that there has been implicit support for low-income expansion from these other service agencies even if *barrios* have only occasionally been serviced. Politicians and officials of these more partisan agencies have been prepared to promise services to low-income *barrios* whether or not they had the technical ability to provide them (see below).

(c) *The Banking Superintendency and the National Housing Institute*

In 1968, a law was passed to control the financial rectitude of all urban development projects with more than four houses. Responsibility was placed in the hands of the Banking Superintendency, SIB, which had similar authority over banking, insurance and financial institutions. From the start there was some doubt whether it was the most appropriate institution to control and regulate the pirate urbanization process given that its experience was in accountancy rather than in the servicing and planning of housing. Nevertheless, it was given the powers to rigidly control the illegal subdivision of land: it can put pirate urbanizers in jail for up to six years and it can freeze the assets of an urbanizer until he can demonstrate that he is capable of running the company properly. As Losada and Gómez (1976) and Doebele (1975) point out, however, the SIB does not apply the law rigorously. Only during one period of two years did the SIB take effective action on low-income subdivisions. Even then, as the authors of this more intensive action have been at pains to point out, they acted only against the worst urbanizers not against all (Paredes and Martínez, 1977). If the SIB had acted to totally suppress the pirate urbanization process, the cure would have been worse than the disease. In any case, Losada and Gómez (1976) are surely correct in pointing out that the housing division of the SIB has consistently had too few resources to act effectively and that the qualifying decrees make it difficult for the SIB to take over a pirate urbanizer effectively.

Nevertheless, between 1976 and 1978 the SIB intervened on numerous occasions and handed over pirate urbanizations to the National Housing Institute (ICT). Unfortunately, ICT have consistently had difficulty administering confiscated urbanizations. Various arguments have been put forward as to why ICT have failed to regularize the situation of the intervened *barrios*. The special agency of ICT in charge of intervened *barrios* claims that it has an impossible job because the assets of the intervened urbanization are always too limited to provide the services expected by the population. By the time the assets of the urbanizer are actually frozen he has had time to protect them. In addition, once a *barrio* has been taken over by ICT most of its inhabitants cease to pay what they owe to the urbanizer and are reluctant to pay the agency. On the other hand, critics of ICT accuse it of inefficiency and claim that a much better job should have been done. Frequent changes of administrators and the frittering away of the assets of the urbanizer have slowed servicing. Indeed, a major critic of ICT has been the SIB; so bad did relations become in 1979 that the SIB ceased to hand over intervened *barrios* to ICT and appointed their own agents. The SIB believe that they do better in terms of servicing the *barrios* by putting pressure on the pirate urbanizer, or through intervention and the appointment of their own agents, than by handing over the urbanization to ICT.

Whatever the merits or weaknesses of the two national agencies it is clear that they have been faced with an impossible task. At best, control could only prevent the worst excesses of the pirate urbanization system; to do more would have cut the safety valve that pirate urbanization provides. The SIB have realized this and have tended to intervene only when the population of the *barrio* or some influential actor (such as a major politician) have complained about the *barrio* situation. Where the *barrio* population have accepted the situation and have failed to create a noticeable problem, the urbanizer has been permitted to carry on.

(d) *Local and national political influence*

Low-income urbanization forms part of the wider system of political patronage and clientalism that operates in Bogotá. Politicians in search of support seek to help *barrios* with their servicing and legalization problems. The politician may represent the *barrio* before the officials in the servicing agency, he may find funds from the council budget to build a community hall or pave a road, he may ask political allies to put pressure on high-level personnel in the servicing or planning agencies. This kind of function helps increase and legitimize pirate urbanization and it serves individual *barrios* insofar as they receive a few more resources. On the other hand, it is not unknown, indeed it is quite common, for politicians to promise to do much more for the low-income settlements than they can in fact provide. Many instances can be cited of politicians belonging to the boards of directors of the servicing agencies who have gone to *barrios* promising to help bring light or roads knowing full well that the agency has just agreed to provide that very service. Our experiences and discussions in Bogotá strongly suggest that the ability of politicians to supply their electorates with services was rather limited (Gilbert, 1981a). They did provide certain benefits but the total budget available to them was normally very limited.

In addition, it became clear in our investigations that the three major service agencies operated relatively autonomously of partisan political processes. For reasons that are elaborated elsewhere (Gilbert, 1981b; Cepeda and Mitchell, 1980), the water and electricity agencies have been given the funds to expand capacity providing that they remove the worse excesses of partisan political activity. The bureaucracy has been protected largely by the appointment of non-partisan directorates. This does not mean that partisan influence has been absent, that politicians have not sought to favour one settlement before another, only that most decisions have been made on broadly technical criteria. By contrast, other service agencies operate much more on partisan political lines. The bus company, the refuse service and the education agency are well known for affording patronage both to *barrios* and to individuals within the *barrios*. Jobs are provided for supporters, services are laid on preferentially and partisan political favours awarded. But, even here there are two major limits. The first is that these are not critical resources with respect to the development of low-income settlements: water, light and drainage are much more essential. The second is that the budgets of these more partisan agencies are much more limited. In 1979, for example, the projected budget of the water authority was around $33 million and that of electricity around $100 million compared to $1.6 million for the bus company and $4.8 million for the garbage company (Bogotá, 1979a).

Our argument, therefore, is that the scope of the partisan politician to win friends and influence low-income populations is limited. Indeed, it has become less influential through time. The growth of the non-partisan agencies has increased much more rapidly than that of the partisan, especially during the 1970s. This means that although individual politicians and political parties seek support in the *barrios* and encourage the pirate urbanization process in certain ways, they are far less effective than in other cities where they control most of the servicing agencies and indeed control access to land. Partisan politics is a critical ingredient to Bogotá politics and urban policy, but it operates at higher levels than the politician–*barrio* intercourse. 'Councillors have a few jobs to offer, some funds to allocate, they can speed up servicing in some cases or may get a bus service, but the key decisions which really affect the way that the poor live are decided at the highest political levels' (Gilbert, 1981a).

This argument is further supported by the experience of community action programmes in the city. Organized since 1968 as a decentralized agency of the city administration, the Department of Community Action (DAAC) is widely viewed as a good example of partisan political patronage at work. The agency has frequently been criticized from outside and within of excessive paternalism, of compliance and of following over-legalistic procedures. Clearly, it has provided funds and organized self-help efforts in the *barrios*. But its limited budget ($0.7 million in 1979) means that it can allocate very little to individual settlements (Bogotá, 1979b).

Partisan politican activity is ever present in Bogotá at all levels of administration. But, it is our contention, that the resources available to politicians to pass on to low-income groups are very limited. For this reason most services and activities administered through partisan political agencies have been limited and ineffective.

The changing policy response

In broad terms, the State's response to low-income settlement has changed from overt opposition with sporadic covert encouragement to overt support within a broad body of simplified rules and regulations. These rules do not permit the invasion of land, but seek to channel the illegal pirate movement into the legal land market. The other major change is that the servicing agencies have increased their capacity to deal with the growth of low-income settlement but one condition of their being able to do so has been that they act in a technical, bureaucratic manner.

There are, of course, innumerable explanations of specific changes in State policy. Nevertheless, there are broad trends in Colombian economy and society which parallel and complement the changes in housing policy. Without going into great detail about either Colombian politics or economic development, we believe that changes in housing policy can only be explained satisfactorily in that context.

The most adequate explanation of the increasingly relaxed attitude to the formation of low-income housing and the attempt to incorporate that housing into the legitimate land and housing market, is that there was really no alternative. Bogotá has grown rapidly on the basis of industrial, commercial and government employment. Cheap labour has been required and some form of housing had to be available to that population. In the early 'sixties, it was hoped that the State would be able to house that population through public sector construction programmes. The example was the ICT construction programmes in Ciudad Kennedy and other parts of Bogotá which were financed largely through the Alliance for Progress. ICT built more houses in Bogotá in 1962 than it has done in any year since; by the middle 'sixties the flow of foreign funds declined and ICT's ability to construct housing was limited thereafter (CENAC, 1975; Stevenson, 1979). Despite attempts to encourage self-help and community participation, the supply of housing fell consistently behind the demand.

In Bogotá, the pressure on housing is clearly demonstrated by the high incidence of renting and overcrowding. In 1973, some 51 per cent of all families rented a home, as often as not a single room. Continued urban growth was creating major housing pressures. In addition, there were significant political developments. The late 'sixties saw the rise of a populist political movement known as ANAPO. Led by ex-dictator Gustavo Rojas Pinilla and his daughter, María Eugenia, the movement was very successful in mobilizing the low-income population of the city in opposition to the National Front alliance of the Conservative and Liberal parties. Having won numerous seats on local councils throughout the country in 1968 Rojas Pinilla almost won the 1970 National Presidential election.[21] In Bogotá, Anapistas won 45 per cent of the popular vote, which represented a major defeat and something of a surprise to the established parties; Misael Pastrana Borrero, the eventual winner received 40 per cent of the vote (DANE, 1972). We interpret this defeat and the period leading up to it as something of a crisis period for the political system. The alliance of the Conservatives and the Liberals was based on the deliberate playing down of partisan political conflict but had the both desired and undesired corrollary of increasing political apathy in the low-income areas

(Losada, 1980). It was on this apathy towards the existing political alliance that ANAPO largely fed (Dix, 1980).

The response of the traditional parties was to pay greater attention to the needs of low-income areas. A dramatic shift in the allocation of resources to these areas did not take place but a clear response was apparent. It would seem to us that the efforts through the SIB to control the worst excesses of the pirate urbanization movement, the attempt to reduce unrealistic planning policies regulations to incorporate many low-income housing areas, and the efforts to step up servicing even in areas which had previously been declared technically unserviceable is largely explicable in these terms. Less attention was paid from this time on to community-action programmes and more to large-scale, centrally directed servicing programmes. Water, electricity and drainage were increasingly provided to the *barrios* as of right rather than as a mixture of patronage, community action and luck.

The fact that the Bogotá authorities were able to react in this way, however, was in part because, for other reasons, highly efficient public utilities had emerged (Cepeda and Mitchell, 1980). The demands of industry and commerce during the 'sixties had required that the relatively small-scale public utilities increased both the scope of their activity and their efficiency. Major expansion plans were launched with the financial assistance of the World Bank and the Inter-American Development Bank. These funds did not come without strings; the loans were conditional on the exclusion of partisan politics from the service arena and the tightening up of pricing policy and commercial practice. As a consequence of these changes the capacity of the electricity and water utilities increased dramatically. Electricity consumption rose threefold between 1965 and 1977. The huge increase in capacity meant that industry and commerce could be satisfactorily serviced, the major motivation behind the expansion, but it also meant that some spare capacity was available for servicing low-income areas. The political developments led to this spare capacity being used to try to win back the support, or at least the compliance, of low-income groups. This attempt was not successful in gaining popularity for the National Front but it may have made it more difficult for non-establishment parties to win popular support in the future. Certainly, attempts to service the low-income communities accelerated still further in the late 'seventies financed by the World Bank.

A similar kind of argument can be used to explain the transformation of the Banking Superintendency (SIB) into a method of controlling errant pirate urbanizers. Law 66 of 1968 was to a large extent the result of several companies building middle- and higher-income housing estates going bankrupt. Prospective homeowners lost money, including it is said certain prominent politicians. The SIB found its powers extended to include the affairs of builders. One outcome of this extension was that power was given to control low-income settlement. For several years that power was not effectively used but it eventually came to be used responsibly to control and channel the pirate urbanization process.

The other major change, the introduction of the minimum standards decree, is also compatible with this interpretation. The idea had emerged from the international literature and had been first tried out in Cali when the government had faced a potential crisis connected with the land invasions in that city. The architect of that programme was a prominent advocate of adopting the policy in Bogotá. In one sense, minimum standards were merely a continuation of the gradual relaxing of standards in the city. The strict servicing requirements laid down by Acuerdo 57 of 1945, were watered down in 1961, still more in 1967 and culminated in *normas minimas*. As usual in Bogotá, specific circumstances precipitated a response. In this case 30 priests complained to Mayor Urrea about the poor servicing of the low-income *barrios*, probably as a reaction to the wider political contest going on in 1969 and 1970. A major study was commissioned which recommended minimum standards and the regulations were approved without problems by the City Council. The only opposition seems to have come from the water authority. In fact, the intention of the authors of the study was that ICT would become actively involved in sites-and-services schemes, taking the initiative away from the private sector. This has not occurred and ICT have done little in Bogotá; the only institutional response was a small scheme near Suba (La Manuelita) and the notorious Guacamayas development, both established by the Bogotá Housing Agency (CVP).

In Bogotá, therefore, the changing response to low-income settlement is explicable in local and national terms but does not easily fit into the theoretical frameworks described in our introduction. Structural explanations of State action can certainly accommodate the changes in policy but do not explain why they occurred when they did. Instrumentalism helps to explain why the electricity and water services were expanded in the late 'sixties, but this expansion can also be explained by a number of other theories. Ideas such as those of Castells (1977: 1979) about collective consumption are partially correct, but are erroneous insofar as they suggest that the only important stimulus to State action was the need to reproduce labour power. The most plausible explanation of water and electricity service expansion is the requirements of industrial and commercial interests. Clearly, the changes that have occurred are those required to maintain the existing economic, social and political system. A political threat was posed to the system in the late 'sixties by ANAPO, an economic threat was posed by the lack of infrastructure and public services and a social threat was apparent given the low-income areas' support for the non-establishment ANAPO. The outcome was a response by the political authorities both to increase the efficiency of the city economy and to improve the servicing and legalization possibilities of the low-income settlements. It has been partially successful but no more. It is likely that a new crisis will appear soon which will require new responses of the authorities. The difficulty with the available theories is that they neither suggest the form of that crisis nor the likely response to it.

CONCLUSION

Our concluding remarks are brief for two reasons: first, many points have already been presented in our review of the literature and within the two case studies; second, much of our analysis forms part of a wider study that is, as yet, unfinished.[22] Our intention is merely to draw some tentative conclusions concerning theory about the nature and role of the State and about the role that low-income housing plays in the Latin American urban economy.

Earlier, we expressed doubts about the ability of any single theory or perspective to account for the complexity of State intervention in cities such as Mexico and Bogotá; we believe our case studies confirm our original doubts. In neither city have we found evidence wholly consistent with an instrumentalist perspective. Certainly, the State has sometimes acted to favour particular groups among the dominant classes. However, the evidence suggests that on occasion non-dominant groups have also benefited and the ability of particular groups or even of the dominant class as a whole to manipulate the governmental system is limited. In particular, the interests of one group is normally constrained by the actions of rival groups and by the regular change of government every four or six years. The change of government personnel rarely allows one favoured group to continue its privileged access to the State machine across administrations. Certain groups always maintain better access to the State than others, but the State can hardly be described as an instrument of those groups.

Structuralist explanations are more consistent with our evidence. In both cities, the State has favoured the massive accumulation of capital by maintaining social and political stability, by squeezing wage levels and by creating profitable opportunities for the private sector. The State has also acted in a legitimizing capacity; in order to facilitate the social reproduction of the labour force, tactical retreats have occurred and improvements have been made in the physical conditions of low-income groups. Such modifications in policy have normally occurred only after political or social stability has been threatened. Unfortunately, it is the weakness of structuralist theory that evidence of compatability is insufficient proof of its viability as a theory. The fact that the general conditions for capital accumulation are maintained by the State is consistent with the theory but the theory is incapable of explaining why specific actions took place at specific times. Structuralism is capable of explaining both the grinding down of the working class by authoritarian governments and the improvement of conditions for the poor. Since nothing is precluded, nothing is explained.

Earlier, we pointed to the shortcomings of both pluralist theoretical approaches, which emphasize the political autonomy of State institutions from society, and more recent managerialist perspectives which credit the bureaucracy with power to articulate policies according to its own rules. A principal weakness of the latter approach is indeterminacy: who or what shapes the rules of the bureaucracy? Although we eschew many of the assumptions embodied within both sets of arguments we feel that any theory of the State should allow for the very significant impact that autonomous institutions and individuals may make upon the urban process. Of course, such groups are normally drawn from dominant social groups. Nevertheless, our case studies demonstrate that at particular conjunctures, specific institutions and individuals play critical roles. Obviously, such policies do not occur in a political, economic or social vacuum. We are also aware that State institutions may exercise covert functions which undermine or counteract the overt tasks for which they were created, but despite this many of the institutions which we studied could not conveniently be located within either a structuralist or an instrumentalist design.

In short, we are arguing that no single theory alone is adequate. This is an unsatisfactory conclusion given that we are unable to offer any suitable alternative: perhaps, however, any satisfactory theory must embrace different elements of several strands of analysis (Saunders, 1980). Perhaps, the nature of the contemporary State is so complex and ever changing that it is an impossible task to try to pin it down? Perhaps, we can go no further than to identify the main forces shaping policy at any given point in space and time?

In our two case studies we have demonstrated the ways in which the development of low-income housing has benefited different sectors of society, both rich and poor. Whatever the problems facing the poor the low-income housing system is an integral element of the Latin American urban economy. Of course, there is no doubt that the needs of the poor rank low among the priorities of the State. At worst, their poverty is accentuated, at best the State intervenes to protect them from the worst excesses of exploitation and misery. In our analysis of the allocation of land we have observed how the Mexican and Colombian States have favoured private landowners at the expense of the poor and even of middle-income groups. As such, little effort has been made to tax land speculators or to harness the innovativeness of the poor through State-sponsored land developments. Actions against the private sector have been limited and usually directed to control individual excesses rather than to modify the wider process. State help for low-income settlements is most likely under the following circumstances.

Firstly, where the poor have raised a serious threat to social stability or the legitimacy of the political system. In the first instance, the State will seek to appease the demands of the poor and to 'defuse' any threat of subsequent demands, through cooptation, institutionalization and/or repression. In both

Mexico City and Bogotá, political crises which threatened the established order resulted in major policy changes.

Secondly, where the State has acted to foster capital accumulation the poor have sometimes benefited as a secondary outcome of that process. Both cities saw massive increases in the capacity of the water and electricity agencies during the last decade, primarily in response to the demands of industrial and commercial capital. As noted for Bogotá such improvements were made primarily to allow economic expansion but in the process, spare capacity was created which could be used to help low-income communities. These agencies employed technical, bureaucratic criteria in their operations and charged the poor for services. And where, as in Mexico, the widespread illegality of land tenure prevented the recouping of installation costs, the pace of servicing was slowed. Nevertheless, the services arrived and an interesting paradox is posed. Unlike the situation in many Latin American countries where it is arguable that bureaucratic authoritarianism has been a force harming the poor, in the special circumstances pertaining in Bogotá and Mexico, such technically-based institutions have probably helped them. By contrast, the policy of those organizations which have been overtly designed to help low-income groups, have often been guided by considerations of social control, manipulation of demand making, the reduction of public expenditure and, sometimes, the enlisting of partisan political support.

Thirdly, State help is more likely where the government can combine assistance to low-income groups with furthering its own interest. For example, in Mexico City, where there has been growing realization that land regularization could help remedy the doubtful tenure situation of many low-income groups while helping to recoup the costs of service installation, increasing land and registration tax revenues and reinforcing the ideology of the 'good citizen'.

It is important to note that neither the needs of the poor nor the ideal of greater social justice has been the prime motive of State action. The three circumstances which favour State intervention have all helped the poor incidentally as the outcome of other priorities. However, if we are correct, over the next few years the level of State involvement in low-income settlements is likely to rise, become more technically bureaucratic, more sophisticated in its approach and, perhaps, even to lead to substantial physical improvements for the urban poor. Structural changes may be desirable, but it is not inevitable that the poorer groups in society will actually get poorer.

GLOSSARY

ANAPO   Alianza Nacional Popular
AURIS   Acción Urbana y de Integración Social
BNHUOPSA   Banco Nacional Hipotecaria Urbano de Obras Públicas, S.A.

CAR   Corporación Autonoma Regional de la Sabana de Bogotá y de
              los Valles de Ubaté y Chiquinquirá
CNC   Confederación Nacional de Campesinos
CNOP   Confederación Nacional de Organizaciones Populares
CODEUR   Comisión de Desarrollo Urbano
COPEVI   Centro Operacional de Poblamiento y de Vivienda
CoReTT   Comisión para la Regularización de la Tenencia de la Tierra
CTM   Confederación de Trabajadores Méxicanos
CVP   Caja de Vivienda Popular
DANE   Departamento Administrativo Nacional de Estadística
DAPD   Departamento Administrativo de Planeación Distrital
DDF   Departamento del Distrito Federal
EAAB   Empresa de Agua y Alcantarillado de Bogotá D.E.
EEEB   Empresa de Energia Electrica de Bogotá
FIDEURBE   Fideicomiso de Desarrollo Urbano
FINEZA   Fideicomiso de Netzahualcóyotl
ICT   Instituto de Crédito Territorial
INDECO   Instituto de Desarrollo de la Comunidad
INDERENA   Instituto de Desarrollo de los Recursos Naturales Renovables
INFONAVIT   Instituto Nacional del Fondo de Vivienda para los Trabajadores
INVI   Instituto Nacional de Vivienda
PRI   Partido Revolucionario Institucional
SAHOP   Secretaría de Asentamientos Humanos y Obras Públicas
SIB   Superintendencia Bancaria
SRA   Secretaría de Reforma Agraria

ACKNOWLEDGMENTS

This paper is the outcome of a major research project underway at University College entitled 'Public Intervention, Housing and Land Use in Latin American cities'. The project, directed by the authors, is financed by the Overseas Development Administration and involves a comparative analysis of the cities of Bogotá, Mexico City and Valencia. Fieldwork took place between September 1978 and October 1979. Thanks and recognition are due to Dr. James Murray, Ms. Ann Raymond, Mr. William Bell and Dr. Carlos Zorro Sánchez for their contributions to the project's success and vitality.

NOTES

1. We will use the term low-income settlement throughout this paper. Although it is
    an inadequate term it does avoid some of the innuendos implicit in such adjectival
    epithets as irregular, illegal, spontaneous, shanty, and unconventional settlements.
    In this paper we are including only those settlements which have been formed in

some state of illegality; whether that illegality be an outright land invasion or merely infringing the regulations on building standards or zoning. We are specifically excluding rental areas formed in what was once conventional middle-income or élite housing.

2. The project is concerned essentially with how resources connected to housing are distributed in Latin American cities. It examines the relationships between the urban poor and the State in the housing context.

3. Footnote on the Poulantzas–Miliband debate summarized in Lukes (1978: 666–7).

4. In 1979 the minimum wage in Mexico City was approximately 170 U.S. dollars a month.

5. The recipients of land allocated to an *ejidal* community under the Agrarian Reform Programme. *Ejidatarios* have usufruct rights only over their agricultural land parcels.

6. The imposition of rent controls appears to have been a strategy aimed primarily at reducing inflation and pressure upon wages rather than an attempt by real-estate developers to pull the carpet from under the rental market (COPEVI, 1977: 30). Nevertheless, the effect was to reduce turnover of inner-city rental accommodation and to accentuate the centrifugal movement outwards (Ward, 1976b).

7. Our fieldwork in one settlement in Ecatepec suggests that the then Governor embargoed lands after the failure of the owners to improve the agricultural status of the lands. Part of the area was then made over to a development company (*Cia. Constructora Texcoco S.A.*) which, from 1962 onwards began to sell off plots as *granjas*—a sort of market garden. This ploy avoided the requirement to install services. At the outset, settlement leaders were paid by the company officials and there were also clear financial overlaps with the municipal authorities.

8. See articles 90 and 91 of the Agrarian Reform Law the provisions of which allow carpenters, school teachers, etc. who play an integral role in the ejido to own a residential plot in the urban zone. It is the liberal interpretation of these provisions by the *ejidal* community that often leads to the influx of large numbers of residents whose jobs and place of employment bears no relation to the *ejido*.

9. Data collected from the Agrarian Reform Ministry Archive on Padierna and from discussions with Lic. Eduardo Miranda, currently engaged upon a detailed historical account of the area.

10. Lands which are particularly subject to threats of invasion and subsequent attempts at eradication are those located in the southern districts and especially Tlalpán. During the period of fieldwork many attempts to occupy the lower slopes of Ajusco were initiated by a maverick farmworkers' union (*Unión libre de campesinos y colonos del Estado de México*). On every occasion they were removed, even ignoring legitimate writs (*amparos*) taken out by some would-be settlers. More recently, there is evidence that a large area held since the mid-1960s by squatters in the infamous settlement of 2 October in Ixtacalco was subject to police removal (*Guardian*, 3 March 1981).

11. This policy is rare in Mexico City, largely for the reasons outlined in the text. The practice was adopted in the Delegación Gustavo Madero where a fence was erected along a certain contour of the Sierra Guadalupe. Above the line shacks were subject to removal and would not receive services.

12. For example: AURIS and FINEZA in the State of Mexico; CoReTT and INDECO nationally; Procuradaría de Colonias Populares and FIDEURBE in the Federal District.

13. For example CODEUR estimated that in order to carry out restricted and selective development programmes that fell within its remit it would require an annual budget of 27 billion pesos a year between 1978–82. Aiming at a realistic figure it

drew up a reduced programme at an annual cost of 7.3 billion pesos. In 1978, it received a derisory 450 millions which barely covered salaries and 'cheap' schemes such as regularization of land tenancy (CODEUR, 1979: 36).

14. The National Front was a sixteen-year coalition between the Conservative and Liberal parties. The parties agreed to alternate the presidency and divide government posts equally. It lasted from 1958 to 1974 but certain components continued during both the López Michelsen and the Turbay Ayala administrations. It was highly successful in re-establishing civilian rule to Colombia.

15. As we shall argue they rarely take such action but it is important for the authorities to have such powers when they require them.

16. Several of these invasions were very close to being pirate urbanizations and opinions differ between the planning authorities, the owners, the population and different political groups about the exact status of particular settlements. We have included all *barrios* which have been referred to as invasions either in the press or in planning documents.

17. Unlike the Mexican *ejidos* which were established by the 1917 Constitution the *ejidos* (*resguardos indígenas*) stem from the colonial period. The *resguardo* was instituted by the Spanish to protect the Indians and to give them an inalienable agricultural base. The land was to be worked and owned communally, it could not be sold or transferred by an individual or by the community.

18. The *Bogotazo* was a major riot brought about by the assassination of the popular Liberal leader Jorge Eliécer Gaitan. It almost caused the fall of the Conservative government and was a principal element in spreading violence in the whole of Colombia.

19. In fact, this successful experiment helped to convince the agency of the value of pumping. It is pertinent to note, however, that Casablanca was especially favoured in its petitioning to the authority by having the Mayor of Bogotá as one of its immediate neighbours.

20. As was indeed suggested under a 1978 proposal for a new city planning ordinance.

21. Many Colombians in fact believe that he did win the election but was unable to take power.

22. Public intervention, housing and land use in Latin American cities — see Acknowledgments.

REFERENCES

Arias, J. (1974). *Estudio de estratificación socioeconómica de los barrios de Bogotá.* Bogotá D.E. DAPD.

Bataillon, C. and D'Arc, H. R. (1973). *La Ciudad de México.* Sepsetentas, México DF.

Bell, W. S. (1981). *Tilting at Windmills: Considerations on the Nature of the State.* University College London, Department of Geography. Mimeo.

Berry, R. A., Hellman, R. G. and Solaun, M. (eds.) (1980). *Politics of Compromise: Coalition Government in Colombia.* Transaction Books.

BIMSA (Bureau de Investigación de Mercados, S.A.) (1974). *Mapa mercadológico del area metropolitana de la Ciudad de México.* Mimeo.

BNHUOPSA (1966). *Obras para México, Numéro especial.* México DF.

Bogotá, D. E. (1979a). *Presupuesto 1979.*

Bogotá, D. E. (1979b). *Proyectos de presupuesto de las entidades descentralizadas y los fondos rotatorios de Bogotá D.E. 1979.*

Bogotá, DAPD (Departamento Administrativo de Planeación Distrital) (1978). *Normas mínimas de urbanización y de servicios. Consideraciones a su aplicación.* Mimeo.

Bogotá, Servicio Seccional de Salud (1977). *Plan de Salud 1977.* Bogotá.

Bogotá, DAPD (1973). *Mercadeo de tierras en barrios clandestinos en Bogotá.* Mimeo.
Bromley, R. J. and Gerry, C. (eds.) (1979). *Casual Work and Poverty in Third World Cities.* John Wiley.
Burgess, R. (1978). 'Petty commodity housing or dweller control? A critique of John Turner's views on housing policy', *World Development* 6, 1105–34.
Cardona, R. (1969). *Las invasiones de terrenos urbanos.* Tercer Mundo.
Carroll, A. (1980). *Pirate Subdivisions and the Market for Residential Lots in Bogotá.* City Study Project Paper Number 7. The World Bank.
Castells, M. (1979). *City, Class and Power.* Macmillan.
Castells, M. (1977). *The Urban Question: a Marxist Approach.* Edward Arnold. Original French edition 1972.
CENAC (Centro Estadístico Nacional de la Construcción) (1975). *Inversiones y Construcciones del Instituto de Crédito Territorial 1942–1975.* Bogotá.
CEU (Centro de Estudios Urbanos) (1977). *La intervención del estado y el problema de la Vivienda: Valencia.* CEU, Caracas.
Cepeda, F. and Mitchell, B. (1980). 'The trend towards technocracy: the World Bank and the International Labour Organization in Colombian politics.' In Berry *et al.* (eds.), 237–56.
Cisneros, A. (No date). *La colonia El Sol.* Mimeo.
Cleaves, P. S. (1974). *Bureaucratic Politics and Administration in Chile.* California University Press.
CODEUR (Comisión de Desarrollo Urbano) (1979). *Programa de acciones y presupuesto 1979–1982.* Mimeo.
Collier, D. (1976). *Squatters and Oligarchs: Authoritarian Rule and Policy Change in Peru.* Johns Hopkins Press.
COPEVI (1977). *La producción de vivienda en la zona metropolitana de la Ciudad de México.* México DF.
COPEVI (1976). *Análisis del Comportamiento del mercado de bienes raices en la zona metropolitana de la Ciudad de México.* Capítulo, F, Mimeo.
Cornelius, W. A. (1975). *Politics and the Migrant Poor in Mexico City.* Stanford University Press.
Cornelius, W. A. and Kemper, R. V. (eds.) (1978). Latin American Urban Research Volume 6, *Metropolitan Latin America: the Challenge and the Response.* Sage.
Cornelius, W. A. and Trueblood, F. M. (eds.) (1975). Latin American Urban Research Volume 5, *Urbanization and Inequality.* Sage.
DANE (Departamento Administrativo Nacional de Estadística) (1978). *La población en Colombia.* Bogotá.
DANE (1977). *La vivienda en Colombia, 1973.* Bogotá.
DANE (1972). *Colombia política: estadísticas 1935–1970.* Bogotá.
DDF (Departamento del Distrito Federal) (1980). *Plan de desarrollo urbano: Plan general del plan director.* Versión abreviada, DF.
DDF (1979). *Plan hidráulico del Distrito Federal.* Report by the Dirección General de Construcción y Operación Hidráulica.
Dietz, H. (1977). 'Land invasion and consolidation: a study of working poor/ governmental relations in Lima, Peru', *Urban Anthropology* 6, 371–85.
Dix, R. H. (1980). *Political Oppositions under the National Front.* In Berry, R. A. *et al.* (eds.), 131–80.
Doebele, W . (1975). *The Private Market and Low-income Urbanization in Developing Countries: the 'Pirate' Subdivisions of Bogotá.* Harvard University, Department of City and Regional Planning, Discussion Paper D75–11.
Dowse, R. E. and Hughes, J. A. (1972). *Political Sociology.* John Wiley.
Durand, J. (1978). *La ciudad invade el ejido.* Mimeo.

Dunleavy, P. (1980). *Urban Political Analysis: the Politics of Collective Consumption.* Macmillan.

Eckstein, S. E. (1977). *The Poverty of Revolution: the State and the Urban Poor in Mexico.* Princeton University Press.

Fagen, R. and Tuohy, W. (1972). *Politics and Privilege in a Mexican City.* Stanford University Press.

Ferras, R. (1978). *Ciudad Netzahualcóyotl: un barrio en vía de absorcion por la Ciudad de México, Centro de Estudios Sociológicos.* El Colegio de México.

Foster, D. W. (1975). *Survival Strategies of Low-income Households in a Colombian City.* Doctoral dissertation, University of Illinois, Urbana-Champaign.

Fox, D. J. (1972). 'Patterns of morbidity and mortality in Mexico City', *Geographical Review* **62**, 151–86.

Frieden, B. (1965/6). 'The search for a housing policy in Mexico City', *Town Planning Review* **36**, 75–90.

Fuentes, A. L. and Losada, R. (1978). 'Implicaciones socioeconómicas de la ilegalidad en la tenencia de la tierra urbana de Colombia', *Coyuntura económica* **8**, 1–28.

Garza, G. and Schteingart, M. (1978). 'Mexico City: the emerging metropolis.' In Cornelius, W. and Kemper, R. (eds.), 51–85.

Gilbert, A. G. (1981a). 'Bogotá: an analysis of power in an urban setting.' In Pacione, M. (ed.), *Urban Problems and Planning in the Modern World.* Croom Helm, 65–93.

Gilbert, A. G. (1981b). 'Pirates and Invaders: Land Acquisition in Urban Colombia and Venezuela', *World Development* **9**, 657–678.

Gilbert, A. G. (1978). 'Bogotá: politics, planning and the crisis of lost opportunities.' In Cornelius, W. A. and Kemper, R. V. (eds.), 87–126.

Gilbert, A. G. (1975). 'Urban and regional development programmes in Colombia since 1951.' In Cornelius, W. A. and Trueblood, F. M. (eds.), 241–76.

Gilbert, A. G. and Gugler, J. (1982). *Cities, Poverty and Development: Urbanization in the Third World.* Oxford University Press.

Grindle, M. S. (1977). *Bureaucrats, Politicians and Peasants in Mexico: a Case Study in Public Policy.* University of California Press.

Guerrero, Ma. T. *et al.* (1974). *La tierra, especulación y fraude en el Fraccionamiento Nuevo Paseo de San Agustín.* Mimeo.

Harloe, M. (1977). *Captive Cities.* John Wiley.

Holloway, J. and Picciotto, S. (eds.) (1978). *State and Capital: a Marxist Debate.* Edward Arnold.

ICT (Instituto de Crédito Territorial) (1976). *Inventario de zonas subnormales y proyectos de desarrollo progresivo.* Bogotá.

Inkeles, A. (1969). 'Participant citizenship in six developing countries', *American Political Science Review* **63**.

INVI (Instituto Nacional de Vivienda) (1958). *Colonias proletarias: problemas y soluciones.* México DF.

Kowarick, L. (1975). *Capitalismo e marginalidade na America Latina.* Paz e Terra, Rio de Janeiro.

Kusnetzoff, F. (1975). 'Housing policies or housing politics: an evaluation of the Chilean experience', *Journal of Interamerican Studies and World Affairs* **17**, 281–310.

Leeds, A. and Leeds, E. (1976). 'Accounting for behavioural differences: three political systems and the responses of squatters in Brazil, Peru and Chile.' In Walton, J. and Masotti, L. H. (eds.), *The City in Comparative Perspective.* Halsted Press, 193–248.

Lewis, O. (1966). *La Vida: a Puerto Rican Family in the Culture of Poverty.* San Juan and New York, Random House.

López Díaz, C. (1978). *La intervención del estado en la formación de un asentamiento proletario: el caso de la colonia Ajusco, tésis de licenciatura*. Departamento de Antropología, Universidad Iberoamericana, DF.

Losada, R. (1980). 'Electoral participation.' In Berry, R. A. *et al.* (eds.) (1980), 87–104.

Losada, R. and Gómez, H. (1976). *La tierra en el mercado pirata de Bogotá*. Fedesarrollo, Bogotá.

Lozano, E. (1975). 'Housing the urban poor in Chile: contrasting experiences under "Christian Democracy" and "Unidad Popular".' In Cornelius, W. A. and Trueblood, F. M. (eds.), 177–196.

Lubell, H. and McCallum, D. (1978). *Bogotá, Urban Development and Employment*. International Labour Office.

Lukes, S. (1978). 'Power and authority.' In Bottomore, T. B. and Nisbet, R. A., *A History of Sociological Analysis*. Heinemann, 633–76.

Mangin, W. (1967). 'Latin American squatter settlements: a problem and a solution', *Latin American Research Review* **2**, 65–98.

Martin de la Rosa (1975). *Netzahualcóyotl: un fenómeno*. Testimonios del Fondo, México DF.

Miliband, R. (1977). *Marxism and Politics*. Oxford University Press.

Miliband, R. (1969). *The State in Capitalist Society*. Weidenfeld and Nicolson.

Millikan, M. F. and Blackmer, D. L. M. (1961). *The Emerging Nations*. Little, Brown and Co., Boston.

Mohan, R. and Hartline, N. (1979). *The Poor of Bogotá: Who They Are, What They Do and Where They Live*. Mimeo. The World Bank.

Montaño, J. (1976). *Los pobres de la ciudad de México en los Asentamientos Espontáneos*, Siglo XXI.

Muñoz, H., De Oliviera, O. and Stern, C. (1973). 'Migración y marginalidad ocupacional en la ciudad de México.' In Castells, M. (ed.), *Imperialismo y Urbanización en América Latina*. Gustavo Gili, Barcelona.

Nalven, J. (1978). *The Politics of Urban Growth: a Case Study of Community Formation in Cali, Colombia*. Doctoral dissertation, University of California San Diego.

Nelson, J. M. (1979). *Access to Power: Politics and the Urban Poor in Developing Nations*. Princeton University Press.

Nelson, J. M. (1969). *Migrants, Urban Poverty, and Instability in Developing Countries*. Occasional Paper 22, Centre for International Affairs, Harvard University.

Nun, J. (1969). 'Sobrepoblación relativa, ejército industrial de reserva y masa marginal', *Revista Latinoamericana de Sociología* **4**, 178–237.

Oliveira, F. de (1972). 'A economia brasileira: crítica à razão dualista', *Estudos CEBRAP* **2**, 3–82.

Pahl, R. E. (1975). *Whose City?* Penguin.

Paredes, L-R. and Martínez, L-G. (1977). *Alternativa para la solución del problema de la vivienda para grupos de bajos ingresos: el sector privado y las Normas Mínimas*. Paper presented to INTERHABITAT Medellín.

Peattie, L. (1974). 'The concept of "marginality" as applied to squatter settlements.' In Cornelius, W. and Trueblood, F. (eds.), *Latin American Urban Research*, **4**, 101–9.

Perlman, J. (1976). *The Myth of Marginality: Urban Poverty and Politics in Rio de Janeiro*. University of California Press.

Portes, A. (1979). 'Housing policy, urban poverty, and the state: the favelas of Rio de Janeiro, 1972–76', *Latin American Research Review* **14**, 3–24.

Poulantzas, N. (1973). *Political Power and Social Classes*. New Left Books.

Pradilla, E. (1976). 'Notas acerca del "problema de la vivienda" ', *Ideología y Sociedad* **16**, 70–107.

Quijano, A. (1974). 'The marginal pole of the economy and the marginalized labour force', *Economy and Society* **3**, 393–428.

Roberts, B. (1978). *Cities of Peasants: the Political Economy of Urbanization in the Third World.* Edward Arnold/Sage.

Saunders, P. (1980). *Urban Politics: a Sociological Interpretation.* Penguin. First published 1979.

Smith, P. (1979). *Labyrinths of Power: Political Recruitment in Twentieth-century Mexico.* Princeton University Press.

Stevenson, R. (1979). *Housing Programs and Policies in Bogotá: an Historical/ Descriptive Analysis.* World Bank City Study Research Project RPO, 671–47.

Svenson, G. (1977). *El desarrollo económico departamental 1960–1975.* Inandes, Bogotá.

Tello, C. (1978). *La política económica en México, 1970–1976.* Siglo XXI.

Turner, J. F. C. (1968). 'Housing priorities, settlement patterns and urban development in modernizing countries', *Journal of the American Institute of Planners* **34**, 354–63.

Unikel, L. (1972). *La dinámica del crecimiento de la Ciudad de México.* Fundación para estudios de población, México DF.

Valladares, L. do Prado (1978). 'Working the system: squatter response to resettlement in Rio de Janeiro', *International Journal of Urban and Regional Research* **2**, 12–25.

Vernez, G. (1973). *Bogotá's Pirate Settlements: an Opportunity for Metropolitan Development.* Unpublished doctoral dissertation, University of California, Berkeley.

Ward, P. M. (1981a). 'Political pressure for urban services: the response of two Mexico City administrations', *Development and Change* **12**, 379–407.

Ward, P. M. (1981b). 'Urban problems and planning in Mexico City.' In Pacione, M. (1981). *Urban Problems and Planning in the Developing World.* Croom Helm, 28–64.

Ward, P. M. (1976a). *In Search of a Home: Social and Economic Characteristics of Squatter Settlements and the Role of Self-help Housing in Mexico City.* Unpublished Ph.D. dissertation, University of Liverpool.

Ward, P. M. (1976b), 'Intra-city migration to squatter settlements in Mexico City', *Geoforum* **7**, 369–83.

Ward, P. M. (1976c). 'The squatter settlement as slum or housing solution: the evidence from Mexico City', *Land Economics* **52**, 330–46.

Webb, R. (1975). 'Public policy and regional incomes in Peru.' In Cornelius, W. A. and Trueblood, F. M. (eds.), 223–38.

Wionczek, M. A. (1971). *Inversión y tecnología extranjera en América Latina.* Editorial Joaquín Mortiz, México DF.

Zorro Sánchez, C. (1979). *Normas jurídicas y realidad social: la evolución reciente de las disposiciones en materia de urbanismo en Bogotá,* Document for ODA financed project on 'Public intervention, housing and land use in Latin American cities.'

Zorro Sánchez, C. and Gilbert, A. G. (1982). 'Tolerancia o rechazo de los asentamientos urbanos irregulares. El caso de Bogotá', *Revista Interamericana de Planificación.* Forthcoming.

Urbanization in Contemporary Latin America
Edited by A. Gilbert with J. E. Hardoy and R. Ramírez
© 1982 John Wiley & Sons Ltd.

6

Cities of tenants: renting among the urban poor in Latin America

MICHAEL EDWARDS

The spread of owner-occupancy among the urban poor has been one of the most striking features of urbanization in Latin America during the past half century. The appearance of 'irregular' settlements on a large scale after the 1940s reduced the cost of housing and brought ownership within reach of a far larger proportion of the urban poor.[1] As ownership became increasingly common, the role of rental accommodation as a major source of low-cost housing declined. In Colombia, for example, the proportion of rented dwellings in the ten major cities listed in Table 6.1 fell from a range of between 55 and 70 per cent in 1938 to a range of between 32 and 53 per cent in 1973. Not surprisingly, research into low-income housing came to be dominated by analyses of owner-occupancy among the urban poor. Initially, these studies concentrated on the social, economic and political characteristics of individual squatter settlements (Butterworth, 1973; MacEwen, 1974; Lomnitz, 1975; Cornelius, 1975; Perlman, 1976). It was tacitly assumed that owner-occupancy lay within reach of all who wanted it, and that those who wanted it formed the vast majority of the low-income population. More recently, investigations of self-help housing have adopted a more abstract or theoretical approach; they have emphasized the links between housing production and the State, and the ideological role of self-help in maintaining the *status quo* in dependent capitalist societies (Pradilla, 1976; Burgess, 1978).

Renting among the urban poor in Latin America has been virtually ignored by the academic community. The little work that exists associates renting almost exclusively with city-centre tenements and often depicts such accommodation as 'slums of despair', in stark contrast to the 'slums of hope' located in the urban periphery with its supposedly upwardly-mobile owner-occupiers (Stokes, 1962; Valenzuela, 1969; Lloyd, 1979). Renting among low-income groups has come to be regarded in a pejorative light; the influential

Table 6.1   Dwellings rented in 10 major cities of Colombia, 1938–78
(Percentages)

	1938[1]	1951[1]	1964[1]	1973[2]	1978[3]
Barranquilla	58.0	51.9	34.9	32.2	28.5
Bogotá	62.2	56.2	47.9	49.9	43.4
Bucaramanga	68.9	50.9	40.9	52.5	44.0[4]
Cali	56.9	46.6	37.6	41.8	39.5
Cartagena	54.4	49.5	35.6	30.7	NA
Cúcuta	50.6	43.3	38.8	32.7	NA
Ibagué	53.3	47.5	46.0	41.0	NA
Manizales	50.9	57.5	54.1	45.8	51.5
Medellín	60.0	48.9	43.9	42.9	38.4
Pereira	61.8	52.0	51.9	49.2	NA

Notes
1. Censo Nacional de Edificios y Población, DANE, 1938–64. Data for Bucaramanga include Floridablanca. In the 1938 census *all* buildings were included in the calculations; in subsequent censuses only dwellings 'destined for residential use' were included. The effect of this difference is to overestimate the proportion of rented *dwellings* in 1938.
2. La Vivienda en Colombia, DANE, 1973. Data for Bucaramanga exclude Floridablanca.
3. Encuesta Nacional de Hogares, stage 16, DANE, 1978. Data for Bucaramanga exclude Floridablanca.
4. 54.5 per cent in 1979. Ten per cent sample survey, Edwards, M., 1979. Data include Floridablanca. All data (except 1979) refer to total urban population regardless of income level.

works on housing in Latin America by Turner (1968; 1976) and others lauded the virtues of self-help ownership and saw renting merely as a preliminary stage in the residential and occupational careers of low-income households. The assumption that access to owner-occupation among low-income groups is unrestricted and the idea that central tenements and their residents are representative of poor renters throughout the city are unfounded.

This paper looks in detail at the large but forgotten group who rent accommodation. On the basis of information drawn from the city of Bucaramanga in north-east Colombia, Section One analyzes the factors which determine the relative numbers of owners and renters among the urban poor. Section Two describes the structure of the rental housing market, the different types of tenant, and the patterns of renting which exist in different kinds of low-income settlement. Section Three investigates the nature and scale of landlordism and looks at the nature of the relationship between landlord and tenant. The wider implications of renting, particularly the effects of differences in tenure on material living standards, social mobility, inequality and political activity, form the conclusion to the paper.

Most of the data used in the paper come from a detailed study of renting in Bucaramanga carried out between December 1978 and March 1980. In 1980, Bucaramanga had around 500 000 inhabitants.[2] As far as the author is aware, this is the first major study of renting in any city of Latin America. The

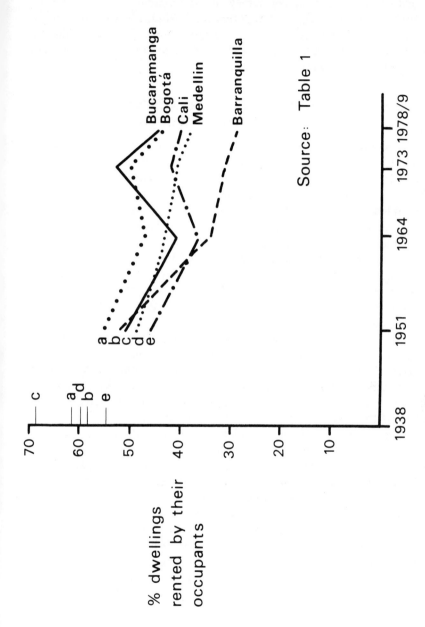

Figure 6.1 Proportion of dwellings rented in Colombia's five largest cities, 1938–79

absence of comparable studies makes it difficult to say whether or not the conclusions of the Bucaramanga survey are representative in any general sense, but similar results have been reported for Bogotá, Mexico City and the Caribbean (Vernez, 1973; Currie, 1978; Clarke and Ward, 1976). While one must be careful in applying the results of the study to urban Latin America as a whole this makes them none the less important.

RENTING AS A MAJOR HOUSING ALTERNATIVE AMONG LOW-INCOME GROUPS

In capitalist economies the satisfaction of housing needs is a positive function of one's ability to pay the market price. Hence, 'choice' in housing is a positive function of income (Molina, 1979; Manrique, 1976). The proportion of the population living in each sector of the housing market, whether rented or owner-occupied, is determined by the distributions of prices of different forms of accommodation and of the incomes of individual households. Those with lowest incomes can afford only the cheapest forms of housing; those with higher incomes have access to a wider range of housing alternatives from which they may make a selection on the basis of personal preference and household needs. Harvey (1973) terms this process 'sequential market bidding', households are forced to compete for the most desirable forms of accommodation in the city.

The results of this bidding process in Bucaramanga are presented in Table 6.2 and shown diagrammatically in Figure 6.2. Each form of housing shown has a different range of prices set by the market, so that the alternatives available to individual households are determined by their level of income. The poorest households in the city are forced into tenement accommodation or to invade land if the opportunity presents itself; better-off families rent rooms outside the tenements where rents are higher; further up the income scale are those who own property in illegal subdivisions ('pirate' settlements), own government housing, or rent an apartment or a unifamily dwelling; at the apex of the hierarchy are those who can afford 'conventional' (commercially-produced) dwellings. A minority of households prefer to rent accommodation even though they are as affluent as most owner-occupiers. Their case is examined in more detail in Section Two, but it is important to recognize that residential decisions are not governed exclusively by income because owner-occupation is not a universal ideal among the urban poor.

However, most households regard renting as a secondary housing alternative: the major role that renting plays in the low-income housing market in Bucaramanga is overwhelmingly a negative response to shortages in the supply of cheap land rather than a positive response to variations in housing preferences among the urban poor. In fact, all the 180 renters interviewed expressed a desire to own property; in this respect the poor of Bucaramanga

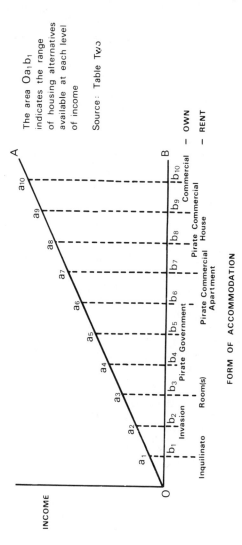

Figure 6.2   The price of different types of accommodation in Bucaramanga

seem no different to their counterparts elsewhere in urban Latin America (Turner, 1968; 1976).[3] The decision of renters is logical given the material and 'existential' benefits conferred by ownership. In the long term, ownership is cheaper than renting.[4] In addition, as John Turner and others have stressed repeatedly, ownership carries with it a series of intangible benefits (such as security, privacy, independence and 'something to leave to one's children') which make it an overwhelmingly attractive housing alternative for poor families.

Table 6.2   The structure of the low-income housing market in Bucaramanga

Submarket	Mean income from employ-ment of head of house-hold/month[1]	Mean household income/ month	Housing costs: mean lot/ house price or mean rent	% of total low-income population
(a) Owner-occupation				
Commercial	4 260	8 450	379 000	16.9
Pirate	4 520	7 480	40–50 000[2]	12.2
Government[3]	5 000	NA	110 000	8.6
Invasion[4]	3 760	4 800	0–20 000	4.3
(b) Rental accommodation				
Commercial (room)	3 630	4 170	896	
Pirate (room)	3 910	4 490	1 057	30.1
Government (room)	NA	NA	1 000	
Commercial (flat)	8 100	10 350	2 558	
Pirate (flat)	6 000	8 270	2 471	8.9
Government (flat)	NA	NA	2 000	
Commercial (house)	7 300	11 800	3 997	
Pirate (house)	5 420	8 400	2 419	13.9
Government (house)	NA	NA	5 000	

Notes
1. Unless otherwise stated all data from the Bucaramanga survey in Colombian pesos of 1979. (Approximate exchange rate: U.S. $1 = 40 pesos.) Housing costs for owners = mean house price in 1979; for renters = mean rent.
2. Mean lot price, 1979, *Barrio* Bucaramanga.
3. Data from ICT, Department of Social Work, Bucaramanga.
4. Data from Lucy de Concha, CDMB, Bucaramanga.

The main advantages of renting, lower short-term housing costs and greater residential flexibility, are of limited importance to most low-income households who see themselves as permanent urban residents. But while ownership is an almost universal ideal it requires a substantial initial capital investment. Unless land is free, ownership is an expensive housing alternative and one closed to the poorest members of the urban poor. Thus, rental housing has a 'residual' character, its importance relative to other forms of accommodation is determined by the factors which limit access to owner-occupation rather than by the number of households who positively prefer renting (Zorro and Revéiz, 1974).

The factors which govern access to home ownership can be grouped into three major categories:

(i) The prices of marketable land and of construction materials, which depend on the pattern of land ownership, the physical amount of land available for purchase, the structure of the building and materials industries, and the prosperity and income levels of the local economy.
(ii) The availability of 'free' land, at root a function of the manner in which the local State and local landowners respond to the invasion of land.
(iii) The supply of new or used dwellings, mainly subsidized public housing since the price of conventional housing puts it beyond the reach of the urban poor.

The ways in which these factors interact vary by city and through time so that levels of ownership vary considerably. Prior to the appearance of irregular settlements in Bucaramanga, the great majority of low-income households lived in rental accommodation.[5] During the late 1940s and early 1950s invasions and illegal subdivisions began to spread over what was then the urban periphery, providing low-income households with the opportunity to acquire a lot on a scale never before experienced. The initial expansion of irregular settlement (nine subdivisions and three invasions) met with little resistance from the municipal authorities. Since the land on which the squatter settlements were founded was owned by the Municipal Council, these invasions did not threaten directly the interests of the local élite; there was still a good deal of vacant land for development in the metropolitan area and the number of illegal settlements was too small to merit intervention by the local state.[6]

The trend towards low-income ownership was reinforced by a boom in the number of houses built by the national housing agency, ICT, during the early 1960s. With the aid of major loans under the auspices of the 'Alliance for Progress', ICT built a large number of cheap dwellings; approximately 60 per cent of all low-income housing units erected in Bucaramanga in 1961 and 1962.[7] Because Bucaramanga had only 225 000 inhabitants at the time, the construction boom had a tremendous impact on the supply of low-income housing. Together with the expansion of irregular settlement it produced a steady decline in the proportion of poor households living in rented accommodation (Table 6.1).

Around 1970, the situation changed dramatically. The plateau over which Bucaramanga had grown was now almost entirely covered by residential development, and in the neighbouring municipality of Floridablanca vacant land was overwhelmingly privately-owned and subject to strict zoning regulations. There was very little land for low-income groups to be found anywhere in the metropolitan area. Only two pirate settlements were founded after 1970, and irregular settlement continued to grow only through 'accretion'. The position was exacerbated by a change in the attitude of local government toward invasions. The 'slum eradication plan' of 1965 aimed to remove every 'squatter settlement' in the metropolitan area and relocate displaced families in new State housing projects in the far east of the city (Valencia *et al.*, 1966; Celis and Vargas, 1975). In contrast to pirate subdivisions, which were legalized quickly and serviced efficiently, invasions were viewed with considerable hostility by the Municipal Council. Indeed, Bucaramanga was made something of a 'test case' in a nationwide attempt to eradicate what were seen as centres of social pathology and potential extremism. No doubt, the fact that most of the more recent invasions in Bucaramanga were founded on privately owned land gave an additional boost to the pretence of philanthropy on the part of the local State. Though only three of the seven invasions were eradicated, the plan signalled the end of the period of expansion of irregular settlement. The demise of the 'Alliance for Progress' during the mid-1960s led to a radical change in the financing of the ICT and forced it to rely increasingly on more expensive private capital. As a result, fewer houses were built, unit prices increased dramatically and low-income households were excluded from government housing, thereby closing a major source of owner-occupied housing for the urban poor (Murillo and Ungar, 1978; Stevenson, 1979). By 1973, the proportion of renters among the urban poor in Bucaramanga had risen to 52.5 per cent, by 1979 to 54.5 per cent (Table 6.1 and Figure 6.1). Today, ownership is the preserve of a minority of low-income families; there is little sign of it becoming more accessible to the poor in the near future.

To what extent can the experience of Bucaramanga be generalized? The proportion of renters among the low-income population varies considerably even among the major cities of Colombia; a range of over 22 percentage points in 1973 (Table 6.1). Theoretically, it should be possible to trace significant interurban variations in each of the major factors which determine access to owner-occupation, but unfortunately the kind of data one requires to make comparisons of this sort are not yet available; temporal variations in real land prices are particularly difficult to identify. One has to be careful in resisting what is essentially a tautological explanation of variations in housing tenure, for example, that certain cities have higher proportions of renters because they have lower proportions of owners, and ask *why* it is that ownership is more accessible in some urban areas than in others.

There appear to be some differences between cities in the physical and social availability of land, in income and price levels, and in the contribution made by central government to the low-income housing stock. But, equally important is the response of the local State to irregular settlement, particularly to the invasion of land. As Gilbert (1981; 1982) has shown, local government attitudes to land invasion vary considerably. Where invasion is strictly controlled or prohibited completely, as in Bogotá and Bucaramanga, larger numbers of low-income households may be forced to live in rented accommodation.

In Mexico City, restrictions on the development of irregular settlement are forcing increasing numbers of poor families to share or rent accommodation (Ward, 1982). However, where squatting is tolerated by local élites, as in Barranquilla, Cartagena and Cúcuta, renting plays a correspondingly lesser role in housing the urban poor.[8] Similarly, in Valencia (Venezuela), where invasions are common, renting is very rare, though in this case legal restrictions on the letting of shacks are an equally important constraint (Gilbert, 1981). The relative importance of each of these factors varies from city to city, but it does seem as if official attitudes toward irregular settlement are crucial in determining what proportion of the low-income population live in rented accommodation.

THE STRUCTURE OF THE RENTAL HOUSING MARKET FOR LOW-INCOME GROUPS IN BUCARAMANGA

Every form of accommodation has a different range of prices. Ownership is cheapest in invasion settlements where costs cover only the building materials, relatively cheap in pirate subdivisions although the land has to be purchased, more expensive in subsidized government housing projects, and most expensive in the commercial housing market. Each of these four sub-markets tends to be occupied by a different income group (Vernez, 1973; Dueñas, 1973; Bender, 1975); among the urban poor there is a broad correlation between household income and type of home ownership (see Table 6.1). But what of the renters? How is the rental housing market structured and how does it correspond to the four submarkets which cater for low-income owner-occupiers?

The few authors who have addressed these questions have usually concluded that each of the four submarkets contains a separate rental sector. Renters in, for example, the pirate settlements can be distinguished from their counterparts in invasions, State housing projects and commercial *barrios* in the same way as owners in each form of settlement can be said to form a distinctive group (Zorro and Revéiz, 1974; Losada and Gómez, 1976). The evidence of the survey shows that this is not true in Bucaramanga. There are only two major submarkets for poor tenants: one for households living in rented rooms (the roomers), and another for tenants of apartments and unifamily dwellings. These two types of rented accommodation have very different prices and there is little movement between them: roomers rarely move to the more expensive forms of rental housing. Whilst the proportions of roomers and higher-income tenants vary considerably between different types of settlement, the form of accommodation in which the tenant lives is more important than the type of *barrio* in which the dwelling is located (Figure 6.3). In practice, this means that tenants living in rooms are very similar wherever they live, while all are very different from the tenants of apartments and

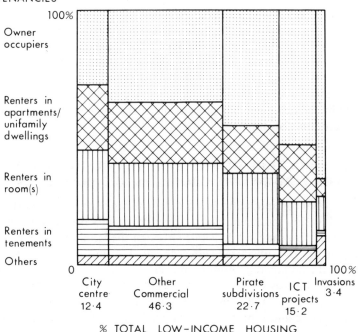

Figure 6.3   The distribution of tenancies in the low-income housing market

unifamily dwellings even in the same street. What differentiates the urban poor is their level of income; not tenure *per se* but the *type* of accommodation which is owned or rented. Also unexpectedly, there are no systematic differences between renters and owners, only between owners and certain types of tenant. The only exceptions to this rule are renters who live in invasion settlements and those who inhabit the tenements of the city-centre, though there are few of the former. Both sets of renters are consistently poorer than owners.

CENTRAL TENEMENTS: MYTH OR REALITY?

Much has been written about tenement accommodation in Latin American cities: *inquilinatos* in Colombia (Giraldo, 1970; Darío, 1970), *vecindades* in Mexico (Lewis, 1961; 1972), *casas de cómodo* in Brazil (Morse, 1971), *conventillos* in Chile (Balanowsky *et al.*, 1974), and *mesones* in El Salvador (SIAP, 1977). Indeed, one might call the central tenement the 'classic' form of urban accommodation for low-income groups in the sense that it is found in most cities and is historically the earliest form of urban housing associated with the poor.[9] However, the image of the decaying urban core, populated by materially and psychologically impoverished tenement dwellers and popularized by Oscar Lewis (1961; 1972) in his descriptions of the 'culture of poverty' in Mexican *vecindades*, is really quite inaccurate. In Bucaramanga, the city centre is an extraordinarily diverse area which exhibits few of the characteristics usually ascribed to it.[10] Central tenements have a character atypical of the rest of the city (Figure 6.4).

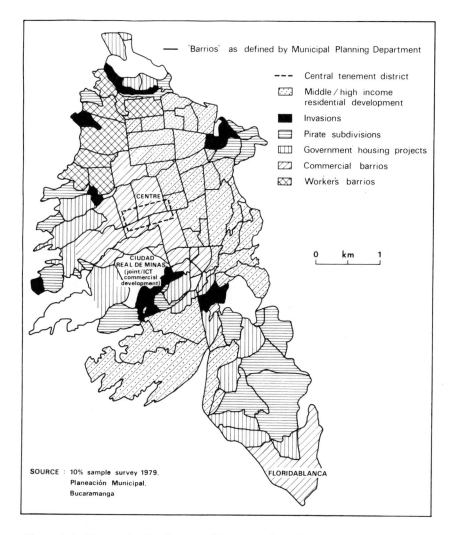

Figure 6.4   The spatial distribution of housing submarkets in Bucaramanga, 1980

As elsewhere in Latin America, the *Bumanguese* élite abandoned the city-centre during the early decades of the present century in favour of detached residential accommodation in the eastern periphery. But, much of what is now the central tenement area never accommodated élite families; in the 1930s and 1940s, the valleys which dissect the city-centre provided low-income households with the opportunity to invade or buy cheaply land in close proximity to the *claustro* dwellings of the élite.[11] A small number of invasion households had no legal tenure until quite recently, though the area was never a 'rental shantytown' like the *ciudades perdidas* of Mexico City (Montaño, 1976; Clarke and Ward, 1976), the *favelas de quinta* of Rio de Janeiro (Morse, 1971), and the *corralones* of El Salvador (SIAP, 1977). Such rental shanty towns are distinguished by the high incidence of renting, the flimsy structure of their dwellings and by the illegality of their tenure, but they seem not to exist in Colombian cities. Nevertheless, variations in land tenure gave the area a diversity which it has never lost.

Former élite dwellings were adapted specifically for subletting. Though floor-plans vary considerably *inquilinatos* are of two basic types: the traditional *claustro* structure with between six and fourteen rooms arranged around a central courtyard; and smaller 'galleries', which developed through sub-division into two or more separate dwellings with between six and ten rooms arranged along one or both sides of the lot. Both types of tenement are single storey with a communal area for washing clothes and a row of shared flush toilets and handbasins. Each family has its own portable two-ring kerosene stove for cooking, though there is usually at least one communal oven for the preparation of larger meals. Ninety per cent of households rent single rooms of 8 or 9 square metres, a tiny space for a family of three or four. Furnishings are spartan: a bed, a small multipurpose table, a few hooks on which to hang clothes, and a few posters and decorations for the walls are the norm. *Inquilinatos* in Bucaramanga are small compared to the tenements reported elsewhere in Latin America;[12] only one-third of those sampled housed over eight families and the largest contained only fifteen households. With rents as low as 500–600 (1979) pesos a month for a single room, the potential rental income even from the largest tenements was only around twice the then current legal monthly minimum wage (3750 pesos). Such low levels of rental income have led to the extreme physical deterioration of tenements in the city centre. Rent controls have had little to do with decay since they have been completely ineffective as regards low-income housing in Colombia.[13] Deterioration occurs despite the fact that over 70 per cent of tenement landlords live on the lot with their tenants; it is an inevitable consequence of the disparity which exists between tenant incomes and the costs of maintaining large dwellings already more than 70 years old. In any case, there is little incentive to maintain tenements since the physical state of the fabric makes little difference to the market value of tenement *land*.

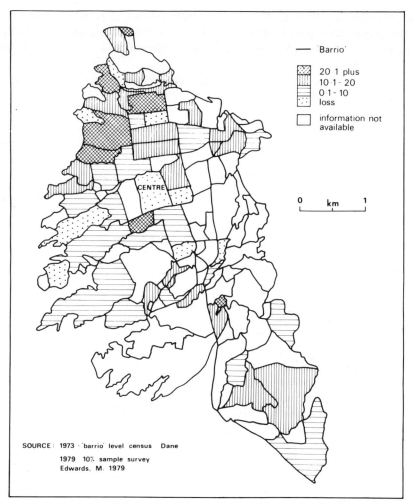

Figure 6.5 Percentage change in the number of households living in rented accommodation by 'barrio', 1973–79

However, *inquilinatos* are uncommon in the city centre and of negligible importance in the low-income housing stock as a whole (Figure 6.5). Twenty-one per cent of tenants interviewed in the centre of Bucaramanga lived in tenements with five or more households, a far higher proportion than elsewhere in the city but much lower than one might expect.[14] The central tenement district is geographically very small: it accommodates no more than nine per cent of the city's low-income population, though even this is higher than the 3 per cent of the 'popular sector' living in the *conventillos* of central Santiago (Balanowsky *et al.*, 1974). It is, therefore, misleading to talk of a central tenement district. The city centre contains a high proportion of the *inquilinatos* but two-thirds of tenants live in rooms with one or two other households, in apartments, or in unifamily dwellings. This is a subtle but important difference.

Pressures from private capital and local government seem set to accelerate still further the decline of the central *inquilinatos* as a source of low-cost accommodation. Although overt co-operation between the local State and private entrepreneurs is rare, both groups wish to see the city centre given over to commercial and high-income residential uses. One of Colombia's most powerful financiers, Carlos Ardilla Lulle, has obtained planning permission to build a covered shopping precinct on vacant land immediately to the east of the main concentration of tenements. This will intensify competition among developers vying for similar sites and inflate land values in the *inquilinato* district. Since the profits to be made from tenements are small when compared to the market value of central land, landlords may be persuaded to sell out and leave the area.

Local government policy reinforces the pressures placed on tenement landlords by commercial redevelopment. Out of a desire to improve traffic circulation in the crowded streets of the central zone the Municipal Council is widening and rerouting the main arterial roads to pass through the tenement areas. In addition, most local planners still view the tenement district as the centre of a 'culture of poverty', crime and prostitution, to be removed in order to make the city centre safer and more attractive.[15]

Most *inquilinato* households are very similar to roomers elsewhere in the city, but there is a small but significant minority whose extreme poverty sets them apart from all other tenants in the city. This minority is found almost exclusively in central *inquilinatos*, hence the area's reputation for containing a 'culture of poverty'. These 5 per cent of households are more disadvantaged than the rest of the urban poor because their household heads have difficulty obtaining higher wage employment. They are much older and are concentrated in the central *inquilinatos* because this was the only form of accommodation available when they arrived in the city during the 1930s and 1940s. They have never been able to leave the central zone because their incomes have remained the lowest in the city, on average one third of the legal monthly minimum wage. Most households rely on a single income. Low-income levels stem partly from the nature of their jobs and partly from the structure of their households. Most of this group are approaching the end of their working lives; the majority of household heads are aged between 55 and 70. Single-person families make up some 40 per cent of the total and over two-thirds of the total are headed by women. Old age and the fact of being a woman in a male-dominated society restrict females to the lowest paid jobs, typically domestic service. Among men, street hawking is most common. In this respect central location has a positive advantage in gaining access to potential customers, but it is also inevitable because wages are so low and rents are lowest in the central tenements (Marris, 1979). Their age and sex condition the kinds of work they do, their occupations determine their incomes, and their incomes decide the kind of housing they can afford. But, they do not belong to a 'culture of poverty'; they are materially not psychologically poor and they exhibit no greater pathological tendency than any other group within the low-income population. Common-law marriages are completely absent, divorce extremely rare, and criminals and prostitutes no more common than elsewhere in the city; most residents of the central *inquilinatos* are too old to be either promiscuous or incestuous!

To view this group as in any sense representative of renters as a whole, or indeed to view tenements as representative of rented accommodation throughout the city, is grossly misleading. Although a minority of young tenants (most obviously single parent families) are similarly disadvantaged in terms of income and employment, the great majority share none of the characteristics of central *inquilinos* and have never lived in a tenement.

RENTING OUTSIDE THE CENTRAL INQUILINATOS: THE UPWARDLY MOBILE TENANT

The second category of low-income tenant is the roomer who does not live in the *inquilinatos*: approximately two-thirds of the renters in the Bucaramanga sample, 30 per cent of the urban poor. They are young families who have spent less than ten years in the housing market, and who are accumulating capital in the hope of purchasing property in the future. Typically, they are male headed nuclear households with two or three young children. Household incomes tend to be some 50 per cent lower than among owner-occupiers because household heads have spent fewer years in the labour market, their spouses rarely work full-time (being engaged in childbearing and childcaring), and their children are too young to work at all. Since the heads earn close to the legal minimum wage they can afford no more than a rented room. Most, however, are likely to benefit from the little upward mobility permitted in Colombia's rigid social structure: age, sex, educational attainment, a foothold in the housing and labour markets, and 'urban experience' are all in their favour (Balán, Browning and Jelín, 1973; Cardona and Simmons, 1977). This does not mean that they will eventually progress to owner-occupation. Rising land and property values may force even upwardly mobile households to remain in rented rooms for longer periods of time. Although the evidence is inconclusive, it seems to be increasingly difficult to find vacant lots in Bucaramanga and increasingly expensive to buy the few that exist.[16] As a result, many households are finding it increasingly difficult to break free from the rental sector.

The third group of tenants, the 20 per cent of the urban poor who rent apartments or unifamily dwellings, are indistinguishable from most low-income owner-occupiers. Both groups of households receive between one and two minimum salaries; their age profiles are very similar; their family structures are identical; and they share common occupational and educational characteristics. Most of these tenants have sufficient capital to buy property but for a variety of reasons they *choose* to rent accommodation. The rationale for this decision is sometimes unclear. Many higher-income tenants are self-employed and invest their savings in small businesses rather than accumulating capital to buy land; they view owner-occupation as a long-term goal but are prepared to sacrifice some measure of independence and security in the short-term. Others value the flexibility of renting and shy away from the responsibilities and commitments of ownership. The important point to note is that ownership is not a universal goal among the urban poor, a conclusion that will come as no surprise to students of low-income housing in Africa and Asia, but which is rarely mentioned in the literature on urban Latin America. The fact that a small group of renters have neither the human nor the material resources to build their own dwellings, and a larger group do not even wish to own land, underlines the need for *flexibility* in the formulation of housing policy.

THE EVOLUTION OF THE RENTAL HOUSING MARKET

The central *inquilinatos* could accommodate the whole low-income renter population only so long as the latter were limited. Despite the fact that vacant lots were available in the periphery during the 1950s and 1960s, demand for rooms inevitably outstripped supply in the city centre. Prior to the foundation of the first irregular settlements in the city the only alternative locations for prospective low-income tenants lay in the 'workers' *barrios*' built during the 1920s and 1930s to accommodate the expanding industrial labour force of the city. They were built specifically for lower-income groups by commercial developers as far as possible from the élite residential areas of the central and eastern city. Between 1973 and 1979, the percentage of households living in rented accommodation in all the workers' *barrios* rose to between 60 and 70 per cent, while the corresponding figures for the city-centre remained stable at, or fell away from, a level of ground 65 per cent. Today, the area houses approximately 60 per cent of all low-income renters in Bucaramanga, two-thirds of the tenants living in rented rooms. Tenements in the area, however, make up only 17 per cent of the rental housing stock because most lots in the workers' *barrios* are small and cannot be further subdivided. In any case, few owners seem inclined to act as tenement landlords (see below): most share the dwelling and its services with one or two tenants but make no effort to attract renters in larger numbers. The limited number of *inquilinatos* means that socially and residentially immobile tenants are rarely found in this type of development.

There are good reasons for thinking that the supply of cheap rooms is beginning to dry up even in the workers' *barrios*. A persistent complaint among tenants is that it is becoming increasingly difficult to find alternative accommodation nearby after eviction (see below). The sample survey revealed that approximately one-third of owner-occupiers in any *barrio* have no desire to let property. Since the housing stock in the workers' *barrios* is now some 65 to 70 per cent rented this suggests that it is almost fully 'saturated' with tenants; there is a net deficit of rooms throughout the commercial sector. This is not an entirely recent phenomenon, for in relative terms the commercial submarket has been declining as a source of low-cost accommodation for many years. According to the sample, between 1941 and 1979 the proportion of in-migrants arriving in *barrios* of commercial origin fell from 93 per cent to 41 per cent. Given that most low-income households live in rental accommodation on, or soon after, arrival, this dramatic fall-off indicates the emergence of rental housing opportunities elsewhere in the city.

State housing projects were natural targets for increasing numbers of low-income tenants during the 1960s and early 1970s. The shift in housing tenure from owner-occupation to a more equal mix of renting and ownership takes place very quickly in the government submarket since dwellings are handed over to their owners more or less complete and fully serviced.[17] Consolidation in irregular settlements is necessarily slower and the housing stock requires a longer period of time before it can begin to accommodate renters. More than one-third of the households in Zapamanga, the newest 'low-income' ICT project in Bucaramanga (completed in 1977), live in rented accommodation.[18] Pirate settlements require between two and five years before renters enter, and invasions even longer.[19]

Letting government-financed dwellings is illegal in Colombia.[20] Although there are certain exceptions to this rule (for example, when a family has to leave the city in order to take up employment elsewhere), the illegality of renting in ICT projects is quite clear. Equally clear is the fact that legal restrictions have little or no effect; most ICT projects have between 35 and 40 per cent of their households living in rented accommodation (Zorro and Revéiz, 1974; Medina and Navas, 1974). While ICT officials are aware of widespread illegal letting in the city they take no action, ostensibly because they lack the resources to deal simultaneously with delays in the monthly payments for the dwellings and with the problems of tenants. It was also stressed privately that any attempt to halt the process by evicting landlords would have little effect. The highly politicized nature of the State housing bureaucracy and the partisan allocation of ICT dwellings means that it is extremely difficult to evict landlords with political influence.

Although renting has increased substantially throughout the government sector over the past decade, ICT projects are not major suppliers of rental accommodation to low-income groups. It is unlikely that more than one-third of residents in public housing are renters. Many owners of public housing are reluctant to rent rooms, partly due to the size of the units and partly because their higher household incomes do not require supplementation. Not only is rental accommodation limited in this submarket but it is also dominated by more expensive forms of housing; 35 to 40 per cent of all tenants rent apartments and unifamily dwellings and many fewer rent rooms. In addition, the physical structure of public housing means that tenements are extremely rare; for the poorest families in the city the government submarket offers little in the way of rental accommodation.

Less than 4 per cent of the city's low-income population live in invasion settlements. Local government remains strongly opposed to the invasion of land in Bucaramanga and no invasion has yet been legalized by the Council, none have piped water or drainage, and few dwellings have been consolidated. As a result, invasions are a last resort for most low-income households; they house the poorest 'owners' in the city and are extremely unattractive to prospective tenants. Owners in invasions have at least minimized expenditure on housing by escaping the payment of rent and they possess some of the advantages which stem from 'ownership'. But renters in invasions have few advantages. Outside the invasion submarket they can at least count on reasonably adequate levels of servicing and are free from the threat of eradication. By contrast, renters in invasions must endure the disadvantages of squatting and the problems of renting at one and the same time. Not surprisingly, only 14.8 per cent of households in invasion settlements are renters, the vast majority living in rooms or shacks. Unless the supply of rooms is drastically reduced elsewhere in the city the number of tenants seeking rented accommodation in invasion settlements is unlikely to increase.

The pirate subdivisions are the major source of new low-cost rental housing in the city, with their share of tenants rising from seven per cent in 1973 to around one quarter in 1979. Most pirate settlements have around 50 per cent of their residents in rented accommodation ten years after foundation, the proportion increasing with the age of the settlement.[21] But the forms of rental accommodation are highly diverse; tenements have not spread through the subdivisions in the same way as happened in Mexico City (Montaño, 1976; Ward, 1976; Connolly, 1982), which reflects the variety inherent in Colombian irregular settlements where dwellings develop slowly and to no set plan.[22] The usual pattern is for owners to let a single room in their house: 62 per cent of renters in pirate settlements live in dwellings with one or two other households. Tenements are very rare, and where they do occur they are usually stepped up the hillsides; if the gradient is sufficiently steep it is possible to build rooms or small apartments one on top of another in order to squeeze in five or six tenants on a lot of 100 to 150 square metres. Once a second storey has been constructed it is usually let rather than occupied by the owner's family.[23] Renting here is a highly innovative process in which the need to let property is tailored to the restrictions of the physical environment and the gradual rhythm of dwelling construction; it is very different from the kind of tenancy exemplified by the central *inquilinato*.

The role of the pirate submarket in housing low-income tenants seems certain to grow in importance as subdivisions consolidate and increasing numbers of owners begin to let property. Seventy-five per cent of those interviewed in pirate settlements not already landlords intended to let once they had sufficient room. In the near future there should be no shortage of cheap rental accommodation for those prepared to live in pirate subdivisions. Pirate settlements are taking on the mantle once worn by the commercial sector. They are housing increasing numbers of low-income tenants, usually with the landlord sharing house and services with one or two renters. Though more owners are letting than ever before there are now few large-scale absentee landlords. The intriguing question is whether this has altered the nature of landlordism and the landlord–tenant relationship in any *fundamental* sense.

LANDLORDISM AMONG THE URBAN POOR: ILLEGALITY AND PETTY CAPITALISM

Surprisingly little research has been carried out into the characteristics or behaviour of landlords in either 'developed' or 'less developed' countries.[24] The popular image of the powerful capitalist reaping excessive profits from dilapidated property owes much to the Victorian novel, the 'myth of the slumlord' as it is sometimes called (Sternlieb and Burchell, 1973). In fact, landlordism among low-income groups in Bucaramanga shows few of the characteristics which marked it out as a hated symbol of capitalism throughout the industrial world; it is altogether a smaller-scale and more flexible activity.

The motive for letting property is overwhelmingly financial: 90 per cent of resident landlords accommodate renters in order to generate additional income.[25] As one would expect, landlords earn lower average incomes than nonlandlord owners; they also tend to be older, have smaller families and own larger dwellings with vacant space. Rent forms a very important adjunct to income from employment, contributing approximately 50 per cent of total household income for landlords in the city centre and 22 to 41 per cent for those in pirate settlements. The former figure is lower because a high proportion of landlords in the city-centre have retired from the labour market and are living exclusively on rental income, and because the potential rental value of dwellings in irregular settlements is far below that of the central tenements. This is the only significant difference between landlordism in its traditional tenement form and landlordism elsewhere in the city. Most landlords live on the same lot as their tenants in every type of low-income settlement.

Landlordism in Bucaramanga is a small-scale phenomenon; few landlords own more than one rented dwelling and in the city-centre the property records show that only one person owns more than one *inquilinato*.[26] Property ownership in irregular settlements is similarly widely distributed; only one owner out of 100 owned more than one property anywhere in the city.

It is difficult to estimate rates of return on rented property since one is comparing current income from rent against the costs of land purchase and construction over a number of years. In any case, since few landlords invest in special facilities to accommodate tenants one has no base from which to calculate the returns. At the time of the survey, landlords were receiving between 900 and 1000 pesos for a single room (slightly less in the central *inquilinatos*), 2000 to 2500 pesos for an apartment, and 2500 to 4000 for a house. The great majority therefore received less than 3000 pesos per month from rent, less than the legal minimum wage. While the income is insufficient to buy other property elsewhere in the city, it covers maintenance and helps to pay off repayments on the initial cost of the lot.[27] But the profits to be made from landlordism are clearly very small when compared to other forms of capital accumulation.[28] As such it remains a small-scale activity even though demand for rented accommodation remains high. Low profit levels also explain why so few tenements are being built in the irregular settlements. But another part of the answer lies in the financial and fiscal responsibilities which accompany legal construction and in the nature of the renting contract itself. The addition of rooms and the improvement of toilet and washing facilities increases property taxes charged by the municipal authorities. While it is relatively easy to disguise the letting of one or two rooms, the development of tenements inevitably increases tax payments to the local authority. This was a common complaint among potential landlords in Bucaramanga. Equally important is that most landlords let property as a temporary economic expedient rather than as a permanent use for the dwelling or occupation for its owner. It is a convenient method of supplementing a household's income which requires little capital investment, supervision or risk. Few landlords make any modifications to their dwellings, no contract is signed, and no external agents are involved. The construction of tenements alters the casual character of letting; it demands that the landlord spends a good deal more time and energy in overseeing the dwelling and its inhabitants. While the potential profits are attractive to those who have retired from the labour force they are less than what most younger households can make from their jobs. As a result, petty landlordism shows no sign of developing into a larger scale, and more avowedly capitalist, activity.[29]

Under Colombian law every renter and landlord must sign a contract (*Contrato de Arrendamiento*) and have it registered with a recognized renting agency (Castro, 1979; ANIF, 1979). This contract sets out the terms of the tenancy and, in theory, protects the rights of both tenant and landlord. In fact, only a minority of low-income tenants have contracts and even fewer registered contracts: among roomers only 5 per cent have contracts and among renters of unifamily dwellings 50 per cent. These proportions might be expected given the characteristics of the two types of tenant: contracts require the signature of two property owners in the city to act as guarantors, a qualification which puts the poorer and younger roomers at an immediate disadvantage. Landlords do not want to sign contracts since it reduces their ability to evict tenants and raise rents. Similarly, renting agencies are reluctant to register contracts for rooms because the profits are insignificant. Few tenants are even given monthly receipts for rent. Consequently, few tenants, and practically no roomers, are protected by the law; since there is no supervision of rented properties not covered by contracts landlords act with impunity in contravening State rent controls.[30] Although most arrangements between landlords and tenants are illegal, rents are paid at regular intervals and are set by the market rate.

Landlords can evict tenants in the knowledge that they will soon find a replacement. Nevertheless, landlords do not have complete power. Since incomes are low it is in their interest to adopt a relatively flexible attitude toward the collection and setting of rents. One generally finds that there is a trade-off between the desire to maximize rental income and the knowledge that rents cannot be pushed too high.[31] It is common, especially in the central *inquilinatos*, for landlords to vary rents according to the economic capacity of each of his tenants; the poorest pay perhaps half the rent of higher-income tenants for a room of similar size. Since landlordism is such a small-scale activity there is no general attempt to fix rents and there is considerable variation around the mean rent even for the same type of accommodation.[32] Rents are on average 10 per cent lower for tenants with resident landlords than for tenants without, and one-third lower among the 10 per cent of renters related by kin to their landlords. Most landlords are well aware of the need for flexibility where tenant's incomes are low or unstable, but this is little more than enlightened self-interest. Landlordism among the urban poor is small-scale capitalism exemplified. While few landlords can be said to be *maximizing* profits from the use of their property, this does not alter the fundamentally capitalist character of the relationship between landlord and tenant. Land and capital are being used to generate unearned income. The fact that most landlords live with their tenants appears to make little difference to the nature of renting itself. Renting has an exploitative character, but the prime source of exploitation lies in the inability of poor families to own their home, not in the landlord–tenant relationship itself.

HOUSING TENURE AND SOCIAL STRUCTURE: THE WIDER IMPLICATIONS OF RENTING

It would be wrong to end this paper without looking briefly at the wider implications of renting for the urban poor. Specifically, what effect does renting have on physical living conditions, material inequality, social mobility and political mobilization?

This is not the place to look in any detail at the *ideology* of tenure.[33] Suffice it to say that the evidence from Bucaramanga indicates that there is no direct relationship between tenure and social class, nor even between tenure and income group. Families earning the same level of income choose different types of housing, and others with very different incomes choose the same form of tenure. All low-income groups surveyed in the city, regardless of tenure, stand in roughly the same position *vis-à-vis* the dominant classes in Colombian society. There is, however, one respect in which tenure may reinforce and accentuate income inequality *among* the urban poor: the redistribution of income embodied in the payment of rent. Though the evidence for redistribution is not as straightforward as is often claimed (Zorro and Revéiz, 1974), in most cases the payment of rent does widen the disparity between the net incomes of owners and tenants; in Bucaramanga by an average of 40 per cent in the case of roomers and 15 per cent among higher income tenants.[34] The distribution of income among the urban poor is that much more unequal after the purchase of accommodation is incorporated into the calculation. This is an undesirable consequence of the spread of landlordism among low-income groups in a market economy but unavoidable because the taxation of rental income would remove the monetary incentive behind letting and thereby reduce the supply of rental accommodation.[35] It is undesirable because renting has a serious effect on the material living standards of low-income groups. Since tenants have to commit between 25 and 30 per cent of their budgets to the payment of rent, the amount they have available for expenditure on food, clothing and education is obviously limited. The enforced payment of rent reduces the 'investment surplus' of the household, limiting their ability to become homeowners or indeed to use their surplus for any other purpose. In a material sense, tenants are undoubtedly worse off than owners and tenure *itself* plays an important part in perpetuating differences in material living standards and in widening income inequalities among the urban poor.

Many authors have taken this argument one step further by stressing the political or ideological role of housing tenure in dividing the urban poor and weakening their potential for collective action (Janssen, 1978; Walton and Lubeck, 1979). The strength of community action is said to decline as settlements become increasingly heterogeneous, low-income landlords being pitted against low-income tenants (Cornelius, 1975; Montaño, 1976; Goldrich *et al.*, 1970). Renters themselves are often held to be less involved or politically active than owners (Havens and Flinn, 1970; Darío, 1970; Giraldo, 1970). There are two related lines of argument here. The first concerns the impact of variations in housing tenure at the collective or community level. It centres on the conflicts of interest between owners and renters which weaken the ability of the urban poor to act cohesively in the political arena. The second concerns the relationship between tenure and politicization at the individual level; are tenants more apathetic politically than owners, and, if so, why?[36] Underlying both arguments is a more fundamental question: does tenure exert an important and independent influence on politicization or is it a minor influence compared to other variables such as the nature of work and national political organization?

Although most political demands are overwhelmingly parochial, concerning the material necessities of life rather than wider issues of government or participation, conflicts of interest among owners and renters do arise. Owners are more interested in changes at the city and the community level, for example, the regularization of land tenure or changes in land taxes. Renters are more concerned with their individual problems, levels of rent, eviction and so on, and are less interested in community-level issues from which they derive little direct benefit. Regularization, for example, is of little interest to those without a permanent 'stake' in the community; hence renters participate less often in the activities of *Acción Comunal* (neighbourhood councils), are less active in demonstrations for community improvements, and vote even less regularly than owners. As such, a fall-off in political involvement and communal activity at the *barrio* level is the likely result of increasing numbers of renters living in the community. Poor tenants as a group do not engage in organized activities to fight for their rights; few know of the *Asociación de Destechados* (Association for the Homeless), an organization which exists to protect the interests of tenants but does little to help low-income groups in the city.[37] In part the 'apathy' of tenants derives from their youth, lower incomes, and shorter periods of residence in the *barrio*; age, income and residence as well as tenure produce the difference. But the difference in political and community participation between renters and owners should not be exaggerated. Even the most active group in the sample, owners in the city centre, are less than enthusiastic in community and political activities; they help their *barrio* council but do not attend meetings, only 50 per cent vote, and few take part in political campaigns or attend party meetings. While owners are more politically active, political organization and mobilization is limited *universally*, discouraged by the nature of the Colombian political system (Gilbert and Ward, 1982). Two decades of coalition government have successfully alienated the vast majority of poor families from the political process (Berry *et al.*, 1980).[38] In this context housing tenure plays a very minor role in further weakening their potential for political action and community involvement.

CONCLUSION

This chapter has shown that more than half of the urban poor in Bucaramanga live in rented accommodation. Low-income tenants fall into two broad groups: those who live in apartments or unifamily dwellings, and those who rent rooms. Both types of tenant are found throughout the city, but increasingly rental accommodation is to be found outside the traditional rental tenements in the city centre.

Outside the *inquilinatos* landlordism is a small scale and hardly exploitative activity. It is a temporary financial expedient to supplement an owner's income from employment and one which involves a minimum of risk and capital investment. Profits are limited because few landlords have more than one or two tenants and rents are fairly low. Although eviction of tenants occurs frequently there are usually other rooms available nearby. Given the basic shortage of housing and the low levels of income in Bucaramanga, the rental market for low-income groups appears to allocate accommodation fairly well.

This is not to say, however, that renting has no undesirable consequences, nor to suggest that the spread of renting is generally desirable. For although renting has a limited effect on political activity and community involvement it does create differences of interest between owners and tenants. Renting also widens existing disparities in income between tenure groups and further limits residential mobility. But, politicization, income inequality and residential mobility, are not primarily determined by tenure; the principal determinants are of course the social, economic and political structures within which all poor families must live and work.

ACKNOWLEDGEMENTS

The fieldwork was carried out as part of the author's doctoral research programme at University College London and financed by a grant from the Social Science Research Council of Great Britain. The research was carried out under the umbrella of the project on 'Public intervention and land use in Latin American cities' financed by the Overseas Development Administration and directed by Alan Gilbert and Peter Ward. The author wishes to thank Alan Gilbert, Peter Ward, Bill Bell and Ann Varley for their comments on an earlier draft of this paper.

NOTES

1. Throughout this paper the term 'irregular settlement' is used to cover dwellings located on land invasions and pirate subdivisions. Land tenure in invasions is illegal; subdivisions are illegal only in the sense that they contravene certain planning regulations established by the Municipality. The term 'low-income' settlement includes the above along with State housing and areas of commercial origin where the urban poor live.
2. Semistructured questionnaires were applied to 2004 randomly selected household heads in sampling fractions directly related to the importance of each type of

settlement in the city (if 10 per cent of households lived in invasions, 10 per cent of the sample was taken from invasions). The sample is therefore taken to represent the 'urban poor' in Bucaramanga. More detailed questionnaires were applied to 180 randomly selected household heads in a pirate subdivision in the urban periphery, and 180 in 'Chorreras de Don Juan', a small settlement in the city-centre.

3. In contrast to the urban poor in Asia and Africa, a far higher proportion of whom prefer renting to owner-occupation. See, for example, Peil (1976) and Muench (1978).

4. Shelton (1968) estimates that ownership is cheaper than renting if a household remains in the same dwelling for more than 3.5 years. This is almost certainly true in Bucaramanga.

5. Burgess (1978) gives a useful account of variations in modes of housing production.

6. The debates of the Municipal Council in Bucaramanga make no mention of any form of low-income housing prior to the early 1960's.

7. My calculation is from data supplied by ICT's Bucaramanga office and by the Municipal Planning Department. To give some idea of temporal changes in the real price of ICT financed dwellings, the cheapest house cost the equivalent of 29 minimum monthly salaries in 1963, 66 in 1972, 75 in 1975 and 47 in 1979 (this last figure refers to one small project of 240 units). Rising real prices stemmed from a switch away from 'self-help' under the Alliance for Progress programme toward more expensive forms of construction and financing and towards direct contracting to private capital.

8. Gilbert (personal communication) has calculated that for ten cities in Colombia in 1973 there is a correlation (R^2) of −0.58 between the percentage of low-income households living in rented accommodation and the proportion of dwellings in unregularized invasion settlements.

9. Throughout this paper 'tenement' and 'inquilinato' are used interchangedly to denote a dwelling which contains five or more households sharing washing and toilet facilities. This follows Colombian statistical convention.

10. The central cores of many African and Asian cities are known to be very diverse. See Drakakis-Smith (1981).

11. This came out of our interviews with owners in Chorreras who had arrived in the city in the 1930s and 1940s. *Claustro* was the name given to the traditional form of house introduced from Metropolitan Spain; an open courtyard surrounded by a single storey of between 5 and 15 rooms.

12. Tenements housing over 30 families have been reported for both Bogotá (Darío, 1970; ICBF, 1978) and Mexico City (Lomnitz, 1975; Montaño, 1976).

13. Rents were originally frozen throughout Colombia in 1943, though legislation was not enacted until 1956. The law was reintroduced in December 1976 but had little effect on low-income groups. Between 1977 and 1978, for example, rents for 'workers' rose by 20 per cent in Bucaramanga, as measured by the Retail Price Index (my calculation from tabulated results, Indice de precios al consumidor, DANE, Bogotá).

14. The 'city centre' defined by the Municipal Planning Department and used in this paper consists of seven *barrios*.

15. As in Bogotá, where many tenements around the main bull ring and what is now the Tequendama hotel were pulled down to make way for high-income residential and commercial developments.

16. There is very little land available for subdivision anywhere in the Metropolitan area. It is possible to find vacant lots in existing subdivisions but they are rare and

expensive; a lot of average size (100–150 square metres) costs between 40 000 and 50 000 1979 Colombian pesos (a figure of 500 pesos/square metre was quoted in three separate subdivisions). In 1979 the U.S. dollar was worth 40 Colombian pesos.

17. Methods of finance and construction vary considerably in the state sector; only one 'site-and-service' scheme exists in Bucaramanga. Even in so-called self-help projects, dwellings are handed over to their owners more or less complete. Tenants can therefore be accommodated very quickly.

18. Two projects financed by ICT were completed after the author left Colombia: Bucarica (for middle-income groups) and Villaluz. No data are yet available on tenancy.

19. It is impossible to judge exactly when each settlement begins to accommodate renters; the mean number of years between foundation and the entry of the first tenants *in the survey* was 5 for pirate subdivisions and 10 for invasions.

20. Interview with ICT, Bucaramanga.

21. A stepwise regression analysis was performed on the survey data using the percentage of renter households as the dependent variable, and the age of the '*barrio*', the size (number of households) and level of service provision (percentage of dwellings lacking piped water and drainage) as independent variables. Age 'explained' 28 per cent of the variance using the 64 *barrios* in the sample and 34 per cent for the 20 pirate settlements. The correlation coefficient (rank) between the percentage of renters and age was $+0.53$ for the total sample, and $+0.59$ for the pirate submarkets (significant at 5 per cent level).

22. See the forthcoming results of the Gilbert and Ward project.

23. Under the *Plan Terrazas* the Banco Central Hipotecario (BCH), the Central Mortgage Bank, aims to facilitate this process by granting low interest loans to those wishing to add another storey to their dwellings. However, there is no evidence to suggest that this was ever a major factor in most people's decisions.

24. The author knows of no substantive research on landlordism among low-income groups in Latin American cities. Some work has been carried out in Africa (see Muench, 1978; Peil, 1976; Brand, 1973; Marris, 1979; Lloyd, 1979), and good summaries of recent work in the U.K. may be found in Clarke and Ginsburg (1975) and Elliot and McCrone (1975).

25. No absentee landlords were interviewed in Bucaramanga: 27 per cent of owners in Chorreras were absentee landlords; 22 per cent in the pirate settlement.

26. This figure was calculated using the number of properties listed under each name (surname and initials). It is unlikely that more than one property owner in such a small area will have exactly the same name, but obviously the calculations cannot be exact.

27. For Bogotá, Currie (1978) estimates that the cost of constructing 1 square metre of a dwelling could be covered by two months income from rent.

28. Investment in the finance market, particularly in exchange certificates, is far more lucrative, but alternative forms of investment are irrelevant to the vast majority of low-income owners; they have far too little capital to make rational judgements about which form of investment carries the maximum return.

29. Bucaramanga presents a contrast to Nairobi, for example, where renting is fast becoming dominated by large-scale private capital. I am grateful to Phil Amis of the University of Kent at Canterbury for this information.

30. In force in their present form since December 1976. See also Note 13.

31. Similarly flexible or lenient attitudes among landlords have been reported by Muench (1978) and Brand (1973).

32. The mean rent for rooms in Chorreras is 896 pesos, with a standard deviation of 441; for the pirate settlement the corresponding figures are 1057 and 573.
33. The political and ideological implications of housing tenure are discussed in Saunders (1977, 1978, 1979) and Conference of Socialist Economists (1975, 1976).
34. Net income is defined as total household income minus rent for tenants, and total household income (including income from rent) minus monthly debt repayments for owners.
35. Any attempt to impose fiscal restraint on capital gains from property ownership or exchange meets with intense opposition. Successive attempts to reform the land tax system in Colombia, and particularly taxation of lots held vacant for speculative purposes, have met with failure. Opposition from the Municipal Council in Bucaramanga has been particularly fierce (Council minutes, debate 052, 1978).
36. 'Political' activity or action is taken here to include any action or demand which is articulated via the existing machinery of local and national politics in Colombia, however narrow or parochial it may be.
37. Its full title is the *Unión Nacional de Inquilinos de la Vivienda y Destechados de Colombia* (National Union of Tenants and Homeless Families). It is a middle-class organization which represents its 1800 members in court actions and provides assistance in finding vacant properties for purchase (usually in ICT projects). It does not (unlike 'Provivienda' in Bogotá) organize land invasions or keep a register of low-income tenants.
38. During the coalition years of the National Front (1958–74) the Presidency alternated between Liberal and Conservative parties, so there was little incentive to vote. Although the Front ended officially in 1974 élite power-sharing remains in force (Gilbert and Ward, 1982).

REFERENCES

ANIF (Asociación Nacional de Instituciones Financieras) (1979). *Control integral de arrendamientos: una pieza en la política de vivienda*. Paper given at the Chamber of Commerce, Bucaramanga, by Jaime Córdoba Zuloaga, President of ANIF.

Balán, J., Browning, H., and Jelín, E. (1973). *Men in a Developing Society: Geographical and Social Mobility in Monterrey, Mexico*. University of Texas Press.

Balanowsky, V., Pingeot, F., Recabarrén, J. and Vanderschueren, F. (1974). 'Movilización urbana en los conventillos de Santiago.' In Castells, M. (ed.), *Estructura de Clases y Política Urbana en América Latina*. Ediciones SIAP, Buenos Aires.

Bender, S. (1975). *Low-income Housing Development in Bogotá*. Rice University, Program of Development Studies Paper 66.

Berry, R., Hellmann, R. and Solaún, M. (eds.) (1980). *Politics of Compromise: Coalition Government in Colombia*. Transaction books, New Brunswick.

Brand, R. (1973). 'Migration and residential site selection in five low-income communities in Kumasi (Ghana)', *African Urban Notes* 7, 73–94.

Burgess, R. (1978). 'Petty, commodity housing or dweller control? A critique of John Turner's views on housing policy', *World Development* 6, 1105–34.

Butterworth, D. (1973). 'Squatters or suburbanites? The growth of shanty-towns in Oaxaca, Mexico', in Scott, R. (ed.), *Latin American Modernization Problems*. University of Illinois Press.

Cardona, R. and Simmons, A. B. (1977). *Destino la metropoli: un modelo géneral de las migraciones internas en América Latina*. CCRP, Bogotá.

Castro, J. (1979). *El Contrato de Arrendamiento*. Ediciones Biblioteca Actualidad Jurídica, Bogotá.

Celis, C. and Vargas, G. (1976). *Estudio socio-antropológico de una zona de tugurio en la ciudad de Bucaramanga*. Mimeo, Universidad Industrial de Santander.

Clarke, S. and Ginsburg, N. (1975). 'The political economy of housing.' In *Conference of Socialist Economists* (1975).

Clark, C. and Ward, P. (1976). 'Stasis in makeshift housing: perspectives from Mexico and the Caribbean', *Actes du XLII Congrès International des Americanists*, **X**, 351–58.

Conference of Socialist Economists (1975). *Housing and Class in Britain*.

Conference of Socialist Economists (1976). *The Political Economy of Housing*.

Connolly, P. (1982). 'Uncontrolled settlements and self-build: what kind of solution?' In Ward, P. (ed.), 141–74.

Cornelius, W. A. (1975). *Politics and the Migrant Poor in Mexico City*. Stanford University Press.

Currie, R. (1978). *The rental market within the context of the development of the housing market for low-income groups in Bogotá, Colombia*. M.A. Thesis, Institute of Latin American Studies, University of London.

Darío, R. (1970). *Ensayo de metodología sobre 'inquilinato' y cambio familiar en Bogotá*. Departamento de Antropología, Universidad Nacional de Colombia, Bogotá.

Doebele, W. (1978). Selected issues in urban land tenure, *World Bank Staff Working Paper*, No. 283, 99–207.

Drakakis-Smith, D. (1981). *Urbanization, Housing and the Development Process*. Croom Helm.

Dueñas, H. (1973). *La demanda por vivienda en el submercado comercial en Bogotá: un estimativo*. Tésis de grado, Facultad de Economía, Universidad de Los Andes, Bogotá.

Edwards, M. A. (1981). *Cities of tenants: renting as a housing alternative among the Colombian urban poor*. Unpublished doctoral dissertation, University College London.

Elliott, B. and McCrone, D. (1975). 'Property relations in the city: the fortunes of landlordism', *Centre for Environmental Studies, Conference Paper* **14**, 31–64.

Gilbert, A. (1981). 'Pirates and invaders: land acquisition in urban Colombia and Venezuela', *World Development* **9**, 657–678.

Gilbert, A. (1982). 'Housing the urban poor.' In Gilbert, A. and Gugler, J. (1982), *Cities, Poverty and Development: Urbanization in the Third World*. Oxford University Press.

Gilbert, A. and Ward, P. (1982). 'Low-income housing and the state.' In Gilbert, A. *et al.* (eds.), *Urbanization in Contemporary Latin America*. John Wiley, 79–127.

Giraldo, R. (1970). *El inquilinato, causas y implicaciones*. Mimeo, CENAC, Bogotá.

Goldrich, D., Pratt, R. and Schuller, C. (1970). 'The political integration of lower-class urban settlements in Chile and Peru.' In Horowitz, I. (ed.), *Masses in Latin America*. Oxford University Press.

Harvey, D. (1973). *Social Justice and the City*. Edward Arnold.

Havens, A. and Flinn, W. (1970). 'The power structure in a shantytown.' In Flinn, W. and Havens, A. (eds.), *Internal Colonialism and Structural Change in Colombia*. Praeger.

ICBF (Instituto Colombiano de Bienestar Familiar) (1978). *El Gamín: su albergue social y su familia*. UNICEF, Bogotá.

Janssen, R. (1978). 'Class practices of dwellers in barrios populares: the struggle for the right to the city', *International Journal of Urban and Regional Research* **2**, 147–59.

Lewis, O. (1961). *The Children of Sánchez*. Penguin.

Lewis, O. (1972). *A Death in the Sánchez Family*. Penguin.

Lloyd, P. (1979). *Slums of Hope? Shanty Towns of the Third World.* Penguin.

Lomnitz, L. (1975). *Networks and Marginality; Life in a Mexican Shantytown.* Academic Press.

Losada, R. and Gómez, H. (1976). *La tierra en el mercado pirata de Bogotá.* Fedesarrollo, Bogotá.

MacEwen, A. (1974). 'Differentiation among the urban poor.' In De Kadt, E. and Williams, G. (eds.), *The Sociology of Development.* Tavistock publications.

Manrique, R. (1976). *El mercado de vivienda en Bucaramanga y su área metropolitana.* EDUB (Empresa de desarrollo urbano de Bucaramanga), Bucaramanga.

Marris, P. (1979). 'The meaning of slums and patterns of change', *International Journal of Urban and Regional Research* 3, 419–41.

Medina, C. and Navas, A. (1974). *La vivienda compartida en arrendamiento en el submercado guvernmental: estudio de caso.* Tésis de doctorado, Facultad de Economía, Universidad de Los Andes, Bogotá.

Molina, H. (1979). 'El problema de la vivienda en Colombia', *Teoría y práctica en América Latina* 14.

Montaño, J. (1976). *Los pobres de la ciudad en los asentamientos espontáneos.* Ediciones Siglo Veintiuno, SA.

Morse, R. (1971). 'São Paulo; case study of a Latin American metropolis', *Latin American Urban Research* 1, 151–88.

Muench, L. (1978). *The private burden of urban social overhead: a study of the informal housing market of Kampala, Uganda.* Doctoral Dissertation, University of Pennsylvania.

Murillo, G. and Ungar, E. (1978). *Política, vivienda popular y el proceso de toma de decisiones en Colombia.* Departamento de Ciencia Política, Universidad de Los Andes, Bogotá.

Peil, M. (1976). 'African squatter settlements: a comparative study', *Urban Studies* 13, 155–66.

Perlman, J. (1976). *The Myth of Marginality: Urban Poverty and Politics in Rio de Janeiro.* University of California Press.

Pradilla, E. (1976). 'Notas acerca del problema de la vivienda', *Ideología y Sociedad* 16, 70–107.

Saunders, P. (1977). *Housing tenure and class interests.* University of Sussex, Urban and Regional Studies Working Paper 6.

Saunders, P. (1978). 'Domestic property and social class', *International Journal of Urban and Regional Research* 2, 233–51.

Saunders, P. (1979). *Urban Politics: a Sociological Interpretation.* Penguin.

Shelton, J. (1968). 'The cost of renting versus owning a home', *Land Economics* 44, 59–72.

SIAP (Sociedad Interamericana de Planifición) (1977). *Seminario inter-regional sobre 'asentamientos humanos marginados.' Conclusiones generales.* Mimeo, Bogotá.

Sternlieb, G. and Burchell, R. (1973). *Residential Abandonment: the Tenement Landlord Revisited.* Centre for Urban Policy Research, Rutgers University, New Brunswick.

Stevenson, R. (1979). *Housing Programs and Policies in Bogotá: an Historical/ Descriptive Analysis.* World Bank City Study Research Project RPO 671-47.

Stokes, C. (1962). 'A theory of slums', *Land Economics* 18, 187–97.

Turner, J. (1968). 'Housing priorities, settlement patterns and urban development in modernizing countries', *Journal of the American Institute of Planners* 34, 354–63.

Turner, J. (1976). *Housing by People.* Marion Boyars, London.

Valencia, A., Valderrama, S. and Mestres, J. (1966). *Control y erradicación de tugurios en Bucaramanga.* Universidad Industrial de Santander, Bucaramanga.

Valenzuela, J. (1969). 'Barrios populares en América Latina.' In Cardona, R. (ed.), *Migración y desarrollo urbano en Colombia*. Bogotá.

Vernez, G. (1973). *The Residential Movements of Low-income Families: the Case of Bogotá, Colombia*. Rand Institute.

Walton, J. and Lubeck, P. (1979). 'Urban class conflict in Africa and Latin America: comparative analyses from a world systems perspective', *International Journal of Urban and Regional Research* 3, 3–25.

Ward, P. M. (1976). 'The squatter settlement as slum or housing solution: the evidence from Mexico City', *Land Economics* 52, 330–46.

Ward, P. M. (ed.) (1982). *Self-help Housing: a Critique*. Mansell.

Zorro, C. and Revéiz, E. (1974). *Estudio sobre los inquilinatos en Bogotá*. Centro de Estudios sobre Desarrollo Económico, Universidad de Los Andes, documents 010 and 034.

Urbanization in Contemporary Latin America
Edited by A. Gilbert with J. E. Hardoy and R. Ramírez
© 1982 John Wiley & Sons Ltd.

7

A home of one's own: squatter housing strategies in Guayaquil, Ecuador

CAROLINE O. N. MOSER

INTRODUCTION

Conceptualization of the characteristics, nature and function of 'self-help' housing and illegal squatter settlements in the Third World has advanced considerably in the past two decades; progress that has been reflected in important changes in government housing policies. This paper examines some of the concepts emerging from recent research on 'petty commodity' or 'self-help' housing, and considers their relevance for understanding squatter housing strategies in a low-income community in Guayaquil, Ecuador.

Analysts of Latin American urbanization in the 1950s and early 1960s were primarily concerned with the failure of conventional government housing programmes to satisfy low-income housing demand. The direct consequence of this failure, the proliferation of low-income squatter and shanty settlements, was viewed nevertheless as a temporary phenomenon, a consequence of extremely rapid urban growth. These newly established, makeshift settlements were identified as reception areas for recently arrived migrants who were still 'unintegrated' into the city. Within each city, however, squatter settlement formation and the process of house construction were seen to be homogeneous; the socioeconomic characteristics of the population, the method of land acquisition, and the form of house consolidation varied little. The illegal nature of land occupation and the failure to pay rent or to compensate the 'owner', meant that squatters were seen as existing outside the capitalist land and housing market and developing in spatially 'marginal' locations (Bonilla, 1961; Leeds, 1969). 'Squatter settlements were seen as zones of total social breakdown: . . . policy-makers equated the problem of marginality with that of substandard housing . . . marginality was seen as something to be physically eradicated, a manifestation that had a simple cure' (Perlman, 1976: 103).

Government intervention based on these assumptions often involved the bulldozing and clearance of whole settlements.[1] Such action was justified on the grounds that the settlements constituted 'public eyesores', were 'insanitary' or represented a form of 'urban cancer'. Demolition occurred in cities as far apart as Hong Kong, Nairobi and Rio de Janeiro, with displaced squatters sometimes being relocated in new, more distant and usually inappropriate housing areas. Rarely did governments consider whether the housing was suitable to the occupations and incomes of the resettled population; as often as not the result was that public housing was too expensive for the 'target group' for which it was intended (Bryce-Laporte, 1970; Ashton, 1972).

That 'self-help' housing was a rational response by the expanding low-income urban population to the growing shortage of conventional housing was widely recognized by the late 1960s. In particular, the formative work of Turner (1968, 1969) and Mangin (1967) led to 'self-help' squatter settlement being viewed as a sensible and viable alternative to the housing shortage; it allowed the poor the opportunity to incrementally build their own home, relating their investments to their income level, giving them 'freedom' to decide on size, standard and style according to their individual family needs. Although the entire process of upgrading could take ten years or more, sub-letting and cottage industries were seen as mechanisms which could be utilized to increase the homeowner's income. Widespread acceptance on the part of international agencies and national governments that the process of 'self-help' housing did not represent a problem and might even be a solution to the housing situation had important policy implications; a number of governments soon shifted from formal housing policies to 'self-help' alternatives, particularly 'site-and-service' schemes (Ward, 1978: 38).[2]

By the 1970s, 'self-help' housing had become part of the general debate about the 'informal sector'.[3] Unfortunately, the lack of any clear formulation of the concept led policy makers to regard the informal sector as being synonomous with the urban poor, with people living in squatter settlements, and with the self-improvement of housing in 'informal' areas (Moser, 1978: 1051). The informal sector concept, with its *a priori* dualist division of the urban economy into two autonomous sectors, has had particular appeal to policy-makers because of its emphasis on the productive role of the informal sector to generate growth and employment.[4] It is this role that recent literature has sought to question: can the informal sector generate autonomous growth or is the rate of accumulation constrained by the structural factors inherent in the wider socioeconomic system? An alternative framework based on petty commodity production (a form of production existing at the margins of the capitalist mode of production but integrated and subordinate to it) has been identified as having greater utility for handling the complexities of internal differentiation (Moser, 1978: 1055).[5] This approach conceptualizes the urban economy in terms of a continuum of productive activities, with complex linkages and dependent relationships between production and distribution systems and with the petty commodity sector occupying a subordinate position in the system.

The 'self-help' approach to housing has been criticized within the informal sector debate because of its implicit tendency to view 'self-help' housing mainly in terms of its use value. Turner (1972) suggested that the choice of housing represents a compromise between the three universal housing needs: access, shelter and tenure. The value of housing to its *user* depended upon the degree to which it satisfied these priorities; priorities which varied among different low-income groups such as 'bridgeheaders' or 'consolidators'.[6] Such an approach has tended to exaggerate the independent nature of squatter housing (and its potential for autonomous growth) and hence failed to see either how the housing process functions in the valorization of capital or how the various fractions of capital become involved in the process of land and housing development.

In the debate concerning the commodity status of housing Burgess (1978: 1108) has argued that 'the status of land and housing cannot be understood purely or even primarily in terms of its use values. This would mean that the principal activities and processes involved in housing and settlement would be placed "outside the sphere of investigation of political economy"' (Marx, 1859). The importance of recognizing the commodity status of housing relates ultimately to the need to analyse the ways in which alternative housing strategies articulate the interests of the various fractions of capital tied to their production, consumption and exchange, and consequently the implications for 'solving' the housing problem. Thus, the debate between 'State-assisted self-help' and 'official housing' policies needs to be 'situated in the context of the conflicting interests of the different fractions of capital tied to the housing problem' (Burgess, 1978: 1105) and understood in terms of the conflicting interests of groups and classes struggling for housing resources.

In the process of transformation into its commodity form, 'self-help' housing differs from other housing commodities in that it is constructed for the immediate use of the producer, rather than for exchange by agents different from the consumer.[7] This does not mean that it can be understood outside the process of commodity formation. Burgess (1978: 1112) maintains that 'self-help' housing is cheaper neither because of the absence of bureaucratic systems and legal housing norms, nor because building systems are autonomous rather than heteronomous (Turner, 1976). It is cheaper because the squatter is 'operating in a different sphere of circulation of capital — that covered by petty commodity production of housing. He has not escaped capitalism: he is merely in another part of it'.

In his elaboration of the commodity status of housing, Burgess adapts Pradilla's (1976: 77–83) distinction between industrial, manufactured and self-help forms, by emphasizing the importance of identifying the relationship between the three 'forms' in terms of the dominant capitalist mode and the dependent petty commodity form of production. In the *industrialized* form the relationship between production and consumption is carried out through the mechanism of commercial exchange. This industrial sector dominates housing production through its control over housing budgets and the industrialized building-materials industry, and through State and finance company dominance of the supply of land. Burgess suggests that the petty commodity production of the housing object assumes two forms — the *self-built* and the *manufactured*, with the distinction that the first is produced for its use-value, the second for its exchange value. In the manufactured form, middle-class houses are produced by small architect-led firms, using standardized raw materials and a differentiated labour force. These firms are dependent on the industrialized housing sector for capital, technology and building materials. Characteristics such as these suggest that the manufactured form, within the strict categorization of petty commodity production, is more accurately defined as small-scale capitalist production.[8]

In the case of the 'self-help' housing form, the producer and the consumer are the same and construction if financed by savings from income. Labour is provided free by the household, kin and neighbours, with paid labour called in for specialized jobs. Construction materials are recycled throwaways valorized through the labour input, although manufactured building materials are purchased at later stages. Construction involves rudimentary technology, large labour inputs and traditional techniques. Production is for 'self-consumption' with the status altered when the house is used in the market as a commodity for sale or rent. Despite its production for use-value, 'self-help' housing is dependent on the industrialized form through building materials linked to the modern sector. Commodity relations develop on invaded land through illegal subdivisions and self-improvements producing ground rents. Burgess' distinction between the capitalist and the two petty commodity housing production forms provides a basis for the analysis of housing and settlement processes. However, identification of the relationship between the dominant capitalist mode and the dependent petty-commodity forms assumes a level of generality which requires considerable clarification and modification if the process of transformation of 'self-help' housing into its commodity form is to have any empirical applicability.

In the process of squatter settlement formation two contradictory tendencies are evident which are fundamental to the debate concerning the petty commodity production of housing. The first tendency is towards increased penetration and transformation of the sector by the capitalist mode of production, the second is its long-term conservation and survival in a petty commodity form. These contradictory tendencies are identified by Burgess (1978: 1109) in the following passages: 'it is in the nature of the capitalist mode of production (as the logical development of Marx's Capital demonstrates) that there should be a constant expansion of the sphere of commodity production for capitalist exchange. Such an expansion is a necessary condition of capitalist development and not an effect of it'. But, 'the survival of the self-help form ultimately derives from the conditions of undervalorization of labour endemic in Third World capitalist development, and from the ineluctable necessity of low-income groups for some form of shelter. Insofar as housing is necessary for the maintenance and expanded reproduction of social labour the dominant capitalist mode of production is satisfied to allow the self-production of such activities' (1978: 1115).

In a different analysis of the conflicting interests around squatter housing, Peattie (1979) identifies the housing problem in Third World countries as reflecting the multiplicity of organized interest groups and their different alliances which advocate conflicting and often contradictory policies to which government policy is forced to respond. For instance, the interests of the industrialist are to keep a pool of labour available at a minimum cost ignoring the growth of squatter settlements, the pressures from real estate interests are to develop land for more profitable purposes, while government interests are to give the city a 'respectable face'. As such, 'much of the zig-zagging of government policies towards such settlements is explicable in terms of the irreconcilable competition between the policies suggested by these two sets of pressures' (Peattie, 1979: 1021).

Although in the macro-level debate, individual micro-studies can provide no more than examples, with a much wider series of studies necessary if any more general conclusions are to be reached, the following case study examines some of the implications of the underlying debate concerning the petty commodity production of housing. First, it describes the 'self-help' housing strategies of a low-income community in Guayaquil and examines the manner in which families acquire floodland plots (*solars*) and then incrementally build and consolidate their own houses. It identifies and analyses the role of 'professional' squatters, commercial retailers of raw materials and local-level neighbourhood (*barrio*) leaders in this process. It describes how 'self-help' housing develops, the conditions under which it is transformed into its commodity form, and the way in which this manifests itself. The intention is to examine the utility of a distinction between manufactured and self-help forms of petty commodity housing and to clarify the extent to which petty commodity production of housing is operating in a different sphere of circulation of capital. Secondly, it examines some of the conflicting interests in squatter housing in a particular temporal and spatial conjuncture. The intention is to examine some of the issues raised by the assumptions concerning the homogeneity of the 'self-help' housing sector, defining the process whereby 'self-help' housing is transformed into its commodity form, and identifying the interests involved in the valorization of land and housing in the informal housing market (that is, the extent to which it establishes an entrepreneurial élite). In this manner the paper aims to identify the specific social, economic and political conditions under which either the rapid penetration of capitalism into the 'self-help' housing sector or the conservation of petty commodity production of housing is the dominant feature.

HOUSING STRATEGIES OUTSIDE THE FORMAL MARKET: THE CASE OF INDIO GUAYAS, GUAYAQUIL

This case study is about a community known locally as Indio Guayas, located on the far edge of Guayaquil's *suburbio* (Figure 7.1).[9] Clearly, the housing strategies of one small area of the city's squatter settlements cannot be viewed in isolation. If the data collected in an anthropological micro-study is to have any wider significance it must be positioned within the socioeconomic formation of which it forms a part. Specifically, the settlement's formation and evolution can only be understood in terms of external economic and political factors. These include the nature of the housing market, the structure of land ownership and the relationship between the State and poor concerning land and services, all of which directly or indirectly determine the strategies of low-income housing. However, in a paper of this length it is possible only to provide a brief resumé of this wider context.

The growth of Guayaquil

Guayaquil is Ecuador's largest city, chief port and major centre of trade and industry. It was founded by the Spanish in 1537, on low land subject to periodic flooding, 160 kilometres upstream from the Pacific Ocean at the confluence of the Daule and Barboyo Rivers. Its growth stemmed from its optimal location at the point where tropical produce transported from the hinterland by rivercraft could be transferred to seagoing vessels for export. Therefore, its growth has been closely linked to Ecuador's primary export-oriented economy and has been critically dependent on shifts in the world market structure (MacIntosh, 1972). It has grown during both booms and slumps: the decline in the traditional export crop of cacao in the 1920s resulted in a massive in-migration with the city's population growing from 45 000 in 1890 to 116 000 in 1930 (Moore, 1978: 184). Urbanization after the Second World War was even faster, resulting partly from the decline in the banana boom in the 1960s, but also from import-substitution industrialization policy after 1950. Historically, Guayaquil's economy has been controlled by a small number of élite families. This group accumulated capital through the export of agricultural products and the importing of machinery, diversified their

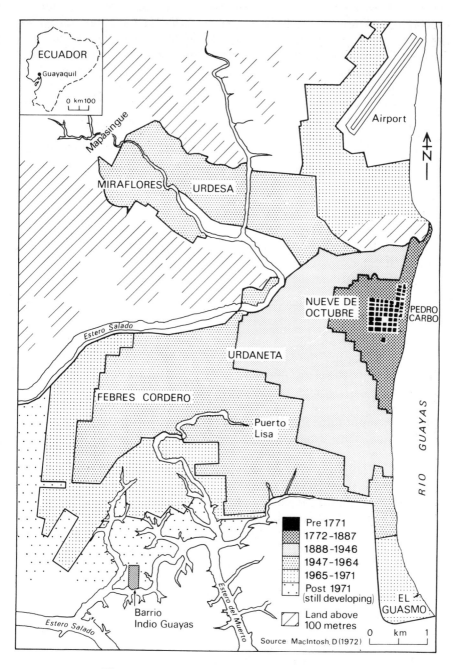

Figure 7.1   Guayaquil: pattern of urban growth

business by investing in commercial banks (such as Filanbanco and La Previsora) and moved finally into the industrial sector concentrating on agricultural processing plants (such as Secafe) (Navarro, 1976). One consequence of the enormous political and economic power based in Guayaquil has been to ensure that the city remained the first port of the country even after its natural advantages disappeared. The city has benefited from a disproportionate amount of national State investment which has been used to modernize the city's port, airport and urban infrastructure (MacIntosh, 1972). Unfortunately, the highly skewed distribution of income in Ecuador and the low level of *per capita* income has limited the possibilities for industrial development (JUNAPLA, 1973). As a result, Guayaquil has remained an industrial enclave with limited industrial employment. Urban growth, therefore, has not only been a reflection of job creation but also of the agricultural sector's declining capacity to retain its population (Cuera, 1972; Hurtado, 1969; Moore, 1978). Today, Guayaquil has a population of over one million with 30 per cent of its annual growth produced by in-migration. These migrants are mainly *mestizos* from the surrounding littoral departments but also include a limited number of Indians from the highland *Sierra*.

Spatial development of the city

Commercial activity in Guayaquil is focused around the forty gridiron blocks which broadly formed the Spanish colonial city in 1771. On the edge of this area are the inner-city slums, the *tugurios*. These rooms, either subdivisions of decaying middle-class houses or purpose-built tenements, accommodate up to 15 people per room in appalling overcrowded and insanitary conditions. Although many of these slums lie within the 1887 city limits (Hamerby, 1973), over time they have extended outwards along with the city's development. However, few of the buildings date from before the 1890s when the last of a series of fires swept through the city. To the north, separated on higher hilly ground, are the predominantly middle- and upper-income areas (Figure 7.1). To the west and south, stretching towards the river estuaries which bound the city, is an area of tidal swampland with little commercial value in its natural state, which provides the predominant area for low-income expansion. Settlement in this peripheral zone involves two processes—the creation of solid land as well as the construction of squatter housing. This area is known as the *suburbios* and has grown at a far faster rate than the rest of the city (Crook, 1978: 107); in 1950 it contained 12 per cent of the population, compared to 60 per cent in 1975 (Departamento de Planeamiento Urbano, 1975).[10] The *suburbio* is heterogeneous in terms of housing structure, type of tenancy, density of population and provision of services. The older more consolidated parts are virtually indistinguishable from the *tugurios* with upgraded brick and cement housing, high population densities, a high incidence of rented accommodation and some services (but no sewerage).[11] A transitional zone gradually gives way to kilometre after kilometre of small, incrementally built, bamboo and timber houses standing on poles above the mud and polluted water. The houses are interconnected by a complex system of catwalks (*puentes*) which also link them to the nearest solid land, in some areas as far as a forty-minute walk away. This newer area of the *suburbio* which stretches to the Estero Salado and its tributaries, has a much higher incidence of 'ownership', lower population densities and virtually no services.

The supply of housing in Guayaquil does not meet the demands of the poor. The urban population has expanded rapidly, and, particularly since the discovery of petroleum during the 1970s, a construction boom has resulted in rapid development of the city centre involving the destruction of many old inner-city houses to make space for new offices, banks, shops and apartment blocks. Consequently, tenement accommodation has become increasingly scarce, rents have increased and housing densities have risen to the point where conditions in rooms are insanitary and overcrowded. Because they cannot afford the prices most of the urban poor are effectively excluded from the conventional (public or private) housing market (Banco Ecuatoriano de Vivienda, 1975: 7). In 1975, for example, the average cost of public housing was approximately U.S. $920, as compared to the monthly *per capita* income in the city of U.S. $25 (Moore and Caruso, 1975: 27). As a consequence, many public housing programmes have tended to provide 'units on the whole occupied by middle-income groups' (Van Fleet, 1969: 5). The critical factor determining the size of the rental sector is the extent to which low-income families are able to build their own accommodation. This is determined by a number of factors of which the most important are the availability of land, the attitude of the State and the income levels of the poor. 'Where these factors operate against "self-help solutions" then the rental market is likely to contain a high proportion of urban poor' (Gilbert and Ward, 1978: 297). As in certain other Latin American cities, the illegal 'invasion' and settlement of land has been the predominant means by which the poor in Guayaquil have obtained housing — by which is meant both land and some form of shelter.

Invasions and the growth of the Suburbios

Indio Guayas is one such squatter settlement, situated on the far edge of the *suburbio* (Figure 7.1). Although it is over one hour by bus from the city centre, with its access to employment and educational establishments, and is located on floodland right at the edge of one of the tributaries of the Estero Salado the *moradores* (literally inhabitants) have moved there because of the high costs of rental accommodation and the advantage of owning *de facto* a plot of land.

In order to understand both the manner in which commodity relations have developed in relation to this mangrove swampland and the process of land valorization, it is necessary to refer briefly to the question of land ownership in Guayaquil. It is especially important to comprehend the relationship between the structure of land ownership, alternative uses of land and the extent to which the State and/or private sector tolerates squatting.

Although there is no universal pattern of land ownership, an extensive literature on patterns of ownership in Latin America has identified that 'where land has limited alternative use values or is publicly owned, squatting tends to be more common' (Gilbert and Ward, 1978: 298). Therefore, in cities such as Lima, which is surrounded by State-owned desert land, or Valencia with large areas of low-lying municipal land, wide-scale squatting has occurred (Collier, 1976; Gilbert, 1981). However, where the private sector or State is highly resistant to the threat of invasion, as in Mexico City, São Paulo and Bogotá, illegal subdivisions are then the only alternative strategy for the poor. Equally important is the manner in which governmental attitudes towards invasion vary, not only between cities but also between regimes and different periods within a specific city.[12] Consequently, both the alternative uses of land and the State's attitude towards invasion need to be identified in the case of Guayaquil.

Historically, the ownership of land in Guayaquil has varied according to the type of terrain. For centuries the higher land to the north and south of Guayaquil's commercial centre was owned by a few families. Gradually, they have speculated with this land, selling off plots in some areas for middle-class housing estates, in others for industrial estate development. Until fairly recently, squatting was actively discouraged, with the police used to remove invaders. However, with the exhaustion of municipal land in the late 1970s (see below), invasions have occurred on private land in Mapasingue and Durán in the north and on partly municipal land in Guasmo in the south. By contrast, the lowland mangrove *suburbio* to the west and south-west of the city, which has been largely developed since 1946 through the process of gradual in-filling (primarily with quarried rocks and rubble and to a much lesser extent with the city's garbage), has a complex history of ownership. In 1880, the Municipality bought a large area of land, fronting on the river, from the Banco de Crédito Hipotecario for 14 500 pesos. All of this land 'is today known as the *Barrios Suburbanos*' (Estrada Ycaza, 1973: 23). Although part of this land was appropriated by a Peruvian (Miguel Terencio Gutiérrez) in 1905, in 1928 it was returned to the Municipality by supreme decree.

In 1950, some 13 hectares of *suburbio* land were mistakenly declared to be unsettled (*terrenos baldiós*) and in a national government contract of sale this 'land' was sold by the *Parroquia Urbana* of Ayacucho to five private individuals.[13] However, in 1967 the National government, in a new decree (No. 151) declared the 1950 sale 'invalid' and the land was returned to the Municipality. It is important to emphasize that powerful political pressure from the CFP Party of Assad Bucaram provided an important influence on the enactment of this legislation. Although the rights of the Municipality were reaffirmed by this decree (Saavedra and Loqui, 1976: 147–56), municipal control was limited in several ways.[14]

Firstly, the Municipality was required to *sell* land for 5 sucres per square metre to the existing occupier, provided he had been there one year or more, owned no other property in the city, and the plot (*solar*) was not larger than 300 square metres. Secondly, all the so-called shore zone (*zona de playa*), which the State had given irrevocably to the Municipality, was in turn to be donated to those settlers with more than one year's occupancy. In fact, the politically motivated use of the term *zona de playa* for much of the suburbio area forced the Municipality to hand over much of the land without payment (Estrada Ycaza, 1973: 24). Although the 1967 decree consolidated the *de jure* ownership of *suburbio* land, it was only with the 1974 Municipal Ordinance for the allocation of *solars* that provision was made for legal title to land. This ordinance established an Office for the Distribution of *Solars* to allocate and administer titles to the land, as well as prohibiting the invasion or occupation of empty *solars* located in the *zona de donación*. However, the process set up for acquiring permanent title was highly complex, involving several government offices (Moore, 1978: 190); by 1978 only 2 000 out of an estimated 60 000 titles had been distributed.[15]

The different types of invasion onto *suburbio* land occurring during the 1940–70 period can be clarified if placed within the context of the changing patterns of land ownership. Lutz (1970) distinguishes between three main types of invasions. Firstly, politically motivated and organized land invasions, tending to occur near elections: 'When a political party wins an election but cannot deliver on promises on jobs, housing and improved standards of living, it may "give away land it doesn't own" ' (Lutz, 1970: 60). This use of land as a source of political patronage is a well-known and widely identified phenomenon particularly in the case of publicly-owned land.[16] In the case of Guayaquil, this process first began during the 1940s on what was widely reputed to be municipally owned *suburbio* land. Estrada Ycaza (1977: 231) claims that in Guayaquil 'the process of invasion is essentially political' and this was certainly the case with the first large-scale invasions of *suburbio* floodland which occurred during the Second World War. Initially, they were promoted by the political party of Velasco Ibarra, while later the Concentration of Popular Forces (CFP) was responsible for a much more organized squatter settlement invasion on a block-by-block basis. During the 1960s, 'self-help' campaigns to make the mangrove swampland habitable were promoted by two politicians, first Carlos Guevara Moreno and after him Assad Bucaram. Both used the invasion of the *suburbios* as a strategy to enlist supporters both prior to, and during, their terms of office as Mayor of Guayaquil.

A second type of invasion is manipulated by real estate interests, with landowners prompting the invasion of generally unsaleable land in order to raise its compensation level on expropriation. In Guayaquil, "there have been six sizeable areas of Guayaquil held by large landowners—five of them in the *barrios suburbanos*. Since such unimproved mangrove swamp can only be developed commercially at considerable cost landowners have . . . covertly hired professional *barrio* leaders to organize invasions on their own land. Leaders help invading squatters demand fill, electricity, bus lines, and other services which increase the value of the formerly unusable land. When the barrio leaders ask the municipal government to expropriate the land and provide titles to squatters, the landowner "victim" may denounce the invasion of private property and raise the price. But the municipal government is unfortunately deep in debt and cannot afford such expropriations' (Lutz, 1970: 61). Since Lutz identifies neither the landowners nor the area they owned, his description remains at a very generalized level. The earlier discussion on changing land ownership patterns in the *suburbios* and the so-called 'illegal' ownership of some of the area between 1950 and 1967 would suggest a somewhat more complex process than Lutz describes.

The third type of invasion is that of 'professional squatters' who resettle in a new invasion every few years and rent their previous squatter homes. Their role approximates to that of 'pirate' urbanizers in Bogotá and 'professional invaders' in Valencia, insofar as all open up new land for low-income, 'self-help' housing. In all three cities a considerable debate exists relating to the extent to which these 'urbanizers' make large profits, exploit the poor and are involved in a process which cannot be controlled either by politicians or the planning authorities (Gilbert, 1981: 6). Moore (1978: 201) mentions land speculators in the case of Guayaquil 'who make from 50 000 to 100 000 sucres "selling" lots to participants'. This contrasts markedly with evidence from Bogotá that 'for the most part the pirate market successfully and competitively supplies a relatively low-quality good for which there is a high demand at a modest price and for which there is no satisfactory alternative' (Carroll, 1980: 91).

No overall survey of *suburbio* land at the level of Guayaquil exists, nor any detailed descriptions of the process of acquisition of *solars* and incremental house construction.[17] From the various survey sources[18] it would appear that the first two types of organized invasions were more common in the *suburbios* before the 1967 legislation and that it is the third type, the 'professional squatters', which has predominated since then. Politically organized invasions now occur on the higher-value private land as referred to earlier. Where the invasion of land is controlled by pirate invaders the Municipality has limited, if any, control over the price of *solars*. Therefore, this case study examines not only the process of valorization of land but also the extent to which it provides a lucrative area for those fractions of capital said to be tied to the expansion of petty commodity housing and squatter settlements.

The *moradores* of Indio Guayas

Indio Guayas is the name by which the local residents call an area on the very far edge of Cisne Dos, in the Parish of Febres Cordero (Figure 7.1). Indio Guayas covers an area of about ten blocks (*manzanas*) stretching about one and a half miles. The settlement has no clear physical limits and is named after the *barrio* committee to which the majority of residents belong. The areas over which these *barrio* committees hold jurisdiction vary in size and frequently overlap each other, although one committee tends to predominate in each area. The data are based on participant observation, from living in the area seven months, and on a 244 household survey of three different block groups.[19] The block groups were selected to show changes in the settlement and consolidation process; A is the longest established area (with occupation of up to ten years) and C the most recent (some of whose households had been in the area no more than a few weeks).[20]

The population of Indio Guayas is young, with a mean age of both men and women of only thirty years. It is representative, not of the population of the city as a whole, but of a young, aspirant petty bourgeois group (74 per cent own radios, 34 per cent televisions and 38 per cent sewing machines). Very few couples go through a formal marriage ceremony and free unions (*compromisos*) are the predominant form of relationship. A number of different household arrangements can be identified; nuclear and extended families are predominantly male headed and have a mean household size of 5.8. This is a low-income community, representative of the lower end of unskilled labour. Virtually all workers are excluded from unionized proletarian employment but survive in highly competitive small-scale enterprise, underpaid and irregular 'casual' work in a variety of marginal service sector activities. The men in the survey fall within the census categories of artisan/machine operators (32 per cent), comprising tailoring outworkers, mechanics and skilled construction workers, sellers (20 per cent) and unskilled factory workers and labourers (18 per cent). The women work in personal services (39 per cent), as domestic servants, washerwomen and cooks, as sellers (35 per cent), and as artisans (14 per cent), all of whom are dressmakers (Moser, 1980a; 1981). None of the workers fall within the income groups capable of buying their own conventional homes since their incomes are well below that required even for a house constructed by public agencies (Moore and Caruso, 1975).

The motivation to 'invade' this municipal floodland and acquire a 10 by 30-metre plot is primarily to own a home of one's own, a sign of upward mobility and 'consolidation' in the city. This is reflected in the fact that 85 per cent of lots are occupied by the owner, with a further 10 per cent owned by another member of the family, and there is very little renting or subletting. The residential histories of the *moradores* are heterogeneous. Although 80 per cent of women and 75 per cent of men were born outside Guayaquil a considerable proportion had migrated with their families to the cities as children. Fifty-eight per cent of women had come to Guayaquil when under 20 years of age as had 30 per cent of the men. More than half the sample (55 per cent) had lived in rental accommodation prior to coming to Indio Guayas; often in the inner-city *tugurios* but also in the longer established *suburbio* areas where individual rooms are let. Some had moved through a number of different rental areas and most often (88 per cent) had lived in one room.[21] The fact that 44 per cent of the sample had not previously lived in rental accommodation indicates the increasing tendency for families to stay with relatives not only when arriving in the city but also when first setting up home with a partner. It is not just the expense of inner city rental accommodation which forces people out into the *suburbios*. Some could never gain access to this increasingly scarce form of rental accommodation while either were forced, or 'chose', to remain with relatives as a short-term strategy to save money to buy their own lot in the *suburbios*; 55 per cent of the sample paid for their *solar*/house in Indio Guayas entirely with their own savings.

Acquisition of a lot

Potential inhabitants heard about vacant plots almost entirely through their families (37 per cent) or friends (40 per cent) and over 54 per cent had families living in the area. A distinct process can be identified whereby an extended family settles in the area over time. Most frequently an elder son establishes a house for himself and his nuclear family. After a few months, or even a year or two, he will acquire a second plot in the same street or slightly further out. He will move to the new plot and bring in his mother and/or siblings to the older plot which he transfers to their name. In this way extended systems of families settle in close proximity, with 10 per cent of later members coming directly from the countryside to join their kin in the suburbios, thereby bypassing the rented accommodation stage discussed above.[22]

Although many of the *suburbios*, particularly in the 1950s and 1960s, began as large-scale politically or privately motivated invasions, Indio Guayas was settled primarily through incremental plot by plot squatting. Both individuals and groups were involved in the initial process of cutting back the mangrove swamp and marking out the area, some were associated with political groups while others acted primarily for personal profit. For example, Antonio, an ex-leader of the banana ship loading union, was aligned to a political group but was also intent on setting up his own store in the area. He recalls with nostalgia the hazardous process of wading through mud, water and mangrove with white flags on the end of long poles, meticulously ensuring that the gridiron layout was correct (Moser, 1980b).[23] Each individual has the right to own only one 10 by 30 metre plot, but so-called 'professional squatters', once they have staked out plots for themselves and their family, 'advise' others how and where to acquire *solars*. It is necessary to describe this process in detail if the nature and function of the 'professional squatter' is to be clearly defined.

The inhabitants of Indio Guayas identify eight different categories of *solar* acquisition, making a clear distinction between paid and unpaid acquisition (Table 7.1).

Table 7.1   Categories of *solar* acquisition

Category of acquisition	Total number	Barrio percentage	Percentage of owners in each *manzana* group		
			A	B	C
Cutting mangrove without paying	35	14	17	14	8
Paying for cutting of mangrove	45	19	19	10	34
Buying *solar* without house built	73	30	27	31	33
Buying *solar* with house built	26	11	12	13	2
Invasion-group without paying	3	1	—	2	2
Invasion-individual paying	14	6	—	10	10
Invasion-individual not paying	23	9	11	10	6
No information	6	2	10	7	3
Renting *solar*—not owner	11	5			
	244	100	100	100	100
Characteristics of payment					
Total paying to acquire *solar*	158	65	58	65	79
Total not paying to acquire *solar*	69	29	32	30	19
Other	17	7	10	5	2
Total	244	100	100	100	100

Cutting mangrove without paying: 14 per cent of the sample opened up the land for themselves. In this pre-capitalist form of land acquisition, unvalorized land was acquired for use-value. Comparisons between three different *manzana* groups show that this arduous method of land acquisition was more common in the earlier period, the late 1960s, when large areas of uncleared swampland existed.

Paying for cutting the mangrove: 19 per cent paid a 'professional squatter' to cut down the mangrove and mark out the perimeter of the plot with a few poles. This is seen as legitimate payment for labour with charges relating very specifically to labour-time; only a brief period is involved between the cutting by the 'professional' and occupation by the owner. Here the ingredients of capitalism are present with the introduction of value into the land.

Buying the solar without the house: 30 per cent bought their *solar*, the most common method of acquisition. In this case, the land has a specific exchange value. In this category are included 'professional' speculators who own the plot without building on it, sometimes for a number of years, and then sell it at the market price in a direct capitalist exchange. However, there is a limit to the time a speculator can retain a *solar* in this way (see below), and it most commonly occurs when a resident acquires a second plot free in a new area. Because he cannot own two plots he quickly sells the second, a process found more or less equally throughout all three block groups.

Buying a solar with the house built: 11 per cent bought their *solar* with a house already constructed, a capitalist exchange at the market price. This type of acquisition is more common in the longer established blocks where the owner is often moving to another area of the *suburbios* to live or is selling for speculative reasons.

Gift from family or others: 3 per cent of households had received the lot as a gift from other members of the family. The most frequent examples are when sons give land to their parents, as described earlier, and when parents help a son or daughter to establish an independent household. Sometimes, too, men establish a new house for a woman on starting a second household.

Group invasion without payment: Only 1 per cent obtained plots in this way.

Individual invasion with payment: 6 per cent of all cases in Indio Guayas.

Individual invasion without payment: 9 per cent of all cases.

The last three categories of 'invasion' are similar in many respects with payment the critical distinction. Although these are termed 'invasions' they do not refer to the invasion of the uncleared mangrove swamp as discussed above. Here 'invasion' refers to a much later stage in the process of land valorization, the occupation of plots 'owned' by other individuals who neither live on nor have built upon the plot. This is a recent trend in land acquisition, more common in the newly opened up *manzanas*, which reflects the increasing shortage of unoccupied State land. Although the 'invasion' of empty plots in this manner is prohibited by the 1874 Municipal Ordinance (Saavedra and Loqui, 1976: 153), the lack of legal, documented titles means that *de facto* ownership is by possession. Thus those who do not live on, or protect, their plot are liable to usurpation especially since it is virtually impossible to evict an individual once he has invaded.

Frequently plots are not occupied immediately but are held either for speculative purposes or, more commonly, as an investment in a potential future home to be lived in when infrastructure has reached the area. The distance from the city centre, the lack of electricity and running water, and, above all, the lack of roads and the perilous system of bamboo catwalks, all deter owners from living on their plots. Women, in particular, are reluctant to move because of the dangers to their children and the added burden of domestic labour under such primitive conditions. The arrival of in-fill is therefore often the central factor affecting their decision.

Invasions are often the outcome of the conflict in interests between absentee owners of plots and those owners resident in the *suburbios*. The conflict arises because of the way the Municipality of Guayaquil allocates its limited resources to the provision of infrastructure. The allocation is sometimes made on the basis of a patron-client exchange. Political leaders allocate resources to those settlements which can promise them electoral support. Clearly, settlements with large populations have greater negotiating power than those with few inhabitants. For this reason it is in the interest of settlement leaders, and indeed the whole *barrio*, to increase the settlement's population. One way of doing this is to encourage the clandestine invasion of unoccupied plots. Although there may also be a direct financial benefit to the leader for tipping off the invaders, the principal motive is undoubtedly the wish to have as many people as possible living in the area. The invasion itself is carried out at night when a family will occupy the lot and build a rudimentary shelter. Absentee owners have few ways of countering such an invasion.

Since most absent owners generally pay a resident neighbour a small sum to keep an eye on the plot, news of the invasion reaches the owner rapidly. He immediately rushes to the scene and attempts to oust the new occupants: abuse and violence frequently occur. The police are sometimes called in from other areas for assistance, although it is widely recognized that this action is unlikely to achieve concrete results. In a community such as Indio Guayas, where there is no police station, the community itself has the responsibility to maintain internal social order on a day-to-day basis. In this situation it is the local leaders whose unofficial, but accepted, function it is to arbitrate 'invasion' disputes. In almost all cases the matter under discussion is not eviction of the new occupant, which the leaders have neither the power to effect nor the desire to do so, but the cash compensation payment to the former owner for the loss of the *solar*.

Negotiations are often protracted and throughout the invader must ensure that a member of his family is permanently in residence as he hastily attempts to consolidate the flimsy plastic sheeting and bamboo structure. Although the final price paid bears some relationship to market value it is more accurately a reflection of the financial resources of the invader, with the old owner desperately trying to get as much compensation as he can. However, as Table 7.1 shows, he fails more often than he succeeds.

In the three 'invasion' categories, land is valorized after acquisition (or revalorized if it was initially bought) when there is financial payment. Although there is an exchange, the lack of legal ownership of land means that the whole process described is unsanctioned by the State and outside the arena of legality. The fact that 74 per cent of the sample occupied their *solar* the same year as they acquired it would suggest that the lack of legal title acts to reduce large-scale speculation and limits the length of time an owner can risk owning but not living in a *solar*. *De facto* ownership by occupation means that it is very difficult for absentee owners to guard their plots by 'lending' them to others since the person once installed may simply claim the plot. Similarly, the very low incidence of renting in Indio Guayas is a direct result of the same phenomenon occurring with rented accommodation.[24]

The price of plots

In order to clarify the extent to which an entrepreneurial class emerges to dominate the exchange of land in the *suburbios* it is necessary to examine not only the process of acquisition but also the price paid in the exchange (Turner, 1967: 178; 1968: 358; 1976: 29). Table 7.2 provides a breakdown of the prices of plots. Despite the very wide range of prices provided by informants in the

Table 7.2   Price of *solars*[1]

| Price | Number | Percentage | Percentage in each *manzana* group | | |
			A	B	C
Less than 600 *sucres*[2]	67	50.0	47	51	52
601–1200	22	16.5	12	17	22
1201–1800	5	3.7	2	4	5
1801–2400	9	6.7	0	8	15
2301–3000	10	7.5	11	6	6
3001–5000	8	6.0	10	6	0
5001–7000	7	5.2	12	2	0
7001 plus	6	4.4	6	6	0
Total	134	100.0	100	100	100
Not bought	69				
Other	17				
Price under dispute/ no information	24				
Total	244				

[1]In the case of the 26 solars bought with house built the price quoted is for the solar with the cost of the house deducted.
[2]In 1978 the exchange rate was approximately U.S. $1.00 = 25 sucres.

survey (from under U.S. $8 to the reputed price of $1200), half the owners paid less than $24. Although Table 7.2 has not been adjusted to account for inflation the indication is that the price of land has remained remarkably stable over the ten years during which *barrio* Indio Guayas has been established. The fact that prices for recent plots in *manzana* C at the very edge of the Estero Salado are less than the price of *resold* plots in upgraded areas indicates the critical importance of infilling in the expansion of the *suburbios* and in the changing price of land (Table 7.3). The process of valorization,

Table 7.3   Date of acquisition of *solar* and arrival of infill

	Number in each *manzana* group		
Date	A	B	C
1965	1		
1966	1		
1969	1		
1970	10		
1971	17		
1972	19[1]	2	
1973	11	8	
1974	9	32	6
1975	8	16[1]	12
1976	8	11	8
1977	10	17	21[1]
Subtotal	96	86	47
Not bought/no information	9	6	1
Total	104	92	48
Percentage with infill in 1977	98	87	10

[1]Date when infilling began.

therefore, is related not only to the supply and demand of uncleared swampland, but also to the infrastructural provision, which in turn is linked to the process of political petitioning in Guayaquil.[25]

Seven per cent of owners had purchased plots from other members of their family. The vast majority, however, had bought from a third person; 42 per cent from local people they could name and 21 per cent from other local but 'unknown' persons. Tabulations of named individuals selling plots revealed that none had sold more than three and the majority, one or two. Although there are obviously some entrepreneurs who have made large profits out of the speculative sale of *suburbio* land in Indio Guayas, land sale is predominantly a small-scale petty activity. Numerous locals have made small profits by illegally acquiring an extra plot or two when they first arrived, clearing it of mangrove and holding it speculatively for a period of time before selling it off to later arrivals. In addition, the fact that more than half the owners bought their plots with personal savings, a further 15 per cent with money lent by family or friends, and only 13 per cent used formal credit agencies (employers, loan or credit companies) provides further evidence that the economic activities in this low-income sector of the city do not offer the potential for large-scale profit on the part of those involved in the provision of credit.

By law, every individual is allowed to own a 10 by 30 metre plot but is not allowed to subdivide it. It is clear, however, that subdivision is common in Indio Guayas; Table 7.4 shows that 35 per cent of the sample had engaged in

Table 7.4   Subdivisions of *solars*

Category of solar	Number	Percentage	Percentage in each *manzana* group		
			A	B	C
Solar not divided	123	50	44	54	56
Subdivision of *solar*	87	36	35	33	42
Sale with owner leaving	19	8	10	8	2
Not bought	5	2	4	1	1
No information	10	4	7	4	—
Total	244	100	100	100	100

some form of subdivision. Generally, the subdivision of land in low-income settlements is associated with increasing consolidation and rising land values. As the population increases and services improve the land becomes more valuable so that families can benefit more from selling part of their plot. In Indio Guayas subdivision is occurring in all blocks, whether consolidated or not. This suggests that increased pressure on municipal *suburbio* land in general is leading to higher prices for the newer land or at least to greater pressure on individual households to subdivide. Nevertheless, the process is not far advanced since the mean size of plot in the sample was 231 square metres with little variation between the three block areas (Table 7.5).

From the detailed description of plot acquisition it is apparent that the process by which this municipally owned swamp has become valorized is neither homogeneous nor straightforward. Almost all the inhabitants had been involved in an exchange relationship in the acquisition of their plot prior to building their house. Burgess refers to housing (by which he means the physical house plus the land) in the self-help form as 'operating in a different sphere of circulation of capital' (1978: 1112). The evidence from Indio Guayas shows that although the process of valorization of land has involved neither the penetration of large-scale capital nor accumulation at any significant level, it is clearly capitalist exchange. The extent to which it is useful to define it as being in a different sphere of the circulation of capital because of its *scale* is not clear. The most significant characteristics of the process are the low prices charged for plots, the limited labour charges for cutting down the mangrove swamps, and the small 'tip offs' paid for the selling off of unoccupied, or illegally acquired, plots. Inhabitants of the area buy and sell to one another and use their profits to acquire larger or better positioned plots and to improve their houses. Land prices for the *suburbio* swamp have not increased as much as might be expected over the ten year period. The fact that a powerful entrepreneurial class has not emerged means that caution is necessary when referring to the scale of profits made; certainly they do not reach anywhere near the figure of 50 000 sucres cited by Moore (1978: 201). Two factors

Table 7.5   Size of *solars* in the three *manzana* groups

Solar size (square metres)	Percentage	Percentage in each *manzana* group		
		A	B	C
Less than 50	2	1	2	—
51–100	7	11	4	2
101–150	24	29	24	11
151–200	14	15	16	11
201–250	13	11	11	24
251–300	31	24	36	39
301–350	2	2	3	—
351–400	2	4	1	—
401–450	1	1	4	—
451 and over	1	—	—	1
No information	3	2	—	3
Total	100	100	100	100

determine the process of valorization of land in this particular community: firstly, the supply of land, which since it is now decreasing may lead to prices rising in the next ten years; secondly, the system of land ownership, where the lack of land titles or of a policing system to protect property means that *de facto* possession by occupation is the concrete form of 'ownership'. The extent to which this acts as an effective limit to land speculation has important implications in terms of the present trend in Third World cities towards giving squatters land titles (Andrews and Phillips, 1970). While such a policy satisfies squatter owners as individuals, encouraging them to 'consolidate' and invest both capital and labour time in their own homes, at the same time it increases the speculative market for land. As Burgess (1978: 1129) succinctly remarks, 'the problem of legality in other words is fundamentally the issue of market valuation of land'.

The process of house construction

The vast majority of *moradores* (84 per cent) bought their plots without a house, while of the 10 per cent who bought an existing house half and substantially altered or extended it. Consequently, this is a community heavily involved in the process of house construction. A wide range of knowledge exists not only among professional construction workers but among most family members; women make small repairs to their houses as they live in them and children repair the roof when the rain comes in and paper the bamboo walls with newspaper to keep out the wind. The constant movement of building materials, brought in on donkey carts, pick-up trucks or on bicycles, gives a strong visual impression of an area permanently involved in construction and repair.

Contrary to the popular conception of self-help housing as a process lasting for an extended period of time, in Indio Guayas two-thirds of the inhabitants built their houses within a three-month period. This suggests that sufficient capital was saved prior to the acquisition of the plot. However, insofar as this is atypical of Latin American squatter settlements, it may be a consequence of the tropical climate conditions of Guayaquil and the relatively inexpensive cost of a basic living structure. The most important building materials are standardized: 86 per cent of houses have corrugated iron roofs, 76 per cent split-cane walls and 82 per cent wooden floors. The house is built on top of an intricate foundation made from thick mangrove poles which do not rot in water. Bamboo-walled houses have a life of six to ten years. The next stages in the incremental process of house construction are the filling in of the swamp under the house, replacing the wood floor with cement and substituting the bamboo walls with brick or breeze blocks. In the more established areas this process of upgrading is occurring slowly. It is, however, very costly and the fact that only 6 per cent of houses in the sample had brick walls and 2 per cent cement floors (even then retaining the original mangrove poles) indicates that upgrading is neither automatic nor inevitable. In fact, for many 'the settlement did not provide a vehicle of upward socioeconomic mobility but merely a means of survival' (Gilbert and Ward, 1978: 302), with both personal and general economic conditions limiting improvements beyond the mere replacing of badly worn bamboo walls (Harms, 1976).

None of the products used in house construction are recycled throw-aways but are produced by capitalist enterprises for exchange. Corrugated iron roofs are manufactured in the city's industrial zone and bought from commercial retailers of building materials. The bamboo comes from the Barbayoya area north of Guayaquil while the poles come from the mangrove islands surrounding Guayaquil. Although the wood is sometimes produced by pre-capitalist systems of production, it is shipped by merchant entrepreneurs and stored in large warehouses close to the low-income *suburbio* area, particularly at Puerto Lisa where the Las Casitas Estuary ends. Local entrepreneurs buy from these wholesale warehouses and retail to the local residents in Indio Guayas. These are valorized commodities then, coming in to the *suburbio* through merchant capital. The retailers are certainly successful entrepreneurs since most local residents buy from them; 64 per cent of the inhabitants bought their building materials from outlets within the *suburbios*, more than half of them from the four located within the survey area. It is the need for credit in buying housing materials, even over a period as short as three months, which often forces them to use the local entrepreneur. The relatively large number of competing retailers within a limited area helps to keep down both the prices of building materials and the profit levels of the retailers. Up to now there has been insufficient demand for these retailers to stock cement or the other materials necessary for brick housing. It may be that more monopolistic practices are involved in the production and sale of these more expensive building materials but we have no evidence to study this possibility.

Houses are built with varying amounts of paid labour (Table 7.6). The producer and the consumer were the same in 55 per cent of the cases. Construction is undertaken at weekends, during periods of unemployment or after work (although this is uncommon in Guayaquil since it is dark by 7.00 p.m.). In Indio Guayas, each individual works on his own house. Turner's description of the resilient poor who joint together to build their own homes is inappropriate in this highly individualistic community

Table 7.6   Labour utilized in house construction

Category of labour	Percentage in survey
No labour (either wage or family)	55.5
Nuclear family (unpaid)	3.0
Extended family (unpaid)	4.5
Builder (wage labour) less than 50 per cent	11.0
Builder (wage labour) completely	24.0
Other/no information	2.0
Total	100.0

where the utilization of unpaid kin or neighbourhood labour is uncommon.[26] Paid labour is usually employed in the first crucial and skilled stage of sinking and joining together the mangrove foundation on which the whole house rests. Many of the so-called 'professional squatters' who clear the swampland are also construction workers. They work in cooperative gangs of two to four skilled carpenters who share their profits equally and who hire casual unskilled assistants on an hourly basis. Not only are these gangs involved in digging foundations but they also construct entire houses for a pre-negotiated price in three to five days. A quarter of the houses in Indio Guayas were built through this artisan/petty commodity form of production to the direct order of the client. There is intense competition for contract work of this sort among the large number of construction workers living in the area. Hence, most construction workers tend to move between this petty commodity sector and the manufactured and industrial construction sectors outside the *suburbios* where they are employed as bricklayers. They prefer to work in the petty commodity sector not only because they earn more but also because they are independent of contractors and bosses.

Insofar as the house is constructed for self-consumption it has a use value. Nevertheless, in the process of its construction it has been valorized through the incorporation of the costs of labour and raw materials and consequently it has a commodity form which may be realized when it is brought onto the market for sale or rent. The costs of house construction vary with the size of the house, the extent to which paid labour was involved in its construction and the date at which the house was constructed. A breakdown of total costs between materials and labour shows the latter to be a relatively small component. Of those using paid labour in the construction of their houses, one quarter paid less than 1000 sucres (the cost of installing the structural *palos*) and 60 per cent no more than 3000 sucres. Not allowing for inflation, 16 per cent paid up to 4000 sucres, 25 per cent between 4001 and 8000 sucres and a further 20 per cent between 8001 and 12 000 sucres. At the other end of the spectrum, 9.7 per cent paid over 40 000 sucres, the owners of upgraded brick-built houses. This variation in housing costs reflects the heterogeneity of the community in terms of occupation and earning power.

One-third of houses in the survey area are used also as a place of production, providing an additional, if unspecified, commodity value. Although the use of the home for petty commodity productive activities is more commonly associated with inner-city slum areas, even in this peripheral area 32 per cent of the homes were used as shops. These shops embraced a wide range of activities: 34 per cent were tailors, dressmakers or shoemakers and a further 16 per cent prepared and sold cooked foods.

Two-thirds of the houses are less than 40 square metres in area, with the newer houses, built further out, smaller than those in more established areas. Over time, a certain amount of internal house upgrading has taken place. In the newest survey block (C), 83 per cent used a hole in the floorboards for the family toilet, while the remaining 17 per cent had a separate structure at the end of a small private catwalk at the back of the house. In both of the older survey blocks, half the homes had holes and half separate structures. Where houses are located on catwalks the twice-daily tidal flow deals quite hygieni-cally with the sewage. However, once perimeter roads are built, they stop the tidal flow and the interior of the block becomes a cesspit. There is little the inhabitants can do without government help; it is easier to cope in a self-help manner with some services than with others. In Indio Guayas, neither water nor electricity is officially supplied to individual households, although Guayaquil's one electrical company, owned by a North American firm, had been pressurized into providing street lighting along the settlement's main road. This electricity line was being extensively tapped by the community: 72 per cent of the houses were illegally tapping the mains and running cables across the swampland. The cost of cable is considerable, often costing as much as 2000–3000 sucres, and neighbours sometimes share a cable as well as jointly guarding it against theft. Water is supplied by a private transport co-operative. This monopoly owns 44 tankers and has complete control over the price, hour of delivery and selection of clients to whom it delivers water (Predam, 1976b: 55). The profits are considerable since the tankers fill up free from municipal supplies located at five points designed to serve the *suburbio* area of the city.

Each tanker holds 55 gallons of water and sells it at 5 sucres per barrel.[27]

It is in the provision of infrastructure, and particularly of infill, that the penetration of larger scale capital into the *suburbio* can be identified. During the past 20 years, the *suburbios* have been gradually transformed from a tidal swampland by the construction of a system of perimeter roads, reclaimed slightly above the tidal level, with individual households left to fill the interior plots if and when they have the necessary capital. Although the municipality has filled in some areas of the *suburbio* with garbage (such as in Plan Piloto) this practice has met with considerable resistance from local communities and infilling is now primarily with rocks, stones and gravel.

The process of decision-making about infilling in the *suburbio* is highly complex and can only be referred to briefly in a paper of this length. It is a process, however, in which political and economic interests predominate over those of the local inhabitants. This was clearly shown, for instance, in the decision not to implement the recommendations of a USAID financed technical study of the flooding problem undertaken in 1966–67. The study showed conclusively that dyking was a better method of flood control than infill, with the consultants proposing that levées be built around the land to the south and southwest of the city. In addition, the estimates showed that filling in the land would cost nine times as much as the levée scheme.[28] The fact that the levée scheme was not implemented was primarily for political reasons. As MacIntosh (1972: 57) has argued: 'Firstly, it required a long-term outlook by the implementing agency, which the general political instability of Ecuador does not engender. The average national president is in office for only 28 months, and the average mayor of Guayaquil for only 6 months (1950–65). Secondly, dyking would be impartially beneficial to all squatters whereas the method of fill allows each political regime to aid only those neighbourhoods that support it'. The latter argument is very relevant to understanding the allocation of infill between communities. Although, there is some relationship between the length of residence and the acquisition of infill, the latter is not allocated in a routine manner but tends to coincide with changes in local or national political circumstances. Thus, the inhabitants form themselves into self-help committees to petition for infrastructure. These committees are then co-opted by the political parties which exchange services in return for votes and political support (Sepulveda, 1977).[29] However, this relationship changed between 1972 and 1977 during a period of military rule. Under this government few resources were allocated to infill in Guayaquil since the regime did not consider the political support of the *suburbios* to be a high priority. At this time, local self-help groups became rather dormant but soon regrouped when local and national political activity again offered them the opportunity for obtaining infrastructure.[30]

Infill comes mainly from private stone quarries to the north of the city. The owners of these quarries benefit not only from the business of selling crushed stone, but also from the fact that they can later sell the flattened hillsides for residential development. Infilling requires earthmovers and lorries and is generally undertaken by large companies rather than by the municipality. It is a highly profitable business both for the contractor and for the quarries and it is widely recognized that political party affiliation is a major factor in the choice between tenders. In sum, both the allocation of contracts and the choice of settlements to benefit from infill is a highly politicized process.

CONCLUSION

This detailed description of the different stages involved in acquiring a home of one's own within a squatter settlement is intended to identify, within one community, the process by which so-called 'self-help' housing is transformed into its commodity form. It is recognized that it is difficult to generalize from this case study, not only because it is based principally on micro-level, rather than on city or country, data but also because it examines at one point in time a complex process which in reality stretches over a number of decades. Consequently, the aim has merely been to provide examples on which to judge whether rapid penetration of capitalism into 'self-help' housing, as against the conservation of the petty commodity production of housing, is the dominant form in the squatter settlements of Third World cities. Recognition that 'self-help' housing, even though it is constructed for the immediate use of the producer rather than for exchange by agents different from the consumer, cannot be understood outside the process of commodity formation, means that clarification of the relationship between the dominant capitalist mode and the dependent petty commodity form is necessary.

The detailed description of plot acquisition and house construction in Indio Guayas shows the manner in which 'self-help' housing is transformed into its commodity form. The intention has been to indicate some of the limitations of viewing 'self-help' housing only in terms of its use value. In fact, the eight different categories of plot acquisition identified form a continuum: from the 'pre-capitalist' form of land acquisition through pioneer invasion to acquisition through capitalist exchange in the case of buying a plot with a house already built. Different degrees of valorization accompany each stage. In the case of Indio Guayas, the most important commodity is not the house but the land on which it stands. Although this is in part an outcome of climatic conditions which make the actual house cheaper to build than it would be, for instance, in a cold Andean climate, nevertheless it does suggest that greater emphasis in the analysis of 'self-help' housing should be placed on the issue of land. In Indio Guayas, for instance, most plots had been valorized by market forces even before the house was built.

In the construction of the house the same type of continuum can be identified, with artisan production for use value at one end and petty commodity production for exchange value at the other. In this case commodity relations develop through the use of paid labour (Table 7.6), although insofar as the owner of the means of production is involved in the cooperative based production process this is petty commodity production. The main construction cost comprises the building materials. These are linked to the modern sector, not only in the case of manufactured parts such as corrugated-iron roofs, nails and cable, but even in the case of the more traditional products such as bamboo which is used not only for the walls in *suburbio* houses, but in the industrial construction sector as scaffolding. While the Burgess/Pradilla typology is useful in distinguishing between industrial and petty commodity housing, the further distinction between the manufactured and the 'self-help' form is not clarified sufficiently to make it definitionally useful. The only totally 'self-help' component is labour; land is valorized through the process of its acquisition and house building materials are bought on the market. Housing in Indio Guayas has a valorized commodity form. Its exchange value on the market reflects not just the human labour time involved in its construction but also independent factors such as the price of raw materials and the supply of land, over which the 'self-help' builders have no control.

'Professional squatters', commercial retailers of raw materials, and local-level *barrio* leaders all benefit financially from the opening up and consolidation of areas such as Indio Guayas. However, it is important not exaggerate the importance of what Burgess refers to as the 'petit bourgeois' element. In a heterogeneous community with a limited amount and range of work available, there is mobility between one form of employment and another. For the male labour force of Indio Guayas entry into construction gangs is often far easier, for instance, than it is into some sectors of the manufacturing sector. As such the 'petty bourgeois' element who benefit from the housing process are in no sense a powerful capitalist class but small-scale, local entrepreneurs. Like most other petty producers they make so little profit that they are unable to increase the scale of their business over time. To date, there has been little penetration by large-scale capital into squatter settlement housing; the process has not been one of increasing marginalization but of conservation of the small-scale sector.

The petty commodity production of housing in the various forms identified in Indio Guayas is integrated into the capitalist sector in a complex but subordinate way. As long as it is not sufficiently profitable for large-scale capital to penetrate this housing sector, it will remain a 'moving frontier' for local entrepreneurs to open up (King, 1974). However, this does not necessarily mean, as Burgess suggests, that 'self-help' housing is operating in a different sphere of capital. The fact that *suburbio* housing is dependent on the capitalist sector is amply illustrated in two ways. Firstly, large-scale capital controls more profitable areas of infrastructural provision such as water, electricity and infill. Secondly, and more important, the land market in the *suburbios* is entirely controlled by the interests of large-scale capitalism, in this case articulated through the conflicting interests of different political parties. To date, *suburbio* land has been seen essentially as a source of patronage. The 1967 decree giving the *moradores* the right to own their plot was effected essentially by a populist party seeking votes. The fact that titles have still not been granted, though it may inadvertently keep down the level of speculation on land, is more likely a consequence of political neglect rather than design. The situation in Guayaquil is common to many Latin American cities. The extent to which it will persist in its present form depends on two critical factors either of which might soon change: the continued availability of municipal swampland which, in fact, is already rapidly diminishing; and the attitude of emergent interest groups in Guayaquil towards *suburbio* land. Whether the *suburbio* is treated as a source of political patronage or as a source of economic exploitation, will determine the future position of the 'self-help' housing form in the capitalist economy of Guayaquil.

NOTES

1. The theoretical justification for such policies were particularly influenced by the concept of the 'culture of poverty' as developed by Oscar Lewis (1961, 1965, 1966).
2. See Harms (1976) and Peattie (1979) for critiques of the 'sites-and-services' concept.
3. See Moser (1978) for a comprehensive examination of the concepts and methodology employed in the 'informal sector approach'.
4. See, in particular the ILO country study on Kenya (ILO, 1972), the city studies on São Paulo (ILO, 1976) and Bogotá (1978) and the sector studies on Calcutta (Bose, 1974) and Dakar (Gerry, 1974).
5. Lebrun and Gerry (1975), Bienefeld (1975), Gerry (1978) and Scott (1979).
6. See Gilbert and Ward (1978: 291–92) for a resumé of this debate.
7. This paper is limited to the arena of the informal rather than formal housing market, in other words to 'self-help' housing as initiated by the poor rather than 'self-help' housing controlled by the State through such means as 'site-and-service' schemes. It is recognized that in reality the distinction between the two types is often by no means clear-cut.
8. Scott (1977) provides a detailed definition of petty commodity production which helps avoid some of the inconsistencies in Burgess's use of the concept.
9. *Indio Guayas* is the name of a self-help *barrio* organization founded in its presently constituted form in 1975. Since it is not a specific geographical area it does not appear on any map of Guayaquil.
10. During the intercensal period 1962–74 the population of the *suburbios* grew at the rate of 9.1 per cent per annum.
11. Because of the limited area of non-swamp land Guayaquil is very compact with a net density in the city centre of over 600 hundred people per hectare.
12. This brief account of differences in the State's attitude to squatting is largely based on a detailed description by Gilbert and Ward (1978).
13. National Assembly Decree number 151 of 14.7.67 stated that the contract of sale of 30.6.50 was between the National Government, represented by the Governor of the

Province of Guayas and Mr. José Santiago Castillo, Raúl Maruri, Manuel María Cevallos and Carlos Ronaldo Repeto. The amount of land sold was 13.02 hectares, at a price of 10.00 sucres per hectare (Saavedra and Loqui, 1976: 147–8).

14. Both Estrada (1973, 1977) and Saavedra and Loqui (1976) in their analyses of the Decree 151 emphasize the double-edged nature of the legislation, which while it required 'illegally' owned land to be returned to the Municipality, then required the Municipality to either sell it or give it to the *moradores*, with sale depending on whether or not it was *zona de playa*.

15. Personal communication with Alfredo Rodríguez, October 1977.

16. Comparable experience of the use of land for political purposes has been identified in Lima (Collier, 1976), Chile in the last years of the Frei Government (Cleaves, 1974), and Valencia (Gilbert, 1981).

17. See Estrada Ycaza (1977: 234).

18. See Acción Internacional Técnica (AITEC) (1976), Junta Nacional de Planificación y Coordinación Económica (1973b), Lutz (1970) and PREDAM (1976a, 1976b).

19. The fieldwork for this case study was carried out between September 1977 and March 1978. It was based on the anthropological technique of participant observation, while the author and Brian Moser were living in the community, and on a 244 household survey. The research was financed by Granada Television and was the basis of a documentary film, 'People of the Barrio', on the survival strategies of a Third World urban community.

20. The sample survey covered three groups of two *manzana* blocks set at equal distances apart, stretching over an eleven block area. Block A was located in the oldest area and C in the most recent area.

21. Even in *Indio Guayas*, households are frequently very overcrowded with extended families, with as many as six to eight adults, living and sleeping in an area of less than 40 square metres.

22. In a detailed analysis of one street in *Indio Guayas* it was found that 26 per cent of the respondents had kin living in the same street, of which 68 per cent were extended family, while 54 per cent had kin in the survey area.

23. Plots laid out in this manner in Guayaquil's *suburbios* wastes considerable land: 'All the suburbio roads are at least twice as wide as is necessary and take up 40 per cent of the land' (MacIntosh, 1972, 58). This can then cause immense problems of costing when infrastructure, particularly infill, is provided (Crook, 1978).

24. Since invasions occur at night one method employed to avoid an unoccupied house being invaded is for one member of the family (generally a son) to literally 'sleep' there, without participating in the community at all. The large number of conflicts of ownership which have arisen with 'house minding' arrangements means that this method is far less common than it used to be. The same is also the case with renting (Scrimshaw, 1974).

25. For a detailed description of the process whereby local self-help organizations are co-opted by political parties during periods of national political activity in the country and then revert to their essential nature, see Moser (1980b).

26. The extent to which the inhabitants in streets lacking infill are willing to provide the capital and labour time on a communal basis for the building of a catwalk system varies widely. It depends a great deal upon the level of trust between neighbours. While some streets have a communal catwalk running down the centre of the street, in other streets a series of parallel catwalks run to each house.

27. 'The water in Guayaquil costs 2 sucres per cubic metre for the rich, while its price

in the suburbios is 16 sucres per cubic metre' (Diario 'El Expreso' of 14 March 1976: 5) quoted in PREDAM, 1976b: 56).
28. See Tudor Engineering Company (1967) and JUNAPLA (1967).
29. This is a widespread phenomenon in Third World cities and is described aptly by such writers as Cornelius (1973), Portes and Walton (1976) and Nelson (1979).
30. See Moser (1980b).

REFERENCES

Acción Internacional Técnica (AITEC) (1976). *El Otro Guayaquil: servicios sociales del suburbio intimidades y perspectivas*. Publicaciones de la Junta Cívica de Guayaquil, Guayaquil.

Andrews, F. M. and Phillips, G. W. (1970). 'The squatters of Lima: who they are, what they want', *Journal of Developing Areas* 4, 211–24.

Ashton, S. (1972). 'The differential absorption of two slum subcultures to a Colombian housing project', *Urban Anthropology* 1, 176–94.

Banco Ecuatoriano de Vivienda (1975). *Informe de labores, 1972–74*. Quito.

Bienefeld, M. (1975). 'The informal sector and peripheral capitalism: the case of Tanzania', *Bulletin of the Institute of Development Studies* 6, 53–73.

Bonilla, F. (1961). 'Rio's favelas: the rural slum within the city.' In Mangin, W. (ed.) (1970). *Peasants in Cities*. Houghton Mifflin.

Bose, A. N. (1974). *The Informal Sector in the Calcutta Metropolitan Economy*. ILO–WEP working paper, Geneva.

Bryce Laporte, R. S. (1970). 'Urban relocation and family adaptation in Puerto Rico: a case study in urban ethnography.' In Mangin, W. (ed.), *Peasants in Cities*. Houghton Mifflin, 85–97.

Burgess, R. (1978). 'Petty commodity housing or dweller control? A critique of John Turner's views on housing policy', *World Development* 6, 1105–34.

Cleaves, P. S. (1974). *Bureaucratic Politics and Administration in Chile*. California University Press.

Collier, D. (1976). *Squatters and Oligarchs: Authoritarian Rule and Policy Change in Peru*. Johns Hopkins Press.

Cornelius, W . A. (1975). *Politics and the migrant poor in Mexico City*. Stanford University Press.

Crooke, P. (1978). 'Housing and Settlement.' In Cassen, R. and Wolfson, M. (ed.), *Planning for Growing Populations*. OECD Development Centre, Paris, 103–31.

Cueva, A. (1972). *El proceso de dominación política en el Ecuador*. Ediciones Críticas, Quito.

Departamento de Planeamiento Urbano (1975). *Esquema política de Guayaquil*. Municipalidad de Guayaquil.

Estrada Ycaza, J. (1973). 'Desarrollo Histórico del Suburbio Guayaquileño', *Revista del Archivo Histórico del Guayas* 3, 14–26.

Estrada Ycaza, J. (1977). *Regionalismo y Migración*. Publicaciones del Archivo Histórico del Guayas, Guayaquil.

Gerry, C. (1974). 'Petty producers and the urban economy: a case study of Dakar.' ILO–WEP working paper, Geneva.

Gerry, C. (1978). 'Petty production and capitalist production in Dakar: the crisis of the self-employed', *World Development* 6, 1147–60.

Gilbert, A. (1981). 'Pirates and invaders: land acquisition in urban Colombia and Venezuela', *World Development* 9, 657–78.

Gilbert, A. and Ward, P. M. (1978). 'Housing in Latin American cities.' In Herbert,

D. M. and Johnston, R. J. (eds.), *Geography and the Urban Environment*. John Wiley, 285–318.

Hamerly, M. (1973). *Historia social y económica de la antigua provincia de Guayaquil, 1763–1842*. Archivo Histórico de Guayas, Guayaquil.

Harms, H. (1976). 'Limitations of self-help', *Architectural Design* **46**, 230–31.

Hurtado, O. (1969). Dos mundos superpuestos: ensayo de diagnóstica de la realidad ecuatoriana, INEDES, Quito.

ILO (International Labour Office) (1972). *Employment, Income and Equality: a Strategy for Increasing Productive Employment in Kenya*. Geneva.

ILO (1976). *Urban Development and Employment in São Paulo*. Geneva.

ILO (1978). *Bogotá, Urban Development and Employment*. Geneva.

JUNAPLA (Junta Nacional de Planificación) (1967). Tudor Engineering Company, *Projecto de Rehabilitación de Terrenos*. Guayaquil.

JUNAPLA (1973a). *El desarrollo urbano en el Ecuador*. Quito.

JUNAPLA (1973b). *El estrato urbano popular: informe de investigacion sobre Guayaquil*, Quito.

JNCP (Junta Nacional de Planificación y Coordinación Económica) (1973). *Plan integral de transformación y desarrollo 1973–77*. Quito.

King, K. (1974). 'Kenya's informal machine makers: a study of small-scale industry in Kenya's emergent artisan society', *World Development* **2**, 9–28.

Lebrun, O. and Gerry, C. (1975). 'Petty producers and capitalism', *Review of African Political Economy* **3**, 20–32.

Leeds, A. (1969). 'The significant variables determining the character of squatter settlements', *América Latina* **12**, 44–86.

Lewis, O. (1961). *Five Families—Mexican Case Study in the Culture of Poverty*. Random House.

Lewis, O. (1965). *La Vida: A Puerto Rican family in the culture of poverty—San Juan and New York*. Random House.

Lewis, O. (1966). 'The culture of poverty', *Scientific American* **215**, 19–25.

Lutz, T. M. (1970). *Self-help neighbourhood organization, political orientations of urban squatters in Latin America: contrasting patterns from case studies in Panama City, Guayaquil and Lima*. Unpublished Ph.D., Georgetown University.

MacIntosh, D. (1972). *The politics of primacy: political factors in the development of Guayaquil*. M.Sc. Thesis, Columbia University.

Mangin, W. (1967). 'Latin American squatter settlements: a problem and a solution', *Latin American Research Review* **2**, 65–98.

Moore, R. J. (1978). 'Urban problems and policy responses for metropolitan Guayaquil.' In Cornelius, W. A. and Kemper, R. V. (eds.), *Latin American Urban Research*, Volume 6, *Metropolitan Latin America: the Challenge and the Response*. Sage, 181–204.

Moore, R. J. and Caruso, R. (1975). *Estudio de investigación del mercado Guayaquileño*. Meals for Millions Foundation, Guayaquil.

Moser, C. O. N. (1978). 'Informal sector or petty commodity production: dualism or dependence in urban development?', *World Development* **6**, 1041–64.

Moser, C. O. N. (1980a). 'Women's work in a peripheral economy: the case of poor urban women in Guayaquil, Ecuador.' Mimeo.

Moser, C. O. N. (1980b). 'Popular participation and the politics of access to infrastructure in Guayaquil's suburbios.' Mimeo.

Moser, C. O. N. (1981). 'Surviving in the suburbios', *Bulletin of the Institute of Development Studies* **12**, 19–29.

Navarro, G. J. (1976). *La concentración de capitales en el Ecuador*. Ediciones Solitierra, Quito.

Nelson, J. (1979). *Access to Power: Politics and the Urban Poor in Developing Nations.* Princeton University Press.

Peattie, L. (1979). 'Housing policy in developing countries: two puzzles', *World Development* 7, 1017–22.

Perlman, J. E. (1976). *The Myth of Marginality.* University of California Press.

Portes, A. and Walton, J. (1976). *Urban Latin America: the Political Conditions from Above and Below.* University of Texas Press.

Pradilla, E. (1976). 'Notas acerca del problema de la vivienda', *Ideología y Sociedad* 16, 70–107.

PREDAM (1976a). *Plan de rehabilitación de las areas marginales de Guayaquil.* Junta Nacional de Planificación y Coordinación Económica, Tomo uno, Quito.

PREDAM (1976b). *Plan de rehabilitación de las areas marginales de Guayaquil.* Junta Nacional de Planificación y Coordinación Económica, Tomo segundo, Quito.

Saavedra, E. C. and Loqui, L. C. (1976). *Estudio de la legislación de desarrollo urbano del Cantón Guayaquil.* Guayaquil.

Scott, A. M. (1977). 'Notes on the theoretical status of petty commodity production.' Mimeo.

Scott, A. M. (1979). 'Who are the self-employed?' In Bromley, R. J. and Gerry, C. (eds.), *Casual Work and Poverty in Third World Cities.* John Wiley, 105–129.

Scrimshaw, S. C. (1974). *Culture, environment and family size: A study of urban in-migrants in Guayaquil, Ecuador.* Unpublished Ph.D. thesis, Colombia University.

Sepelveda, J. R. (1977). *Algunos elementos de socialización política en el area suburbana de Guayaquil.* Departamento de Publicaciones de la Universidad de Guayaquil, Guayaquil.

Tudor Engineering Co. (1967). *Feasibility Report for Land Reclamation Project.* Guayaquil, Ecuador, San Francisco.

Turner, J. F. C. (1967). 'Barriers and channels for housing development in modernizing countries', *Journal of the American Institute of Planners* 33, 167–81.

Turner, J. F. C. (1968). 'Housing priorities, settlement patterns and urban development in modernizing countries', *Journal of the American Institute of Planners* 34, 54–63.

Turner, J. F. C. (1969). 'Uncontrolled urban settlements: problems and policies.' In Breese, G. (ed.), *The City in Newly Developing Countries.* Prentice-Hall, 507–31.

Turner, J. F. C. (1972). 'Housing as a verb.' In Turner, J. F. C. and Fichter, R. (eds.), *Freedom to Build.* Collier Macmillan, 148–75.

Turner, J. F. C. (1976). *Housing by People.* Marion Boyars, London.

Van Fleet, J. (1969). *Urban Development.* Inter-American Development Bank. Mimeo.

Vernez, G. (1973). *Bogotá's pirate settlements: an opportunity for metropolitan development.* Unpublished Ph.D. dissertation, University of California, Berkeley.

Ward, P. M. (1978). 'Self-help housing in Mexico City: social and economic determinants of success', *Town Planning Review* 49, 38–50.

Urbanization in Contemporary Latin America
Edited by A. Gilbert with J. E. Hardoy and R. Ramírez
© John Wiley & Sons Ltd.

8

Who shall do what about housing?

JOHN F. C. TURNER

In countries with very large proportions of low- and very low-income populations, government budgets are bound to be extremely small. Centrally administered housing production in such contexts is a pretence; a sort of charade to distract attention from reality. Most of the real producers, of course, are the people themselves. This is immediately obvious in rapidly growing, large, low-income cities; it is even becoming obvious in relatively stable or decaying cities of high-income countries now that the consequences of excessive monopolization by the market, by the State, or by both together are evident. The reality to which I refer is the same for all contexts: no society can afford to suppress the capacities and will of its people for long; low-income societies can hardly begin to substitute mass housing for housing by the masses; rich societies can only do so for a while, as we are discovering in Europe today.

For those with open eyes and minds, it seems obvious that unless the people and the organizations and institutions involved in housing are properly related, as self-managing entities with sufficiently equal powers to negotiate, resources are bound to be wasted. True material economy, in other words, depends on autonomy (self-management, that is, not to be confused with self-sufficiency or autarchy). As economy, in the final analysis, is the issue of energy use, it either delays or accelerates entropy—it is a matter of life or premature death. However many accessible mineral resources the earth may hold, it should be as intellectually clear to every informed person as it is intuitively clear to every religious believer, that modern civilization is breaking both the inner and outer limits of life: people cannot and will not tolerate alienation from the roots of their being and can never be satisfied by compensatory consumption; and the energy demands of modern consumer societies are bound to exceed biospheric tolerance even if their polarizing tendencies do not precipitate catastrophic conflicts. When these facts are seen it is obvious that we are on the threshold of a profound change: the third energy crisis which is forcing the abandonment of corporate urban-industrial society, just as the previous crisis forced the change from agriculture to industry and as the first crisis forced the change from hunting and gathering to agriculture. Whatever form the next development in man takes, it has to be based on the principle of autonomy in order to achieve a viable economy, social justice and symbiotic relationship of man and the biosphere.

This is the premise from which the discussion of the particular question of determining responsibilities follows. The underlying question of who actually produces what must be answered first. All I can do here is to present the answer I assume and to summarize the argument that I have developed elsewhere; this underlying argument is echoed and amplified by the following discussion but, unless the assumption is recognized, my reasoning may seem obscure.

It is obvious who provides most homes and neighbourhoods in low- and very low-income contexts: the mass of the people house themselves with whatever the rest of society leaves them and with what they can take on their own initiative (Ramón, 1976). Paraphrasing a famous rhetorician, one can say, when contemplating housing by the masses in large, rapidly growing, low-income cities, that: 'Never before did so many do so much with so little.' And, when contemplating the mass-housing projects by corporate agencies for low-income people, one can say: 'Never before can so little have been done for so few with so much.' This is the message of my books, *Freedom to Build* and *Housing By People*: the vastly greater capacity for creating and maintaining useful things that people have when they can get hold of the land, materials and tools they need; a capacity for using their own skills and material resources that is far greater than centralized organizations or the heavy, capital-intensive and centralizing technologies that these prefer. Only those who still believe that the satisfaction of human needs depends on centralizing technologies and ever-larger pyramidal organizations can honestly ignore the lessons the poor teach us all; only if one sees no virtue or use in getting more from less can one suppose that interest in self-managed development by the poor is in the defence of wealth. Those of us who have realized that even our own future, and certainly that of our children, depends on producing far more with far less, have an entirely different understanding and appreciation of what people do when they are free to decide and act for themselves within the limits of their own capabilities. Ironically, it is the poorest and materially most deprived that make the greatest demonstration of this truth. If they can do so much with so little, so much less than is their due, all of us can produce vastly more with far less than is actually used by the rich. The triple pollution of which Illich (1973) speaks, the dirtying, defilement and desecration of the world, is the direct consequence of the counterproductive and unsustainable way of life we rich peoples and classes still maintain.

All present-day establishments, I believe, divide contemporary society into a public sector and a private sector. These are not phrases one often hears on the street and their lack of common sense is becoming evident to many who have long supposed that modern society really can be described in these terms. The modification, if not the abandonment of this assumed dualism, is apparent in the increasingly frequent use of terms such as 'non-governmental', 'non-profit', and so on. Non-State and non-market institutions, organizations and activities are receiving increasingly frequent recognition as part of a third sector.[1] In England, it is often referred to as the 'voluntary sector', somewhat inappropriately as many working in it are wage or salary earners. In France, one reads and even hears the phrase '*la société civique*'. There can be few countries in the world today where there is no discussion of the so-called 'informal sector' and the 'household economy'. Although these last two terms are not a 'third sector' in the sense that I understand it, they refer to realities largely subsumed by it and that cannot be identified with either the private or public sectors as conventionally understood.

Robertson's (1976) book, *Power, Money and Sex*, asks whether it is possible to ignore the third force in human affairs and still understand them: he answers that it is obviously not. Sex is as powerful an instrument of oppression and exploitation as money or power itself. A balanced view not only demands recognition of all three basic motives but also of their complements. There are positive corollaries to each: power carries responsibility; gain can be creative, and sex is the mainspring of loving care. It is absurd as well as blasphemous to ignore the basic facts of life. By ignoring activities, organizations and institutions based on caring and that are neither commercial nor governmental, one is left with the equivalent of only two primary colours. Without the third, it is impossible to paint pictures of what one sees; attempts to do so result in immensely convoluted misrepresentations, typical of most current political and ideological debate.

Of course, there are reasons why many prefer the simplistic dualism: it justifies or, at least, defends the interests of those served by the profits or powers of the predominant systems. Those with vested interests in financial capitalism naturally fool as many as they can, not excepting themselves, that peace and plenty depend on control being in the right hands. On the other, left-hand side of the same general corporate urban-industrial system, those with vested interests in centralized State power have also succeeded in fooling many people for quite a long time. But 'actually existing socialism', as Rudolf Bahro calls it, is as discredited as financial capitalism.

The principal motive of the 'third sector' is care for one's dependants and one's neighbours. Most of us do most things in order to provide what we and those near us need for personal use or consumption. Even though many of the ways of getting the money to do things with are organized for commercial profit or political power, neither of these motives predominate in most people's personal, domestic or neighbourhood activities. As Burns (n.d.) and others point out for the United States, very large proportions of services and, even, goods are produced by people in their own homes and neighbourhoods. The OSTI investigations of owner-builders in that country showed how large the 'third sector' remains even in such a highly industrialized and commercialized context (Grindley, 1972). In much less industrialized, monetized, institutionalized and professionalized countries of the Third World, the 'third sector' is of even greater importance. These observations do not imply that motives are not mixed; the principles of capital gain and political power may necessarily penetrate predominantly personal and local activities. To eliminate the motives of profit and power is as unrealistic as the elimination of sex; all the evidence suggests that creativity, responsibility and love depend on a proper balance or equilibrium which can only be achieved when the third principle predominates. If people cannot or do not care, life soon becomes intolerable and, eventually, the first and second laws of thermodynamics make sure that it becomes impossible.

The duopoly conventionally assumed by the market and the State, and imposed by them to the maximum possible extent, rests on the alienation of production, distribution and use. The language of the corporate establishments inculcates the disabling habit of dividing people into producers and consumers; a habit reinforced by reducing the meaning of resources to money, by calling work employment and by reifying as many activities as possible. These falsehoods are evident in the activity of housing, especially when carried out by people through their own local organizations and institutions that have avoided incorporation into the market or State sectors. It is absurd to call most housing users, residents or occupiers 'consumers'. People only consume their homes and neighbourhoods when they are so deprived of responsibility, freedom and control that they or, more commonly, their children vandalize their surroundings, compounding the neglect that usually follows attempts to substitute central for local control (Ward, 1977). Whenever people are responsible for their own homes and neighbourhoods, even when they have few material resources, they are generally both caring and creative.

The principal producers of the housing stock are the users, whether the first users built it themselves, or had it built for them, or whether it was built by third parties. Unless buildings have exceptionally short lives, because they are provisional or built from highly industrialized systems, users are likely to put more time and effort into maintaining and improving their homes than the original builders. Even if the first builders were general contractors to commercial or government agencies for developments in which users had no part, the continued existence of dwellings, at least, depends as much or more on the work of the users as on the original builders—anyway when dwellings are designed and built in ways that allow for changes and improvements, as practically all traditional forms do. Certainly, the great majority of terrace houses in my own home street in London, built about a century ago, have undergone several radical changes of use, mostly from middle-class single family homes to working class rooming houses, to flats for small modern households; many external walls as well as internal partitions have been removed and rebuilt; almost all roofs have been renewed and so have most windows, most now have central heating as well as modern bathrooms, kitchens and, of course, electricity as well as gas installations. By no means all of these improvements have been carried out by occupiers but most of the minor repairs and almost all the decorations and redecorations have been done by them as well as the vitally important everyday care. In most climates, the deterioration of empty structures, even when unassisted by vandals, is very rapid; and so, very often, is the deterioration of occupied buildings which the users do not care for or whose design and construction do not allow for changes or improvements, even when unassisted by technical faults in the building system.

When and where households share land and amenities in common, as in most original forms of settlement, and where semi-private space is complemented by cooperative management, the productivity of users is substantially increased. As the Caminos (1977, 1980) show, the deterioration of settlement layout in modern times and the consequent social and material losses, have been even greater than those caused by deterioration following the alienation of house design and construction. Those who look to the recovery and reassertion of personal and local powers overcoming domination and alienation by market and State forces, must start with local groups and communities. As the vast numbers of successful squatters' associations in Third World countries prove, they can do a great deal, even when exceptionally poor and oppressed.

The conventionally assumed division of labour and the consequent alienation of producers and users, and the conventional public/private sector dualism must be rooted out of our minds, along with other disabling notions such as the identification of resources with money. We can start, at least, with a recognition of the 'third sector' based on the vital principle of personal care and neighbourliness. Until better words are suggested, I refer to the 'third sector' as the 'community sector' when speaking English; the predominantly profit-seeking commercial sector I call the 'market' sector and the predominantly political, power-seeking sector the 'State'.

Power, money and sex, or responsibility, creativity and love are really principles, not sectors. Realities cannot be split off into sectors like segments or slices of a cake. Activities of individuals are rarely, if ever, expressions of one principle alone; those of organizations or institutions in complex societies are bound to have mixed motives. This three-dimensional concept of social reality and the generalizations it allows us to make, is useful only insofar as we see it in terms of balances or, better, of equilibria as we are dealing with change. For reasons that follow, I join those who argue that equilibrium cannot be achieved through the destabilizing forces of financial capitalism or State socialism. The polemics of privatization and collectivism are essentially meaningless and insoluble without the 'third sector' or principle. Stability and life itself depend on the pre-eminence of caring people.

It is still common to find that huge areas of new urban settlement in rapidly growing, large, low-income cities do not appear on official maps or city plans. In one capital city of the Mahgreb which I visited recently, I was told that the higher authorities were unaware of the largest area of current settlement; this is several kilometres long, at least 1 kilometre wide, and largely built up with houses of brick, block and reinforced concrete. Like so many similar developments in quite different parts of the rapidly urbanizing world, it is neither commercial speculative housing nor State housing. I am not suggesting that the failure to map this or other similar areas in other places is because it cannot be classified. I am arguing that the existence of these largely non-market and non-State, predominantly community or third sector, settlements threaten the interests of corporate organizations or institutions; understandably, their dependants and defenders try to maintain the duopoly with the double think and double talk exposed by George Orwell and by ignoring inconvenient realities as long as they can.

Official and professional jargon locks thinking into the categorical programmes of corporate institutions and organizations. Conventionally, all authority over housing is in the hands of government or of capitalist State institutions or corporations. If people's programmes cannot be ignored or suppressed, then strenuous efforts are made to incorporate them into the market or the State. Both systems are bound to categorize the subjects and objects of mass-housing: corporate industrial systems must standardize for mass-production and marketing; centrally administered State systems must also categorize the subsidized 'consumers' or 'beneficiaries' for reasons of political and fiscal accountability. Both impose an order of settlement that inhibits the self-realization of people's own housing and settlement programmes. It goes without saying that State and market housing take scant notice of people's own programmes.

When thinking or speaking or housing programmes one must be aware of whose programmes they are. Assuming that a programme is 'a course of action' and that courses have objectives, it is useful to recognize the common alternatives, especially the people's or community sector alternatives. I suggest that there are three general objectives that determine anyone's desired course of action, or housing programme: to stay put by resisting eviction and subsequent dislocation (often breaking up an established community and its members' families and often causing the premature death of the elderly);

to improve one's more or less secure home and neighbourhood (often a way of increasing one's security of tenure); or to find another home and neighbourhood in a more appropriate place or with more compatible neighbours. As these are not mutually exclusive goals there are seven combinations of goals or alternative programmes. The classic Peruvian *barriada* builders' programme combines all three objectives; the settlers' first act and objective was to squat an area of land and resist eviction; having done that they then improved; but the overall objective was to establish a new settlement.

Housing programmes are still widely assumed to be new developments carried out by State or market organizations, although there has been a significant change of emphasis in many countries during recent years; these changes are partly due to the influence of international funding agencies but mainly to increasingly organized community demands for the establishment and improvement of existing neighbourhoods. Even though rapidly growing populations obviously need more new homes and neighbourhoods than relatively stable areas, market and State agencies have neglected people's needs for maintenance and improvement. Among the natural reasons for this is the fact that there are more commercial and political interests in new developments: there are more legitimate and corrupt profits to be gained; new developments on new sites can be large, highly standardized and easy to administer; whether correctly or not, they are widely believed to be popular with the intended beneficiaries or users as well as with other social classes impressed by their photogenic quality on completion; not least is the fact that new developments carried out by corporate agencies do not involve negotiations with community groups, anyway until after they are built.

For these and other reasons, the 'order of settlement' imposed by the market and State systems departs from the traditional norm (Beresford, 1967) in which the planners 'devise, order and array' the settlement; that is, in which they allocate the land, invite the citizens and ensure orderly development (by the citizens). Modern developments have reversed the sequence of resident organization, or community formation, and physical improvement or investment. When developments are programmed by market or State organizations, improvements are carried out before the residents are selected informed or organized. The supra-local agencies decide where the people will live, who they will live with, what they will live in and with what forms of financing and tenure, even if they do not also decide how the development will be managed and maintained. All this can seem reasonable and even necessary to those who assume that the market or State agencies' knowledge of what people need is superior to the people's self-knowledge, and when it is assumed that market and State agencies have greater productive potentials. Whether based on sincere or hypocritical justifications of commercialization, institutionalization or professionalization, this historically anomalous order of settlement is a natural consequence of the alienation and reification of housing. In England, this was done first by landlords enclosing the people's commons and subsequently housing them in tied cottages or landless peasants' barracks; the early industrialists followed suit, often forced to house next to their factories their workforce of displaced rural workers with nowhere else to go; speculative developers took over in the expanding industrial cities and, as inflation made renting unprofitable, governments were forced to take over where they could afford to do so; where they cannot and when they cannot, the people take over once again.

When people, or the community sector, take over as the market and State sectors fail to provide, another order of settlement arises: people organize themselves first; they then take the land and, finally, they build. Although the social and economic costs of uncontrolled and unplanned settlement tend to be as exaggerated as the capacities of official planners, it is anomalous for the uses of large areas of urban land to be decided by users without the authorization of those with legitimate powers over city development.

If even partial advantage is to be taken of all sectors' capacities, then the historically normal and traditional order of settlement must prevail. Only if there is an appropriate balance of the three complementary sectors' capacities can persons, households and small groups or associations have the essential freedom to act on their own self-knowledge. To use one's own human and material resources for housing (and for other activities) one must have sufficient freedom of choice as to where one lives; who one lives with; how and on what one spends one's money, time and effort; and how one uses, manages and maintains what one acquires or shares with neighbours. These freedoms demand a sufficiently open market for the exchange of what one has for what one needs; this, in turn, demands law and administration that guarantee sufficient equality of access to resources, goods or services subject to monopolization.

The 'necessary order of settlement' places responsibility for guaranteeing access to locally scarce or unobtainable resources, goods or services, needed for building, improving or maintaining homes and neighbourhoods, on government and State; it places responsibility for the organization of the settlers on the people themselves and it demands cooperation of all three sectors for the improvement. A more specific discussion on which particular kinds of actor can and should make what kinds of decision in the housing process requires definitions of specific kinds of tasks and decision-makers. I have already referred to three general tasks: acquiring land, organizing people and making improvements; and I have also referred to three general kinds of decision-maker: government and State, commercial or market, personal and community. In very broad and general terms I have suggested that, in a mixed economy, control over land is the self-managed business of the people themselves; and that carrying out improvements is, necessarily, a cooperative task for all sectors — with the implication that the market may predominate without monopolizing housing so long as it does not control land and so long as people are not heavily dependent on the market sector for employment.

In a short and general discussion it is not possible to describe the full range of alternatives but an illustration of the patterns at a more specific level is necessary. The most appropriate area or phase of action in the housing process, for this purpose, is implementation: that is, the conception or planning and design of what is to be built and installed; its construction, reconstruction or improvement; and its management and maintenance. In order to see more clearly who should do what, one must identify the kinds of actions demanding decisions and the levels at which they may be made. I suggest three kinds of action: those which lead to the acquisition of resources, or the elements from which all things are made (land, work and technics); those actions which lead to the acquisition or installation of services, infrastructure or other components from which the built environment is assembled; and the assembly of the resources or elements and components on the site. Although there are ambiguities in this as in any such general classification, I have found that it is generally accepted as a way of clarifying what is or should be done in any context. Two kinds of characteristics distinguish each of these three levels of action: scale and complexity. By definition, the assembly of particular buildings and built environments is at the scale of the home and neighbourhood; it is also highly complex, involving all social sectors and many skills. The acquisition or installation of any particular component, on the other hand, is likely to take place at a larger scale or to involve a larger system; water supply, for example, is generally the extension of a municipal network; it is also a simpler operation, involving fewer skills. The acquisition of basic resources, whether particular elements, components or whole assemblies, usually involves country-wide or even international systems. But, whether buying cement or borrowing money, such operations are relatively simple although they do involve very large organizations in many, if not most cases. I am careful to qualify these generalized categories as they are variable; some elements or resources are local and even personally possessed; sometimes complex assemblies providing complete dwelling environments are built and managed by large organizations. Levels of action and levels of organization for decision and control must, therefore, be fully differentiated if the alternatives are to be clearly seen and evaluated.

In my view, one that is shared by many and which is by no means original, the most desirable and ultimately essential patterns or combinations of levels of action and authority, are those in which assemblies are controlled locally; components are supplied or installed by municipal bodies and enterprises of similarly intermediate scale; and in which access to elements or basic resources is controlled by regional government, country-wide or international State agencies. When these necessary relations are inverted, as so often in the modern world, social conflict, material diseconomy and chaos ensue. When housing projects or assemblies are centrally administered, or when resources are privately controlled, most people are excluded. Deprived of access to resources or freedom to use what they have, the majority become either passive consumers or, in societies that cannot afford the massive subsidies needed, the mass of the people must do what they can for themselves in spite of the established systems and with whatever resources they are left with or can seize.

Local autonomy and user-control or interdependent self-management, which must not be confused with autarchic self-sufficiency, is essential for socially, economically and physically viable homes and neighbourhoods. This is not to say that everyone must be responsible for the management or maintenance of their dwellings or surroundings, let alone for their design and construction. It simply means that these responsibilities must be localized. No tolerable system could impose the obligations of homeownership on every household, nor could any acceptable system deprive anyone of the right to self-management or, even, of self-building in appropriate places. I do not believe any general housing system can serve most people properly unless it provides for both short-term and easily transferable tenures as well as for security of tenure and ownership or equivalent rights. It is absurd to suppose that everyone can or wants to be responsible for managing and maintaining their own homes; everyone should have the option of passing the responsibility onto others, as long as they are prepared to pay the increased costs — and, of course, this can be done in two ways: through increased rents or subsidies, or through accepting lower standards, as in the occupation of deteriorating buildings in areas of transition or awaiting improvement. Autonomy or control at the local community level is not at all incompatible with a full range of tenures and degrees of individual responsibility. On the contrary, it is only at this level of collective and individual decision-making that a sufficient variety of options can be achieved — as Ashby (1956) explains in his Law of Requisite Variety.

Ashby states that: If stability (of a system) is to be attained, the variety of the controlling system must be at least as great as the variety of the system to be controlled. All the evidence from the experiences of housing that I have seen and heard of supports this proposition. When large organizations monopolize the design, construction or management of homes and neighbourhoods, users' resources are ignored and wasted; consequently, larger proportions of other resources have to be substituted. These other resources, making up for the loss of users' and local knowledge and skills, imagination and initiative, energy and time, are always scarcer and more expensive. A house built by a large building firm contracted by a large administrative organization, demands a large proportion of professional and clerical work. It is certainly convenient and usually profitable for organizations to standardize their operations and products and, therefore, to use capital-intensive technologies as well as centralized and professionalized management systems. The highly standardized end products, whether goods or services, are usually aggregated in the form of large housing projects with standardized forms of financing and tenure as well as dwellings and often in just one location. The imposition of standardized forms of shelter, tenure and renting or amortization, with little or no choice of location and neighbours, is bound to create mismatches between supply and demand; the poorer the people the greater the stresses and tensions created and the greater the resistance to paying or even caring for unsatisfactory goods and services. The usually poor levels of management and maintenance consequently decline still further unless they are even more heavily subsidized, in which case they are likely to increase the expectations and demands of people whose dissatisfactions are exacerbated by the frustration of having no control or responsibility. In extreme, but increasingly frequent cases, new or recently built projects remain empty or become vandalized and have to be abandoned and demolished long before they are amortized and many decades, or even centuries, before their potential life is exhausted. These highly centralized systems are proving excessively unstable, either financially and socially and often physically as well.

Self-management, local and personal control over housing, can only be properly established and maintained so long as it is supported by organizations providing supra-local services and by regional, national or international institutions guaranteeing access to locally scarce resources or to those, like land, which can be monopolized unless real users' rights are protected.

In principle and in general terms, the functions and decision-making powers of intermediate or municipal scale and central or country-wide levels of authority and organization should be limited to specific spheres: the higher the level of authority, the more it should be limited to regulation and the less it should be involved in specification. In other words, the essential responsibilities of central Government or State agencies in housing, is the setting of limits to what may be done at intermediate and local levels at which works have to be carried out. State or inter-State legislation and administration must avoid laying down lines which lower levels of authority and action must follow. Central planning should be an activity which regulates through law and the exchange system, not through master plans (with the partial exception of regional or even larger infrastructures).

Regional, municipal or intermediate levels of authority are, of course, both better placed and often needed for specific investments and their management, anyway when these serve areas and populations larger than those of particular neighbourhoods. While regulatory functions are properly Government or State preserves, productive activities may be carried out effectively and economically by any sector or combination. Although predominantly commercial, successful industrial enterprises can be carried out by State agencies, ideological faiths notwithstanding, as well as by non-government and only semi-commercial worker-controlled, cooperative organizations. As persuasively advocated by Berger and Neuhaus (1977), what they call 'mediating structures' (or community sector organizations) should be supported by governments as alternative providers of social services for learning, health care, care of the elderly, and so on. Self-managing persons and groups, building or improving and maintaining their own homes and neighbourhoods often need specialized advice as well as particular goods or services that they cannot obtain locally or provide for themselves. Most of these can be satisfactorily supplied through local government, commercial, or non-government, non-commercial organizations. Which are the most appropriate suppliers in any particular case depends on that case and its context.

This answer to the question—Who should do what?—is implicit in the positions taken on the three preceding issues: the community sector must predominate but both market and State structures are essential supports and complements. People in their own localities can only be guaranteed access to scarce resources through law and its administration and people can have no freedom of choice and action without a market system. A viable equilibrium of the three sectors is essential for a sustainable civilization. Both commonly touted alternative futures, the one based on corporate capitalism and the other on State socialism, are versions of the same unsustainable system. Both stem from faith and vested interests in material progress and consumer economies led by industrial science and technology. Both dominant ideologies alienate people in practice; both waste land, destroy its flora and fauna, pollute the air and the sea as well as the land; they ignore the constant energies of the sun, the winds and tides and both are willing to risk all life for the sake of their self-destructive systems. Separately or together, capitalism and actually existing socialism cannot possible serve more than a minority of the world's actual or potential population at currently expected levels of energy consumption. It is probable that they cannot even maintain existing levels for much longer without ending the world with a nuclear bang caused by political tensions or with an entropic whimper from ecological collapse.

WHO CAN DO WHAT NOW?

The International Foundation for Development Alternatives (IFDA) Dossier Number 17 summarizes the needed new balance as follows: 'Two contributions are essential: that people reassert their rights to determine and act upon their own needs and priorities, and that government policies increase personal and local access to resources. Thus people in their own communities will be more able to cultivate the habit of direct action instead of waiting on "them" to do things for "us". What is required is a new balance between community, market and State, not the hegemony of any one sector or system. The complement and corollary of personal and local freedom to act is the guarantee of access to basic resources which only central government, planned production and controlled markets can provide.'

This change means deep changes of attitude and values, and of language and understanding as well as political changes of social structures and institutions. What one can do, depends, of course, on one's situation: anyone aware of the need for these changes should do what they can to practise ways of increasing local and personal control over local and personal affairs in everyday domestic, social and working life; one must be careful to use means that also increase and retain wealth where it is needed while reducing waste and excess; and they must not pollute in any of the three senses of fouling, defiling or desecration. Professionals or specialists of any kind must act to increase the decision-making powers of those they serve, not their own powers. Those in positions to influence legislation or its administration must be sure to make or use proscriptive rules that liberate by setting limits to what people may do, instead of prescriptive rules that oppress by laying down lines that people must follow. Those in positions to influence investments made or services provided by government must use it to replace categorical housing projects and programmes with resources and enabling services which self-managing households and cooperating groups can use in their own ways. The conventional packages of housing goods and services must be disaggregated into 'loose parts' that can be made separately available; and so they can be packaged by the users according to their own demands rather than the suppliers' convenience.

Communication and the exchange of experience and knowledge are essential for the dissemination of the practice and understanding of the 'third system' or 'another development' (to use the IFDA terms). Widespread dissemination and rapid learning demand non-hierarchic, autonomous networks of people and small groups who are practising these alternatives in their own communities or who are enabling others to do so. My own first priority is to assist the extension of these networks, increasing the ripple effects of ever-increasing access to information by those who need it most.

ACKNOWLEDGMENT

This paper was presented at the First International Congress of Major Cities' Planning organized by the Departamento del Distrito Federal of Mexico in June 1981.

NOTE

1. Such sectors may also be conceived as systems and are referred to as such in the IFDA Dossier copies of which may be obtained from IFDA, 2 Place du Marché, CH 1206 Nyon, Switzerland.

REFERENCES

Ashby, W. R. (1956). 'Self-regulation and requisite variety.' In Emery, F. E. (ed.) (1969). *Systems Thinking*. Penguin Books.

Bahro, R. (1978). *The Alternative in Eastern Europe*. New Left Books.

Beresford, M. (1967). *New Towns in the Middle Ages*. Butterworth.

Berger, P. and Neuhaus, R. (1977). *To Empower People: The Role of Mediating Structures in Public Policy*. American Public Enterprise Institute, Washington, D.C.

Burns, S. (n.d.). *The Household Economy*. Beacon Press.

Caminos, C. H. (1980). *The utilization of the land and systems of circulation in urban dwelling environments*. Doctoral dissertation, University College London.

Caminos, H. and Caminos, C. (1977). *El precio de la dispersión urbana*. Facultad de Arquitectura, Universidad de los Andes, Mérida, Venezuela.

Grindley, W. (1972). 'Owner builders: survivors with a future.' In Turner, J. F. C. and Fichter, R. (eds.), 3-21.

Illich, I. (1973). *Tools for Conviviality*. Marion Boyars, London.

Ramon, F. (1976). *Alojomiento*. Información y Publicaciones S.A., Madrid.

Roberton, J. (1976). *Power, Money and Sex: Towards a New Social Balance*. Marion Boyars, London.

Turner, J. F. C. and Fichter, R. (eds.) (1972). *Freedom to Build, Dweller-Control of Housing Process*. Macmillan, New York.

Turner, J. F. C. (1976). *Housing by People: Towards Autonomy in Building Environment*. Marion Boyars, London.

Ward, C. (ed.) (1977). *Vandalism*. Architectural Press, London.

Urbanization in Contemporary Latin America
Edited by A. Gilbert with J. E. Hardoy and R. Ramírez
© 1982 John Wiley & Sons Ltd.

9

The law and home ownership in the *barrios* of Caracas

ROGELIO PEREZ PERDOMO AND PEDRO NIKKEN WITH THE ASSISTANCE
OF ELIZABETH FASSANO AND MARCOS VILERA

Low-income housing figures extensively in the social science literature but hardly at all in legal writing. A probable cause of this neglect is that the origin of low-income housing is normally illegal. In fact, Leeds (1972: 323) suggests that it is illegality which is the common denominator linking Latin American low-income housing areas. These areas normally offend the planning regulations, in some cases they have been founded through land invasions.

In this paper we use the Venezuelan term *barrio* to refer to these unplanned, low-income areas. Venezuelan cities are typically divided into three kinds of residential area: the *urban core* which is the oldest part of the city following closely the original Spanish gridiron town pattern; the *urbanizaciones* which are the newer, planned and serviced suburban areas built mainly by developers for higher and middle income groups but which also include government housing areas; and the low-income *barrios*. The *barrios* remain outside the area legally designated for housing and the individual homes lack building permits; the services are laid on gradually after the dwellings have been occupied; the buildings themselves are often of inferior quality and many can be classified as *ranchos* or shanties; needless to say, they are occupied by the poorer people of the city. These terms, *barrios*, *urbanizaciones* and *ranchos* are used both officially and unofficially in Venezuela. *Barrios* and *urbanizaciones* are listed separately under those headings in the Caracas postal zone classification and *rancho* is used both as a legal term and as a census definition. These terms have clear social connotations; the social class of an individual can be assessed by virtue of his living in an *urbanización* or a *barrio*. These categories persist even if the line between them is sometimes blurred; the older and more affluent *barrios* have comparable income levels to government housing areas, many have considerable numbers of fully consolidated dwellings and are fully equipped with public services.

Leeds (1972) describes clearly the structural conditions underlying *barrio* formation. *Barrios* are a feature of societies with high rates of demographic growth, low wages and changing relations between urban and rural areas. Industrialization in these societies creates an urban labour market, generates a dual market and stimulates migration to the cities. Since large areas of urban land are in private hands and the price of this land is generally rising in real terms, *barrio* formation is a natural outcome.

This process is very apparent in Venezuela and has been characteristic of the post-1935 phenomenon of oil-fuelled urban expansion. Between 1936 and 1971 the proportion of urban dwellers rose from 22.1 to 73.1 per cent and the population of Caracas increased approximately ten times in that period. The pace of growth and the form of land tenure and urban expansion have increased the real price of urban land (Urdaneta, 1971; Acedo *et al.*, 1979). Given the wide disparity in urban incomes (UN, 1971), a large number of urban dwellers have little opportunity to occupy architect designed housing in serviced, legal residential areas. The inevitable response has been the evolution of the *barrio*. In 1971, almost one million Venezuelans occupied 191 163 *ranchos*; 9.1 per cent of the total population and 8.9 per cent of the country's houses. In Caracas, 20 per cent of the housing units were classified as *ranchos* in 1971 and by 1990 it is estimated that 31 per cent of the population will occupy such dwellings (OMPU, 1972).

Studies of *barrio* populations have sometimes produced surprising conclusions (Brett, 1976). It is often nor the poorest who occupy the *barrios* for they are concentrated in hostels and lodging houses in rundown parts of the city centre or in older established *barrios*. These who form new *barrios* are normally people who have lived some years in the city and who have obtained some form of stable employment. For these groups *barrio* formation represents a means of achieving rent-free accommodation at a stage in their life and family cycle when they require space more than physical access to unskilled work opportunities (Turner, 1966; 1976).

What is surprising in Turner's analysis is that the *barrios* can offer a degree of personal security; a sense of ownership which may be contrasted either with the situation of the recent migrant ('the bridgeheader') living in rented rooms and liable to eviction if the rent is not paid punctually, or with the situation of those living in government housing (Montero, 1976). In government-built housing the need to make monthly payments, the restrictions on the sale or the renting of the property and the paternalistic management of the estates, appear to cause a feeling of estrangement which in many cases leads to vandalism and the destruction of communal facilities. In contrast the feeling of ownership seems high among those living in *barrios*. Karst *et al.* (1973) found that in Caracas *barrios* more than five months old, 74.2 per cent of owner occupiers had made a major improvement (built a sound roof, walls constructed with breeze blocks, a cement floor or an extra room) and 37.3 per cent had arrived out at least two such improvements.

More than half of those interviewed intended to remain in the dwelling even if the owner of the land were to appear and lay claim to it; only one-fifth said that they would move if this were to happen. Ninety per cent expected to receive compensation in the event of the government appropriating the zone for a public project. The same feeling of security and ownership was also revealed by the expenditures made on the dwelling. What is surprising in this finding is that *legally* status is very insecure, mainly because the dwellings are usually built on someone else's land and do not comply with the planning regulations. Legal transactions in invasion areas are specifically prohibited and dwellings cannot be entered in property registers. Legally the houses are viewed as *res extra commercio* and may be demolished simply by order of the administrative authorities. The intriguing question is: how is security of tenure possible in the absence of legal rights? The proximate answer is that the law is ineffective, but why is it ineffective and how is the security of tenure attained? In our judgement, these questions merit the research which form the basis of this chapter.

In the first part of the paper we analyse the legal restrictions to building on someone else's land and the way these regulations are typically interpreted and administered in the *barrios*.

BUILDING ON OTHER PEOPLE'S LAND: LIMITS TO THE FORMAL LEGAL SYSTEM

We are concerned with the ownership of the *barrio* dwelling; without doubt the most valuable possession of the *barrio* inhabitants. The great majority of dwellings in Venezuelan *barrios* have been built on land owned by someone else, generally land occupied through squatting. According to Karst's data (1973: 98) title to the dwelling and the land were vested in the same person in only 28.2 per cent of the cases investigated, 80.7 per cent of the respondents said that they, their wives or their relatives owned the dwelling of whom only 21.6 per cent also owned the land. The proportion of dwellings built on land belonging to someone else would be even greater, perhaps almost 100 per cent, if the title deeds were examined since Karst's data reflect what the respondents believed the position to be.

Legal regulations governing building on other people's land

There are no laws in Venezuela expressly dealing with building dwellings on invaded land. As a consequence the regulations applicable are those which appear in the civil code relating generally to building on other people's land.

In this part of our paper we are not going to embark on a discussion of the detailed clauses of that law but limit ourselves to giving a general idea of its aims.

Despite the fact that the Venezuelan civil code underwent a general and detailed revision in 1942, a year when the first *barrios* had already begun to proliferate in Caracas, the regulations relating to building on somebody else's land still derive from traditional European law set down, for example, in the French civil code of 1804. The situation envisaged by such legislation is apparently that of a country estate where some person other than the owner, either in error or bad faith, erects a building on the land or cultivates it. Basically the trespass is envisaged as the act of a single person or at most one family. Such legislation did not contemplate the kind of collective invasion, usually politically organized, that normally establishes *barrios* in Venezuela.

In this context it is not surprising that it is the law of accession which is applicable, summed up by the Latin tag *superficies solo cedit*. In other words, the owner of the land becomes the owner of whatever is built on or planted on his land. The code contains relatively detailed regulations governing the relationship between the landowner and the builder which basically deal with three main points: the good or bad faith of the builder; the landowner's right to demolish the building; possible compensation to the builder.

In the kind of case we are concerned with here, where the buildings are unauthorized and constructed with unsuitable materials, the effect of the regulation appears to be that the landowner becomes the owner of the dwelling and does not have to compensate its builder. Let us bear in mind that from the point of view of market economics adopted by this legislation, a building of this kind does not increase the value of the land (on the contrary, it diminishes its market value). It is also implicit that the builder is acting in bad faith because he is well aware that he is squatting on land owned by someone else. The legislation we have referred to is far from straightforward and our summary may be too simple but the main issue is to determine whether a law of this kind can be enforced. From this perspective the main consideration is one of quantity: there are many squatters, they are well organized and they act together simultaneously. In accordance with a well-known dialectical premise quantity can be transformed into quality and the landowner's position can be altered by procedural obstacles (Santos, 1977).

The way in which a *barrio* comes into being needs to be taken into account for an understanding of the functioning or nonfunctioning of the legal system. Squatting is an act that is the culmination of a carefully prepared plan: specialists within the political parties select the land to invade, taking into account who the owner of the land is, to what use it has been proposed to put the land, its present state and so on. At dawn, on the day chosen for the squat to start, a large number of people arrive in lorries bringing the materials needed to erect initial, rudimentary dwellings. The organizers parcel out the land and lay out the footpaths. On the chosen morning, then, there will be a large number of persons on the site all well aware that they are carrying out an unlawful act but who are prepared to resist any attempt to make them move (Ray, 1969).

What action can a landowner take when confronted with this sort of situation? The direct use of violence by the landowner is precluded because he cannot stand up to a large group of well-organized people determined, even if it involves the use of force, to stay put on his land. If he should attempt it single-handedly or with other private individuals it would cause a major breach of the peace which would require the immediate presence of the authorities. From the landowner's point of view there seems little option but resort to the State and its coercive machinery.

The obvious legal tool for defending his property is an action for recovery of land, which has to be heard by a civil court. Confronted with the squatters, the landowner must first start proceedings against *each* of the squatters in a civil court action. Venezuelan legal procedure differs from Roman law in that it requires each of the accused to be identified even when property claims are concerned. Now, bearing in mind that we are normally dealing with a large number of squatters with more or less frequent changes in the actual persons involved, carrying out this procedure poses insuperable difficulties. In addition, the claimant has to establish that he is the owner of the land, a task considered to be virtually impossible because it entails establishing perfect continuity in the title deeds. Even if he should accomplish these two tasks there would be serious questions about whether the decision of the court could be carried out. Quite simply the magistrate would have to consider the consequences of a major police operation against persons who would be being deprived of their homes.

The other legal approach for the landowner would be to defend possession rather than ownership. This is somewhat easier than proving that he owns it but is still difficult technically. In any event, the other difficulties remain.

The owner has a further, though nonjudicial course of action; to persuade the political authority to view the squat as a breach of the peace and to take action to evict the squatters or to move them on. It should be noted, however, that the action of the political authority is discretional. The landowner cannot compel the political authority to act the way he wants it to. The political authority may take action, but in doing so it will assuredly take many other matters into consideration: the possibility of there being a physical conflict between the police and the squatters, its own electoral interests or those of its party, the public approbrium which might result from its actions and so on. To sum up, action by the police against the squatters does not often commend itself and there are generally more reasons for political authority to sidestep such action than to undertake it. Thus, in order to understand when the political authority takes action and when it does not, it is necessary to analyse government policy towards the *barrios*.

Lastly, the municipal authority can order that the erected building be demolished, not on the grounds that is is on someone else's land or because of a possible breach of the peace, but because it has been built without complying with the municipal byelaws. The landowner could no doubt bring influence to bear to get the municipal authority to act in this way. Once again the landowner has no power or right, official action is discretional.

In conclusion, it may be said that the landowner faces difficulties in actually achieving the advantageous position which the formal legal regulations award him. The machinery of justice fails to function, he finds it physically impossible to evict the squatters himself and his only recourse is the discretional action of the political authority, action which takes into account factors beyond the pure rights of the individual landowner. Let us now look at the actual reactions of different government bodies.

Legal and administrative practice

In this section we analyse the administrative and judicial decisions involving the construction of unplanned urban dwellings on other people's land.

(a) An important ruling handed down by the Supreme Court of Justice on 1 May 1970 established that transactions relating to buildings constructed on other people's land cannot be registered without the express consent of the owner of the land. In our view, this ruling gives protection to a landowner since it deprives the illicit builder of whatever legal protection he could derive from registering the building as real property. Given that the ruling resulted from a reference by a Recorder rather than from a legal dispute, we are not aware of the nature of the buildings or the land that the Recorder or the Court had in mind, but it should be noted that it is of general application and not specifically limited to problems relating to the building of urban *ranchos*.

A meticulous search of the available records and archives at the Institute of Coding and Jurisprudence of the Ministry of Justice revealed only one civil court action. Thus was a judgement of 1958 which did not correspond with the situation we are considering because it was not concerned with dwellings in *barrios* in Caracas. The case concerned a building erected with the permission of the municipal authorities on land which was in no sense marginal. At the hearing it was found that the accused erected the building despite the plaintiff's objection and the defendant was ordered to demolish it and restore the land to its previous condition.

We would stress the few cases in this field and in particular that we were unable to discover a single judgement relating to the building of illicit *ranchos* in an urban area where the number of people and economic interests involved in this sphere must have been considerable.

(b) Rulings made by administrative bodies are more abundant. Firstly, we examined actions taken by the State and municipal authorities. In order to see whether there had been any police actions to evict squatters we searched through the two main Caracas newspapers, *El Nacional* and *El Universal*, for the years 1975 and 1976. There was a well-publicized police action in connection with the demolition of some buildings erected in green zones without the permission of the municipal authorities. The buildings involved were not *ranchos* but dwellings involving a considerable outlay of money. There were also police actions aimed at evacuating parts of *barrios* threatened by landslides. The actions were to move the inhabitants out of danger and to locate them in other *barrios*. There were protests because the place where they were to be moved lacked adequate communications and the available dwellings were of very poor quality. The press devoted plenty of news space to the efforts and achievements of the government in the provision of services for the *barrios*.

We had interviews with officials of the Rating Department, the Surveyors' Department and the Registry of the Federal District Municipal Council whose job it is to take care of matters relating to property owned by the council. We asked them what action they took when squatters occupied land owned by the council. They made a distinction between areas intended for community projects, when they called the police to move any squatters, and other areas, when it was Municipal policy to rent the land to the person occupying it. The rent was fixed in accordance with the area of land and the ability of the occupant to pay.

(c) A very important form of administrative action is the expropriation of land, on the grounds that it is to be put to public use or that it is in the social interest, when that land is occupied by *ranchos*. Here it is useful to distinguish between land that is owned by the State and land owned by private individuals.

The former appears straightforward enough from the legal point of view. Applying the general principles of civil law that we examined earlier, the State becomes the owner of the building erected on land it owns and pays the owner of the building zero compensation. The State could also compel the owners of the building to demolish it and to clear the ground. It is also possible for the State to take direct police action against the occupiers of the *ranchos* and demolish them on the grounds of noncompliance with the municipal regulations on housing construction. A policy that allowed the owners or occupiers time to demolish the *ranchos* and to dispose of the materials and which, once the time period had elapsed, involved forcible eviction and demolition, would appear to be legally well founded. Let us ignore for the moment the fact that such a policy could be implemented only by an authoritarian government able to control public opinion and free from electoral control.

A case involving the construction of *ranchos* on private property is more complex. The State could acquire the ownership of land in accordance with the law of appropriation and then proceed as the owner of the land. According to that law, the State would have to pay the owner compensation equivalent to the market value of the real estate. However, it is arguable whether land on which urban *ranchos* have been built has any market value since in effect the owner could not sell it; the State might appropriate the land paying the owner zero compensation. An alternative approach would be to pay the owner an amount equal to the market price of adjacent land, reduced by the cost to the State of removing the squatters. The State would have to pay the *rancho* dwellers the same sort of compensation as to occupants of *ranchos* on State-owned land; it would be unjust if the State were to compensate those in possession of *ranchos* built on privately-owned land but not those who built on land owned by the State.

The justification for paying the occupants of *ranchos* is clearly in itself a way of getting the squatters to move voluntarily and to compensate in some way people on low incomes who are being deprived of a very important possession. However, it is difficult to justify it within the legal framework because a *rancho* cannot be viewed as an improvement. In accordance with the very terms of State legislation it cannot be bought or sold. Legally, therefore, it has no marketable value; it has only use value for those who actually live in it or who are prepared to live in it.

What actually happens in practice? What action is taken by State bodies carrying out expropriation orders made in the public interest? Our research led us to the National Housing Institute (INAVI) which frequently expropriates land occupied by *ranchos* in order to build government housing. Officials in the section dealing with land acquisition and expropriation indicated that they always apply the law relating to expropriation and pay compensation *both* to the landowner for the value of the land *and* to the owner of the building. Qualified surveyors estimate the value of the building at the date of expropriation taking into account the quality of the materials used. The market value of the land is assessed on the basis of recent transactions involving the same or adjacent land. Officials pointed out that they offer an individual the amount assessed by the surveyor, minus 10 to 15 per cent. In the event of agreement not being reached within this negotiable 10 to 15 per cent limit, the case is taken to court in accordance with the procedure set down in the law relating to expropriation.

The officials mentioned that the occupants of *ranchos* are extremely hostile to expropriation and eviction, far more so than the owners of legally constructed dwellings. The only way open for the Institute to overcome this hostility is to offer to rehouse the families with compensation for the *rancho* acting as the down payment on the new dwelling. Where the occupant of the *rancho* is a tenant, he is rehoused and required to sign an agreement enabling him to acquire it. Because it is illegal to let a *rancho*, the case is passed on to the appropriate Civil Commissioner's who take action against the owner of the *rancho*; under no circumstances is the owner paid compensation.

INAVI officials noted that a dwelling vacated by one family was often reoccupied without authorization by a different family if it was not demolished immediately. In order to get the new occupants to move voluntarily, the Institute pays the new squatters compensation equal to three times an imputed monthly rent for the dwelling in question. To sum up, INAVI's expropriation policy is very favourable towards both the landowner and the people living in the *rancho*, whatever their standing. It is unfriendly only towards the owner of the *rancho* where he is not also the occupant.

The loss and recovery of ownership rights through the law

The State's response to the invasion of private land and property by squatters is important because it is one illustration of how the State and the law view class conflicts. In this case it is a conflict between landowners and low-income groups. The former do not constitute a dynamic element within the bourgeoisie, but they share an interest in defending private property, they belong statistically to that class, and they are connected to it by friendship or family ties. On the other side is a group of persons who are unemployed or employed in low-paid occupations and who clearly fall into the lower class. What role do the State and the law play in this conflict over land? Are the law and the State instruments of the ruling class? Do they serve to protect landowners and their property rights? Or, as officialdom would have it, do they serve the interests of the impoverished and the exploited?

The above analysis can be summarized as follows:

Firstly, the legislation and legal principle relating to building on other people's land entirely favours the interests of the landowner. Although not specifically related to the building of *ranchos*, the only court judgements on the subject clearly favour the landowner against the interests of persons who build on his land. But, the first paradox is that by virtue of Venezuelan judicial procedures and lack of action by the administrative machine this favourable legislation is virtually unenforceable. The legal statutes put the landowner in a very advantageous position while simultaneously the bodies charged with the duty of setting it in motion render it ineffective. Why has the State not changed the law and controlled access to urban land? If it supports the landowners, why does it not make their legal rights effective?

Secondly, this paradox seems to reflect a broad ambiguity in State policy. On the one hand, the State recognizes that a significant proportion of the population lacks adequate housing and resorts to squatting. Plans are drawn up to resolve the problem, different measures introduced and substantial resources are invested in low-income areas. At the same time, however, the State pays generous compensation both to the landowners and to the occupants of *ranchos*. One interpretation of this reaction is that rather than trying to solve the problem effectively, officialdom is concerned to dispense resources as favours to its chosen beneficiaries. Thus, due to the State's generalized lack of action, the landowner loses his ownership rights but, due to its selective action, favoured landowners regain their rights through expropriation in the public interest. Official reaction cannot be explained if we view the State as a single undifferentiated entity divorced from society at large. It is necessary to examine who controls the machinery of State and how they attempt to resolve and mitigate the problem of squatting.

Lastly, let us note a final paradox: the State which claims to protect the poor prohibits transactions relating to urban *ranchos* in order to make this protection effective. By law it is forbidden to build *ranchos*, to rent, to sell them to to do anything of a similar nature. This ruling, intended to protect the poor from entrepreneurs who build and trade in *ranchos*, means that those whom it ostensibly favours find that one of their most important possessions is not negotiable on the market. What does this prohibition really entail? Does it imply that the only rights relating to a *rancho* are those of the actual occupant, regardless of the means by which he acquired it? Does this not force the inhabitants of *ranchos* into a sort of legal jungle in which only the strongest survive (Brewer, 1975: 603)?

THE STATE AND CONFLICTS OVER BARRIO DWELLINGS

Our aim in this section is to examine official action over conflicts concerning dwellings in the *barrios* of Caracas. We have seen that a ban has been put on the renting or sale of dwellings which do not satisfy official planning and sanitation requirements: a ban which makes unmarketable an extremely useful and valuable commodity. The ban poses problems of very great interest for those who study the interrelationship between the law and society. The owner of a *rancho* might temporarily cease to need it, might wish to move, might die or might otherwise need to engage in some transaction connected with the house: what happens then?

The letter of the law, places the builder or owner of a *rancho* in an insecure position: he lacks any legal title and has no legal rights to transact, there is no machinery by which he can prevent anyone depriving him of the dwelling. For this reason it is tempting for the middle class to label the *barrio* as a jungle where only the fittest survive: the only possible right to a *rancho* comes from living in it, disputes of any kind tend to be resolved by force, hence *barrios* are a living example of a Hobbesian state of nature.

In fact, the available research shows that the level of respect for property and one's neighbours in the *barrio* is no different to that elsewhere in the city. The usual experiences of anyone who has lived in a *barrio*, visited one or spoken to those who live there, is that the behaviour and expectations of the inhabitants are similar to those of the rest of the population. How is this situation possible when there is no legal security attached to the population's most important possession and no legal means of preventing or resolving disputes?

One answer is that a spontaneous law has evolved, a joint approach to expectations held in common having its own bodies for resolving disputes (Karst *et al.*, 1973). This common law is not something which has survived from a rural culture, given that many families have lived in cities for generations. Rather, it has evolved from the social situation of the *barrios* and from the influence of formal law with which *barrio* inhabitants come into frequent contact. In Karst's view, the barrio *junta*, a body having no official standing but which is elected, sometimes less than democratically, by those who live in the *barrio*, takes the principal role in resolving disputes. Its methods of creating and applying the law is similar to that of a judge in common law.

Our starting point is different. We do not believe in the distinction between society and the State or at least we do not consider it to be applicable to the study of Venezuelan society today. We know that the political parties permeate every aspect of social life; they dominate not only local and national government elections but also elections for the management of a social club or for the deanship of a university faculty; the parties have intimate ties with economic and social groups and with the machinery of State. In our judgement, it is meaningless to make distinctions between autonomous sectors or levels of society in modern Venezuela. It would be unthinkable for the political parties not to intervene in the life of the *barrios* and in particular for the party in power not to use the machinery of State to do so (Ray, 1969). Karst (1973: 84) himself noted a tendency which supports our view: 'After the original settlement — whether by invasion, acquiescence or invitation — a governing *junta* assumes both legislative and adjudicative functions. Then within a relatively short period of time, as the *barrio* merges into the larger metropolis, the residents increasingly look to more traditional government authority for support and for the enforcement of their rights.'

Karst concentrated his attention on life in the *barrio*, gathering information through interviews and directly observing the patterns of life there. It was, no doubt, this experience that led him to attach such extreme importance to the *barrio junta*, the sole political organization directly representing the *barrio*. According to his own data, however, only 14 per cent of the inhabitants of the *barrio* interviewed would turn to the *junta* in the event of there being a dispute over their dwelling whereas 48 per cent would turn to some official body: 36 per cent would not know to whom to turn (Karst, 1973: 99).

Our aim is to examine official intervention in preventing and solving disputes connected with life in the *barrios*. Obviously the specialized bodies, that is the courts, would not intervene because of the nature of most *barrio* dwellings and because of the high cost of justice. The people are well aware of this because only 3.1 per cent of Karst's sample declared that they would resort to a court in the event of a dispute over their dwelling. Our first task, therefore, was to select which official bodies to study in our research.

After a preliminary survey of bodies involved in preventing and settling *barrio* housing disputes we selected two municipal agencies: the Community Boards and the Legal Aid Department of the Federal District Council. The Community Boards are bodies which have a good deal of contact with the life of the *barrio* and form the base of the municipal power pyramid. The Legal Aid Department forms part of the Municipal administration. We cannot assert that these bodies play the major role in the settlement of housing disputes because we did not study the actions of all the other official bodies. This would have been an extremely complex piece of research. Instead, we visited all relevant public bodies and chose the above because they seemed to handle a considerable number of disputes in the *barrios*, because they were concerned primarily with the *barrios* and because their officials were willing to help us.

The Community Board and the prevention of conflicts

The Community Boards occupy the lowest tier in the municipal power hierarchy, below the Federal District Municipal Council at the top and the *juntas departamentales*. They are official local government bodies and are not to be confused with the *juntas de barrios* (also known as *juntas pro-mejoras*), which are non-official representative bodies formed by those living in the *barrios*.

The Community Boards have jurisdiction over a parish sometimes containing both *barrios* and conventional housing areas. The Board's interest mainly centre on the former as the *barrios* have the fewest services and contain the inhabitants most susceptible to political patronage. The Community Boards consist of five members nominated by the Municipal Council. The members of the Board, or *comunales* to use the name they themselves adopt, are normally activist members of the political parties of the parish concerned. The party composition of the Board reflects that of the Council.

The authority vested in the Board is laid down in article 48 of the 1936 Federal District Act. Most of the functions set down in that Act have been absorbed by the Municipal Council administration and the Board has retained only a general political function in the life of the parish. This is why Board functions and activities differ considerably from one parish to another.

Two Boards were selected for detailed study, El Valle and La Vega, both of which oversee a large number of *barrios*. Interviews were arranged with both sets of *comunales* and the Board records were examined in the case of El Valle; lack of co-operation from the *comunales* made this impossible in La Vega.

We noted that the Community Boards have no specific responsibility for housing issues and that they have other functions in the life of the *barrio* such as helping with social and sporting activities and actually solving disputes.

Nevertheless, it seemed to us that the Board's most important area of activity is to prevent conflicts breaking out and to set up machinery to help resolve any conflict that does break out. In El Valle we studied the board's files for the first six months of 1975, finding 51 official communications relating to dwellings: 43 authorizations, 4 attestations and 4 referrals.

Authorizations are the documents most frequently issued by the Board and have the effect of allowing specified persons to carry out specific acts. Of the 43 authorizations, 35 were related to land occupation, 2 to the occupation of *ranchos* and 5 to matters concerning nuisance to neighbours.

The Chairman of the Board indicated that an authorization is issued only when a plot is empty and when the claimant is homeless or is living in rented or borrowed accommodation and has been given notice to quit. Authorizations are made only to those who do not have the wherewithal to buy a house.

Surprisingly, the Board renounces any responsibility for any claim that the landowner may make. What value, therefore, does the authorization have? In our judgement, its main use comes in dealing with others who live in the *barrio*. It may be that an inhabitant of the *barrio* thinks that a relative or friend might build a dwelling on unoccupied land. As far as he is concerned, the Board's authorization is definitive. In the same way, the Board's authorization would be convincing evidence if the police should attempt to eject the occupants from the land. It is important to note that the Board's authorization applies to an individual not to a group and applies only to land in an existing *barrio*.

It should also be noted that the authority is only given to construct a '*rancho* of lightweight material': normally planks, and sheets of zinc or cardboard. Only lightweight materials are specified, we believe, because the Board is unsure whether another person has a better right to occupy the land. For this reason, it does not encourage the occupant to invest a lot of money in the dwelling which ensures that if there is any dispute in the future the Board will not be automatically compromised in favour of the builder of the *rancho*.

Lastly, we should note that the Board's authorization is for the construction of a *rancho*, that is to say, a dwelling which does not satisfy the minimum housing standards laid down by the Municipal Council itself. However, it is extremely unlikely that the Municipal Surveyor would intervene to order the demolition of the *rancho*; the Community Board and the Surveyor modify their actions according to the urban area involved. The Board would not authorize anyone to build a *rancho* in the regulated sector of the parish. Two authorizations allowed people to take over unoccupied *ranchos*. In one instance, the takeover was justified on the grounds that 'having been abandoned, the dwellings offer a refuge to rogues and people of ill repute'. In both cases it was stated that in the event of the lawful owner appearing, he would be permitted to reoccupy the *rancho*.

The five authorizations concerning nuisance to neighbours allowed repairs or improvements to be made to the dwellings. In several of these authorizations it was stated expressly that the construction or repair work involved should not be detrimental to the interests of others. This type of document is curious because nobody in a *barrio* normally considers it necessary to seek official permission to carry out a repair or to build something. These cases involved people who foresaw the possibility that their neighbours would complain about the work and got a member of the Board to verify that the work would not affect the rights of their neighbours. In two cases, a dispute had already occurred and the Board verified that no nuisance to neighbours was being caused.

Attestations are the documents not having any specific addressee but which are given to the person requesting them and which bear witness to the claims or statements made. One attestation was issued to a woman who had occupied a *rancho* and who subsequently wished to testify that she had done so. It stated that her occupancy was provisional and laid down that if the lawful owner of the dwelling should appear the occupier 'should hand it over without let or hindrance and without seeking payment of any kind whatsoever'. Two attestations concerned the renting of dwellings: one witnessed that the owner needed the tenant to vacate the dwelling so that he could live there himself, and the other recognized that a tenant was doing his best to find alternative accommodation and gave a month's extension of his tenancy. The final attestation declared that a woman was the legitimate owner of a dwelling since she held the receipt of purchase.

Referrals are communications addressed to other official bodies remitting cases to them for action. Of the four referrals we found, two were addressed to the Tenancy Department and involved cases of renting *ranchos*. One asked for legal action to be taken against the landlord on behalf of a tenant. The other involved a case in which the Board had authorized a tenant not to pay rent on the grounds that the dwelling was built of zinc and cardboard. The two other referrals asked other authorities to deal with cases of nuisance being caused to neighbours. Apparently the Board had been unable to achieve an amicable settlement in these cases.

It is doubtful whether the Board's actions are coherent or that there are fixed rules determining their decisions. For example, a general notice was found which drew the public's attention to the continued force of law prohibiting the sale or renting of *ranchos* and subjecting those who broke the law to the danger of arrest. Despite this general notice, however, in individual cases the Board acknowledges contracts of sale of *ranchos* and requires that occupiers leave *ranchos* in the event of the owner appearing. The thought arises that the personal relationships between the most active *comunales* and individuals in the parish are very important in resolving disputes, in particular when they are members of the same political party. It was well known, for example, that one *comunal* with whom we talked was fond of visiting the *barrios*, checking up and solving problems as a means of furthering himself and his party. He did not hesitate to identify his political party nor to accuse members of the other parties as being lazy and failing to do anything for the *barrios*. In documents giving reference of good conduct for parish inhabitants, we found attestations which had a note saying that the person concerned was a member of the party and had been active on its behalf. In such a climate membership of a political party may be a decisive factor in winning support in a dispute or in getting a *rancho* classified as a proper house and therefore rentable.

The Legal Aid Department of the Municipal Council

The Legal Aid Department of the Federal District Municipal Council gives free legal advice to those too poor to pay lawyers. A senior lawyer and four legal advisers currently work full time. They have two secretaries and support staff and are not overloaded with work. The office is in the centre of Caracas together with other municipal offices. The unit is small: there is nothing to distinguish it from any other government office in Caracas.

In view of the Department's title, we assumed that its aim was to prevent conflicts in the same way as a private lawyer's office or the El Valle Community Board. From the first visit, however, it was clear that they were mainly concerned with the resolution of disputes.

How a legal aid office became transformed into a body for resolving conflicts is a very interesting subject for study. Our hypothesis is that since the *rancho* is officially non-negotiable, the Department would have had practically nothing to do if it had not assumed this role. If title to the dwelling cannot be registered, if the courts do not recognize the validity of any contract, and if going to court or to other legal bodies is costly and time-consuming, it is logical that the Department should forsake giving legal advice and start resolving the conflicts itself. The Department's registry was set up in 1968 and contained approximately 2500 files at the beginning of our investigation. We decided to take a simple random sample choosing systematically one case in every 20. We also obtained information by direct observation and through informal interviews with the Department's lawyers.

Our sample finally consisted of 115 cases or 4.6 per cent of the total. Of these, 34 concerned the occupation of dwellings, 20 the renting of dwellings, 19 nuisance to neighbours, 13 problems between couples living together relating to the dwelling, 10 the occupation of or squatting on land and 10 contracts of sale for land or dwellings. The ordinance which established the Department neither lays down the sort of cases to be dealt with nor the procedures to be followed. The most frequent cases involve disputes. The Department lacks authoritative jurisdiction nor is it officially in a position to act as adjudicator to resolve the conflict. It is thus destined to be a conciliation service; its decisions need not be recognized either by the parties concerned or by State bodies. The principal force behind its decisions derives from the mutual consent of both parties to the dispute. The Department is not assigned any special field of competence nor is it excluded from acting in any particular field. The sole guidance is that it should cater only for those with insufficient economic resources to be able to use the services of private lawyers. The lawyers zealously comply with this guidance and do not help anyone who by the nature of the case or from his appearance seems able to use a private lawyer. The Department is familiar with the field of civil law and refuses to handle criminal cases; cases concerning the civil status of individuals are referred to the competent official bodies. Many cases are remitted to the Department by the Community Boards or the local police but many others come directly.

The record of the case opens with a summary, generally a very succinct one, of the oral statement made by the person seeking legal assistance. Mirroring the terminology of a formal legal case we will call him the plaintiff. Next, an entry is made indicating that 'the claim is accepted' and a summons is issued against the defendant. The plaintiff and defendant are usually neighbours. The plaintiff himself is given the task of handing the summons to the defendant. If, on the day and at the time appointed in the summons, the plaintiff attends but the defendant does not, the latter is summoned again using the same procedure. If he once again declines to appear and the plaintiff wishes to proceed with the claim, a police summons will be served on him. This is served by a policeman but direct force is not used to make the defendant attend nor is he found guilty of the charges laid by the plaintiff if he does not co-operate; lack of co-operation does not carry a penalty.

It is usual for the defendant to turn up following the first or the second summons. On the first occasion that the defendant attends the legal adviser informs him of the charges laid against him. Following this the defendant states whatever he thinks fitting, doing so in the presence of the plaintiff if he is present. In the event of both being present an argument frequently arises between the two parties, sometimes a heated one. The legal adviser maintains order, sometimes with the help of a police officer, and endeavours to get both parties to reach a settlement. It can happen that the defendant agrees on the facts of the plaintiff's case. In this case the legal adviser confines himself to suggesting bases for agreement to the two parties. Once agreement has been reached the case is closed. The other possibility is that the defendant totally or partly disagrees with the plaintiff's version of the facts and with his claims. In such cases the legal adviser attempts to bring the parties closer together, proposing an agreement comprising the points on which their views coincide. In the event of agreement not being reached the next step in the procedure is to seek evidence.

Evidence was obtained in only 42 per cent of the cases we analysed; the rest consisted only of allegations by the parties concerned. Evidence is most frequently obtained by an inspection from which the State of the places or objects causing the dispute are ascertained. What is important is how the evidence is handled. It is not a case of proving allegations so that a judge can settle a matter because the legal adviser can only suggest solutions on which both parties can agree. The evidence is to help suggest a settlement; at the same time the expert report or valuation gives a special authority to the lawyer's proposals.

The solution to the dispute is always an agreement between the parties but 58 per cent of case records did not contain a final solution. In fact, a solution was reached in many cases that appears to have been inconclusive, but agreement between the two parties was reached away from the Department and without its intervention. The summons itself can be instrumental in persuading a neighbour to cease a nuisance or making somebody comply with a contract. In other cases the office ceased to be involved in a matter because one of the parties took the dispute before another State body such as a law court or a tenancy office. It is also possible that many of the agreements reached have not resolved the conflict, perhaps because they were not carried out or because the roots of the conflict were deeper than was revealed. But this is unlikely because in such cases one party would usually return to the Department to renew his action.

The lawyer always wears a jacket and tie and is addressed as *doctor* by the junior personnel. The parties involved have to wait in a reception office before seeing the lawyer and a secretary informs them that he is going to receive them. This is of interest because even the role of the lawyer is that of a mediator or private arbitrator, his opinions carry considerable weight because he has the authority which power and knowledge confer on him. In the eyes of the parties he is a doctor of law, his statements are made in official surrounding and when they are written official paper is used. He can have the police called in and can give instructions to police officers. This authority is transferred to his opinions and we have no doubt that it must be very difficult for the parties concerned to reject any solution he might finally put forward.

We have classified the cases studied into two broad and not entirely discrete categories: those cases involving the acquisition, retention or use of real estate, which we have labelled 'property relationships'; and those cases concerning the alienation or renting of land and property which we will consider to be 'conceptual relationships'. In the following discussion we have discussed only some of the range of cases dealt with by the Department.

(i) *Property relationships*

Ten cases of squatting or occupying land were studied: seven of which were brought by the occupiers, one by the community, one by the community board and one initially by the landowner, with the occupants making a counterclaim later on. Rather than trying to get the occupiers evicted, the actions intended to prevent eviction or sought assistance against possible future administrative or legal action.

Seven cases involved the occupation of small plots or strips of land, generally by neighbours, and three concerned squatting on quite large areas of land by groups of people intending to set up a *barrio*. When the person claiming to own the land cannot prove his ownership beyond doubt, which is no easy matter, the Department backs the squatters. Only in one case was conciliation achieved. It involved a claim brought by the El Valle community board against a person who, it was alleged, bought the land on which a *barrio* was being founded and threatened its inhabitants with eviction or arrest if they did not sign a contract. The defendant went along to the Department and handed over a photocopy of the contract denying having made the threats with which he was charged. He proposed selling plots to those able to buy so that they could build brick houses; not *ranchos* 'because the President of the Republic did not want that'. He claimed that he did not mind those who were not in a position to buy staying there until they had found the means to do so.

Twenty cases dealt with the occupation of dwellings. 'Occupation' is not used here in its technical legal sense but encompasses all cases where one person takes possession of a dwelling but another party claims to have a better title. This category includes cases of failure to return a dwelling to its owner at the end of a contract, pure and simple cases of dispossession, and instances of temporarily abandoned *ranchos* reclaimed by returning owners. Solutions were given in only 13 of the 32 cases involving a dispute.

In 23 cases the plaintiffs were the occupants, generally in conflict with the owners who were attempting to evict them; in nine cases the plaintiffs were the owners; in two cases they were third parties, an individual and a Community Board. When the occupant brings the action he usually confines himself to saying that he moved into an abandoned *rancho* and now the owner has returned who wants to get him out. He claims that he needs a roof over his head and frequently argues that he has made improvements to the *rancho*. The owner usually denies that it had been abandoned and argues that he needs the *rancho* to live in himself. Seven cases were resolved by the property being vacated and six through purchase from the owner; in all these cases both parties were in agreement. Purchase resulted only when the owner was interested in selling. When he was not willing to sell he sometimes agreed to look for alternative accommodation and on other occasions accepted that the occupier had carried out improvements to the *rancho* and recompensed him or offered him a sum of money to leave the dwelling.

Problems between unmarried couples were involved in 13 cases, of which four were resolved. In every case the action was brought by the woman; the husband believed himself to be the owner of the *rancho* and wished to get her out. In various cases the man sold the *rancho* or threatened to do so; in others he asked the woman to get of the *rancho* or harassed her in some way.

Two cases ended in amicable agreements; in one it was agreed that another dwelling should be bought for the woman to live in and in the other it was proposed that the ex-partner would stay in the house but that the property would be conveyed to their children.

(ii) *Contractual relationships*

Although Venezuelan law considerably limits the number of legal cases involving *ranchos*, there is no doubt that unscrupulous dealers take advantage of the needs of the poor and carry out illegal transactions. We came across cases involving renting, buying and selling *ranchos* as well as giving land away.

Twenty cases involved renting; 16 actions were brought by the tenants and four by the landlords. The tenants sought assistance because: they could not pay the rent and they were being asked to leave; they thought they did not have to pay the rent in view of the official prohibition on renting *ranchos*; rents were very high; the landlord wanted to sell the dwelling and asked them to get out; the landlord wanted to get them out and did not want to return their deposit; the landlord would not acknowledge improvements made by the tenant. For their part the landlords argued that the tenants had not paid the rent or that the tenant had refused to move out. The tenant had been asked to leave, sometimes because the rent had not been paid, sometimes because the landlord needed the dwelling and sometimes because of the undesirable conduct of one of the tenant's family who was living in the rented dwelling.

Renting is a much greater source of conflict than occupation for the tenant is generally much more opposed to moving out than the plain squatter. However, in the only four cases where a solution was found it was for the property to be vacated. This solution implies some co-operation on the part of the landlord; he offers the tenant money or a period of abeyance or he pays for the improvements that the tenant has made to the property.

Ten cases involved disputes about buying and selling; six brought by the purchasers, two by the vendors and two by the owners of dwellings bought from vendors who did not own them. Five of these cases were resolved. The allegations made by the purchasers included claims that: the vendor refused to move out of the *rancho*; he was sold a *rancho* belonging to somebody else; part of the *rancho* had been destroyed by rain; the purchase price should be refunded because the sale of *ranchos* is forbidden; the title deeds to the property had not been handed over. In the case of the vendors the actions were brought because the purchase price had not been paid.

Concerning an informal official system of regulations

Official bodies deal with the problems connected with *barrio* dwellings but not in accordance with the letter of the law; both the Community Board and the Legal Aid Department act *ultra vires*. In one sense this situation is worrying. In its favour is the fact that common sense has been used to sidestep regulations that would otherwise condemn the inhabitants of *barrios* to violence and chaos; a relatively equitable system of regulation has been established to which there is easy access, in which litigants participate and where decisions are reached quickly. For reasons we will analyse later, the central bodies of the State have not been able, or have not wished, to respond to the needs of *barrio* inhabitants through the formal legal system. It has been left to bodies at the bottom of the State's power pyramid to respond outside the law.

What has clearly evolved is an informal, official system of regulations. It is official because those who prevent and resolve conflicts are public servants; it is informal because it lies outside the framework of the conventional legal system. It is also a system which is highly politicized and as such we need to examine the influence of the political parties in the process of decision-making.

An important feature of the system is that these official bodies take the side of the *barrio* inhabitants when they are in dispute with the presumed owners of the land on which they have built even if our informants said that they rarely had the opportunity to do this. This tendency can be seen very clearly, however, in the case where the Community Board brought an action against a landowner because he had threatened to evict the inhabitants of the *barrio*. In this case the Community Board did not feel confident of opposing the owner head on; it therefore authorized a plot of land to be occupied without prejudice to the rights of others knowing that the Legal Aid Department is very exacting in its demands for proof of ownership.

More difficult to evaluate are the criteria used in disputes between *barrio* inhabitants. Intensive partisan activity by the members of the Community Board, especially the president, suggests that membership or support of a political party may be very important factors. In so far as the Board's chief role is to prevent disputes, it is tempting for them to make definitive decisions about noncontroversial cases. When no dispute is actually involved they authorize the occupation of an empty plot or an abandoned *rancho* and present it as an act of goodwill, thereby helping the *comunales* build up political clienteles. As no reason for reaching the decision is recorded, it would be difficult to cast doubt on such a decision at a later date.

The Legal Aid Department has a less partisan political complexion. At least two of the lawyers were active party militants but the subject of politics was never raised during the interviews. During the interviews between lawyers and people from the *barrios* at which we were present, there was never any allusion to the subject of political militancy. This does not preclude the possibility of political favours, but it suggests that the situation may be similar to that in formal law where political militancy operates in a subtle and concealed fashion.

What is clear is that the lawyers in these offices do not adapt the experiences of formal law to the resolution of *barrio* conflicts. Proceedings are not those of the ordinary law nor are conflicts resolved through adjudication. We should not be misled by the terms used by the legal advisers in filing lawsuits, summons, evidence, etc. It is also important to note that the rules differ from the law on *ranchos* which views simple possession as the only title. Thus, the renting of *ranchos* is considered to be valid; implicit recognition that possession is insecure and the renting of *ranchos* cannot be prohibited.

Because no general principles exist, the basis of ownership is unclear. Sometimes the criterion applied is long-standing possession, sometimes the *rancho*'s construction and sometimes the need of the occupant or owner. Many solutions are extremely ingenious and many decisions involve some co-operation between the two sides. To sum up, while continuing to use legal terms, the lawyers have created solutions appropriate to the needs of *barrio* life.

URBAN POLICY AND USES OF THE LAW

Housing in Venezuela falls into three discrete categories: high-income, conventional solutions in planned residential areas, government housing and low-income dwellings in illegal, unplanned settlements. The first category is distinctive because of its high degree of commercialization. Land is the object of private appropriation and speculation and housing construction is an important business activity. A whole institutional system exists to attract savings and to invest them in housing, mobilizing large amounts of capital and producing considerable profits. Rapid economic growth, private land owner-ship and the lack of price controls have fuelled rapid increases in land prices. High prices and blatant speculation have limited access to this commercial housing, a problem which successive governments have tried to tackle by restricting credit for luxury housing and by giving tax incentives to the builders of moderately priced dwellings. These policies have been introduced both to help middle-income groups and to sustain activity levels in the construction industry; Venezuela's largest industrial employer and second only to the petroleum industry in terms of turnover.

This housing sector is regulated by formal law. Civil law controls the drawing up of contracts, mortgages, registration, sales, etc. and the special regulations govern tenancies in this sector. At the same time recent developments in the housing and real-estate industries have reduced the amount of formal legal work. Private firms have taken over the regulation and administration of construction, financing, publicity and selling. The standardization of documents has increased the work done by solicitors and the government bureaucracy and not the work of the courts.

The public housing sector is ostensibly intended for those too poor to make use of the conventional, commercial market. This aim has not been achieved in so far as the people occupying public housing generally have medium rather than low incomes; a large proportion of this group could satisfy their accommodation requirements in the commercial sector if speculation were controlled. In addition, most of those who succeed in getting public housing do so through political patronage. Even though the public housing sector is covered by formal law, most matters are regulated by the State bureaucracy rather than by the courts.

It is the third housing sector that has been the focus of this chapter. The principal point that we wish to emphasize is that squatting and the formation of *barrios*, as well as the existence of informal legal systems to control those groups, are neither exogenous to the Venezuelan institutional system nor a pathological element within it (Hernández, 1972). Squatting is necessary given that so many poor people are excluded from the conventional and government housing markets. Organized power groups, notably the dominant political parties, became aware of this situation and took charge of squatting and controlled the political life of the *barrios*. Land invasions are not spontaneous, a product of disorganized individual initiative, but are meticulously planned. The land to be occupied is selected carefully, taking into account who the owner is and his capacity for resistance: at different times land owned by foreign corporations has been favoured, at others land owned by local Venezuelan industrial interests, and in other periods the land of public or semipublic bodies such as the Catholic Church has been preferred (Ray, 1969: 42). Existing plans for the use of the land are also taken into account. Those who plan the squat get precise information from government officials and can make a precise estimate of the likelihood of resistance. The press, which might otherwise give coverage to efforts to evict the squatters, is also controlled through the political parties and they may put pressure on the authorities to permit an invasion. In exchange for these carefully planned operations the parties naturally expect to get the beneficiaries' political support.

What is surprising at first sight is that the same political groups maintain private land ownership and allow land speculation, while promoting invasions and protecting the squatters and illegal builders. Such a contradiction can only be explained in terms of the way the social and political system works. The Venezuelan political regime is based on compromise. Urban reforms nationalizing or significantly limiting land or house prices would be extremely controversial and might even be interpreted by some groups as an act of confrontation. Moreover, as land use is closely connected with the country's productive and political structures, it is natural that the State should wish to avoid controls of this kind. At the same time, systematic repression of squatters and a total failure to provide housing alternatives for those on low incomes would be socially and politically explosive. Thus, squatting and the servicing of *barrios* are not inconsistent with private ownership and speculation in land and housing. In a country like Venezuela where politics is not excessively repressive, they represent two sides of the same coin.

In such a social context the retention of inadequate or inapplicable laws plays an important political role. Possible conflicts are dealt with by the State on an individual basis. The invasions of public land or of land owned by individuals with little power to resist is accepted. In the latter case, real conflict with the landowner can always be avoided by the State's purchase of the invaded land.

For the political parties in power the present situation affords them an extensive system of patronage. Squatting and the formation of *barrios* do not burden the State (or the party in power in local or national government) with any kind of obligation to provide land or services nor the task of sharing them. On the contrary, the State is granting a favour by not evicting the squatters for which those who promote the squat are paid in political power. The provision of public services implies a new round of favours. As for the landowners, squatting can be used as a weapon to punish undesirable behaviour on their part, and expropriation in the social interest or protection against squatters can be offered as a reward.

It is tempting to conclude on this evidence that the Venezuelan State neither constitutes a welfare state nor upholds the rule of law. It is not a welfare state because its objective is less to satisfy the needs of the population than to take advantage of those needs for political ends. It does not uphold the rule of law since it does not implement existing laws and regulations nor has it shown any interest in making use of the legal system, through changes in legislation, to tackle social problems. But such a conclusion is only partly true. A more general assessment would note that current urban policy has satisfied the population: systematic repression and a policy of destroying the dwellings of those without means have been avoided; there is also little sign of a political explosion or of violence and squalor in most *barrios*. Land invasion, *barrio* servicing and the informal legal system have satisfied many housing needs.

This general statement finds support in two sets of data from a study on conflict and consensus among *rancho* dwellers and university professors (CENDES, 1967). These groups are interesting because the first is the group most directly affected by current housing policy, the other constitutes one of the main critics of that policy even though it belongs to a different social class. Both groups (70.9 and 64.5 per cent respectively) broadly agree that the State should control the prices of land and dwellings, but only 1.6 per cent of those living in *ranchos* and none of the university professors viewed housing policy as 'one of the most annoying aspects' of official policy.

Lastly, let us note that the scanty legislation has effectively avoided some forms of commercial speculation in *barrio* dwellings; most notably the prohibition of the renting of *ranchos*. Moreover, the informal systems have avoided the mountainous and cumbersome paperwork which surround conveyancing in the commercial and bureaucratic sectors. If the high cost and the lethargy of the formal legal system in preventing and resolving conflicts is considered, the present system has resolved many of the essential housing problems connected with security of tenure and conveyancing.

The foregoing should not be taken as a description of an ideal situation. The steep slopes and the lack of proper site preparation, brings the danger of landslides and during storms not a few people are made homeless or killed. Sanitary conditions are often poor and the risk of fire is great. But in assessing the *barrio* situation we need to be aware of two dangers: the first lies in applying the high standards of urban living of the ruling class and viewing *barrio* life as miserable, the second in praising a system which although it avoids the most straightforward forms of exploitation and repression rewards over generously a privileged minority. We hope that this study has demonstrated the need for more exhaustive studies of this problematic. Most of all we hope to have demonstrated to social scientists the need to incorporate a legal element into their study of social phenomena and to have persuaded lawyers that texts of law and jurisprudence need to be supplemented by the insights and studies of social science.

NOTES

1. Article 20 of the Rent Act makes it illegal to rent accommodation not meeting minimum sanitation and living requirements. 'Specifically included in this category are dwellings commonly known as *ranchos* which are those constructed of inadequate or perishable materials such as planks, tins and cardboard, which lack running water and a sewage disposal system.' Such a definition does not add anything to everyday language and does not diminish the difficulty of classifying a dwelling as a *rancho* or as a house. For a consideration of the problem of value judgements in the definition of slum housing see Friedman (1968: 3).
2. Other bodies, such as the Tenancy Department of the Ministry of Development, also intervene. We did not consider them because our intention was not to be exhaustive but to focus on important examples of State action in housing conflicts.

REFERENCES

Acedo, C. M. de, Pacheco, E. and Palacios, E. P. de (1979). *Estructura económica y poder político en Venezuela*. OESE, Caracas.

Brett, S. (1976). 'Low-income urban settlements in Latin America: the Turner model.' In de Kadt, E. and Williams, G., *Sociology and Development*. Tavistock 171-96.

Brewer-Carias, A. R. (1975). *Cambio político y reforma del Estado en Venezuela.* Técnos, Madrid.

Friedmann, L. (1968). *Government and Slum Housing: a Century of Frustration.* Rand McNally.

Hernández, O. (1972). *La planificación urbana y el desarrollo urbano no controlado.* Fondo Editorial Común, Caracas.

Karst, K., Schwartz, M. and Schwartz, A. (1973). *The Evolution of Law in the Barrios of Caracas.* University of California Press.

Leeds, A. (1972). 'Las variables significativas que determinan el caracter de los asentamientos no regulados.' In Funes, J. L. (ed.), *La ciudad y la región para el desarrollo.* Comisión de Administración Pública, Caracas, 313–87.

Montero, M. (1976). 'Un estudio psicosocial de la propiedad', *Psicología* 3, 229–34.

OMPU Oficina Municipal de Planeamiento Urbano del Distrito Federal (1972). *Caracas, 1990.* Caracas.

Ray, T. (1969). *The Politics of the Barrios of Venezuela.* University of California Press.

Santos, B. de S. (1977). 'The law of the oppressed: the construction and reproduction of illegality in Pasagarda', *Law and Society Review* 12, 5–126.

Sánchez, M. (1974). 'Estructura social y política de las viviendas en el area metropolitana de Caracas.' In Castells, M. (ed.), *Estructura de clases y política urbana en América Latina.* SIAP, Buenos Aires, 142–63.

Turner, J. F. C. (1966). 'Asentamientos urbanos no regulados', *Cuadernos de la Sociedad Venezolana de Planificación* 36–7, 1–6.

Turner, J. F. C. (1976). *Housing by People.* Marion Boyars.

United Nations (1971). *La distribución del ingreso en América Latina.* New York.

Universidad Central de Venezuela—CENDES (1969). *Estudio de Caracas,* Volumen III. Ediciones de la Biblioteca, Caracas.

Urdaneta, A. (1971). 'Costos de urbanización en Venezuela', *Cuadernos de la Sociedad Venezolana de Planificación* 84–6, 119–24.

Urbanization in Contemporary Latin America
Edited by A. Gilbert with J. E. Hardoy and R. Ramírez
© 1982 John Wiley & Sons Ltd.

10

Urban Renewal and expulsion in São Paulo

RICHARD BATLEY

The population of Greater São Paulo, which stood at 4.8 million in 1960, exceeded ten million by 1975. The annual rate of growth was about 5.5 per cent between 1960 and 1970 compared to six per cent during the previous decade. Something of the order of half a million people were joining the population of Greater São Paulo each year during the 1970s — about 60 per cent of them by migration.

The metropolis (Figure 10.1) was growing rapidly but this was not simply a matter of the settlement of poorer newcomers in the expanding periphery; only the most central districts had a relatively stable or declining population. Beyond the centre, the populations of most areas of the city more than doubled between 1960 and 1970, while some, in the east (Itaquera), south (Diadema) and west (Taboão), quadrupled.

Rapid growth was normal; what has to be explained is the relative stability of the central and inner suburban areas and their relationship with the rest of the city. In one obvious way they were distinctive; the wealthiest groups of the population were heavily concentrated in these areas. A special run of the 1970 census demonstrated that over three-quarters of families in the top income bracket (those earning over about U.S. $1100 monthly in 1970) lived in seven districts within a radius of approximately 7 kilometres to the south and west of the city (IBGE, 1973).

The picture that seems to emerge is of an island of calm surrounded by a turbulent sea of urban development. This picture would, however, be false; there is no island of calm. The relatively slow population growth of the central districts of São Paulo is due to the form rather than to the absence of urban development in those areas. Indeed, the higher income districts of the city are the areas of most obvious 'modern' construction and the constant replacement of older buildings by roads, offices, shopping centres and newer, higher apartment blocks. Behind the relative stability in population was a process of considerable change promoted by the investments of financial institutions and large-scale construction firms.

231

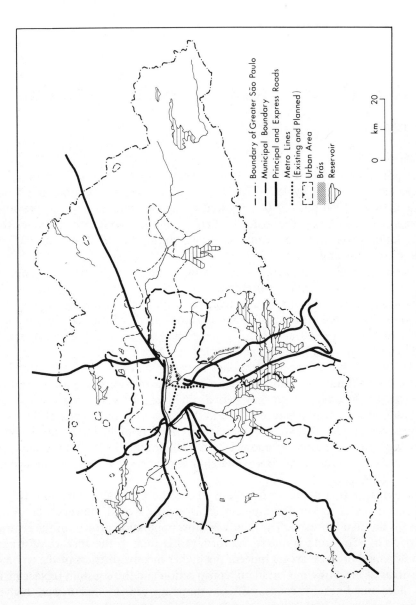

Figure 10.1 São Paulo urban area

What was being built in the centre and the inner suburbs was certainly not accessible to the mass of the population; indeed, it positively contributed to their expulsion. The continuous process of urban redevelopment, backed by high-income demand and institutional finance, stimulated rapid increases in land and housing prices in the centre and the displacement of poorer groups from previous areas of low-income housing (Bolaffi, 1975; Governo do Estado de São Paulo, n.d.). The removal took place through the eventual increase in housing costs or through the direct eviction and demolition which followed private building or public works projects.

For poorer groups, removal from central areas implied the loss of a relatively favoured situation, almost certainly in terms of access to public services and employment and probably also in terms of housing standards. The São Paulo State metropolitan planning company (EMPLASA), assessing the situation of families newly entering the housing market, judged the prospects in 1975 for the two-thirds who earned less than five minimum salaries (then about U.S. $300 monthly) as follows:

'. . . the larger part of this population will be forced to choose between installing themselves precariously and clandestinely in the most central urbanized areas (in *favelas* or *cortiços*), or seeking to accommodate themselves in rustic houses made with their own hands, in the distant periphery without urban services, where there are the worst conditions of sanitation, transport, provisioning and social services' (EMPLASA, 1975: 1–2).

PUBLIC ADMINISTRATION AND THE MARKET

In the particular case of expulsion from the city core which this chapter examines, it will be clear that no simple distinction can be made between the private interests and the governmental actions which are responsible for urban development. Market and administrative factors are closely intertwined. Public agencies involved in urban planning and resource allocation do not only operate within the context of the property and finance capital markets; they also affect these markets. For example, in the Brazilian case, they allocate housing credit, promote investment in the construction and materials industries, install infrastructure, zone land use for residential and industrial developments, and prohibit certain forms of housing settlement. These kinds of controls and resource transfers create new opportunities in the urban property market, discriminating between economic sectors and differentiating between groups of the population. Benefits for some are penalties for others. In the field of housing, some people, depending on their income or housing type, are more able to claim the administrative categorization which renders them eligible for cheap credit, public services, residential zoning, security of housing tenure and controlled rents. Similarly, some are more able than others to avoid punitive administrative action in the shape of penalties, insecurity, harrassment or eviction.

The practice of public agencies may thus be supportive to the very process of speculation and concentration which they apparently intervene to resolve. Selective access to State benefits and protection tends to benefit those already favoured by the market. In a situation of great inequality, of rapid urban expansion, of speculative property investment and of insecurity of tenure (whether due to the conditions of rental or of illegality of occupancy), even the extension of public utilities implies increased property valuation and direct administrative or market-enforced expulsion of residents (Bolaffi, 1975).

Directly, or indirectly, public agencies are of fundamental importance in negotiating transfers between different groups of the population and in distributing bureaucratic permissions and penalties. The relationship between bureaucracies and their public, and the factors which condition it, are therefore crucial (Schaffer and Huang Wen-hsien, 1975). This relationship is not, of course, peculiar to States where overt political action is suppressed, but the terms of the exchange between administrators and the administered are modified where independent avenues of organization, mobilization, appeal and redress are restricted. Administrative contacts are anyway important, but the power of assertion of administrative definitions becomes greater. For those who are subject to them, the officially established rules of the game permit little dispute. This does not mean that individual applicants must always lose out: the needs and capacities of some may accord well enough with administrative definitions; others may be able to manipulate the rules of procedure to gain favoured treatment (Valladares (1978) on squatter removal; Wygand (1966) on water distribution; Leeds (1966) on political interventions in *favelas*; Leeds, Leeds and Morocco (1966) and Leeds and Leeds (1970) on water and electricity distribution in Rio de Janeiro). The point for those subjected to authoritative bureaucratic action is, however, not to alter the rules but to find their way through and round them in what has been described as 'a rational adaptation to what structural circumstances permit and encourage' (Portes, 1976: 108). Thus, as Cardoso (1975: 195) argues, the very practice of authority establishes its own legitimacy by asserting the power of the values which underlie the practice. Conformity is the condition of favoured treatment.

The questions are then: how organizational practice comes to be established and whose interests it reflects? The explanation is not to be found simply in technocratic values or conspiracies of officials. It is, anyway, not policy as devised which is important but policy as implemented. In implementation, as opposed to planning, officials are not free agents; they operate in a context which is itself organized, constrained and rule-bound. There are requirements on them from other levels of the organization and from outside it. These are the conditions which have to be respected if the official and his organization are to survive. Organizational routines appear as anonymous requirements on actors at all levels, but they are the product of, and biased towards, certain interests.

The concern of this chapter is therefore with 'the unconscious mobilization of bias' (Lukes, 1977) in governmental action. The point is to identify how this bias is mobilized in established patterns of administrative action, in 'mundane interaction' (Saunders, 1979: 61), in 'the mere encounters of everyday life' (Schaffer, 1975: 4) and 'uneventful routine' rather than in the 'conscious and active exercise of will' (Westergaard and Resler, 1976: 144). The further point is to explain under what constraints, reflecting what interests, this bias comes to be expressed in practice.

The particular case which is examined in this chapter relates to the building of an over- and underground mass transit railway in São Paulo and the effect which this had on a part of the city which previously accommodated a low-income population and a wide range of small-scale enterprises.

THE SÃO PAULO METRÔ COMPANY

The effects of the Metrô Company's operations extend well beyond its official remit—construction and operation of a mass transit railway system for São Paulo. Because of its vast financial and physical impact it is possibly the major urban agency in the city. As one Metrô official expressed it, in the absence of any other effective official planning agency, the Metrô seeks to take the opportunities (which it creates) to direct the growth of São Paulo and to integrate the plans of different authorities.[1]

The impact of the Metrô's work is concentrated along the two railway lines of the mass transit system which were planned for construction during the 1970s. The North–South line was completed in 1975. Work on the East–West line began that year and was expected to be completed by 1981. The construction cost of the first line was estimated at U.S. $1000 million, and the cost of the second line was estimated in 1976 at U.S. $1500 million. The National Housing Bank (BNH) was a major source of finance; in September 1976 it loaned the equivalent of U.S. $80 million to sustain the works for three months until the end of the year. By comparison, its budget for 'social interest' (PLANHAP) housing in the entire country was less than U.S. $130 million.

The Metrô Company is a 'mixed' enterprise in which the São Paulo State government and the city prefecture have majority shareholdings. The prefecture of the municipality of São Paulo has direct responsibility for receiving loans and finance and passing them on to the Metrô Company. It therefore takes on responsibility for the repayment of debts. Since the Metrô runs at a loss and is expected to continue to do so, the prefecture has in fact to pay off these debts out of fresh loans, State government grants and out of its own capital. These payments are converted into shares in the Metrô company;

the capital so raised is used to pay off the loans contracted nationally and overseas. In August 1976, the State was the largest shareholder, but the municipality by then had committed capital of approximately U.S. $460 million.

The municipal budget for 1977 included the equivalent of U.S. $45 million to cover the Metrô's running costs and 65 million for the continuing repayment of debts incurred on the North–South line. For the new East–West line in 1977, the State government budgeted U.S. $55 million and the municipality allocated 73 million loaned by the BNH in addition to its earlier 80 million.

What was new and beneficial to the prefecture in the BNH loan was that (a) it carried an interest rate (about 20 per cent annually) which was below the inflation rate (about 50 per cent) and below the rate for borrowing on the money market (about 60 per cent); and (b) it could be made self-financing. The terms of BNH's finance would allow it to be used in the purchase from the Metrô company of swathes of land along the line of the railway. Housing would be built and the returns on sales used to repay BNH's loan. The Metrô would be capitalized and the prefecture would cover its costs through the purchase and resale of the land.

In this chapter, I will examine the effects of these works on the inhabitants of the areas along the route of the East–West line; I will give special attention to one particular area, Brás, which was being directly affected by expropriation and demolition at the time that this work was undertaken. I am concerned not with the eventual effects of the railway's operation but with those related to its construction. The immediate consequences on the existing population receive less attention in official statements than do the anticipated benefits from 'urban renewal' and more effective passenger transport. However, several official agencies enter into contact with the resident population in the administration of information, expropriation, eviction, compensation, demolition and rehousing. I will argue that, whatever the official plan or intention, these processes have their own differential effects on groups of the population, that in turn the processes which touch the population are conditioned by organizational relationships and that these relationships are themselves conditioned by the terms of finance.

BRÁS

The transformation of Brás from a rural area on the edge of a small town to an inner suburb of the largest city in Brazil began to occur from the middle of the nineteenth century. The building of the railways from the interior of the State to bring coffee and cotton to the port at Santos signalled the development of the City of São Paulo as a trading centre and eventually as a focus for the investment of the new wealth in urban development and industrialization.

Poorer neighbourhoods like Brás grew up along the line of the railways as the city's population increased from less than 30 000 in 1872 to about 240 000 in 1900 (IBGE, 1971). A quarter of a million European migrants, three-quarters of them Italian, passed through the port of Santos between 1882 and 1891. Many of them stayed temporarily in a newly established hostel for immigrants near Brás, and many did not move into the coffee plantations as expected but stayed or returned to the city. During the 1890s Italians were said to outnumber Brazilians in São Paulo, and the particular focus of their settlement was Brás (Torres, 1969: 119).

This period lays the basis for the present day reputation of Brás as an Italian working-class neighbourhood of small industries and mixed housing ranging from slums to rooming houses, hostels and terraced housing. But, the development of new industries, the opening of new streets and the growth of the population continued well after the end-of-the-century waves of European migration. By 1920, Brás had reached its maximum population of 67 000.

Decay and decline is also part of the reputation of present day Brás. On the one hand, there has been periodic municipal concern at the standard of housing (and morals) in Brás and surrounding areas (Torres, 1969: 168, 181, 212). On the other hand, the municipality has itself promoted radial and viaduct road improvements which have given impetus to precisely the phenomena which attracted municipal attention, that is the industrialization and commercialization of Brás and its decline as a residential neighbourhood in favour of areas further to the east. By 1966, Brás had 1106 manufacturing establishments, the highest number among the districts of São Paulo. They were small-scale enterprises, employing a total of 33 000 workers, scattered throughout the area and representing a wide variety of industries from textiles and clothing, to precision engineering, metal works, carpentry shops, motor spare-parts, jewellers and shoe shops. The population had declined only fractionally to 62 000 by 1967 but it was commonly supposed, often with pejorative implications, that the original Italian inhabitants had given way to migrants from the poor north-eastern states of Brazil (PLANASA, 1976).

In the view of the municipal authorities, the problem of Brás, was its inappropriate commercial activity, its obsolescent housing and its rundown infrastructure. The opportunity offered by the construction of the Metrô line was to 'recuperate' an area of 7½ square kilometres including Brás and parts of the neighbouring areas of Belenzinho and Moóca containing a population of 73 000 people (PLANASA, 1976).

THE PROPOSALS

Brás was affected by two interlinked plans—one for the construction of the Metrô line and the other for the development of the area. In both cases the prefecture of São Paulo municipality had an important governmental responsibility, first through its participation in the ownership of the Metrô company and then through the municipal urban development agency's (EMURB) involvement in planning the future of the area.

Prefect Olavo Setúbal, appointed in 1975, regarded the construction of the East–West line as 'the work which will distinguish the administration of the present prefect' (O Estado de São Paulo 16/1/76). Transport in São Paulo was a problem without solution but as the 'gravest problem . . . I gave it most time and resources' (O Estado de São Paulo 14/4/76). It was to be 'the biggest urban project in the history of the city' (O Estado de São Paulo 28/2/76); it was even 'the biggest ever project of urban intervention in Brazil and one of the most important in the whole world' (O Estado de São Paulo 28/2/76). In the first, eastern stage, 12 stations and 9 viaducts would be built between the centre of the city (Sé) and the terminus (Itaquera); the station at Brás would be the biggest, being the junction with the North–South line and the suburban and main-line railways. The Metrô line would run above ground following the line of the radial highway to the east (Radial Leste) and suburban railway system. The technicians of the Metrô and the prefecture talked of a 'multi-modal corridor' which would mean that the residents of the eastern part of the city, hitherto deprived, 'would be privileged in transport, access roads and urban development' (O Estado de São Paulo 14/3/76).

Initially, the prefecture announced that 3000 houses would be expropriated in a 20-metre strip along the line of the East–West route. Later, it was added that through Brás a further 70 metres each side of that strip would be cleared for development (Figure 10.2). This implied that in Brás, 600 properties would be demolished in addition to the 350 directly affected. It was to this wider area of 'urban recuperation' that the second loan of the National Housing Bank applied; indeed the loan *depended* on the inclusion of a sufficient area of land (a) to permit the construction of a significant housing project, and (b) to allow the municipal planning agency to make gains on the purchase and resale of the land.

The Metrô's president argued that the local people would benefit from improved transport and services, from the removal of industries and from 'social and financial upward mobility' (O Estado de São Paulo 26/9/76). Expropriation would be quick and cause the minimum of 'social traumas'; it was expected that in most cases 'friendly agreements' would be reached; in any case, according to the vice president of the Metrô, an information office in the area would be able 'to guide people in the purchase of new property to replace the old' (O Estado de São Paulo 6/1/76 and 11/3/76).

From the moment of demolition, EMURB (an enterprise whose shares are held by the prefecture and which is concerned with the urban planning and development of the municipality) would, according to the official proposals, take over the redevelopment of the wider area cleared through Brás. The president of EMURB argued that, in general, redevelopment could be left to

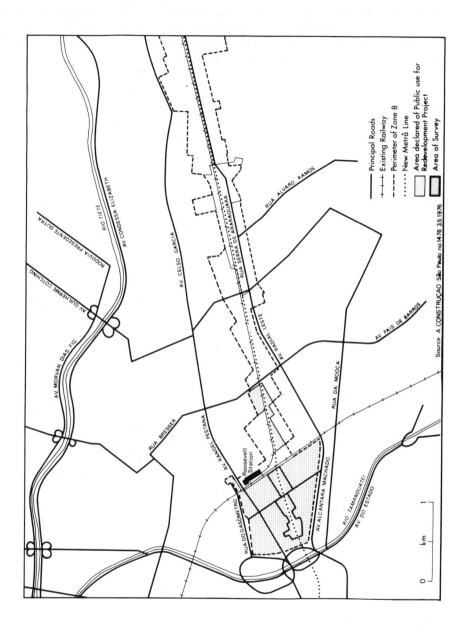

Figure 10.2   Brás-Bresser urban redevelopment area

private initiative (as along most of the North–South route) but that due to the complexity of the street system in Brás, public sector intervention was required to achieve a comprehensive rearrangement of the area (Folha de São Paulo 10/1/76). Diagrams produced by EMURB were published in the press to illustrate the president's argument that minimal expropriation and redevelopment would result in 'an urbanistically unacceptable solution', in 'problems of security' and in 'aesthetic problems'; comprehensive 'recuperation' on the other hand would allow car parking, green space, play areas, schools and health posts and a housing programme. Moreover, the president of EMURB argued that this intervention was necessary if the entire area around Brás was to participate in a process of redevelopment based on private enterprise: 'Private enterprise will thus have in the area a magnificent source of undertakings which normally it would only get with great difficulty because it would have to buy one by one all of the houses which will be expropriated by the Metrô works' (Folha de São Paulo 10/1/76).

The framework of such a project existed in CURA ('urban communities of accelerated recuperation'), a line of credit established by BNH for special comprehensive projects. The case for CURA projects on the route of the North–South line (at Santana and Jabaquara) as well as on the East–West line was argued fundamentally on the grounds that EMURB was party to a process of universal historical necessity, 'an historical force which we cannot stop' (A Folha de São Paulo 10/1/76): 'In São Paulo, as in other big centres, urban areas are subject to phases of evolution, a beginning, development, maturity, decline and death' (EMURB, 1973: 16).

EMURB's role in this process was therefore to renovate deteriorated areas and fit them to new uses. In a defence of its Santana and Jabaquara projects, EMURB officials argued that the function of the public sector intervention was to prevent private speculative gains in this historical process and to turn any advantages (of urban improvement and increased property values) to the benefit of present residents and owners (EMURB, 1973: 19–20).

In the case of Brás, however, the president of EMURB's argument rested precisely on the possibility of stimulating the activity of private developers and on the need to introduce new middle-class residents who would have the resources to finance the transformation of an industrial area into a commercial and residential neighbourhood just 1 kilometre from the city centre (O Estado de São Paulo 9/10/76). This required the replacement of 'obsolescent' housing. The president argued that he could understand that there was a 'nostalgic attachment' to Brás but the fact that 'three generations may have lived in one house only went to show that they are obsolete and old dwellings'. The people may change but 'Brás will not die' (A Folha de São Paulo 10/1/76).

By 1979, the idea of public sector intervention to renovate a larger area than that immediately affected by the Metrô line had been abandoned, but by that time the purchase and demolition of the scheduled areas of Brás had been undertaken on that pretext.

BRÁS—OCCUPATIONAL AND HOUSING CONDITIONS

The 1976 redevelopment proposals referred to three areas (Figure 10.2):
  (i) the largest was the entire area of 7.5 square kilometres around Brás which it was hoped would be eventually affected by private redevelopment following the public intervention. The area was given a special zoning category (Zone 8) which could be used to prevent all physical change for 3 years until the phase of public intervention had been terminated;
  (ii) within the area of Zone 8, there was the wider strip of approximately 70 metres on each side of the Metrô line scheduled for demolition and redevelopment;
  (iii) lastly there was the priority area for immediate demolition to make way for the line itself.

A feasibility study commissioned by EMURB surveyed the population, its work and housing conditions in a sample of 677 households in the area of Zone 8. It also included a universal survey of public services, firms and the age of houses in the area. The study (PLANASA, 1976) produced data which contradicted several of the assumptions expressed in official pronouncements on the redevelopment of the area.

Firstly, it was not true that a previously stable area was now characterized by a wave of recent migration from the poor north-east of Brazil. Two-thirds of family heads had been born in the city or in São Paulo State and 15 per cent had been born abroad; only 11 per cent were migrants from the north-east. Secondly, it was not true that the housing was old and inadequate; 82 per cent of housing units had been built or fundamentally reconstructed since 1940; 96 per cent were in a 'good' or 'reasonable' state of conservation. The sample survey showed that two-thirds of the housing was rented and one-third owner-occupied. Among owners the vast majority (93 per cent) had completed their purchase and only 16 per cent had required any sort of credit.

About half of the households were within the income range (from 1 to 5 minimum salaries) defined as the market of BNH's 'social interest' housing programme (Table 10.1). But whereas COHAB, the agent of that programme in São Paulo, could only serve the top end of the income range, nearly a quarter of the families surveyed in Zone 8 earned less than 3 minimum salaries. Moreover COHAB, in its own struggle to equate its clients' spending power with market conditions, had managed to build only 6000 housing units in the ten years to 1976.

The area was not only able to shelter a population which COHAB could not reach, even in estates located on the periphery of the city, but also to do so in an area which:

(a) was entirely served by all public utility, transport and communications services (PLANASA 1976: 20);
(b) offered education within their neighbourhood to 76 per cent of schoolgoers (PLANASA 1976: Anexo II);
(c) offered employment in the same neighbourhood or in the nearby centre of the city to 69 per cent of employed people (PLANASA 1976: Anexo II).

A more detailed survey was carried out by the writer.[2] This second survey applied to the area within Brás which was scheduled for immediate or eventual demolition (see area (ii) at the beginning of this section); it was based on a 1 in 3 sample of the approximately 780 addresses (household and business) within the area.

Table 10.1   Family incomes in the area of zone 8

Family income range in minimum salaries	Per cent of families
Up to 1	2
1.01–2	8
2.01–3	13
3.01–4	16
4.01–6	15
6.01–8	19
8.01–10	8
10.01 +	19
	100

Sample Number (593)

Source: PLANASA (1976).
Note: One minimum salary at end 1975 = Cr 532.8 (about U.S. $60 or £30).

Although the area covered was smaller, the characteristics of the population in terms of stability, housing conditions and employment were almost precisely the same as in the PLANASA study. The population was not only overwhelmingly from São Paulo State and city but also more than a quarter of the population was born in Brás itself. In a city of continuous destruction, expansion and rebuilding, Brás was characterized by a high degree of population stability; 62 per cent of survey respondents had lived there for more than 11 years.

Brás is part of a ring of inner urban areas which is primarily occupied by tenants. Two-thirds of all houses and businesses are rented. Both surveys found that 80 per cent of households paid rents of under two minimum salaries (about U.S. $120) per month—approximately the same proportion as applied to the city as a whole (Instituto Gallup 1971: 44). Given these standard rent levels, the comparative distinction of Brás from many other areas is in the 'reasonable' or 'good' standards of maintenance of local buildings, access to public services and proximity to employment.

The importance of Brás in the employment situation of local people is indicated in two ways. Firstly, high proportions of employed residents find jobs in Brás (46 per cent) or in the surrounding areas (21 per cent) (Table 10.2).

Table 10.2   Proximity of residents' employments to Brás (percentages)

Location of work[2]	Employed heads of households[1]
Brás	46
Neighbouring districts	6
City centre	15
North and eastern districts	4
South and western districts	13
No information	16
	100

Sample: All residents employed (128)

[1]Includes local business owners who are also *resident*.
[2]Areas are listed in descending order of proximity to Brás — 'neighbouring districts' are Mooca, Belenzinho, Pari and Parque Dom Pedro — 'city centre' are other areas within 3 km of Praça da Sé.

Secondly, a large number of small firms are located in Brás. The PLANASA study identified 2183 industries and 3243 commercial establishments in Zone 8. My survey in the demolition area covered 72 enterprises employing 844 people (including the employer); the implication is that in this small area of demolition more than 216 enterprises (3 × 72) and 2532 jobs (3 × 844) are affected at least by disruption, if not elimination. A further 75 firms could be added to the total to account for the 25 where the owner could not be traced for interview.

Most of the Brás firms employ less than 15 people (Table 10.3); 47 per cent are family firms in the sense that they employ at least one other member of the owner's family; in 42 per cent of the cases, the owner of the firm lived in the Brás area. However, there is nothing uniform in the range of activities carried out by the firms, although there is an emphasis on the manufacture of mechanical parts (cogs, motor parts, metal pieces) for larger producers and on manufactured and trading services to other commercial and industrial enterprises. These enterprises are therefore often by their nature both interconnected and dependent on a network of outside suppliers and entrepreneurial clients.

So the population's stability in the area seems likely to rest not only on nostalgia or sentiment, as the president of EMURB suggested, but also on the material facts of relatively favourable housing conditions, employment chances, public services and capital investment in firms.

Table 10.3   Size of local firms

No. of workers[1]	Per cent of firms
0–2	36
3–4	15
5–14	34
15 +	15
	100

Sample Number: 72

[1]Not including employer.

THE PROCESS OF CONTACT BETWEEN THE POPULATION OF BRÁS AND THE METRÔ COMPANY

Although the possibility of an East–West line to complement the North–South line had been spoken of at least since 1968, when an international consortium (Hocthief–Montreal–Deconsult) produced its proposals for both, it was only in November 1975 that the exact route of the first stage of the East–West line passing through Brás came to be known. The Metrô Company then began to apply the procedure for expropriation to the owners of the 950 properties affected in Brás.

Once it begins, the process of expropriation is rapid. It starts with the visit of a surveyor to each of the affected properties. He confirms the identity of the owner, measures the building and assesses its state of conservation and material quality. In a large operation, such as that in Brás, a private firm is employed to do this work; the surveyors therefore know nothing officially about the Metrô's plans and indeed are enjoined not to attempt to give information. On the basis of their reports and of complex formulae the Metrô's expropriation department calculates each property's value and then calls the owner to appear within three days at the Metrô's headquarter office to hear the offer price. This is not negotiable, unless the owner can demonstrate that the data on which the valuation is based is false. If the owner disputes the valuation itself, he must take court action.

Within three to five days of the first meeting, the owner must return to indicate his acceptance or rejection of the offer, to produce documentary proof of ownership and to sign a sale agreement. In the case of a tenanted property, the Metrô then (as owner) takes court action to require the original owner to evict tenants. If the owner accepts the offer, he receives the full purchase price within the following 30 days. He then has normally up to 20 or

30 days to leave the house unless he can argue an 'exceptional' case for extension. When the owner has tenants he is allowed a further 20 days and they must be given at least 10 days to leave.

From the moment that the letter is received by the owner informing him of his expropriation, the whole process takes between 56 and 68 days (plus 20 days in the case of rented property). Legal action, which would delay the process was rarely taken by owners; 75 per cent entered into what the Metrô described as 'friendly agreements' (O Estado de São Paulo 28/2/76). However 'friendly' these agreements were, it was certainly true that they were negotiated under pressure of time. Demolition of the approximately 350 properties in the direct line of the railway through Brás was begun on 22 January 1976 and scheduled to be completed by 15 February.

At the time of my survey (6–20 March 1976), some demolition had taken place. The area was divided by a strip of half demolished, half empty houses. Life outside the immediate area of rubble, dust and cranes seemed to proceed routinely, but what was striking was the residents' uncertainty about what was happening and about what they should do in the face of a threat which was both certain and imminent.

Authoritative information was not easily available to residents. Practically all respondents to the survey had known that there were some plans for the construction of the metrô railway line through Brás, even before the expropriations began to be announced. However, the sources of information on the plans and their effects were largely unofficial (Table 10.4). Residents (and especially tenants) largely depended on the press and on local people or rumour for their information. Among the more official sources, only the visiting surveyors and the Metrô's local information centre had any importance. But as was noted earlier, the surveyors were themselves not acquainted with the plans and had been ordered not to give advice.

Table 10.4   Main sources of information on the Metrô plans (percentages)

Source	House owners	House tenants	Business owners	Business tenants	All respondents
Newspapers	63	36	65	55	48
TV/Radio	29	16	13	31	21
Local population	32	41	26	31	35
Rumour	29	38	30	31	32
Surveyor	14	11	13	18	12
Information centre	20	8	17	10	12
Official letter	5	1	4	0	2
Other sources	7	4	0	12	6
Sample numbers	(59)	(114)	(23)	(49)	(215)

Note: The question allowed several responses. The columns do not therefore add up to 100 per cent.

Officials of the information centre could respond to requests for advice only in the most general terms. Although it received 8000 calls in the seven months up to August 1976, the only information the centre could give was (a) to confirm whether a house was included in the area to be demolished, (b) to recommend a list of estate agents, (c) to indicate the documents needed to prove ownership and (d) to advise people not to sell to speculators. As the head of the centre argued, it was to 'improve the Metrô's image and to calm people'. At no time was any information given on occupants' rights to compensation, to legal representation, to refuse the first offer, or to appeal, nor was the basis of valuation disclosed. Firm advice on the level of valuation and on dates for leaving was only available as individual cases came to be treated by the disappropriation department. Tenants (two-thirds of the population of Brás) were entirely outside even this limited information system since official agencies had no need to contact them; they were due no compensation and they were to be evicted by the ex-landlord and not the Metrô. The receipt of information largely depended on the subject's involvement (or not) in these two other processes of compensation and eviction.

Certain information on dates for leaving present accommodation was thus limited to little more than a quarter of the population, that is to those 29 per cent who had been offered a price for their property and to their tenants. Even the transmission of information from landlords to tenants was uncertain; as a study by the Metrô Company showed, proprietors sometimes '. . . do not advise the tenant, or encourage him to stay on so as to continue receiving rent' (Metrô 1976: 4).

So the requirement to leave came on the whole without official warning, either in the shape of a letter from the Metrô which would normally allow the owner 2–3 months to find alternative accommodation, or in the shape of a court order for the eviction of tenants within ten days. At the time of the survey, of those 79 respondents who could give dates half had to leave within one month and a quarter in less than ten days.

COMPENSATION

Most residents were tenants who do not qualify for any right to compensation for removal although a few were offered certain discretionary help. In law, tenants of buildings used for business, like the owners of business premises, can claim for 'lost profits', that is profits remaining after payment for the use of the premises. In practice, they were not informed of this right. Owners of property are the only group called by the Metrô to discuss compensation for the loss of their property. Even in their case, however, there was considerable variation in the way this standard principle worked out in practice.

The valuation is based on the measurements and qualitative assessments made by the surveyors and on a complex series of adjustments to take into account local land and building prices. A standard basis of assessment exists in the fixed replacement cost per square metre of *construction* which is used by public authorities throughout Brazil (though the fixed cost varies by State and city). A standard *land* value per square metre is also established by a survey of current land prices in other parts of the city and their transfer to the particular area (Brás) according to a relative weighting based on planning zones of the city. This acts as part of a cycle of cumulative causation—zoning decisions attribute low value to an area and this is confirmed by public purchasing policy.

On the basis of these standard land values and construction costs, adjustments are then made for particular properties. This is partly by comparison with property of similar size and condition in other parts of the city and the use of valuations for property tax (*valor venal*) as a basis for transferring prices from one area to the other. It is also by attributing particular advantages to plots depending on their location, shape and size. Thus corner sites, are given a higher valuation while plots which are narrow and deep or which fall below the municipally permitted minimum (of 10 metres frontage by 25 metres depth) lose value.

Metrô officials consider that they are offering a fair market price and that this is demonstrated by the fact that three-quarters of owners accept the first offer in a 'friendly agreement': 'we would consider that we are offering too much if for example 90 per cent of people accepted'. Clearly however, the assessment relies a good deal on non-market factors both in respect of the administrative judgement of relative worth and in the exclusion from consideration of the higher values likely to result from the introduction of the Metrô line. Property is assessed at existing zoning and use values.

Whether or not the price is a fair estimate of market value, negotiation about property values is limited in various ways. Firstly, the complexity and covert nature of the evaluation formula put it beyond simple challenge; secondly, owners are called for consultation individually as the valuations are produced, thereby limiting the chances for comparison and organizing a local response; thirdly, the immediate onus is on the owner to prove his possession (a considerable problem for people lacking ownership certificates and title deeds on old and inherited buildings) and to react to the offer within days; fourthly, if he does not accept the offer he forfeits the opportunity of a certain cash payment for an uncertain and very delayed increase.

The first offer by the Metrô is indeed formally non-negotiable except by resort to court action. Nevertheless, officials of the expropriation department agreed that representation of the owner by a lawyer could often result in an increased offer, since the lawyer was likely to be informed of the valuation procedure and able to question the particular outcome. However, only about 5 per cent of owners were represented in this way. 'Everybody,' said a local lawyer in Brás, 'could improve their compensation but most people distrust the authorities and don't know how to do it.'

Court action on the question of compensation occurs in about 30 per cent of cases, that is where no 'friendly agreement' is arrived at. This is either where title to ownership is disputed, or where an owner claims an increased valuation or where owners of businesses claim for 'lost profits'. Claims by owners are indeed risky undertakings. The court action will take eighteen months to two years to be heard; in the meantime the property is demolished (the Metrô demolishes first and negotiates afterwards) and the owner receives temporarily only 80 per cent of the valuation for property tax purposes (about 10 per cent of the market value); the owner who brings an action has to pay at least for his lawyer and for the court expenses if he loses. Moreover, a case based on 'lost profits' has to present accounting evidence that the profits were earned and that the due tax was paid on them. Even then the chances of an increased valuation are small. Of seven cases relating to expropriation on the North–South line, the writer noted only two where, after two years the court awarded an increase which exceeded inflation over that period.

Except where the owner has recourse to good legal advice and representation and has the capacity to await an eventual improved offer or withstand a loss, the logic of the procedure of compensation and expropriation clearly moves the owner in favour of quick acceptance of the first offer. 'Friendly agreements' have to be viewed in this context: the small owner is isolated, under pressure and uninformed.

THE DIFFERENTIAL EFFECTS OF EXPROPRIATION AND EVICTION

Most official statements about the plans for Brás justified them in terms of the physical improvement or re-equipment of the area. Where local people were mentioned it was to suggest either that they would benefit from these changes or that at least they would be protected in the process of transformation. Complaints in that case were to be attributed to 'nostalgia'.

The survey results, however, indicate a high level of antipathy to the impending changes and suggest that this was based on adversely affected material interests, even if also on sentiment. The data allowed some distinction between the effects on and interests of groups according to their position as owners or tenants of housing and business premises.

Local people's assessments of the plans for the demolition and redevelopment of the area were discriminating. Unlike officials in public statements, respondents to the survey made a clear distinction between the advantages which the city population and remaining local people might gain from the development and the installation of the Metrô, and the losses which those directly affected by demolition would incur (Table 10.5). Overwhelmingly,

Table 10.5 Assessment of plans (percentages)

	Good	Bad	Depends	Don't care Don't know	
For the city	82	11	1	6	100 (215)
For Brás people whose house or business will be demolished	12	66	15	6	99 (215)
For Brás people whose house or business won't be demolished	55	27	9	9	100 (215)
For self	26	55	7	12	100 (215)

79 per cent of respondents would have wished to remain in Brás had it not been affected. Even if it were true that 'time will break their emotional links with the neighbourhood' (President of EMURB, O Estado de São Paulo 10/1/76), it was apparently not true that time alone had been responsible for building links up. Younger and more recent residents manifested slightly less but still an easily predominant wish to stay in the area; even among residents of less than 2 years, 68 per cent would have wished to stay. Nor was the commitment less among owners of property and businessmen in general, although these, by comparison with tenants, had access to compensation (Table 10.6).

Table 10.6 Preference for staying or leaving Brás (percentages)

Preference	Residential[1] tenure		Period in[1] Brás		Age[2]		All businesses[3]	All respondents[4]
	Owner	Tenant	0–20 years	21 years +	Up to 39	40 +		
Stay	78	78	72	86	64	87	84	79
Depends	0	2	3	0	4	0	0	1
Leave	22	19	25	14	31	12	0	19
Don't know	0	1	0	0	0	1	16	1
	100	100	100	100	99	100	100	100
Sample number	(59)	(114)	(94)	(79)	(70)	(144)	(72)	(215)

Notes: 1 Total 173 = all residents.
2 Total 214 = all respondents less one who gave no age.
3 Total 72 = all owners of businesses (including tenants of property).
4 Total 215 = all respondents.

Most respondents expected to lose by the change; 56 per cent of owners thought the Metrô's offer for their property was low and only 14 per cent thought that it was at a reasonable level: 'We are not selling, we are being imposed upon'; 'I want to make a friendly agreement. They are very strong, it doesn't help to fight.'

Most tenants of housing (74 per cent) and of businesses (86 per cent) expected to pay much larger rents in their future tenancies (Table 10.7). Of the 74 in the sample who knew their future rent, it would be more than double for three-quarters of them and more than four times as much for one-quarter.

Table 10.7   Expectation of future rent—tenants of property
(residential and business) (Percentages)

Expected future rent by comparison with present rent	House tenants	Business tenants
Much more expensive	74	86
Slightly more expensive	8	5
The same	2	2
Cheaper	3	0
Don't know	3	0
Not applicable[1]	11	7
	101	100
Sample number	104[2]	43[2]

Notes: 1 Present tenants who in the future would buy or share or
          return to owned property
       2 Totals are of those tenants who knew that their property
          would be affected.

In spite of the immediacy of the move, 66 per cent of residents had not yet arranged a place to live. About one-third had found or were looking for accommodation in the areas near Brás and around the centre of the city, but respondents frequently said that they had begun looking near Brás and then found that house prices and rents had forced them further out of the city. One-third of those who had already arranged accommodation had moved out to more distant areas with lower levels of public service provision. The obtaining of a place to live was a product of income and chance rather than choice: 'We have to move. It doesn't help to think whether it will be good or not.'

Most local businessmen, like residents, expected to lose from the move in a direct financial sense, whether from low levels of compensation or from drastically increased rents for premises (Table 10.7). Nevertheless 78 per cent expected to, and presumably indeed had to, continue in business. The enterprises which were most likely to fail were the bars and small stores on rented premises, which depended most on a local network of clients.

Besides the question of the level of compensation, most businessmen had to bear higher costs of new premises and the trading losses and expense incurred in the period when the business was being moved. A third cost, the loss of a known location (*ponto*), could be reduced as far as possible by moving within the area. But, this locational cost was what local businessmen seemed most to fear. For small businesses it implied the loss of a local network of suppliers, trading outlets and workers and the loss of clients who could not easily be recaptured by advertising: 'I will have to close the firm for at least a month. I will lose the location and all my goods. I will lose 80 per cent of my clients and the telephone which is essential to the business. It will ruin my life.'

The Metrô company was apparently concerned to ease these outcomes (a) by paying the market price which would encourage owners into a 'friendly agreement' with immediate cash payments which would allow the purchase of new accommodation, and (b) by offering advice and guidance to tenants as well as owners. The difficulties of local people were then treated (or ignored) as though they were the residual problems of special 'social cases' whose responses were 'inadequate' or who for perverse reasons failed to accept the valuation offered.

The personnel department of the Metrô carried out a survey of ex-propriated people which showed that problems were felt more generally (Metrô 1976): 68 per cent of owners were found to have too low an income to sustain mortgage repayments on a new house; 63 per cent of tenants had insufficient income to pay the rent on housing equivalent to their existing accommodation, and frequently could not pay a three-month deposit in advance nor find an owner occupier to act as guarantor of the rent repayments. Owners had only the few weeks after they had received the Metrô's offer to look for accommodation; tenants had even less warning. Pressure of time and the wish to stay in the area had led to an inflationary increase in local rents and prices. The personnel department proposed that the Metrô should be prepared to arrange transport for people moving, to pay deposits and to make special connections with the municipal housing agency, COHAB, so as to secure places in its next round of house allocations. By August 1976, when most of the removals in Brás had taken place, the Metrô had paid deposits in only twenty cases.

The outcome of the Metrô's intervention was not universally catastrophic for the people of Brás. For some people it represented an opportunity to sell property in an area blighted by industrial activity, busy roads and the uncertainty of the redevelopment proposals, and to use their gains as a down payment on a new house. Though seen by most people as detrimental, the effects of the intervention were variable.

The variability was partly a product of the Metrô's own procedures. Some local people (notably residential tenants) were not eligible for compensation; they were thus effectively disqualified from the receipt of official information and therefore they were less able to prepare for their removal. Businessmen who were tenants of premises were formally qualified to receive compensation for the loss of profit but were not informed of this right.

The ordering and processing of cases had the general effect of imposing conditions of urgency, confusion and isolation on the owners dealt with; it also had the particular effect of relatively favouring those who understood and who could withstand the processes to which they were subject. The basis of the valuation was a mystery beyond dispute except to those who could afford legal representation. The disputing of claims was virtually impossible except for those who could manage without their present accommodation or who could withstand a two-year delay in the receipt of compensation. The registration of a claim for lost profits itself depended on previous conformity with tax and accounting standards which were unlikely to have been respected by small businesses. Moreover, the valuation of, and negotiation with, large firms was not managed through the normal procedures but negotiated personally by the head of the Metrô's disappropriation department.

The outcome for individuals therefore depended on:

(a) their belonging to broad categories (house owners and tenants, business owners and tenants, large and small businesses) for which eligibility for information and compensation differed;

(b) their capacity to deal with the complexity and urgency of procedures and to withstand the costs and delays implied by interrupting the procedures;

(c) their dependence on local housing and employment markets. A move away from the area implied greater costs (in lost access to clients, suppliers, work, schools, services and city facilities) for some than for others. Similarly, compensation which for the young might be sufficient to make a down payment on a new house bought through credit, for the old had no such significance since long-term credit could not be obtained by them. The basis of compensation could not allow for those particular dependencies on local markets. At the same time the intervention in the area itself inflated local property prices (but did not compensate for them) and made it less likely that people who depended on the locality would be able to find accommodation or premises there.

(d) the official standards used to assess the expropriation value of property, which had no relation either to the use value of the accommodation to the occupant or to his capacity to find smaller property at the same price. Thus valuations were downgraded according to the age of the building and according to their nonconformity with space standards introduced *after* their construction. The effect of this administrative reduction in local values was to increase the costs and losses involved in moving house or business.

WHY NO RESISTANCE?

The extension of the Metrô line through Brás clearly did not present itself as a universal benefit. The interests of many people seemed likely to be damaged profoundly. In the survey interviews and in press reports local people expressed their distress openly. Yet there was a complete absence of organized, or individual, resistance, or refusal to co-operate. The fact that most owners fell in with 'friendly agreements' on their expropriation was itself taken by Metrô officials to bear out their view that demolition was proceeding with the goodwill of all but the old, nostalgic and special 'social cases' who presented themselves as 'problems' to the social workers at the information centre.

Distress was very much more general than the official view allowed. There was apparently a common interest in collective action to hold up or postpone the Metrô's plans, to make demands or seek information, to seek joint legal representation or to campaign through the press or the municipal council. All of the 'stakes' in the local neighbourhood, which North American political sociologists (Clarence-Davies, 1966; Kaplan, 1963; Rossi and Dentler, 1961) have found to be associated with an active local response to urban renewal programmes, were present in Brás: economic stakes in business and home ownership, affective stakes in tenancy, social stakes in the 'community', status preservation and 'community consciousness'.

At one level, the absence of organized and overt resistance could be simply explained in terms of the consequences of such action. It would almost certainly have been suppressed by police or military force. It would also have been easily avoided by the authorities. As has been noted in the case of British and American studies of demolition and slum clearance programmes, where the authorities have legal powers to achieve their ends the co-operation of the public is simply not required (Kaplan, 1963; Dennis, 1970; Batley, 1972). This was even more clearly the case in Brás; whatever the public response, demolition was going ahead as a quite self-contained activity.

What is more surprising is that there was scarcely any dispute about compensation or dates of leaving, no objection to eviction, little employment of legal representation, no joint approach to the Metrô to negotiate more favourable terms nor to claim compensation for lost business profits and locations. Several sorts of explanation can be offered.

Firstly, there was the overpowering nature of what was happening. Dennis (1970: 350–2) has identified the disincentives to 'public participation' in British slum clearance situations: the threat at the stage that demolition is announced 'is not immediate enough to form a basis for organized opposition . . .'; the sheer magnitude of the change '. . . the possible ramifications of which may be too complex to grasp and too obscure to be contemplated'; the 'sense of helplessness' engendered by 'the planning machinery and the behaviour and attitudes of the planning personnel'. Any sense of shock or helplessness can be imagined to be the greater in a situation, as in Brás, where the threat was immediate rather than delayed.

Secondly, as Dennis argues for the British case, the expression of official plans and justifications itself promotes the view that the demolition and urban renewal are inevitable, beyond sectional interests and too big to make adjustments to the people of a particular locality. Earlier, I indicated that the Metrô and EMURB saw themselves engaged in a historical process of evolution, acting in favour of progress over decline. The work was massive so that what was happening in Brás was merely an aspect of a general improvement for the city. What was striking was that on the whole residents of Brás, in spite of their personal grievances, appeared to share the view that what was happening was not only inevitable but also that it *should not* be resisted, because it represented progress against which no man could be seen to stand. Although they were aware of the gap between the interests of those who would be expelled and those who would remain to use the line, they behaved as if it were the assumed benefit to the city population as a whole which was paramount (Table 10.5). The association of 'progress' with the construction of the Metrô implied that those who claimed that their interests were damaged would be assigned the unattractive role of 'obstacle to progress'.

Thirdly, and underlying also the first two explanations, is the force of the organizational procedures within which officials and subjects are locked. 'Demolition' and 'redevelopment' may carry general connotations but the programme in Brás only acquired its particular significance as it came to be implemented. The inevitability, urgency, complexity and obscurity which events assumed was a product of the way in which official agencies dealt with the people being affected: the propagation of late and partial information forced people back on reliance on rumour; the mystery of the evaluation procedures and the relentless independence of the process of demolition made people *in fact* helpless. Similarly, the procedures ensured that the primary concern of those affected was (a) with their individual circumstances and (b) with what would happen next rather than with what was happening now. They might have a common interest in staying in Brás, but any consensus was fragmented by the way that the processes of information, compensation and removal treated them separately and even required some (landlords) to act for the Metrô in dealing with others (tenants). The crucial issue of expropriation was conducted case by case (but in no predictable order) on the terms (and on the territory) of the expropriating organization. Attempts to negotiate implied sure delays and, therefore, certain losses for uncertain gains. The abruptness of the procedures meant that people must be more concerned with finding their next accommodation than with negotiating over their lost property: 'to get mixed up with lawyers at this stage only wastes time'; 'We can't say anything in case they pull the house down with us in it'; 'I went to Rua Augusta [the Metrô HQ] and they said that when the notification came we would have to get out — end of conversation.'

CONSTRAINTS ON OFFICIAL AGENCIES

The adverse effects on local people did not pass unnoticed by Metrô officials. The head of the expropriation department was aware that the urgency of their removal did not allow people to find alternative accommodation nor to register their children for new schools; he knew that people were 'often temporarily shocked'; officials in his department knew that owners of large businesses with legal representation got a better deal than small businessmen without assistance. Social workers in the personnel department were aware from their survey that a large population of the population could not find alternative accommodation; they appealed for resources to allow them to meet 'the basic needs of the expropriated population' (Metrô 1976: 16). EMURB officials often privately expressed a commitment to the idea of turning the advantages of public sector investment to the benefit of affected residents; indeed this was *stated* policy in the case of the redevelopment of Jabaquara and Santana through which the North–South Metrô line was constructed.

It was, however, the process of implementation, not good intentions, which determined the outcomes for affected people. It was the Metrô's own procedures which helped to generate local helplessness and confusion. Officials themselves were not independent of, nor wholly able to control, these procedures. There were limits to change. The procedures broadly conformed with the requirements placed on the Metrô company by its relationship with other organizations, including the municipal, state and federal governments, and internal and external creditors. These relations were all thoroughly inter-penetrated so that for example the Metrô's relationship with the federal government was through the municipal government (the prefecture) and the point which underlay this relationship was, on the whole, the question of access to credit.

The Metrô's relationship with the prefecture was especially direct, first because, after the State government, it was the largest shareholder and second because all credit allocated to the Metrô was channelled through the prefecture as guarantor of the repayment of the finance. It was precisely this guarantor role which had forced the prefecture into its significant shareholding; periodically it has repaid the Metrô's debts by purchasing shares, the capital so raised being used to pay off the arrears. On the one hand, the construction of the city's Metrô railway system was a considerable liability of which the prefect as much as local councillors complained; on the other hand, it was a matter of prefectural pride and achievement and a matter in which the prefect could be obviously influential on the development of the city.

The question of prefectural commitment to, and influence on, the Metrô has several contradictory implications. The works offered a rare opportunity for prestige and effectiveness to the prefect; they gave access to large-scale credit in contrast to the usual requirement on the municipality to undertake its commitments out of its own funds; long-term funding, the scale of the works, and the consequent association of the prefect's reputation with the success of the project gave the Metrô a certain promise of continuity. However, the continuity, scale and sophistication of the works and the wide-ranging sources of finance in their turn gave the Metrô administration a greater degree of independence from the prefect's control than other 'mixed economy' municipal-financed enterprises could claim. For example, EMURB, the municipal urban development agency, was subject to continuous alterations in its directorship and its plans with each change in the prefect (there were three changes between 1972 and 1976). The Metrô, on the other hand had had one president in its seven-year life, although he was formally subject to appointment by the shareholders. A slow down in the works, a decline in future levels of finance threatened the loss of the technical team which he had built up; this was a possibility which he was able to employ in budgetary negotiations with government and which worried the federal as much as the local authorities.

The Metrô, therefore, had a particular power to negotiate its survival and the continuity of its works. On the other hand, the factors (the scale, sophistication and wide-ranging organizational connections) which gave it this power, also made the Metrô particularly vulnerable to change—this was precisely its negotiating point. Thus, a new prefect (Miguel Colasuonno) could require the abandonment of detailed plans and already initiated works for the construction of a line under a principal avenue (Paulista), for these plans only to be revived and considered four years later under a later prefect (Olavo Setúbal). Financially, the indebtedness of the Metrô project made it extremely vulnerable to changes in prefectural, state or federal government priorities.

All these factors gave an urgency to the works. The nature of the undertaking carried its own logic in favour of continuity, which the Metrô company was able further to exploit so as to maintain the commitment to and the pace of the undertaking. The uncertainty which nevertheless hung over the works made it that much more imperative to carry out each stage of the programme quickly while funds and governmental commitment were there. Once that stage had been initiated, the prefect and his administration had an interest in pressing for its conclusion during their term of office, and the Metrô company had an interest in maintaining prefectural support by promising success in achieving that objective.

There were other more directly financial reasons for haste. These related partly to the sources and terms of finance and partly to the piecemeal nature of financing; ultimately, these factors required the Metrô company to act quickly and without much regard to local interests in Brás.

The financing of the Metrô work was undertaken entirely through the prefecture which received the finance, guaranteed it and took on responsibility for repayment. It was, however, the federal government which organized internal loans and which contracted foreign loans through the central bank;

the State government's authorization to raise external credit was withdrawn by the federal government in August 1976, six months after the State had contracted a loan of U.S. $175 million on the London money market for investment in the construction of the East–West line. The prefecture was dependent, therefore, primarily on the federal government for raising finance, but also on the State government for obtaining a proportion of the loans and for contributing to their repayment.

Finance raised abroad accounted for more than half the cost of the construction of the North–South line, split almost equally between loans tied to particular purchases and untied credit. The principal creditors were British, North American, German, Italian and Japanese banks, the International Bank for Reconstruction and Development and the Inter-American Development Bank.

The advantage of foreign loans was that they were relatively long-term (between 5 and 12 years). They were also relatively cheap in terms of foreign currency: interest was between 8 per cent and 12 per cent per annum (according to the London Interbank Offered Rate—LIBOR) with an additional 'spread' of 1.76 to 2 per cent, for the Brazilian risk, and of a Brazilian central bank rate of 3 per cent. Against this, repayment of national loans raised through federal agencies was indexed for inflation. However, overseas debts had to be repaid in foreign currency which meant that they also were effectively indexed; in this case the adjustment followed from the devaluation of the cruzeiro on international money markets (which turned out to be a more severe correction than the internal inflationary index calculated by the federal government).

The passage of time was thus crucial to the scale of the debt incurred through loans—with time, the costs of credit, land, materials and works increased. As the president of the Metrô expressed it: 'productivity increases with speed' (O Estado de São Paulo 9/10/76). The figures on the outgoings involved in meeting the Metrô debts are confusing but illustrative. According to a statement by the city prefect, the municipality was committed between 1976 and 1982 to *yearly* outgoings of about U.S. $150 million in repayment of loans and running costs (O Estado de São Paulo 28/8/76). Another statement by the prefect claimed that the Metrô had absorbed 38 per cent of municipal investment between 1968 and 1976 (O Estado de São Paulo 14/4/76). Yet another report suggested that the total debt *remaining* to be paid on the North–South line in 1976 was U.S. $250 million, before any further debts on the East–West line were assumed (O Estado de São Paulo 6/9/76).

Ultimately this repayment could only come from the capital contribution of the prefectural and State governments. The Metrô itself, it was agreed, would offer no return; indeed it was running at a loss which was being subsidized out of new loans and State and municipal grants, as well as by the rundown of the fund intended in the long term for maintenance. The construction of the

East–West line was crucial in that respect because it offered the prospect of increasing the traffic on the system as a whole, in a situation where the North–South line on its own had turned out to be running below a viable passenger capacity.

The need to maximize the use of expensive credit and the need to bring the second line into service to help reduce the net running costs of the whole were two important reasons for haste. They were also reasons for minimizing the costs of expropriation and construction.

There was a further factor; the piecemeal and uncertain nature of the funding favoured the elimination of all costs which were easily dispensable and the continuous demonstration of cost effectiveness to would-be creditors. During 1976, there was a series of threats and counter-threats by the prefecture, State and federal governments addressed each other to the effect that they could not be counted upon to bear the costs of the East–West line's construction. The prefect said that he would contribute 'not a penny more' (O Estado de São Paulo 27/8/76); the State government reserved its position until the second half of the year saying that its budget was extremely tight; the federal urban transport company (EBTU), which was responsible for organizing finance for allocation throughout the nation, argued that the local authorities should take the initiative and that until then even those funds already assigned to São Paulo would be withheld (O Estado de São Paulo 9/10/76). Into this breach stepped the president of the Metrô arguing that the 'accelerated execution' (and therefore reduced cost) of the works was contingent upon a commitment from all three parties (O Estado de São Paulo 9/10/76). Respite came with the second loan from BNH negotiated by the prefecture; this would be used to purchase land from the Metrô company for use in a housing programme.

The product of this uncertain and piecemeal financing was a continuous need for the Metrô to conduct its work urgently as funds became available and while they retained their value, and to demonstrate that it could act as quickly as it had promised to government fund-raisers. Indeed, an official suggested that the wide variety of sources and terms of finance itself led the Metrô administration to spend credit as quickly as it became available so as to reduce confusion with later packages of credit on other terms from other sources.

WHO LOSES?

Under these constraints, protracted negotiations with local people about compensation and dates for removal could only stand in the way of quick action; what was needed was a clear field of expropriated and razed land ready for immediate construction work.

Secondly, what was needed by the Metrô and those who paid for its finance was the minimization of its costs; partly this could be achieved by reducing inflationary increases through speedy action but there was also every reason why the Metrô should attempt to avoid dispensable costs. These included compensation in excess of that needed to remove owners, and compensation for lost commercial profits and sites on which business tenants were ill-informed. More fundamentally, the very decision to build the railway overground through Brás and beyond, but underground in more central areas, was based on calculations relating to the cost of land purchase to the Metrô by comparison with the costs of underground construction. The result was that businessmen and residents of the most central, highly valued areas of the city gained twice: first from non-removal and second from the further increased values consequent upon the improvement of transport. Removed people in other areas lost three times: first by their removal, second by their non-participation in enhanced values, and third by the inadequacy (or non-existence) of the compensation when compared to the cost of purchasing property at standards similar to those they originally enjoyed.

Thirdly, the Metrô and those who organized its finance were interested as far as possible in the recuperation of its costs. The special opportunity which the Brás project provided was in the opportunity to recoup costs by the resale of land at prices which reflected its improved value. This was made possible by the special terms of the loans from the national housing bank (BNH) which, under a special line of credit for 'urban recuperation', allowed the purchase of the swathes of land on either side of the Metrô line for their eventual redevelopment for commerce and middle-class housing, both privately and through the co-operative housing institute (INOCOOP). Metrô and EMURB would gain on the resale of the land.

The BNH was the only financing organization through which such a transfer of mutual benefit to public authorities could be arranged. It carried with it the requirements that sufficient land should be available to make 'recuperation' possible and that sufficiently well-off occupants should be introduced into the housing and commerce to pay off the increased values which the Metrô's arrival would generate.

Ironically, the BNH had come to participate in a process which was not only extraneous to its original purpose of housing provision but one which was responsible for the destruction of the low-income housing which was supposed above all to benefit from the bank's finance. The demolition in Brás alone was equal to one sixth of the units sold between 1966 and 1975 by COHAB, the São Paulo arm of BNH's 'social interest' housing programme.

Moreover, whatever else the advantages of the Metrô to the city and remaining local population, experience suggested that the process of expulsion did not stop with the direct impact of demolition. As the president of EMURB had made clear, the objective was to initiate a process of private redevelopment. In the areas of Vila Mariana and Santana, served by the North–South line, the increase in property values had continued to displace business and residential tenants; after one year, high-rise flats were replacing houses, commercial sites were being bought by large stores at prices five times higher, small businesses which sold 'on tick' to known customers were giving way to firms selling on hire purchase (O Estado de São Paulo 26/9/76).

One effect of urban redevelopment was thus to further incorporate these areas, with their surviving and new populations, into the credit-based housing and consumer goods markets. The new opportunity presented to creditors was marked by the campaign by the Commercial Association of São Paulo to promote hire purchase in the newly 'opened up' areas with the slogan 'credit is the solution'. Through its constraints on the Metrô's operation, credit had already played its part in removing those for whom credit was *not* available as a solution to the new patterns of consumption imposed in the 'recuperated' areas.

The *longer term* expulsive effect of the process of redevelopment was recognized to various degrees by the members of a working party (including the presidents of the Metrô and EMURB, the municipal planning coordinator and the municipal secretary of public roads) set up by the prefect to consider the future of the area along the East–West line. The president of the Metrô was least convinced; in his view the redevelopment presented the east zone population with the possibility of 'social ascent'. The planning coordinator pointed out that: 'for owners it will be a good business [but] for those who live in rented accommodation, prices will rise and probably they will have to move. I see no solution for this' (A Construçao 3/5/76).

The president of EMURB attributed the outcome to the same sort of historical necessity as he had earlier attributed to the life cycle of urban areas: 'To wish to avoid this process [of expulsion] is more or less like attempting to revoke the law of supply and demand. Besides if we reasoned like that we would arrive at the absurdity of proving that the process of development is itself bad . . . . We have to be realistic because this is the process of development' (A Construçao 3/5/76).

CONCLUSION[3]

However impersonal, objective, external and inevitable this development and its effects appeared to the active participant (whether official or member of the public), they were nevertheless the product of social forces or interests operating through organizational procedures. I have argued that the terms of finance are a principal constraint on the action of the public agencies examined, underlying the relationship between these agencies and the public. The constraint, however, does not appear as an external obstacle. In setting the terms on which organizations operate and survive, the logic of capital accumulation through credit comes to be internalized in the action of public agencies and officials. There develops a mutuality between the terms of capital and the operation of official organizations: on the one hand, agencies are able to turn the terms to their advantage, on the other, public procedures become functional to accumulation. The outcome is that redevelopment shifts gains from tenants and small owners back to creditors, to the recipients of large-scale reorganized land and to those who are able to meet the conditions of the extended credit-based land, housing and consumer goods markets. Expulsion is thus related to accumulation.

GLOSSARY

EMPLASA   São Paulo state metropolitan planning company.
BNH   National Housing Bank.
EMURB   São Paulo municipal urban development company.
COHAB   São Paulo metropolitan housing company.
INOCOOP   Co-operative housing institute.

ACKNOWLEDGEMENT

The research on which this paper is based was carried out in 1976 with the financial support of the Institute of Development Studies and the Centre for Environmental Studies.

NOTES

1. Where statements by officials are not attributed they are from interviews by the writer. Interviews were conducted with officials of the Metrô's planning and expropriation departments, its information office and its financial adviser and with officials of EMURB's planning and expropriation departments.
2. The survey was carried out with the help of Dr. Zilton Luis Macedo and Professor Gabriel Bolaffi.
3. There are clear connections between what I have argued here and Castell's analysis of urban renewal in Paris; he identifies its effects in accentuating 'spontaneous' trends towards spatial segregation, in demobilizing demands and in reinforcing the 'consumption dynamic' in renewal areas (Castells, 1978; Chapter 5). I hope to have added an understanding of the way in which interests act through organizational processes.

REFERENCES

Atas da Câmara Municipal de São Paulo LIX, 1873 cited in Torres, 1969: 118.
Batley, R. A. (1972). 'An explanation of non-participation in planning', *Policy and Politics* **1**, 95–114. In Lambert and Weir (eds.) (1976), *Cities in Modern Britain*. Fontana.
Bolaffi, G. (1975). *Habitacão e Urbanismo: O Problema e O Falso Problema*. XXVII Reunião Anual da Sociedade Brasileira para O Progresso da Ciência, Belo Horizonte.

Cardoso, F. H. (1975). *Autoritarismo e Democratização*, 2nd ed. Paz e Terra, Rio de Janeiro.
Castells, M. (1978). *City, Class and Power*. Macmillan.
Clarence-Davies, J. (1966). *Neighbourhood Groups and Urban Renewal*. Columbia University Press.
Dennis, N. (1970). *People and Planning*. Faber and Faber.
EMPLASA (Empresa Metroplitana de Planejamento da Grande São Paulo) (1975). *Diretrizes da Política Habitacional na Grande São Paulo*, Volume 1.
EMURB (Empresa Municipal de Urbanização) (1973). *A Reurbanização de Santana e Jabaquara*. São Paulo.
Governo do Estado de São Paulo (n.d.). *Região Metropolitana de São Paulo: Diagnóstico 75*. São Paulo.
IBGE (1973). *VIII Recenseamento Geral, Censo Demográfico — Sao Paulo*. IBGE Rio de Janeiro (Special run conducted for Metrô).
IBGE (1971). *VIII Recenseamento Geral, Sinópse Preliminar do Censo Demográfico*. Rio de Janeiro.
Instituto Gallup (1971). *O Mercado Habitacional na Cidade de São Paulo*. Instituto Gallup, São Paulo.
Kaplan, H. (1963). *Urban Renewal Politics*. Columbia University Press.
Leeds, E. (1966). *Interaction of National, State and Local Political Structures in the Favela*, Paper presented to the 36th International Congress of Americanists, Mar del Plata.
Leeds, A. and Leeds, E. (1970). 'Brazil and the myth of urban rurality: urban experience, work and values in squatments of Rio de Janeiro and Lima.' In A. J. Field (ed.), *City and Country in the Third World*. Schenkman Publishing Co., 229–85.
Leeds, A., Leeds, E. and Morocco, D. (1966). *Politico-Administrative Power in Relation to Electricity in Rio Favelas*. Paper presented to the American Association for the Advancement of Science, Washington D.C.
Lukes, S. (1977). 'Political, ritual and social integration.' In S. Lukes, *Essays in Social Theory*. Macmillan.
METRÔ (Companhia do Metropolitano de São Paulo) (1976). *Estudo Exploratório e Programa de Intervenção Social nas Areas Desapropriados*. São Paulo. Mimeo.
PLANASA (Planejamento e Assessoria Administrativa) (1976). *Area CURA — Brás/Bresser, Estudo de Viabilidade Económica — Financeira, Relatório Parcial I*. Mimeo.
Portes, A. (1976). 'The politics of urban poverty.' In A. Portes and J. Walton, *Urban Latin America*. University of Texas Press, 70–110.
Prefeitura do Municipio de São Paulo (1969). *Plano Urbanístico Básico de São Paulo*. Secretaría de Obras, São Paulo V3.
Rossi, P. and Dentler, R. (1961). *The Politics of Urban Renewal*. Free Press of Glencoe, Illinois.
Saunders, P. (1979). *Urban Politics: a sociological interpretation*. Hutchinson.
Schaffer, B. B. (1975). 'Editorial', *Development and Change* **6**, 3–12.
Schaffer, B. B. and Huang Wen-hsien (1975). 'Distribution and the theory of access', *Development and Change* **6**, 13–36.
Torres, Maria, C. M. T. (1969). *O Bairro do Brás*. Prefeitura Municipal.
Valladares, L. do Prado (1978). 'Working the system, squatter response to resettlement in Rio de Janeiro', *International Journal of Urban and Regional Research* **2**, 12–25.
Westergaard, J. H. and Resler, H. (1976). *Class in a Capitalist Society*. Penguin.
Wygand, J. (1966). *Water Networks: their Technology and Sociology in Rio Favelas*. Paper prepared for the 36th meeting International Congress of Americanists, Mar del Plata. Mimeo.

Urbanization in Contemporary Latin America
Edited by A. Gilbert with J. E. Hardoy and R. Ramírez
© 1982 John Wiley & Sons Ltd.

11

Regional development policies in Mexico

Luis Unikel

INTRODUCTION

Mexico is a country of enormous physical contrasts whose natural resources are very unevenly distributed. Whereas the south-east of the country contains 40 per cent of the nation's water resources but only 10 per cent of its population, eight million Mexicans live in desert conditions and areas like the Bajío have a large population but few agricultural resources. But, if the resource base has favoured only the development of a few regions, it has not been an obstacle to others, such as the central valley of Mexico, which have received extensive governmental support.

Mexico's contemporary pattern of regional inequalities and urban settlement began to emerge during the colonial period (1519–1821). The Spanish established a hierarchy of urban centres which culminated in the economic, cultural and administrative capital, Mexico City. In the middle of the eighteenth century a well-developed urban system had emerged; important cities had developed along the routes between the capital and the mining centres in the north, along the Mexico City–Vera Cruz access and in the Bajío area of central Mexico.

The war of independence, which began in 1810, temporarily disturbed this pattern. The dominance of Mexico City was undermined and the growth of regional centres throughout the country slowed. If Mexico City regained its former influence with the declaration of independence some provincial cities did not recover until the Mexico–United States War (1846–1848). But the most sustained period of urban growth came during the dictatorship of Porfírio Diaz (1877–1910). Rapid exploitation of the country's mineral resources, the development of ports and railways and the growth of foreign trade stimulated urban expansion in north and central Mexico and accentuated the already dominant position of Mexico City.

The growth of the national capital has been consistently rapid throughout the twentieth century. During the Mexican revolution (1910–17) it provided greater security than most other cities for those affected by the armed struggle. And, in the so-called 'constructive' stage of national development (1921–70), Mexican government policy has favoured the capital in the allocation of private and public investment (Carrillo Aronte, 1971). Industrialization, transport pricing policy, and the development of commercial agriculture have favoured urban growth and especially the concentration of economic and political power in Mexico City (Lavell, Pírez and Unikel, 1978). In 1970, the metropolitan area contained 32 per cent of the nation's industrial plants, 46 per cent of the industrial labour force and 51 per cent of industrial production (Unikel and de la Peña, 1976: 68). In terms of population, 8.4 million Mexicans lived in the city in 1970, 38 per cent of the nation's urban population.

The level of spatial concentration and acute regional income and welfare disparities have long concerned the federal government. This concern reached a peak during the administration of Luis Echeverría (1970–76) when criticism crystalized on the national development model employed by different governments from 1940–70. This model aimed at rapid economic growth through the concentration of capital in large enterprises and the stimulus of public investment to the private sector. The major problems were that the model failed to provide jobs for the mass of the population, failed to raise living standards for this group and polarized economic, social and political interests. These problems increased the danger of violent social conflict.

DEFINING A REGIONAL DEVELOPMENT POLICY

In Latin America, the terms plan, policy and programme are used inter-changeably so that the differences between them become blurred. This means that we are no longer clear what a regional policy is: what should it contain, what distinguishes a government statement from a government policy, what constitutes a policy and what are the instruments to carry it out? For this reason I have tried to extract an adequate definition of regional policy from the regional development literature. Paraphrasing Lebas (1974: 1) regional policy is that part of the State's political process that tries to correct inherent inequalities and contradictions in the spatial economic system. Such a policy is concerned with 'the factors that govern the location of economic activities and population, in accordance with technological and economic requirements, human needs and aspirations, and the characteristics of the area in question' (Commission of the European Community, 1969: 22).

Convinced that not every national government declaration of principles constitutes a policy, I have drawn up a series of requisites which I believe every regional policy should contain. I am well aware of the difficulties facing any government trying to implement such a plan, especially in an underdeveloped and dependent capitalist country such as Mexico. Nevertheless, insofar as a government matches its accomplishments against these requisites, it will be in a better position to judge its real achievements and to satisfactorily modify its policy.

(a) Regional policy should be capable of implementation. If it is not, it will become merely a good intention; a Utopian solution that fails or one that becomes a demagogic exercise.
(b) It should contain clear objectives but ones that are more specific and limited than general social goals, such as raising living standards or housing the population. If the objectives are not precise the policy will become a mere declaration of principle. It is then open to the danger that politicians may interpret any action as satisfying the policy objectives; the essence of demagogy.
(c) A policy should be defined so that government action can be rationally evaluated. It should contain a clear strategy which demonstrates how positive results can be achieved and negative outcomes avoided. It should also provide a framework into which daily tasks and administrative activities can be fitted.
(d) A regional policy should have national scope; the goals and instruments should relate either to every region in a country or to every region with common characteristics, poverty, high unemployment, etc. Regional policy should be an integral part of national development policy. It should be clear how regional policy is expected to contribute to national development and how far it is expected to be successful.

EVALUATING A REGIONAL POLICY

There are two very different approaches to an evaluation of the relationship between the State and the economic system: the positivist, non-theoretical perspective adopted by scholars of many diverse political tendencies, and the Marxist approach which tries to analyse the development of capitalist relationships and the role of the State from a theoretical perspective. The first, sees the State as an exclusively administrative and coordinating agent, whose increasing intervention in the life of capitalist nations can be interpreted through direct empirical observation. The second, perspective stems from the premise that the State '. . . can be considered to operate in favour of the interests of a specific group, that of the bourgeoisie' (Ecker, 1974: 2). It argues that State intervention occurs for essentially economic reasons and relegates the State's political and administrative functions to a second order of importance. This latter perspective is more difficult to support empirically, judgements depend on reading between the lines of newspaper reports and government documents. This is a powerful reason for preferring the first approach to the second.

In many developed countries, such as Great Britain with its 40 years experience of regional planning, policy evaluation is a well developed technique. In Latin America, by contrast, the regional programmes that have proliferated in recent years have been marked by serious deficiencies largely because of a lack of evaluative techniques. Either because they have not studied the assessments made of similar kinds of programmes, because such examinations are lacking, or because existing studies do not offer an adequate basis for comparative analysis, regional programmes are technically deficient. This situation is also due to the fact that few Latin American governments review their policies regularly, let alone welcome public comment, whether those policies have been drawn up by public officials, academics or foreign consultants.

In the case of Mexico, most policy evaluation has been positivist; the State's functions have been assumed to be the administration and regulation of public activities and to be complementary to the activities of the private sector. Despite this assumption, most policy reviews have arrived at conclusions which are very similar to the hypothesis from which the Marxist perspective begins: government 'measures have especially favoured national and foreign entrepreneurs, commercial farmers and the productively employed population living in the country's major urban centres' (Dirección General de Programación y Descentralización Administrativa, 1973: 14).

With the exception of a few recent cases, 'official evaluations' of the public policy are generally descriptive and informative. Government programmes are presented to the public through the President's annual report to the nation and through the speeches and reports published by the different ministries. The federal government spend large sums of money on this process, money that would be better spent on the preparation of an objective and impartial evaluation of government activities.

During the Echeverría administration 'self-criticism' was frequent; high-level officials made public statements noting deficiencies in their own ministry or in specific government programmes. Generally, these comments were intended for political consumption rather than to provide an in-depth evaluation of a given policy or public programme. Nevertheless, this self-criticism, and the attacks and counterattacks on the private sector, gave an idea of the administrative failings and the conflicts of interests within the public sector and of the disputes between the public and the private sectors.

Evaluations of public programmes are also presented in the press and on television. If both media lack the personnel to make adequate socioeconomic and political evaluations, a few scholars and journalists periodically analyse federal government policies in certain newspapers and specialized journals. But, it is clear that social scientists are most critical of the government when writing in academic publications. It is these studies that in the long run have permitted a continuous evaluation of government plans and programmes.

They have sometimes also influenced government decisions, for example, in the repeal of the tax exemption law in the Federal District in 1954 (Romero and Urquidi, 1952) and in the introduction of industrial decentralization and regional development policies in the 1970s (Yates, 1961; Barkin and King, 1970), even if this influence has often taken time to work; Yates' study, for example, had no impact on the policies of the López Mateos and Díaz Ordaz administrations (1958–64 and 1964–70).

NATIONAL AND REGIONAL PLANNING PRIOR TO 1970

Before 1970, most planning in Mexico was directed at specific economic sectors and was limited to the national level. With the exception of certain regional programmes, notably the river basin projects and the national frontier policy, the government had been little concerned with the formulation of a rational, territorial strategy for distributing public expenditure. Resources were allocated not to regions but to those sectors essential for economic development or for raising living standards.

It should be emphasized, however, that prior to 1970 planning was an intermittent activity in the public sector. After the two six-year plans formulated by the Cárdenas administration (1934–40), many years were to pass before the government of López Mateos formulated its action plan, 1962–4. This plan arose from the country's need for external credit; credit which would only be forthcoming if an economic plan were prepared along the lines laid down by the recently established Alliance for Progress. This momentary impulse was gradually forgotten during the Díaz Ordaz administration which had an apathetic, conservative and reticent attitude towards economic planning. *The Economic and Social Development Plan, 1966–70*, prepared by that government was never made public, its 'secrecy' intended to allay possible criticism (Benveniste, 1970). Neither of these plans produced results different from those that would have been attained through traditional sectoral development programmes.

Technical and administrative weaknesses, the limited diffusion of information, the lack of clearly formulated objectives and fear of political commitment opened these attempts at national sector planning to charges of being partial, incomplete, utopian, trivial and secret. The planning of the sixties served only to reduce still further planners' prestige within the government sector; by the end of the Díaz Ordaz administration all the existing plans and planning studies were once again filed away. Disillusion was such that the planning directorate of the President's Secretariat was abolished and a Directorate of Economic Studies created in its place.

Parallel to these undistinguished efforts at planning, governments had introduced isolated measures designed to decentralize industry, to promote the development of selected problem areas and to develop particular natural resources. Undoubtedly, the most ambitious regional programme was that begun by President Miguel Alemán in 1947 with the creation of the Papaloapán and Tepalcatepec River Basin Commissions. The programme did not explicitly attack industrial concentration and population agglomeration but did plan to relieve '. . . the congested central plateau, whose exhausted land should be devoted to the production of crops which colonial policies had denied it . . .' (Mosk, 1954: 220); an aim previously embraced among the goals of the so-called 'March to the Sea' initiated by President Avila Camacho between 1940 and 1946. The River Basin Commissions undoubtedly contributed to national development and acted as a stimulus to agriculture (Barkin and King, 1970). However, the projects have accomplished little '. . . as a strategy to achieve decentralisation of economic activity or to reduce the stream of migrants to urban areas . . .' (Barkin, 1973; 183), partly because the Commissions did not use their full powers to attract industrial activity to their regions. The Valley of Mexico River Basin Commission which was established in the Ministry for Water Resources in 1951 also had little effect in slowing the growth of Mexico City.[1] During its life of 21 years the Commission was the only government agency in which all the federal entities that make up the Valley of Mexico were represented. It was also the only river basin commission that formulated a plan to slow the growth of the metropolitan area. Needless to say, it succeeded neither in coordinating the federal entities nor in dispersing population and economic activity. Indeed, because of the social and political vacuum in which the plan was formulated, it was never accepted officially even by the Ministry of Water Resources itself.

The only programme that directly affected the location of industry was the Guarantee and Development Fund for Small and Medium Industry. Among the credit institutions established prior to 1970 it was the only one that gave preference to companies locating outside the Federal District and Monterrey. Between its foundation in 1953 and 1970 the Fund slightly increased the share of industrial credit going to the states and reduced that of the Federal District. However, because the State of Mexico was not classified as an area of industrial concentration, companies could locate within the Mexico City metropolitan area and still obtain credit. As a result, its share of the Fund's credits increased from an average of 10 per cent during 1953 and 1961 to 20 per cent in 1970 and the metropolitan area's industrial base grew still larger (Lavell, 1972).

The abolition of tax incentives to industry in the Federal District in 1954 while the State of Mexico maintained its incentives until the mid-sixties had a similar effect. Companies could benefit from proximity to the metropolitan area and receive tax relief merely by locating in contiguous municipalities outside the Federal District. Since companies could also buy larger and cheaper lots with good opportunities for land speculation, the urban area spread rapidly into the State of Mexico.

A further attempt at industrial dispersal began with the establishment of the *industrial* town of Sahagún City. Between 1953 and 1970, 22 industrial parks or cities were established, 14 of which were founded by private enterprise. The locations of most of these industrial areas were governed more by market considerations than by decentralization motives. Most of the parks were established in or near a metropolitan area, thus stimulating still further the City of Mexico and its surrounding cities. Finally, the *National Border Programme* achieved a measure of decentralization even if it was instigated more for reasons of international geopolitics than to achieve regional development in Mexico. From 1960 to 1965, the National Border Programme, with the collaboration of the Federal Assemblies for Building Improvement (both under the control of the Ministry of National Patrimony) sought, with little success, to change the physical appearance of the main border cities and to improve their municipal services. During the next seven years greater attention was given to promoting industrial development, accelerating the flow of national products to the border market, and creating new employment opportunities. The main plank of this new strategy was the 'Programme to employ the surplus workforce along the northern border with the United States' which offered major incentives to companies locating 'in-bond' industry along the national border. The programme certainly improved the chronic employment situation caused by the large-scale migration to the northern border after 1940. Unfortunately, it also increased Mexico's dependence on the United States; most of the investment came from that country, and since the goods produced were destined exclusively for the United States the prosperity of the border area was linked to the economic cycle in that country.

In sum, the above programmes had little effect on federal public spending which continued to respond more to the needs of national economic growth than to the goal of income redistribution. For the same reason, policy objectives were never clearly stated and the instruments were too weak to counterbalance the interests of private groups in maintaining economic centralization. On various occasions measures intended to decentralize industry have had the opposite effect.

THE REGIONAL DEVELOPMENT STRATEGY AFTER 1970

Luis Echeverría paid more attention to the issues of regional inequality and urban primacy than previous presidents. In his inaugural speech he declared that his 'governing will mean redistributing evenly the fruits of redoubled efforts; making the more privileged groups and regions contribute to the development of the more backward' (Navarrete, 1971: 180). 'We will prevent the benefits of growth concentrating in a few areas. It is vital that we remodel economic space by creating growth poles . . .' (p.184).

What motives led to this change in strategy from an exclusively 'developmentalist' model to one based on the idea of 'redistribution with growth'? The most logical (although unproven) answer is that several of the richer peripheral States were asking for greater economic autonomy from the federal government. Shapira (1974) argues that these States had begun to apply pressure on the federal government during the sixties when State politicians realized that they might modify their traditional role *vis-à-vis* the federal administration. Instead of acting as intermediaries in the search of a higher State budget or a larger share of the public works investment, they thought that they might begin to weaken Mexico's highly centralized political and economic system to their mutual benefit.

But, there are alternative hypotheses which also merit analysis. Firstly, a regional investment policy might paradoxically be a means of undermining the threat that regional income might bring to the continuance of 40 years' economic growth and social stability (Segovia, 1974). Secondly, it might increase internal political cohesion and improve the federal government's ability both to face up to popular pressures and to channel the benefits of growth towards the majority of Mexicans (Camacho, 1974). Finally, redistribution with growth might have appeared to be the 'only way out of the national crisis of unemployment and low purchasing power among the poor' (Carrillo Aronte, 1971: 441).

Irrespective of the motives Echeverría may have had in formulating his new economic strategy, he introduced a large number of new industrial, agricultural and water programmes as well as encouraging regional development and the decentralization of people and industry away from the Valley of Mexico. The regional policies fall broadly into two chronological groups. The first group of policies were adopted between 1970 and the end of 1973 and were intended to directly encourage the decentralization of economic activities preferably into backward areas. The second group of policies were introduced between the end of 1973 and the beginning of 1975 and consisted primarily of measures to improve government coordination. They aimed to link the various programmes, whether explicitly regional or not, which were concerned with a more integrated, balanced and equitable pattern of social and economic development.

Among the first set of measures the more important were the State Funds for Industrial Preinvestment Studies, the National Fund for Industrial Promotion and a trust fund for the promotion of industrial centres, parks and cities and commercial centres. A substantial increase in funds was made to the Guarantee and Promotional Fund for small and middle-size industries. These funds were allocated according to the area in which companies proposed to locate; in June 1972 three industrial zones were designated with varying levels of incentive and disincentive to location.

Most of these measures were to be administered by *Nacional Financiera*, the

National Development Bank. The Industrial Centres, Parks and Cities Programme was established under the joint auspices of the *Nacional Financiera* and the Ministry of Public Works. The Urban Development Commission (CODURPA) was the executive agency of this programme responsible for the location, design and construction of the projects. The Commission identified a number of 'growth centres' which would help deconcentrate activity from Mexico City, Guadalajara and Monterrey, and stimulate regional development.[2]

The industrial tax, credit and technical assistance programme was put in the hands of the Ministry of Industry and Commerce; the body which also coordinates development in the northern border area. The latter, which despite the replacement of the National Border Programme in 1972, continues to benefit from the establishment of 'in-bond' industry, and the promotion of agricultural and commercial development.

Various efforts were also made in this first period to stimulate rural development, improve regional administration and achieve slower and more coordinated growth in the metropolitan area. A National Water Resources Plan was produced, an Integral Programme for Rural Development, Regional Development Committees for the States of Yucután, Oaxaca and Chiapas established, and a further, unsuccessful, attempt made to establish a coordinating Commission for the Mexico City Metropolitan Area. In addition, the country was divided into nine regions as part of a major effort to delegate authority from the federal government to the local authorities (Dirección General de Programación y Descentralización Administrativa, 1973).[3]

In December 1973, the first of a second set of measures was introduced in the form of the General Population Law. This law had powers that could dramatically affect most aspects of economic and social development. Its first goal, for example, promised to 'match economic and social programmes with the needs posed by the size, structure, dynamics and distribution of the population'; other goals recognized the need for urban and regional planning (Moya, 1974; 125). The National Population Council was established in 1974 to implement this law; a body that became increasingly influential after 1977.

At the beginning of 1974, the Presidential Secretariat created its own General Directorate for Regional Development. This Directorate was intended to help coordinate federal, regional and state investment and expenditure thereby reducing waste and accelerating the pace of economic growth. By January of the following year Developmental Promotion Committees had been established in each of the country's States to coordinate the investment and development plans of the different ministries at the State level. In addition, a National Commission for Regional Development was set up to coordinate action at the regional level; all ministerial subsecretaries and the directors of federal agencies being members. Through these measures a mechanism had been created by which the federal government hoped to coordinate action at the national, regional and state levels.

Government efforts to implement a 'redistributive' economic development programme culminated in May 1976 with the passing of the Human Settlements Law. The passing of this law had required several constitutional changes and considerable discussion with the private sector which felt threatened by a perceived threat to its rights over property. Once the law had been approved a new ministry, the Secretariat for Human Settlements and Public Works, was established.

THE EVALUATION OF THE
REGIONAL DEVELOPMENT STRATEGY

Having summarized government initiatives since 1970 to decentralize industry, promote regional development, and reduce regional inequalities, we must examine whether they can achieve their goals. In short, is the country likely to achieve a more balanced pattern of regional development?

The first point to mention is that there are many inconsistencies between the regional development policy and the aims of other sectoral programmes. Several elements contained in the Federal Water Law, the Agrarian Reform Law, the dam and road construction plan, export policy, and inflation measures and many other programmes are not only inconsistent but also incompatible with more balanced regional development. An important source of conflict is that the public officials in each agency often have different personal objectives or represent different collective interests. As Camacho (1974: 96) argues the multiplicity of interests represented within the public sector makes the adoption of any single coherent political line impossible beyond mere self-defence against popular pressure. Thus even though the Echeverría administration tried to improve government efficiency of the public sector through a new Control and Vigilance Law (Proel, 1973), and the new administration of López Portillo has introduced an administrative reform at the federal level, real cohesion is impossible. These measures may improve administrative coordination within the public sector, but I do not believe that they can prevent the implementation of actions that counter-balance or even oppose the objectives of regional development. Incompatibility between national and regional objectives is very difficult to avoid in practice even in countries such as Great Britain, France and Italy (CEC, 1974). But what is critical, and must be avoided in Mexico, is that these inconsistencies are so marked that they prejudice either national development or development of the poorest regions.

A major dilemma, but one common to many countries, is the wish to maintain rapid economic growth while simultaneously reducing regional and personal inequality. Should development in Mexico City be favoured before that of the periphery? Should higher priority be given to more developed areas within the periphery than to the poorest and most backward? That there is a real conflict here is certain; at present national resources are too limited to raise the living standards of the whole population sufficiently to satisfy their basic needs. In addition, there are major political barriers to helping the poorest regions. While it is accepted that State intervention is necessary to achieve income redistribution, national, regional and intraurban interest groups often oppose any government pressure which promises to reduce disparities. As Brookfield (1975: 123) argues '. . . although the reduction or elimination of inequalities is perhaps the most fundamental of social goals, it is also opposed to the self-interest and group self-interest of those with power, ambition and wealth. Possibly this is the basic dialectic which underlies all others, and should first be viewed at this most fundamental level, taking note of the fact that unequal advantage is an inevitable concomitant of any system of organization, viewed in whatever dimension; the dimension of geographical space is merely one in which unequal advantage is most obvious'.

For these and other reasons I feel that conflict over the appropriate treatment of regional disparities and urban primacy is unavoidable. Consider, for example, the dilemmas posed by the growth of Mexico City. Even if we ignore the drastic possibility of immediately halting the metropolitan area's growth, and adopt a policy of control in stages, the dilemma remains how best to supply water, electricity, drainage and adequate transportation in the long run. In the first place, federal government intervention in the Federal District and the State of Mexico is essential because public investment is necessary but the local authorities have insufficient economic resources of their own to resolve their own problems. Second, the government is subjected to major economic and social pressures which demand continued improvement in the area's infrastructure even if that may be undesirable from a national point of view. Finally, while new infrastructure serves existing social needs, it also attracts more private enterprise which creates still further demands for infrastructure. Since the signs are that marginal costs *per capita* are increasing in the city, an inevitable source of conflict is present.

At the metropolitan level of government, a further dilemma is posed by the lack of agreement between the Federal District and the State of Mexico over the desirability of further growth within the metropolitan area. The Federal District is willing to help growth providing this does not cut its tax base or the number of jobs available in the city. On the other hand, the State of Mexico feels, rightly or wrongly, that it has served as an escape valve for many of the Federal District's problems. It is willing to discourage industrial activity within the already industrialized parts of the metropolitan area (Unikel, 1972), but wants to maintain industrial expansion not only in its rural areas but also on the less-developed northern fringe of Mexico City (Cuautitlán and Tultitlán).

Difficult questions also arise over whether to favour regional versus spatially concentrated development. How, for instance, can demographic and economic concentration in the metropolitan area be reduced if the social forces favouring its growth continue to operate? If, despite growing urban diseconomies, structural changes fail to modify the advantages which individuals and groups gain from continued concentration, migration from the countryside will continue as will the establishment of new economic activity (Instituto de Desarrollo Urbano y Regional, 1974). It seems impossible to reduce concentration without:

   (i) imposing measures which deter large-scale private investment in certain areas of the metropolitan area and the Valley of Mexico;[4]
  (ii) exercising effective control over public investment principally benefiting low-income groups within the metropolitan area;
 (iii) eliminating federal subsidies which reduce metropolitan living costs such as subsidies to public transport (Yates, 1960);
  (iv) complying with atmospheric and water contamination laws;
   (v) negatively affecting employment, especially that provided by small and medium-sized companies;
  (vi) relocating important federal government functions outside the Valley of Mexico;
 (vii) attempting to increase governmental efficiency and coordination in the metropolitan area through the establishment of tripartite institutions in which the Federal District, the State of Mexico and the federal government are represented.

There seems little doubt that the introduction of these policies would meet with public hostility and political resistance, at least in the short run; a point noted 20 years ago by Yates (1960) in his still valid recommendations for regional policy in Mexico.

But even if development of the poorer areas is favoured over that of the metropolitan areas another dilemma is apparent; the process of regional development does not guarantee that it will be the poorest groups who benefit (Gilbert and Goodman, 1976). This point is well demonstrated in Mexico in the case of the generally successful River Basin Programme. Barkin and King's (1970: 185) study of the not untypical Tepalcatepec Commission concluded that the Programme clearly accelerated the pace of regional growth and raised *per capita* income. But, 'a considerable part of increased production was financed by groups who migrated from the wealthier parts of the country. There resources and experience spurred the rate of growth, but also fostered a high level of income concentration in the region'. Similarly, I believe that the decentralization decree of June 1972 will improve the spatial distribution of income but will not favour the poorest people in the country. Since subsidies are given to industries locating in growth centres or in municipalities closest to the metropolitan centres income will become concentrated in those regions already receiving the largest share of public spending, having the greatest resources and which have easiest access to credit. In other words, it seems impossible to avoid the dilemma between spatial and personal income redistribution unless poor people are given large subsidies, are provided with social services and are granted access to credit facilities.

Politically, of course, this is difficult since in a national environment of limited resources the transfer of income and subsidies to poorer groups demands that 'those areas, sectors and individuals with greater resources cover a substantial part of the cost of providing vital social services in depressed areas' (Navarrete, 1974: 200). But these areas also demand better treatment from the federal government. Relatively affluent regions such as the north and north-west, which have traditionally received the greatest federal contribution, that are highly politicized and which are most opposed both to Mexican governments and to the PRI, also contain substantial numbers of poor people. If the gap between Mexico City and regions such as these is closed, regional income redistribution will go hand in hand with rapid economic growth, but the cost will be the continued neglect of the periphery.

In the short term, there is a conflict between growth and the spatial redistribution of income in societies such as Mexico. It is a structural characteristic that cannot be ignored but frequently is ignored in the formulation of regional policies. Mexican regional policies have been formulated in a social vacuum, they have considered economic and spatial factors and not political and social realities. If we continue in this way the price is clear, it is to condemn regional policies to failure.

CONCLUSIONS

1. The Echeverría administration introduced a more determined programme to decentralize industry and stimulate regional development than any of its predecessors. Many of these initiatives have been supported by the government of López Portillo. The programme attempted to reconcile national strategy objectives, redistribution with growth, and the subnational, state and region, investment programmes. It instituted a series of attempts at administrative reform and a continuing concern for regional problems within the public sector. I believe that the basis for a realistic and effective national policy of regional development has been established in Mexico for the first time.
2. Nevertheless, the studies, plans and programmes produced have been formulated in a 'social vacuum'; the economic, social and political viability of the proposed measures has not been carefully examined.
3. As a result, the institutional changes can guarantee only the use of planning as an instrumental technique. With luck, the strategy can be implemented

although innumerable sociopolitical and economic factors oppose it, but an attack on the causes of territorial and personal income inequalities requires more than administrative reform.

4. This signifies that indicative planning is insufficient to achieve the formulated objectives and incapable of solving the basic problems. The government must not only offer incentives to the private sector to locate in peripheral regions but it must also channel resources to the poorer strata of society.

5. Latin American, and even European, growth-centre policies have demonstrated that the centrifugal diffusion of development from the centre to the periphery have a limited effect. Measures to create jobs and to improve living conditions among the poor are needed in the peripheral regions. If such efforts are not directed at the poor, Mexico's wealth will continue to be concentrated among more privileged groups even if that wealth will now be spread among a greater number of regions. Such a 'redistribution' may ease tensions between the centre and the periphery and may reduce the chances of serious interregional confrontation. What it will not do is to significantly improve either interregional or intraregional income differences.

6. The Echeverría administration have greater priority to regional inequality than previous governments, a tendency that has been maintained by the present government. However, it is still too early to predict the outcome of this strategy or to know whether future governments will be willing, or will be persuaded, to pay the economic and social price to maintain and reinforce this commitment. If the government's declared objectives are to be achieved major structural reforms are urgently needed. The question is: are those reforms imminent or even possible? There are signs of progress, for example the recent approval of the Law of Human Settlements and the National Plan for Urban Development. But such progress is very limited given the magnitude of the task and, as we have demonstrated, it is less than certain that all the changes are in the right direction.

ACKNOWLEDGEMENT

I am indebted to Diana Rumsey and Allen Lavell for their help in correcting and translating the paper.

NOTES

1. The Valley of Mexico is a hydrological basin which contains the whole of the Federal District and parts of four contiguous States. By Mexico City we mean the metropolitan area which included in 1970 all but one of the Federal District's delegations plus eleven municipalities from the contiguous State of Mexico.
2. The growth centres included several submetropoles, 14 regional metropoles,

30 intermediate metropoles, 12 urban centres and 74 urban subcentres (Secretaría de Obras Públicas, 1973).
3. All of the regions consisted of at least two States; the central region was divided into two, the metropolitan area and the rest.
4. Yates (1960: 249) considered that it is 'much more efficient, much fairer for the companies, and much less dangerous in other respects, to use deterrents . . .', for example, '. . . to encourage the industry to contribute a higher proportion of the real social costs in the Valley of Mexico so that each company will choose the location that most suits it'.

REFERENCES

Barkin, D. (ed.) (1973). *Quienes son los beneficiarios del desarrollo regional?* SEP/Setentas.

Barkin, D. and King, T. (1970). *Desarrollo económico regional: enfoque por cuencas hidrológicas de México.* Siglo XXI Editores.

Benveniste, G. (1970). *Bureaucracy and National Planning: a Sociological Case Study in Mexico.* Praeger Publishers.

Brookfield, H. (1975). *Interdependent Development.* Methuen.

Camacho, M. (1974). 'El poder: Estado o feudos políticos', in Centro de Estudios Internacionales (ed.) *La vida política en México, 1970–73.* El Colegio de México.

Carrillo Aronte, R. (1971). 'La estrategia del desarrollo regional de México: evolución, magnitud y perspectivas.' In Wionczek, M. *et al.* (ed.) *Disyuntivas sociales, presente y futuro de la sociedad mexicana.* SEP/Setentas, Vol. II.

CEC (Commission of the European Community) (1969). *A Regional Policy for the Community.* Luxembourg.

Dirección General de Programación y Descentralizatión Administrativa (1973). *Bases para la regionalización de la administración fiscal federal,* Secretaría de Hacienda y Crédito Público.

Ecker, T. (1974). *Capitalist planning, the State and regional policy, some comments on Britain in the mid-1960s.* Polytechnic of Central London. Mimeographed.

Gilbert, A. and Goodman, D. (1976). 'Regional income disparities and economic development: a critique.' In Gilbert, A. (ed.), *Development Planning and Spatial Structure.* John Wiley, 113–4.

Instituto de Desarrollo Urbano y Regional (1974). *Gravity model of migration, flow division and flow creation for Mexico.* Toluca, Summer Research Project, Report 3.

Lavell, A. (1972). 'Regional industrialization in Mexico: some policy considerations', *Regional Studies* **6**, 343–62.

Lavell, A., Pírez, P. and Unikel, L. (1978). *La planificación del desarrollo y redistribución espacial de la población: el caso de México: 1940–78,* Paper presented at the Seminar on Spatial Redistribution of Population (Centro Latinoamericano de Demografía, Santiago, Chile, August 1978).

Lebas, E. (1974). *Sociology of regional planning and policy: theoretical and methodological problems.* Working Paper 14, Polytechnic of Central London.

Mosk, S. (1954). *Industrial revolution in Mexico.* University of California Press.

Moya, M. (1974). *La revolución demográfica.* Fundación para Estudios de la Población.

Navarrete, I. de, (1974). 'Distribución del ingreso en México: tendencias y proyección a 1980.' In Mir, A. (ed.), *Las ciencias sociales: antología.* Asociación Nacional de Universidades e Institutos de Enseñanza Superior.

Navarrete, J. E. (1971) (ed.). *La política económica del nuevo gobierno*. Banco Nacional de Comercio Exterior.

Proel, J. (1973). 'Los intentos de planificación económica en México', *Comercio Exterior*, **XXII**.

Romero Kolbeck, G. and Urquidi, V. (1952). *La exención fiscal como instrumento para atraer industrias al Distrito Federal*. Mimeo.

Secretaría de Obras Públicas (1973). *Obras públicas*. Secretaría de Obras Públicas.

Segovia, R. (1974). 'La reforma política: el ejecutivo federal, el PRI y las elecciones de 1973.' In Centro de Estudios Internacionales (ed.), *La vida política en México 1970–73*. El Colegio de México.

Shapira, Y. (1974). 'La experiencia sinaloense y el federalismo mexicano', *Foro Internacional*, **XV**.

Unikel, L. (1972). *La dinámica del crecimiento de la ciudad de México*, Fundación para Estudios de la Población.

Unikel, L., and de la Peña, R. (1976). 'Consideraciones sobre la concentración económica en México', *Asentamientos humanos* **1**.

Yates, L. (1960). *El desarrollo regional de México*. Banco de México.

Index